Martin Worthington
Principles of Akkadian Textual Criticism

Studies in Ancient Near Eastern Records

General Editor:
Gonzalo Rubio

Editors:
Petra Goedegebuure · Amélie Kuhrt
Markus Hilgert · Peter Machinist
Piotr Michalowski · Cécile Michel
Beate Pongratz-Leisten · D.T. Potts
Kim Ryholt

Volume 1

De Gruyter

Martin Worthington

Principles of Akkadian Textual Criticism

De Gruyter

ISBN 978-1-5015-1325-1
e-ISBN 978-1-61451-056-7
ISSN 2161-4155

Library of Congress Cataloging-in-Publication Data

A CIP catalogue record for this book is available from the Library of Congress.

Bibliographic information published by the Deutsche Nationalbibliothek

The Deutsche Nationalbibliothek lists this publication in the Deutsche Nationalbibliografie; detailed bibliographic data are available in the Internet at http://dnb.dnb.de.

Printing: Hubert & Co. GmbH und Co. KG, Göttingen
∞ Printed on acid-free paper

Printed in Germany

www.degruyter.com

A Giuliana Parodi e Bernard Worthington
miei genitori
nonché Assiriologi onorari

Larga è la foglia, stretta è la via,
Dite la vostra, che ho detto la mia.

Preface

> Nos méthodes de recherche, désormais dûment élaborées, gagneraient à être appliquées au domaine de l'Orient. Aussi bien l'examen d'un manuscrit syriaque, arménien, copte ou arabe ne diffère-t-il aucunement de celui d'un manuscrit grec ou latin. Les règles élaborées par les philologues classiques valent pour l'étude des *Maximes de Phtahhotep* et des *Préceptes de Kagemeni.*
>
> Alphonse Dain[1]

This book's remotest origins lie in my PhD Thesis *Linguistic and Other Philological Studies in the Assyrian Royal Inscriptions, c. 1114 – c. 630 BC*, submitted to the University of Cambridge in April 2006. It was in the course of my doctoral studies that I acquired many of the analytical habits which underpin the present work, and first began to think seriously about many of the questions which drive it. In both respects I owe much to my PhD supervisor, Nicholas Postgate. Most of the ideas about Assyrian royal inscriptions which appear here go back to the Thesis.

My intention after submitting the Thesis was to revise it with a view to publication, but in the course of a Junior Research Fellowship at St John's College, Cambridge, between 2006 and 2010, I slowly became aware that it would make better sense to do something different: to concentrate on a small cluster of issues which the Thesis addressed briefly, namely those devoted to textual change and the kindred subject of orthography, and – with due revision, expansion and systematisation – make them the subject of a book. Other projects prevented work on this front from being more than intermittent during my time at St John's, but the long gestation period in idyllic surroundings was fertile. It resulted in the abandonment of many ideas which at first sight looked attractive, and in the accumulation of copious notes on orthographic anomalies now discussed in these pages. What is more, in the process of working on discrete problems in Akkadian orthography, my findings on which were published separately, I came to see more and more potential in spellings as sources of information about all sorts of things.

In Autumn 2010 I embarked on a Postdoctoral Research Fellowship at the School of Oriental and African Studies, London. My research

1 Dain, *Les Manuscrits* (1949) 8.

plan for the Fellowship was to examine the individual style of Babylonian poems, but as I began to look into this intriguing topic I found I was running into methodological quagmires connected to some of the issues I had been thinking about for several years, in particular the reliability (or otherwise) of our extant manuscripts. Methodologically, the situation of said issues recalled that which, in 1923, Paul Maas sketched for Ancient Greek poetic metre:

> At present little productive research in this field is being done, and the few scholars who are active in it disagree even over basic principles. One can seldom be sure whether the silence of other scholars indicates agreement or disagreement, indifference or incomprehension.[2]

I therefore decided to take the *alû* by the horns, and to make a book on Akkadian textual criticism my sole occupation until it should be completed. Nurtured with generous doses of midnight oil, and battening on the various privations which it inflicted on its author, the present work at last came into being over the course of the calendar year 2011.

The longer and harder I have worked on it, the more forcefully the realisation has struck me that this is a decidedly preliminary study. The issues addressed are so vast, and the process of documenting them so laborious, that I could do little more than scratch the surface. Future research will very likely unearth all sorts of complexities currently unsuspected, and solutions to problems which at present seem intractable. Nonetheless, one has to start somewhere.

The word 'principles' in this book's title thus embodies two meanings: I shall indeed attempt to lay out some theoretical foundations for Akkadian textual criticism, which I hope will be useful to future researchers; but at the same time, 'principles' hearkens back to its Latin sense of 'beginnings'.

* * *

It is a very pleasant duty to thank the institutions which supported me while I thought about the issues tackled in this book, and eventually wrote it: the Master and Fellows of St John's College, Cambridge, first for a Benefactor's Scholarship, then for a Junior Research Fellowship; the DAAD (German Academic Exchange Service) and the Altorientalische(s) Institut of the Universität Leipzig for three very stimulating months spent in Leipzig during 2006; the British Academy and the School

2 Cited in the translation of Hugh Lloyd-Jones: Maas, *Greek Metre* (1966) 6.

of Oriental and African Studies, London, for my current Postdoctoral Research Fellowship.

The project took a step towards fruition at the Rencontre Assyriologique Internationale in Barcelona (2010), where Michiel Klein-Swormink of De Gruyter expressed an interest in seeing my work on textual criticism. When I eventually had a draft fit for sending to him, in June 2011, he responded with invigorating enthusiasm. The manuscript then passed into the expert hands of Gonzalo Rubio, the series editor, who saw it through the refereeing process and tendered wise advice. Florian Ruppenstein of De Gruyter oversaw the book's production, and I am especially grateful to him for being so tolerant and accommodating in respect of my excesses at proof stage. I thank Michiel, Gonzalo and Florian for their openness, patience and professionalism.

I am indebted to various scholars for agreeing to share writings with me in advance of publication: Fredrik Hagen sent me the introduction to his book *The Instruction of Ptahhotep*; Jim Adams sent me two drafts of chapter 12 from his *Social Variation and the Latin Language*; Philippe Talon allowed me to use his *Partitur* transliteration of *Enūma eliš*, which greatly expedited work on that composition; Paul Delnero sent me two drafts of his *JNES* article on memorization, and indulged me in correspondence about it; Martin West sent me the proofs of his paper on critical editing; Rim Nurullin sent me his two *Gilgameš* papers now published in *Babel und Bibel*; Kirk Grayson and Jamie Novotny allowed me to quote from their forthcoming Sennacherib volume (RINAP 3/1). To all of them I extend my grateful thanks.

I am grateful for the opportunity of soliciting feedback on my ideas in seminars at the Universities of Leipzig, Venice, Udine, Göttingen and Oxford, at the kind invitation of Michael Streck, Lucio Milano, Mario Fales, Annette Zgoll and Fran Reynolds; and at the 2011 Rencontre Assyriologique Internationale, in Rome.

I was also immensely fortunate in having a large number of friends and colleagues who with great generosity gave of their time, learning, and critical acumen to my writings at several stages of their development: Mikko Luukko, Werner Mayer and Viv Prescott commented on early drafts of what I did not yet know would end up being this book. During 2011, as the manuscript limped towards respectability, it benefited enormously from the warm encouragement and good-humoured criticism of readers of successive drafts – in order of reading: Daniela Bedin, Nathan Wasserman, Yoram Cohen, Aage Westenholz, Kai Lämmerhirt, Mark Weeden, Gonzalo Rubio, Nicholas Postgate, and Martin West. They saved me from errors, provided me with bibliographical references, encouraged me to think and think again, and, by providing stations along the way, helped me get to the end of what would otherwise have been an impossibly long and arduous journey. To all of them I express my heartfelt thanks.

Oliver Stadon and my father read an early draft of the Introduction. Unnerved by their unanimous pronouncement ('incomprehensible'), I duly set about redrafting – both the Introduction and much else besides. Should the non-Assyriological reader (if any) find the exposition comprehensible, this will be due in no small part to their input.

Two anonymous referees commented on the manuscript, and one of them made useful suggestions for how to improve the structure, which I followed with gratitude. For all remaining faults, as well as for the ideas and arguments presented, I bear sole responsibility.

* * *

My work benefited from many informal chats and discussions, both oral and written, which were wonderful sources of ideas, information, encouragement and human wisdom. In addition to many of the individuals named above – esp. Daniela Bedin, Mario Fales, Werner Mayer, Nicholas Postgate, Viv Prescott, Oliver Stadon, Nathan Wasserman, Mark Weeden, Aage Westenholz and Annette Zgoll – I would like to mention João Abreu, Louise Allen, Annie Attia, Mark Bailey, Riccardo Bernini, Gilles Buisson, Bruno Burger, Augusto Castagnini, Ginny Catmur, Antoine Cavigneaux, i Ceccarini, David Conlon, David Cook, Peter De Ville, Matthew Dolan, Grant Frame, Benedikt Franke, Paul Ganter, Andrew George, Jane Gilbert, the Hamptons, Yağmur Heffron, Christian Hess, Inger Jentoft, the Kessons, Aptin Khanbaghi, James Kinnier Wilson, Bert Kouwenberg, the Lester-Kochs, Amélie Kuhrt, i Maggioni, Simon Malloch, Caroline Martin, Paola Paoletti, Cinzia Pappi, the Parnhams, Luigi Parodi, the Pongs, the Redheads, James Rock, die Scheffers, John Tait, George Watson, Elizabeth Whitton, Henry Zemel, and the other members of the Zgoll family.

A special word goes to Michele Vizzarro. His demise only days before his 53rd birthday, falling victim to the terrible snowfalls which befell the Urbino area in February 2012, is here recorded with infinite sorrow. Michele was unmatched in kindness and charisma, and a hero to me since childhood. *zikiršu lū dari.*

I owe these wonderful people things as varied as inspiring examples of industry and efficiency, exciting discussion about the subordinative ending *-u*, emails of such poetic richness that reading them is like drinking a magical potion, bold support for my wilder-looking initiatives, constant stimuli to intellectual rigour and curiosity, sublime specimens of irony, not a few meals, sound and robust common sense, salvific reminders of the existence of a world beyond the computer screen, apothegms I still chuckle at delightedly years after they were voiced … – in short, *joie de vivre, de lire, de penser et d'écrire*, and lots, and lots, of merriment. This book is incalculably the better for all these things.

I would also, with a delay which renders them all the stronger, like to express my thanks to Sean Higgins, my A-level History teacher. It was he who, all those years ago, devoted hour upon hour, far beyond the call of duty, to initiating me into the mysteries of writing in paragraphs. For any clarity which readers find here, the merit is chiefly due to him.

Finally, with this demanding enterprise at last complete, I now understand why so many researchers dedicate their books to their parents. And indeed it is to mine, ever-resourceful guides and companions on the stormy seas of life, that, with gratitude and admiration, this book is affectionately dedicated.

London, 26. v. 2012

Contents

Abbreviations

Miscellaneous

acc.	accusative
Ah	Atra-hasīs
al.	alii (others)
Ann.	Annals
c	consonant
cols	columns
cv	consonant+vowel
cvc	consonant+vowel+consonant
ed./eds	editor/editors
Ee	Enūma eliš (manuscript sigla after Talon)
esp.	especially
f.	feminine
fn.	footnote
Gbr.	Gottesbrief
Gilg.	Gilgameš (manuscript sigla after George)
gen.	genitive
lit.	literal(ly)
m.	masculine
MS(S)	manuscript(s)
n./nn.	note/notes
no.	number
nom.	nominative
p./pp.	page/pages
pl.	plural
Rass.	Rassam (conventional designation of a Sennacherib Cylinder inscription, no. 4 in Frahm and RINAP 3/1)
sg.	singular
v	vowel
var./varr.	variant/variants
vc	vowel+consonant
vol.	volume
vs	versus

Names of kings

Abk	Aššur-bēl-kala
AD	Aššur-dān
AN	Adad-nērāri
Asb	Assurbanipal
Asn	Assurnaṣirpal
Esar	Esarhaddon
ŠA	Šamšī-Adad
Šal	Šalmaneser
Sar	Sargon
Senn	Sennacherib
TN	Tukultī-Ninurta
TP	Tiglath-pileser

Modern Scholarship

(See also http://cdli.ucla.edu/wiki/doku.php/abbreviations_for_assyriology).

AbB	Altbabylonische Briefe – Leiden
ACh	C. Virolleaud, *L'astrologie chaldéenne* (Paris: Geuthner, 1903-1912)
AfO (Bh.)	Archiv für Orientforschung (Beihefte) – Vienna
AHw	W. von Soden, *Akkadisches Handwörterbuch* (Wiesbaden: Harrassowitz, 1959-1981)
AMD	Ancient Magic and Divination – Groningen / Leiden
AnOr	Analecta Orientalia – Rome
AnSt	Anatolian Studies – London
AOAT	Alter Orient und Altes Testament – Kevelaer and Neukirchen-Vluyn / Münster
ArOr	Archiv Orientální – Prague
ARRIM	Annual Review of the Royal Inscriptions of Mesopotamia Project – Toronto
AS	Assyriological Studies – Chicago
ASJ	Acta Sumerologica (Japonica) – Hiroshima
BAM	Die babylonisch-assyrische Medizin – Berlin
BaM	Baghdader Mitteilungen – Baghdad
BiOr	Bibliotheca Orientalis – Leiden

BIWA	R. Borger, *Beiträge zum Inschriftenwerk Assurbanipals – Die Prismenklassen A, B, C = K, D, E, F, G, H, J und T sowie andere Inschriften. Mit einem Beitrag von Andreas Fuchs* (Wiesbaden: Harrassowitz, 1996)
BSOAS	Bulletin of the School of Oriental and African Studies – London
BWL	W. G. Lambert, *Babylonian Wisdom Literature* (Oxford: Oxford University Press, 1960)
CAD	Various authors, *The Assyrian Dictionary of the Oriental Institute of the University of Chicago* (Chicago: The Oriental Institute, 1956-2011)
CM	Cuneiform Monographs – Leiden
CRRA(I)	Comptes rendus de la rencontre assyriologique (internationale)
CT	Cuneiform Texts from Babylonian Tablets, &c., in the British Museum – London
CTN	Cuneiform Texts from Nimrud – London
GAG	W. von Soden, *Grundriss der akkadischen Grammatik*, 3rd ed. (Rome: Pontificio Istituto Biblico, 1995)
HdO	Handbuch der Orientalistik – Leiden
HSAO	Heidelberger Studien zum Alten Orient – Heidelberg
HSS	Harvard Semitic Studies – Cambridge, MA
JANES	Journal of the Ancient Near Eastern Society of Columbia University – New York
JAOS	Journal of the American Oriental Society – New Haven
JCS	Journal of Cuneiform Studies – New Haven
JEOL	Jaarbericht van het Vooraziatisch-Egyptisch Genootschap Ex Oriente Lux – Leiden
JMC	Le Journal des Médecines Cunéiformes – Saint-Germain-en-Laye
JNES	Journal of Near Eastern Studies – Chicago
KAL	Keilschrifttexte aus Assur literarischen Inhalts – Wiesbaden
KAR	Keilschrifttexte aus Assur religiösen Inhalts – Wiesbaden
LAS II	S. Parpola, *Letters from Assyrian Scholars to the Kings Esarhaddon and Assurbanipal. Part II: Commentary and Appendices* (AOAT 5/2; Neukirchen-Vluyn: Neukirchner Verlag, 1983)
MDOG	Mitteilungen der Deutschen Orient-Gesellschaft zu Berlin – Berlin
MDP	Mémoires de la Délégation en Perse – Paris

MSL	Materialien zum Sumerischen Lexikon / Materials for the Sumerian Lexicon – Rome
NABU	Nouvelles assyriologiques brèves et utilitaires – Paris
OBO	Orbis Biblicus et Orientalis – Göttingen
OECT	Oxford Editions of Cuneiform Texts – Oxford
OIP	Oriental Institute Publications – Chicago
OLA	Orientalia Lovaniensia Analecta – Leuven
PBS	Publications of the Babylonian Section (University of Pennsylvania. Museum) – Philadelphia
PIHANS	Publications de l'Institut historique-archéologique néerlandais de Stamboul – Istanbul
RA	Revue d'assyriologie et d'archéologie orientale – Paris
RIMA	Royal Inscriptions of Mesopotamia. Assyrian Periods – Toronto
RIME	Royal Inscriptions of Mesopotamia. Early Periods – Toronto
RINAP	The Royal Inscriptions of the Neo-Assyrian Period – Winona Lake
RlA	Various authors and editors, *Reallexikon der Assyriologie* (Berlin: De Gruyter, 1928-)
SAA	State Archives of Assyria – Helsinki
SAAB	State Archives of Assyria Bulletin – Padua
SAACT	State Archives of Assyria Cuneiform Texts – Helsinki / Winona Lake
SAAS	State Archives of Assyria Studies – Helsinki
SpTU	Spätbabylonische Texte aus Uruk – Berlin / Mainz
StOr	Studia Orientalia – Helsinki
STT	O. R. Gurney and J. J. Finkelstein, *The Sultantepe Tablets I* (London: The British Institute of Archaelogy at Ankara, 1957); O. R. Gurney and P. Hulin, *The Sultantepe Tablets II* (London: The British Institute of Archaelogy at Ankara, 1964)
TCL	Textes Cunéiformes du Louvre – Paris[3]
TCS	Texts from Cuneiform Sources – Locust Valley, NY
UET	Ur Excavations Texts – London
UF	Ugarit-Forschungen – Münster
VAB	Vorderasiatische Bibliothek – Leipzig

3 'TCL III+' refers to the sole extant manuscript of Sargon's eighth campaign, i.e. TCL III (= Thureau-Dangin, *Huitième Campagne* (1912)) with the addition of fragments realised subsequently to belong to the same tablet (Meissner, *ZA* 34 (1922); Weidner, *AfO* 12 (1937–1939)).

WdO	Die Welt des Orients – Göttingen
ZA	Zeitschrift für Assyriologie und Vorderasiatische Archäologie – Berlin
ZDMG	Zeitschrift der Deutschen Morgenländischen Gesellschaft – Wiesbaden

1 Introduction

> The manuscripts are the material upon which we base our rule, and then, when we have got our rule, we turn round upon the manuscripts and say that the rule, based upon them, convicts them of error. We are thus working in a circle ... The task of the [textual, MW] critic is just this, to tread that circle deftly and warily.
>
> Alfred Housman[4]

It is the aim of this book to raise awareness among Akkadianists of analytical questions and methods which in other fields fall within the province of 'textual criticism'. We will both systematise ideas which already find expression in Assyriological writings, and, thanks in large part to work done in other fields, introduce new ones.

Textual (or 'lower')[5] criticism is traditionally defined as the practice of reconstructing the original wording of a composition,[6] as distinct from that on its extant manuscripts.[7] This involves close philological analysis of several kinds: understanding the extant manuscripts and compar-

4 Housman, *Proceedings of the Classical Association* 18 (1921) 80.

5 'Higher' criticism is otherwise known as 'literary' criticism. While some scholars use 'textual criticism' inclusively, as a cover term for 'higher' and 'lower' criticism together, this book uses the phrase as synonymous with 'lower criticism'. Sometimes, the boundary between the two is blurred (e.g. on issues of compositional logic, cf. § 2.2.1).

6 Cf. Maas, "Textkritik", in Gercke and Norden (eds), *Einleitung in die Altertumswissenschaften* (1927) 1: 'Aufgabe der Textkritik ist Herstellung eines dem Autograph (Original) möglichst nahekommenden Textes'.

7 For example, Wenzel, *Speculum* 65/1 (1990) 14 comments that 'In the case of the *Canterbury Tales*, ... even the earliest surviving manuscripts are felt to have undergone editing on the part of their scribes and therefore must be accepted as more or less intelligent responses by first-generation readers'. West, *Iran* 46 (2008) 125a observes that in the case of the Iranian *Yasna* 'The agreement of the manuscripts is no guarantee of a reliable text, because they all derive from an archetype copy made around A.D. 1000, that is, five or six hundred years later than the Sasanian prototype'. In Assyriology, note the comment by Labat, *Création* (1935) 21 on the extant manuscripts of *Ee*: 'Aucun de ces textes n'est original; ce sont tous des copies de tablettes antérieures qui ne nous sont pas parvenues'.

ing them, choosing between variants, identifying corruptions, and formulating conjectures about how wording might originally have run.[8]

The notion of 'original' wording is not as easy to work with in Assyriology as it is in other fields, owing to vagueness about authors and complexities surrounding the very notion of authorship (see § 2.1). Nonetheless, it is our contention that Assyriology can gain much from borrowing (with due adaptation) the working methods and habits of thought from textual critics in other disciplines.

Two issues will interest us most: the mechanisms through which textual changes arose during transmission, and the rationales of cuneiform orthography. This may seem an odd combination of topics, but ample proof will be offered that they are organically connected in at least two ways: it is necessary to understand the logic of spellings before attempting to gauge whether they attest to errors; and spelling patterns hold the clue to a surprisingly broad range of questions about textual change and related issues.

Central to our method of analysis will be the examination of spellings on individual manuscripts, from several vantage points – ranging from the use of case endings to the distribution of the signs ŠA and ŠÁ. We shall see that the findings of such pedantic-looking examinations can impact on matters far removed from orthography.

Assyriological scholarship is not short of brilliant ideas and insights on the issues which we will discuss, or at least on most of them. Said ideas and insights have, however, tended to go unnoticed. This was because, not being integrated into broader questions, their true worth was not realised – sometimes, it seems, not even by their own proponents. As a result, the knowledge which Assyriology possesses about Akkadian orthography and textual change is neither systematised nor efficiently

---

8 Authoritative guides to textual criticism include Delz, "Textkritik und Editionstechnik", in Graf (ed.), *Einleitung in die lateinische Philologie* (1993); Vinaver, "Principles of Textual Emendation", in (Anonymous) (ed.), *Studies Pope* (1939); and West, *Textual Criticism and Editorial Technique* (1973). Still influential is the work by Maas cited in fn. 6 (revised in several subsequent editions). On Maas's continuing influence see Montanari, *La critica del testo secondo Paul Maas* (2003). Commendable introductory surveys include Bird, *Multitextuality in the Iliad* (2010) (though, as noted in fn. 148, Bird's own contentions are not watertight, the survey of previous work in his Introduction is excellent, and very useful) and Bein, *Textkritik* (2008). (I am grateful to Kai Lämmerhirt for bringing these two works to my attention). For further suggestions on reading see Delz's p. 51.

pooled: with rare exceptions,[9] insights achieved are not widely taken note of and reapplied to new sources, but left to languish in inconspicuous footnotes. In consequence, many opportunities for enhanced understanding are missed. It is perhaps symptomatic of this state of affairs that the phrase 'textual criticism' rarely appears in writings by Akkadianists.[10]

As regards sources, this is not a book about a particular textual corpus. Rather, it seeks to promote and explicate questions and methods of analysis with an applicability to the world of Akkadian cuneiform at large. Naturally, the discussion of textual changes arising through transmission is only relevant to writings which *were* transmitted, such as literature and scholarship, to the exclusion of most letters and utilitarian documents. Therefore, for this topic the sources drawn on are literary and scholarly. By contrast, for the rationales of Akkadian orthography any written source is potentially relevant, and here our source base is broader. Inevitably, there is a bias towards the textual typologies which the author is most familiar with: most of the examples are drawn from literature, medical prescriptions, Neo-Assyrian royal inscriptions, and Old

9 Such as the suggestion by Goetze, "The Akkadian dialects of the Old Babylonian mathematical texts", in Neugebauer and Sachs (eds), *Mathematical Cuneiform Texts* (1945) that certain orthographic traits distinguish the North and South of Babylonia in the Old Babylonian period (but see the cautionary remarks of George, *Literary Texts* (2009) 43).

10 One such exception is Lambert, *BSOAS* 52/3 (1989) 544. Another is Borger, *JCS* 18/2 (1964) 50: 'Es scheint mir dringend nötig, dass die Assyriologie … endlich … eine textkritische "standard operating procedure" entwickelt'. Borger's Assyriological articles on 'Textkritik' – *Orientalia* 31 (1962) and *AfO* 25 (1974–1977 [1978]) – are, unlike his appraisal of text-critical approaches to the New Testament in *Theologische Rundschau* 52/1 (1987), not primarily concerned with 'textual criticism' in the senses which the phrase is generally recognised to possess. Rather, the first deals with textual reconstruction: estimating how much text is lost in lacunae, putting fragments in the right order, identifying duplicate manuscripts, etc. This is of course an immensely important task (and sometimes an extremely demanding one), but it is distinct from textual criticism. The second compares variants across manuscripts, and observes grammatically correct ones to be preferable. This arguably is textual criticism, but of a rather primitive (if again indispensable) variety. The paper entitled "A lesson in textual criticism as learned from a comparison of Akkadian and Hebrew textual variants" by E. B. Smick, *Bulletin of the Evangelical Theological Society* 10/2 (1967) seems to not to have excited reactions in Assyriological literature. (Though it is limited in scope and not always water-tight in its analyses – for example, it is unclear why on Smick's p. 131 the variation across manuscripts attributed to "choice of synonyms" could not be due to inadvertence – it is nonetheless a pioneering and worthwhile contribution).

Babylonian letters. However, many of the methods implemented and ideas proposed are believed to have wider applicability.

Our discussion of transmission will be dominated by first millennium examples. This is partly due to the nature and distribution of the extant sources (many more manuscripts of transmitted compositions, as opposed to manuscripts written *ex nihilo*, are extant from the first millennium than from the second), and partly again to the author's interests. Whether Akkadian textual corruption occurred more frequently in the first millennium than the second is a question which cannot be addressed here.

A significant part of this book is taken up with lists of attestations, from which counts are derived. To some readers, this may seem an excessive level of documentation. A justification is offered in § 2.5.

It was not practical to collate the manuscripts discussed. Our analyses therefore rely on modern editions (cuneiform copies and transliterations). Care was taken to exclude instances which there was reason to deem unreliable.

1.1 Notes on nomenclature and conventions

The word 'manuscript' will be used to mean: an object (usually, but not necessarily, a clay tablet) inscribed with writing.

The word 'text' will be used with two slightly different meanings: 'a sequence of words' and a 'sequence of cuneiform signs'.[11] The distinction between these two meanings is not always important. When it is, we have sought to disambiguate.

The word 'exemplar' will be used to mean: a manuscript which served as the textual basis for the production of another manuscript (not necessarily through one-to-one copying). Assyriologists often use the word '*Vorlage*' in this meaning; some Assyriologists, e.g. fn. 21 and passim in RIMA, use 'exemplar' in the sense which we attribute to 'manuscript'.

We reserve the verb 'to copy' for the process of a person actually copying a written source, as in a medieval scriptorium. When we need to talk about manuscripts being generated by other means (e.g. through dictation), we use less specific verbs, such as 'to produce'.

11 In cuneiform it is possible to render the same sequence of words with different sequences of cuneiform signs, and a given sequence of cuneiform signs can often be read as more than one sequence of words.

We use the word 'transmission' in the broad sense of 'production of new manuscripts of pre-existing compositions', and 'transmitter' to mean someone who does this.

For 'version' and 'recension' we follow Jerrold Cooper in treating the former as superordinate to the latter: a given version of a composition may circulate in different recensions.[12]

When manuscripts with lowercase A as siglum (MS a) are referred to, danger of confusion with the English indefinite article sometimes arises. In such cases the lowercase A is put in quotation marks (MS 'a'). This does not imply scepticism vis-à-vis the siglum.

Our use of the symbol ~ in transliterations (as a marker of sandhi and truncated spellings) is explained in § 4.4.

Royal inscriptions from TP I to AN III are cited after their numbers in RIMA 2 and 3.

In translations from Akkadian, italics signify uncertainty.

1.2 The transmission of Akkadian scholarship and literature

As is well known, Akkadian scholarly and literary compositions were transmitted over long periods of time, in some cases from the early second millennium to the late first (though the vast majority of extant manuscripts come from the first). Unsurprisingly, transmission brought about changes of several kinds, intentional and unintentional. It will be one of the main concerns of this book to describe and explain the mechanisms through which these changes occurred, and to illustrate what can be learned from them.

For these purposes, the question of *how* transmission was effected – the three chief possibilities being copying, dictation, and learning by heart – turns out to be less important than one might think. Nonetheless, since the issue lurks in the background of much which we shall discuss, we here set out a brief survey of the issues as we understand them. For each of the three methods we will assess the feasibility of showing that individual manuscripts were so produced.

12 Cooper, *ASJ* 22 (2005) 50.

1.2.1 Transmission through copying

Clear evidence of copying can present itself in two ways: first, the colophon may say that this is how a manuscript was produced. Second, a manuscript might include annotations by the copyist (see § 1.4.5).

Prima facie there would seem to be other ways of establishing that transmission occurred thorough copying, but on closer inspection they run into difficulties.

a) Some[13] textual changes arose through visual misidentification of cuneiform signs, and these are usually interpreted as evidence of copying.[14] However, copyists need not have been the only transmitters who misidentified the signs on their exemplars – they might also happen to people dictating or learning by heart.[15]

An example of this ambiguity occurs in the Hittite version of *šar tamḫāri.* Volkert Haas comments as follows:

> Die Schreibung *nu-úr-da-aḫ-ḫi* für Nūr-Dagan zeigt, dass der Schreiber ... die Lesung GAN des Zeichens ḪÉ nicht kannte und so den Namen verballhornt hat. Daraus ist zu schliessen, dass der vorliegende Text nicht auf Diktat entstanden, sondern von einer Vorlage abgeschrieben worden ist.[16]

However, it does not seem impossible that the misreading of GAN as ḪÉ was instead perpetrated by someone dictating,[17] so the inference of copying seems overly sanguine.

b) Sometimes, extant manuscripts not only agree in wording, but also exhibit identical or near-identical spellings. Such a situation could be thought to reflect faithful copying of a common source, but matters are not necessarily so simple: shared spellings which are common in the relevant textual typology could reflect what we propose to call 'orthographic convergence' (§ 2.4.2), and shared spellings which are unusual in the rel-

---

13 Not all cases in which one sign is substituted for another necessarily reflect visual misidentification: *lapsus styli* (§ 3.2.1.2) could be responsible.

14 Of course, this would not be evidence that the extant manuscript was produced through copying, perhaps only that copying occurred at some point among the extant manuscript's ancestors.

15 For possible Greek examples see Skeat, *Proceedings of the British Academy* 42 (1956) 193 and 201-202.

16 Haas, *Hethitische Literatur* (2006) 68 n. 1.

17 This appears to be the view of Goodnick Westenholz, *Legends* (1997) 103: the spelling *nu-úr-da-aḫ-ḫi* 'reflects a dictation mistake of the reader, who read aloud the GAN as ḪÉ'.

evant textual typology could have been transmitted through comments during dictation, or even through painstaking memorisation.

The possibility that an extant manuscript was produced by copying has sometimes been ruled out when phonetic-looking errors are present.[18] Such reasoning is of doubtful validity, for two reasons. First, as remarked in the introduction to § 3.2, different types of error could build up cumulatively through different phases of transmission. Second, it is very difficult to distinguish errors caused by dictation from errors of '*dictée intérieure*' (§ 3.2.3).

Ulla Koch notes that late extispicy tablets contain traces of Old Babylonian sign values (KU as *qú*, ZA as *sà*, AB as *ìs*, and BI as *pí*). She infers an 'unbroken written tradition'.[19] This is an interesting idea, but not all extant manuscripts with these sign values can be assumed to be part of such a tradition – once the sign values had become traditional in extispicy, they could have been taught by precept, and used on manuscripts written *ex nihilo*. Hence, while they may do so for the typology as a whole, observations such as Koch's do not help us in reconstructing the modalities of transmission that lie behind individual manuscripts.

1.2.2 Transmission through dictation

For the purpose of elucidating the mechanisms of textual change (i.e. how and why textual changes occurred), the question of whether dictation was practised or not (and if yes, how widely) is not of great importance. For changes such as could have arisen through dictation could equally have arisen while copying, through *dictée intérieure* (see § 3.2.3). Theodore Skeat wisely judged that 'In the last resort, irrespective of whether visual copying or dictation is employed, it is the education and attention of the scribe which is really the governing factor'.[20] Nonetheless, we shall for completeness's sake attempt to assess the relevant evidence.

We will concentrate on the production of complete manuscripts with some claim to be authoritative and useful for future readers, to the exclu-

18 See e.g. Finkelstein, *JCS* 17/2 (1963) 44b: 'The writing of lu instead of lú in the name Ameluanna … suggests the scribe was writing from memory (or possibly from dictation?) and not from a cuneiform prototype'.

19 Koch-Westenholz, *Babylonian Liver Omens* (2000) 18. Other scholars have made similar observations in other corpora from time to time (e.g. Nougayrol in fn. 28).

20 Skeat, *Proceedings of the British Academy* 42 (1956) 189.

sion of exercises from the early stages of scribal education (see § 1.5 and fn. 56);[21] and we are dealing only with the transmission of literary and scholarly works, not with the production of utilitarian documents or letters.[22] Those domains have their own problems.

It has been maintained that the possibility of dictation in Akkadian is precluded *a priori* by 'the complicated nature of the cuneiform script', on the grounds that 'very chaotic copies' would have ensued.[23] This, however, seems unduly negative. Providing a group of writers were schooled in the same orthographic conventions, we see no reason to doubt that they could have applied these conventions independently in the process of writing from dictation, producing very similar sequences of signs.[24] The degree of variability observable across many manuscripts of literary and scholarly works seems fully compatible with such a situation.

If one allows for the possibility that a person dictating gave instructions for rare spellings to be preserved, even more manuscripts become possible candidates. So much *a priori.* Demonstrating whether dictation actually occurred or not is a different matter.

21 Foster, *JAOS* 127/3 (2007) 370 notes that a funerary inscription on clay cones 'survives in so many exemplars [i.e. manuscripts, MW], evidently all written by different scribes from dictation, who in some cases imperfectly drafted them in amateur Old Babylonian script, and one of which is inscribed in the wrong direction'. He comments that 'a school exercise is the obvious explanation'. Cf. Radner, *Macht des Namens* (2005) 20–21 and Foster, "Late Babylonian Schooldays: An Archaising Cylinder", in Selz (ed.), *Fs Kienast* (2003). Chiera, *They Wrote on Clay* (1939) 171 argues that 'Judging from the differing signs used in the same exercises by various pupils, students must also have taken dictation', though the stringency of the inference is doubtful.

22 For the likelihood (suggested by their unpolished and anacoluthic formulations) that some of Šamšī-Adad's letters were written at dictation see Finet, "Allusions et réminiscences comme source d'information sur la diffusion de la littérature", in Hecker and Sommerfeld (eds), *Keilschriftliche Literaturen* (1986) 15 (citing ARM I 28; 31; 52; 73) and Charpin, *Lire et écrire* (2008) 163 and 294 n. 445.

23 Grayson, "Old and Middle Assyrian Royal Inscriptions—Marginalia", in Cogan and Eph'al (eds), *Studies Tadmor* (1991) 266.

24 If a group of Assyriologists well-read in a particular textual typology were dictated a passage from that typology and asked to write it down in transliteration (thereby excluding the need actively to recall the shapes of cuneiform signs, a matter in which they would be less practised than ancient writers), I suspect they would produce results indistiguishable from the transliterations of extant manuscripts.

There is a widespread tendency in Assyriology to assume that substitutions arising through phonetic similarity are evidence of dictation.[25] However, substitutions of phonetically similar words could arise through inadvertence in the writer's own head (*dictée intérieure*).[26] *Per se*, then, an isolated error of phonetic similarity tells us nothing about how a manuscript was produced. Sometimes, errors of phonetic similarity cluster so densely on a manuscript that some scholars believe the balance of probability to favour dictation,[27] but such judgments are subjective and difficult to evaluate when little is known of the individual ancient writers. Sandhi spellings (§ 4.4) have sometimes been regarded as evidence of dictation,[28] and the same is true of orthographic variability across different

---

25 See e.g. Ferrara, *JCS* 28/2 (1976) 93 apropos of a manuscript of the Sumerian composition *Nin.me.šár.ra*: 'There are also several orthographic peculiarities, some of which are suggestive of oral error and therefore indicate dictation'; Al-Rawi and George, *Iraq* 57 (1995) 228: 'The development *aškus* < *arkus* is not unexpected (see *GAG* § 35 c), but the phonetic writing is most unusual, and probably symptomatic of a manuscript written at dictation'; also fn. 82 below.

26 Skeat, *Proceedings of the British Academy* 42 (1956) 202 remarked on this ambiguity as follows: 'The fact seems to be that, just as fifty years ago an editor stumbling on a text full of phonetic errors automatically concluded that it has been dictated, so nowadays he, equally automatically, attributes the phenomenon to 'self-dictation' by the copyist. In other words, there has been no increase in knowledge but merely a change in fashion'.

27 See e.g. Skeat, *Proceedings of the British Academy* 42 (1956) 198 on the Pierpont Morgan *Iliad*: 'I do not think there can be much doubt that Plaumann was right in conjecturing the manuscript to have been written from dictation. The extent and depth of the errors and corrections are so great that it is difficult to conceive a scribe so transforming a text by the mere process of transcription'. Similarly Skeat's p. 203 on MSS A and S of Columella's *De re agricola*: 'It seems difficult to believe that such perversions as the above can in all cases proceed from visual copying'.

28 A tablet from Ugarit (RS 25.460; edited by Nougayrol, "Textes suméro-accadiens des archives et bibliothèques privées d'Ugarit", in Nougayrol, Laroche, Virolleaud and Schaeffer (eds), *Ugaritica V* (1968) 265–273, with improvements in von Soden, *UF* 1 (1969) 191–193) exhibits oddities at word boundaries, including *dal-hat e-re-tum* for *dalhā têrētum* 'the omens are confused'. This prompted von Soden, ""Weisheitstexte" in akkadischer Sprache", in Kaiser (ed.), *TUAT 3/i* (1990) 140 to comment as follows: 'Die Tafel wurde wohl aufgrund einer Vorlage aus Babylon nach Diktat geschrieben und weist eine ganze Anzahl von sinnstörenden Hörfehlern auf'. In his original edition of the tablet, however, Nougayrol's comments on 'les crases – au sens large – exceptionellement fréquentes' (p. 266) maintained exactly the opposite view: 'On eût pu croire qu'elles reflétaient simplement la prononciation réelle d'un milieu donné et qu'en

manuscripts of the same composition,[29] but we see no cogency in these views.

In principle, one could assemble a case for dictation on the basis of *combinations* of features internal to a manuscript.[30] However, instances where this can be done convincingly are few and far between. Other textual arguments for dictation are likewise rarely convincing.[31]

What, then, of meta-linguistic evidence (i.e. explicit statements)? One thinks of course of the few[32] colophons which mention dictation – or appear to. The problem is, that Akkadian expressions translated as 'according to dictation' and the like turn out on close scrutiny to be of uncertain meaning.

For example, the phrase *ana pî* 'to/for *pû*'[33] is generally understood as meaning 'according to dictation',[34] but the accuracy of this translation can

---

conséquence ce texte avait dû être dicté, non : copié. Mais sa rare fidelité à la graphie paléobabylonienne prouve définitivement le contraire, à mon opinion'.

29 See e.g. Borger, *BIWA* (1996) xiv: 'Die Schreiber der Prismen dürften nach Diktat gearbeitet haben. Die Keilschrift lässt sehr viele orthographische Varianten zu, und die Schreiber haben die vorhandenen Möglichkeiten jeder für sich weidlich ausgenutzt'; similarly Jursa, *Bēl-rēmanni* (1999) 21 on the Bēl-rēmanni archive.

30 See e.g. the persuasive analysis by Houwink Ten Cate, *JNES* 27/3 (1968) of a manuscript of a Hittite prayer, where the features suggestive of dictation are not only substitutions of phonetically similar words, but also incomplete sign forms: the writer was struggling to keep up. Singer, *Muwatalli's Prayer* (1996) 135–142 collated and revisited the manuscript, confirming that Houwink Ten Cate was 'basically correct' (p. 141; ref. courtesy Mark Weeden).

31 For example, Læssøe, *Iraq* 18/1 (1956) 61 n. 6 argued that a Neo-Babylonian manuscript of a prayer which used the divider sign where a Kuyunjik manuscript of the same composition had actual line divisions was probably written from dictation. However, the divider signs show that the writer of the Neo-Babylonian manuscript knew where the line divisions should go. Hence not to follow them was obviously a conscious choice, which could have been made during copying.

32 As noted by Hunger, *Kolophone* (1968) 8a, colophons which even appear to mention dictation are few in number ('nur wenige').

33 The most basic meaning of *pû* seems to be 'mouth', though it can also have speech-related meanings, such as 'utterance' and 'wording'.

34 Jursa, *Bēl-rēmanni* (1999) 12; George and Al-Rawi, *Iraq* 58 (1996) 160', top edge; Finkel, "On Late Babylonian Medical Training", in George and Finkel (eds), *Studies Lambert* (2000) 139 (the features cited by Finkel as being suggestive of dictation can be understood as reflecting auto-dictation); Lambert, *JCS* 16/3 (1962) 66: vi.17, translating *a-na pi-i* anše.kur.ra as 'at the dictation of a horse'.

be questioned. If one considers *ana pî* in the light of phrases such as *ana pī tuppi* 'according to the wording of the tablet',[35] which emphasises faithful transmission, then the possibility suggests itself that *ana pî* simply means 'in accordance with the (original) wording', i.e. 'faithfully'.[36] Grammatically, the phrase would then be analogous to the absolute use of *ana libbi.*[37] This interpretation of *ana pî* as 'faithfully' is supported by the use of *pû* in connection with a wall, where wording is not at issue: *kī pī mahrê ušēpiš* 'I had it built just like the previous one'.[38] If the interpretation suggested here were followed, the phrase *ana pî* would be neutral with regard to the question of copying vs dictation.

An example of a more localised problem is furnished by a colophon's phrase *ana qabê liginni*, lit. 'in order to speak the *liginnu*' (a *liginnu* being an excerpt tablet). Following a suggestion by Benno Landsberger that the phrase *liginna qabû* 'to speak the *liginnu*' meant 'to dictate', Hermann Hunger and Wolfam von Soden understood *ana qabê liginni* as 'für das Diktieren'.[39] CAD L 183b believes *liginna qabû* to mean 'to recite from a *liginnu*-tablet' (not: 'to dictate'), but for unclear reasons translates the occurrence in our colophon as 'from dictation' (184a). In the present state of knowledge, the translation 'for *liginnu*-recitation' or even just 'for recitation / to be recited' seems at least as likely as 'for dictation'.

More intricate problems with *pû* appear in the subscript of a Neo-Babylonian tablet of war rituals (Hunger no. 486, provenance uncertain):[40] *ana p[ī] ummâni šaṭir gabarû labīru ul āmur*: 'Written according to the *pû* of the scholar(s), I did not see an old original'. Though we accept as self-evident that the tablet was not written by copying a pre-existing exemplar, what exactly does *ana pī ummâni* 'according to the speech of

35 Examples in CAD P 467 *sub* c).

36 See already Lambert, *AfO* 17 (1954–1956) 320 on the similar expression *ša pī*, lit. 'of the mouth of': 'The phrase *ša pî* means no more than "according to", or "that which is according to"'. Elman, *JANES* 7 (1975) 22 (a reference I owe to Nathan Wasserman) appears to use the fact that *ša pī* means 'according to' as evidence that *ana pī* cannot mean the same, but I see no reason why near-identical expressions should not have near-identical meanings.

37 Thus alreads Finkel, "Adad-apla-iddina, Esagil-kin-apli, and the series SA.GIG", in Leichty, de Jong Ellis and Gerardi (eds), *Studies Sachs* (1988) 149 n. 56: *ša pî ummâni/ummânī*: 'according to the Sage(s)'.

38 Borger, *Asarhaddon* (1956) 25 Ep. 35:40 (now Leichty, *Esarhaddon* (2011) 207, 'I had (it) built as it was before'). For *mahrê* = 'previous one' see § 3.5.6.

39 Hunger, *Kolophone* (1968) no. 416 (see comment on Hunger's p. 12); AHw 552a.

40 The tablet was edited by Ebeling, *ArOr* 17/1 (1949) 178–183; improvements (though not to the subscript) in Elat, *BiOr* 39 (1982) cols. 5–6.

the scholar(s)' mean?[41] We need not suppose that the extant tablet was written under dictation. The mention of the *ummânu* would lend a tablet authority, and *ana pī ummâni* may simply be a declaration that the rituals are reported faithfully in the form that the *ummânu* knew them. The writer of the tablet could have learned the rituals from the *ummânu* over a period of time, by whatever means (copying, rote learning, and – why not? – dictation), and then written the extant tablet from memory, or even using written 'notes' (not necessarily in Akkadian).

Similarly, when the Neo-Assyrian scholar Issar-šumu-ēreš writes to the king that a particular omen is not from the series, but from the *pû* (mouth/speech/wording) of the scholars,[42] we need not suppose this to mean that the omen was not available to him in written form. It seems at least as likely that he refers to a written source which is not part of the 'canonical' series but which nonetheless, he argues, preserves an authoritative oral tradition.[43] Eckart Frahm notes that in first-millennium commentaries much which is labelled *šūt pî* 'the things of the *pû*' (a phrase often understood to mean 'oral lore') was in fact taken from written sources: 'The vast majority of the commentaries with subscripts that refer to *šūt pî* were clearly no spontaneous transcriptions of some teacher's oral lectures, but faithful copies of earlier commentary tablets'.[44]

In view of all these complications, it is extremely difficult, if not downright impossible, to prove in any given instance that a manuscript was produced by dictation.[45] In consequence, it is equally difficult to estimate how widespread dictation was in the transmission of Babylonian and Assyrian compositions generally.

41 Elman, *JANES* 7 (1975) 21 points to the high number of odd sign forms on the tablet, and infers this was 'the examination tablet of a mediocre, advanced student – advanced because of the length and complexity of the text …, mediocre because of the errors he made'. For Elman *ana pī ummâni* means 'by dictation' here. This is plausible, but not the only possibility.

42 *šumu anniu lā ša iškarim-ma šū ša pî ummânī šū* 'This omen – it is not from the series, it is from the *pû* of the scholars' (SAA X 8 r.1-2).

43 Thus also Elman, *JANES* 7 (1975) 26.

44 Frahm, *Commentaries* (2011) 44. One of the indications that these commentaries were copied is their use of *he-pí* annotations (see § 1.4.5.1).

45 It is comforting that Assyriologists do not stand alone in having to deal with obscure meta-textual remarks. Gutas, *Theophrastus* (2010) 77 notes that the term 'diseased' (*saqīm*) applied to a lost Arabic manuscript might have indicated that it was textually unsound, or physically damaged. (I owe my acquaintance with Gutas's book to Jessica Priestley).

We conclude with some thoughts about the effects which dictation would have had on transmission, if it did occur. Dictation is *a priori* likely in contexts where it was necessary to produce a large number of copies in a short space of time. This was the situation e.g. with some royal inscriptions. Sennacherib's Rassam cylinder is extant on 74 manuscripts, produced within a month, perhaps in a matter of days.[46] From the fact that errors of phonetic similarity are rare on the extant manuscripts, one might infer that dictation was rare in this setting.[47] Yet if one bears in mind the possibility that the majority of the relevant writers had ample experience in the writing of royal inscriptions,[48] it transpires there is no reason why dictation should have led them to commit errors of phonetic similarity:[49] they would have known what words and phrases to expect, and been unlikely to mis-hear them. They would, in other words, be no more likely to make errors of phonetic similarity when writing under dictation than when copying. Indeed, owing to the distracting necessity of looking backwards and forwards which is inherent in copying,[50] dictation might have *reduced* the likelihood of errors. This possibility should be borne in mind also for other textual typologies.

1.2.3 Transmission through learning by heart

It is sometimes maintained that Akkadian-speaking scholars knew compositions by heart.[51] If this was so, they could have written them out

46 Frahm, *Einleitung* (1997) 51b.

47 This appears to be the reasoning of Frahm, *Einleitung* (1997) 50b-51a.

48 This was not always the case, see e.g. § 3.3.3 on Šal III 44. But such cases generally appear to involve objects bearing short inscriptions, perhaps because they were assigned to trainees. It would make sense to assign the longest inscriptions to the most expert scribes.

49 For scepticism that dictation would necessarily lead to proliferation of errors on manuscripts in Greek and Latin see Skeat, *Proceedings of the British Academy* 42 (1956) 194, reacting against earlier views.

50 On this see Vinaver, "Principles of Textual Emendation", in (Anonymous) (ed.), *Studies Pope* (1939).

51 E.g. Finkel, "On Late Babylonian Medical Training", in George and Finkel (eds), *Studies Lambert* (2000) 143.

from memory.[52] Unfortunately, it is extremely difficult to assess the extent to which this happened.[53]

We are sceptical that it can be demonstrated for individual manuscripts, on the basis of variants they contain, that they were solely written from memory. In general, many variants which might be errors of erroneous recall (e.g. synonymous substitutions) could equally be intentional variants. But, setting this problem aside, even for instances which are believed to attest to erroneous recall – indeed, in a sense *all* errors of transmission are due to erroneous recall – it is usually difficult to decide whether it is faulty recall of what a transmitter has learned by heart, as opposed to faulty recall of what the transmitter just read on an exemplar, or just heard from a person dictating. For if the chunks are too large, if the language is too complicated or alien, if one's mind is elsewhere, or if one is pressed for time, misrememberings of all kinds occur all too easily during dictation and copying.

A further complication is that, when they produced new manuscripts of a composition, transmitters cannot be assumed to have relied exclusively on external sources (such as an exemplar or a person dictating): they might well have been already familiar with the composition – though perhaps in a different version or recension from that which they were supposed to transmit, and not necessarily to the point of knowing it by heart. This familiarity could affect transmission in several different ways: it might help the transmitters make sense of the external source, improving the accuracy of transmission; but it might also lead them to misinterpret the external source;[54] and they might, consciously or unconsciously, merge wording from the external source together with that which they remembered (for possible examples see § 6.2.5 and fn. 980).[55] This could ac-

52 Note however the contention of Elman, *JANES* 7 (1975) 20 that, even if compositions were known by heart, they might still have been transmitted through copying.

53 George, *Gilgamesh* (2003) 419 comments that 'The part played in textual transmission by the human memory is inherently unquantifiable'.

54 We shall meet examples of how this might happen: at *Ludlul* II 120, someone who knew the recension with *īrim* would presumably have read *i*-LAGAB as *i-rim* even if the writer had intended *i-kil* (see § 2.3.2). At *Gilg.* VI 68-69, readers who knew a recension with *ī nīkul* and *hurdatni* would probably have interpreted *i-na zēri*(kul) and *hur-da-ta-na* as variant spellings of the words they knew, when in fact we believe they reflected a different tradition (§ 4.7.2).

55 On this latter point, compare the remarks of Hanna, *Studies in Bibliography* 53 (2000) 167 on the problematic word *wight* in *The Wife of Bath's Prologue* (D 117): 'Memorial contamination might be at issue. Given the 'bespoke' conditions

count for instances of interference between passages which are far apart in a composition, and also for interference between compositions. Hence we deem neither of these types of interference to be hard evidence of transmission through learning by heart, though both may well be evidence of transmitters' familiarity with the compositions they transmitted.

All in all then, demonstrating the role of learning by heart in transmission is extremely difficult. Once one excludes all the features whose attribution to faulty recall of words learned by heart is open to doubt, there is likely to be very little left. There may be cases where combinations of features in a manuscript add up to a strong argument that it was written solely from memory,[56] but if so Akkadian examples have yet to be found.

We shall see (esp. § 3.3.4) that careful study of extant manuscripts can yield evidence that transmitters did *not* know (the relevant portions of) the compositions they were transmitting (at least in the version they were supposed to transmit), and/or were not familiar with the idioms of the relevant textual typologies. Even so, we should always be cautious about attributing faulty recall to ancient quotations of literature and scholarship, as they may correctly reproduce a version or recension which differs from that reconstructed in our modern composite texts.[57]

1.2.4 Differences in transmission between the second and first millennia?

The first millennium yields large numbers of colophons reporting that manuscripts were produced through copying. Hence one can easily establish that copying was widespread (at least in the settings where our manu-

under which English books were produced until the 1460s, no copyist of this work was ever a virgin; all of them knew the text already, and the text they knew may have overridden in their copying whatever they saw before them in their exemplar'.

56 This is argued in Delnero, *JCS* 62 (2010) 64–67 and Delnero, *JNES* (forthcoming), with reference to scholarship outside Mesopotamian studies, for Old Babylonian copies of Sumerian literary compositions, produced as exercises by learners.

57 Frahm, *Commentaries* (2011) 107 states that many quotations in commentaries 'differ quite substantially from the received tradition, and were apparently reproduced by the commentators from memory, without consulting any actual manuscripts'. Unfortunately, the fact that we usually have very few manuscripts per line means that it is difficult to form an impression of the textual stability of individual passages.

scripts originated), but even here the question of which method of transmission prevailed is cloudy.

For the second millennium, from which far fewer Akkadian manuscripts of transmitted compositions are extant, we are very poorly informed. It is therefore best to reserve judgment about how transmission was conducted. It seems safe to suppose that, at one point or other, all methods of transmission will have been employed, but to pinpoint the dominant ones is impossible in the present state of the evidence.

1.2.5 Manners of transmission: summary

It is hazardous to draw a general picture of how Akkadian textual transmission was conducted. Presumably, copying, dictation and learning by heart all played a role at some point. The only more specific thing we can say is that copying was, in many textual typologies, frequent in the first millennium.

The vagueness of this summary may be a serious obstacle to reconstructing the history of transmission for individual compositions. Happily, however, much in extant manuscripts can be clarified without reconstructing this history. For example, an error of visual misidentification can be corrected without knowing whether it was introduced by the writer of the extant manuscript, or whether it was already present in a textual ancestor. As we shall see, there is much to be done in Akkadian sources at this comparatively simple level.

1.3 Transmission as a source of textual change

It is extremely rare to find any two manuscripts which are perfect duplicates of each other (in the sense that they contain exactly the same sequences of signs). Rather, the normal situation is to encounter differences (often termed 'variants') of various types (orthographic, lexical, morphological, syntactic, etc.) across manuscripts of the same composition. The textual changes which give rise to these differences can occur in error (misunderstanding or inadvertence), or be deliberate.

Textual changes which arise through error are all but unavoidable in cultures which lack modern[58] printing techniques,[59] for inadvertence and misunderstanding produce them even when transmitters seek to be faithful. As is widely recognised in Assyriology,[60] this applied to Mesopotamia no less than to other ancient cultures.

Copyists, in particular, have been observed to corrupt the text they transmit in many cultures and throughout the ages.[61] Countless examples could be cited. Classicist Alphonse Dain maintained that the copyist is subject to *distractions inévitables.*[62] Similarly, Medievalist Elizabeth Bryan remarks that 'one-to-one copying ... necessarily introduced unique scribal error to every book..., so that no two "copies" were exactly the same'.[63] A modern example of the dangers of copying is supplied by

58 The earliest printers were actually less accurate than the best scriptoria, see Saenger, *The Library Quarterly* 45/4 (1975); also (without refs) Cerquiglini, *Éloge de la variante* (1989) 19 and 22.

59 An exception is posed by the Rig-Veda of ancient India, which were transmitted 'with marvellous accuracy even in the smallest details' for over a millennium (see Gonda, *Vedic Literature* (1975) 16–17; quotation from p. 16). But – (a) this was oral transmission, which escapes several pitfalls inherent in written transmission (see fn. 50); and, more importantly, (b) a uniquely rigorous set of mnemonic strategies were used: in addition to linear memorisation as we would learn a poem by heart today, the words of the Vedas were also rearranged and repeated according to various patterns (e.g. ab, bc, cd, de ...; ab, ba, ab, bc, cb, bc ...; ab, ba, abc, cba, abc, bc, cb, bcd, dcb, bcd ...). These strategies gave the textual history of the Rig-Veda a stability unmatched in other traditions.

60 See e.g. Gragg, *JAOS* 92 (1972) 207b: 'Whenever there exists a textual tradition of sufficient length, we know that there exists the possibility of a gradual change in the transmitted text. Signs are misread, overlooked, transposed, repeated, simplified, and then consciously or unconsciously, correctly or incorrectly corrected or restored'; also Falkenstein, *Literarische Keilschrifttexte aus Uruk* (1941) 1 on manuscripts from first millennium Uruk: 'Verschlechterungen des Textes sind auf Rechnung der wiederholten Abschriften zu setzen'. For the Hittites see the brief article by Otten, "Kopien von Keilschrifttexten (bei den Hethitern)", in Edzard et al. (eds), *RlA VI* (1980–1983).

61 The astonishing levels of exactitude in scriptoria which produced manuscripts for the fifteenth century French aristocracy (see Saenger in fn. 58) are exceptional.

62 Dain, *Les Manuscrits* (1949) 16. He elaborated on this idea vividly on pp. 28-29: 'Il n'est pas de travail qui, plus que le travail de copie, soit soumis aux impondérables : l'heure qui ne passe pas assez vite, la faim qui tiraille le cénobite et cette vue sur le monde qu'il aperçoit malgré tout de la fenêtre de sa cellule !'. These frustrations might have been felt all the more keenly by the Babylonian transmitters listed in Fales and Postgate, *SAA XI* (1995) no. 156, one of whom, the son of a *šandabakku*, was kept in irons (*siparrī parzilli šakin*, line 10).

63 Bryan, *Collaborative Meaning* (1999) 8.

the preface to the second edition of Ignace Gelb's *Old Akkadian Writing and Grammar*:

> The older edition contained a number of misreadings and inconsistencies which had crept into the manuscript when it was recopied, during my absence from Chicago and without my knowledge, because the original stencils had been spoiled as a result of the intense summer heat.[64]

One of the reasons for the profusion of changes introduced while copying may be the disruptive nature of the procedure (having to look back and forth), which affords many opportunities for error (see Eugène Vinaver in fn. 50). Copying is of course not the only means of transmission which results in inadvertent changes.

In contrast to the near-ubiquity of inadvertent changes, the incidence of deliberate ones varies across scribal cultures, and also within them. In the Greek world, transmitters 'Tended to be careless of exact quotation or copying', and literary papyri from the early Ptolemaic period are revealing of 'lack of respect for the accurate recording of an author's words', as their 'divergences cannot ... be put down to mere carelessness by the scribe'.[65] Eric Turner further comments on early papyri exhibiting 'wild' variants, contrasting them with more faithful transmission in the Roman period:

> Some [early Ptolemaic papyri, MW] are clearly wild, some less so, and some appear to have quite a good textual basis ... Yet an important point will be missed if one is satisfied with this classification and dismisses the 'wild' papyri as the property of uneducated immigrants and untypical. They are beautiful examples of calligraphy, and they contain good readings as well as a high coefficient of error and a high proportion of change. Their uniqueness will be best realised by comparison with similar texts of the Roman period: in the later texts the coefficient of error is not so high, nor is there so great a bulk of variants. It is tempting to explain these differences on psychological grounds; the writers of these early papyri felt no compulsion to copy accurately because they did not regard the exact expression (especially the order of words) of the author as sacred. It is a sobering explanation. To what corruptions may not classical writers, especially in prose, have been exposed in the copies of the fourth and third centuries?[66]

---

64 Gelb, *Old Akkadian Writing and Grammar* (1961) ix.

65 Turner, *Greek Papyri* (1980) 107, with examples.

66 Turner, *Greek Papyri* (1980) 108. A different view of variants has been adopted by Bird, *Multitextuality in the Iliad* (2010) for early Ptolemaic manuscripts of Homer (cf. fn. 148), but Bird recognises that his reservations do not apply to other authors, 'such as Pindar or Virgil' (p. vii).

Later, the copyists of Medieval Europe normally aimed to transmit sacred writings (especially the Bible) without variation.[67] On the other hand, the same cultures attached less importance to the exact transmission of non-sacred writings, so deliberate changes are proportionately more common in them.[68] Ralph Hanna observes that copyists of Middle English manuscripts sometimes indulged in 'extensive rewriting' from 'a desire to join in the fun and write some poetry too'.[69] In ancient Mesopotamia we must similarly reckon both with situations where the aim was to transmit as faithfully as possible (though even here, as we shall see, the notion of fidelity needs to be examined), and with situations where it was thought appropriate to make changes of various kinds. Examples will be provided in § 3.4.

Textual change, whether deliberate or erroneous, is, then, a phenomenon which pervades virtually all fields of study and research which deal with written sources.[70] In many disciplines, textual changes have long been intensively analysed, with exploration of questions such as how they arose, and what can be deduced from them.[71] We will argue that this rich scholarly literature about textual criticism contains many ideas and analytical habits which – with due adaptation – can be imported into Assyriology with great profit.

---

67 Bryan, *Collaborative Meaning* (1999) 11–15.

68 Though even here Zumthor, *La lettre et la voix* (1987) 114 reports a tendency to transmit the wording of Latin compositions more faithfully than the wording of those in the vernacular.

69 Hanna, *Middle English Manuscripts* (1996) 160. Compare Tarrant, "The Reader as Author: Collaborative Interpolation in Latin Poetry", in Grant (ed.), *Editing Greek and Latin Texts* (1989) esp. 114, arguing that the motivations for interpolation were more varied and colourful than previously realised in Classics.

70 Problems of transmission do not only arise with words. For an example in music see the comment by Schnabel on the first edition of Beethoven's Sonata 29, *Allegro Risoluto*, bar 47 (van Beethoven, *32 sonate* (1988) vol. 3, p. 169): 'Im Originaldruck ist vor das achte Sechzehntel kein b-Zeichen gesetzt; demnach soll es also « g » [g natural, MW] sein. Es mag hier ein Versehen vorliegen; wahrscheinlich ist doch « ges » [g flat, MW] gemeint'.

71 Cross-fertilisation has sometimes taken place, e.g. a Medievalist drawing on handbooks of textual criticism written by and for Classicists (Hanna, *Middle English Manuscripts* (1996) 174, 178, 180); a Homeric scholar drawing on New Testament scholarship (Bird, *Multitextuality in the Iliad* (2010) esp. 4).

1.4 Attitudes to transmission

Did Akkadian transmitters feel obliged to reproduce their exemplars as seen, or did they feel free to change the signs and wording? If so, to what extent, and under what circumstances? How did they cope with damage and obscurities?

These are some of the most important questions of Akkadian textual criticism. Unfortunately, at present the answers can only be rather vague: the details will hopefully one day become clear through the accumulation of detailed studies.[72] In this section we will present the questions and problems, leaving to later sections such study of the evidence as we shall undertake.

1.4.1 Ancient notions of fidelity

Today, with cameras and photocopiers, we can easily make perfect reproductions of writings, and indeed we are used to seeing them mass-produced in identical copies (books etc.). We should however be wary of allowing this to condition our understanding of standards of reproduction in ancient Mesopotamia, where the production of perfect replicas, though possible, was much more arduous.[73]

72 Some interesting observations about textual alterations arising from changing religious ideology are made by Tigay, *Evolution* (1982) 68–71, though here we have to contend with redaction as well as transmission. Tigay (p. 72) also maintains that the 'editors' of *Gilg.* 'felt free to alter its wording and style in accordance with their own sense of clarity and aesthetics', though many isolated instances which fit this picture could equally be due to inadvertence.

73 Cf. Zolyómi, 'Variation in the multiword expression *igi bar* in the Old Babylonian period', in Ebeling and Cunningham (eds), *Analysing Literary Sumerian* (2007) 317: 'In the case of Sumerian literary texts we have no evidence… suggesting that … exact verbal accuracy was aimed at by those who wrote the mss. (except, of course, for the case where a ms. is clearly meant to be an exercise of copying)'. For Old Babylonian manuscripts there are additional complications set out by Delnero, "Pre-verbal /n/: function, distribution, and stability" in the same volume, p. 110: 'Copies of OB literary compositions are the incidental by-product of the educational process, and were clearly not intended to be preserved for posterity. The means by which they were produced, as well as the quality of the texts they contain, is therefore dictated not by the need to create a "correct" copy, but by the specific objectives of the pedagogical exercise from which they result'. (I owe these references to Gonzalo Rubio).

In cultures where identical reproduction is difficult, the notion of exactitude is relativised, or even de-prioritised. Elizabeth Bryan remarks that medieval copyists 'did not necessarily aspire to our modern standards of exact repeatibility',[74] and Paul Zumthor comments that 'copy' is a modern idea: medieval manuscripts are better regarded as *re-créations* of a composition.[75] In their fieldwork on Balkan poets, Milman Parry and Albert Lord encountered an epic singer, Đemo Zogić, who said he could repeat a song 'word for word and line for line', even though this was not literally true – 'Was Zogić lying to us? No, ... to him "word for word and line for line" are simply an emphatic way of saying "like".'[76]

In principle, transmitters might make changes for any number of reasons: because the exemplar used rare or archaic phrasing, which they found unfamiliar or even did not understand; because they thought (whether rightly or wrongly) that the exemplar contained an error; because the exemplar was broken, and they wanted to fill the lacuna; for reasons of subjective preference. The question is, what actually happened in practice? Were conscious changes made, or not? And if yes, under what circumstances, or for what reasons? In other words, what standards of textual fidelity were there in Akkadian scribal culture?

There are cases where exemplars seem to have been reproduced even in matters of detail. We will meet several examples, esp. in §§ 3.4.4 (*Diagnostic Handbook* XVII), 3.4.6.2 (Issar-šumu-ēreš) and 3.5.7 (oracle questions). Nonetheless, we shall see that transmitters were not always punctilious about preserving details of spelling or wording on their sources.[77]

It is likely that standards of fidelity varied with variables such as the type of change (layout, spelling, wording), the period, the textual typology, the reason for which the copy was made (e.g. for the moment or long-term storage), the characteristics of the exemplar (e.g. old or modern), the personal preferences of individual transmitters, and the standards and conventions of individual scriptoria. All this will have to be worked out through a painstaking process of documentation, for which we will outline a simple method in § 3.4.

74 Bryan, *Collaborative Meaning* (1999) 8.

75 Zumthor, *La lettre et la voix* (1987) 114–115.

76 Lord, *The Singer of Tales* (1960) 28.

77 See George, *Gilgamesh* (2003) 429: 'wilful tampering'. Labat, *Création* (1935) 22–24 offers several examples of what he considers to be such tampering in the transmission of *Ee*, though other interpretations (inadvertence of several kinds) are possible.

1.4.2 Non-restoration

Faced with a lacuna, a transmitter might or might not restore it. If restoration of a lacuna was not attempted, the transmitter had (as far as we can see) four main options: **1)** simply to omit the lacuna, and possibly such words as were meaningless without it; **2)** to leave uninscribed clay to represent the lacuna; **3)** to reproduce the visible traces; **4)** somehow to indicate to the reader that the exemplar was damaged.

Of these four procedures, the first would leave no distinctive traces: even if we know (from other manuscripts) that an omission occurs, there is no way of knowing whether it was intentional or not.

The second would leave visible traces (the uninscribed clay), but modern scholars might well be hesitant to interpret uninscribed clay as evidence for a lacuna on the exemplar without corroboration.[78] An unusually compelling example occurs on a late copy of the Gula Hymn (MS a) inscribed by a *šamallû mašmaššu agašgû* 'novice, junior *mašmaššu*'.[79] Lines 76 and 77 of the composition end with ^{d}en.líl and ^{d}nin.líl, but, as noted by Wilfred Lambert, MS 'a'[80] omits en.líl in line 76 and líl in line 77.[81] What is more, the resulting line endings are indented with respect to those of surrounding lines: the writer appears to have left uninscribed clay to represent lacunae on the exemplar.

The third procedure is attested (see fn. 365), though rarely. The fourth can be documented quite abundantly in the shape of annotations (see below).

In the absence of an explicit annotation to the effect that the exemplar was broken, it is rare to be able to point confidently to a case of non-restoration.

---

78 Though note Jacobsen, *King List* (1939) 15 on lines 3-4, MS P_2.

79 According to Lambert, *Orientalia* 36 (1967) 105, the tablet 'probably dates to the Persian period'.

80 For the quotation marks in manuscript sigla see the end of § 1.1.

81 Lambert, *Orientalia* 36 (1967) 103. The copy of lines 76 and 77 is given in Lambert's Tab. XI. Lambert also suggests that in line 166 the UD-*ši-la-a-ti* on MS a (vs *tašīlāti* 'celebrations' on MS c) derives from a misidentification of a damaged Neo-Babylonian TA as UD. While this is possible, one cannot rule out that a transmitter misunderstood a spelling such as *ta-ši-la-a-ti* as representing /taššīlāti/ for *tamšīlāti* 'likenesses' and hypercorrected *ta* to *tam* (=UD).

1.4.3 Restoration

When restoration was performed by a transmitter, the relevant words or signs might be taken from several sources (none of which guaranteed that the restoration would exactly match the lost text): the transmitter's own recollection of the composition, *ad hoc* surmise (potentially informed by acquaintance with the idioms of the relevant textual typology), or an external source – such as a colleague, or another manuscript.

A transmitter might or might not be confident about the accuracy of a restoration. Given how confused some transmitters were by what they were transmitting, it cannot be presumed even of confident restorations that they were always accurate.

It is difficult to establish how often restoration was undertaken: if a restoration was correct, or at least plausible, then usually we have no indication that it happened at all; if it was incorrect, then it is hard to distinguish from substitutions of similar signs or deliberate variants. A case which at present seems exceptional is *Gilgameš* VIII MS m_1, on which Aage Westenholz comments as follows:

> When I inspected the tablet, I thought that I could see a faint outline around the portion with the preserved text: the copyist sketched the outline of his broken *Vorlage*, copied what was written there, and then inserted his restorations in smaller script. (Pers. comm.)

Here the intention would be simultaneously to restore and have the reader know that restoration had taken place. It is likely that future research will reveal more such instances.

We will here present some cases where restoration by transmitters is likely. (As always, we are left wondering whether the restoration was effected by the writer of the extant tablet, or of an ancestor manuscript).

Two duplicate tablets from the archive of Bēl-rēmanni (Neo-Babylonian Sippar) corrupt original *ú-šeb-ši-*: one (BM 43301+) has *ú-ša-šal-*..., the other (BM 42568) has *ú-*[*š*]*ab*$^{?}$*-ši-*. Michael Jursa draws the persuasive inference that the exemplar was damaged, and that the writers of both tablets attempted restoration, the latter more successfully than the former.[82]

An anti-witchcraft incantation has *ilu gít-ma-lu* 'merciful god' where one expects ^{d}*gu-la* 'Gula'. Tzvi Abusch insightfully infers that damaged

82 Jursa, *Bēl-rēmanni* (1999) 19.

^{d}*gu-la* was erroneously understood as *ilu gít-ma*, and emended to *ilu gít-ma-lu.*[83]

Claus Wilcke has compared the beginning of the Old Babylonian and Standard Babylonian versions of *Etana.*[84] He persuasively argues that several differences between them can be attributed to erroneous restorations of a damaged exemplar, probably one written in Middle Assyrian script. The beginning of the Standard Babylonian version is currently extant on one manuscript only (K 2606), so it is impossible to determine how far back in transmission the faulty restoration occurred, or how wide a diffusion it enjoyed.

It is very probable that a significant number of restorations are found among the examples of substitutions of similar signs cited in § 3.3, since some of these were very probably due to damage on the exemplar (see e.g. Nils Heeßel on šu.gidim.ma dingir^{meš}, § 3.2.1).

1.4.4 The use of multiple exemplars

When a transmitter introduces a variant with a remark such as *šanîš ša pī tuppi šanê* 'alternatively, according to another tablet',[85] it is clear that parallel manuscripts of what the transmitter regarded as the same passage were consulted. There are further scattered remarks which attest to this procedure.[86]

By contrast, when one just finds *šanîš* 'alternatively',[87] it may be tempting to suppose that a variant from another manuscript is being reported (as e.g. in § 3.2.10), but in some cases the context is compatible with the variant being a transmitter's conjectural emendation (which could have ended up being transmitted in its own right). Similarly,

83 Abusch, *Mesopotamian Witchcraft* (2002) 104 n. 12.

84 Wilcke, *ZA* 67 (1977) 211–214, esp. the cuneiform diagram on his p. 214.

85 Gurney, *Iraq* 22 (1960) 223–224: an incantation tablet gives two alternative rituals, introducing the second as reported above. Also von Weiher, *SpTU IV* (1993) no. 129 line 34.

86 Neo-Assyrian *An.gim* is related to both the MA and NB recensions (Cooper, *Return of Ninurta* (1978) 51), probably because the redactor drew on both, blending them. A tablet of the Neo-Assyrian scholar Urad-Gula appears to state in the colophon that it was redacted from broken tablets: *ina pī tuppī hepûti*(gaz^{meš}) *šaṭir* (Hunger, *Kolophone* (1968) no. 498 line 3; the original edition by Gadd, *StOr* 1 (1925) 30 does not translate the colophon), though it is possible that MEŠ simply marks gaz as a sumerogram (§ 5.4.7).

87 See CAD Š/i 387.

when manuscripts provide alternatives which are visually similar, it is possible that a transmitter was unsure what to restore, and so provided the reader with multiple possibilities (see e.g. § 3.3.3 on Neo-Assyrian ka-*šú* and eme-*šú*).

It is not always easy to know what to read into colophons' statements that multiple exemplars were used.[88] The different exemplars might have been used in parallel and blended into each other, to produce a 'composite text' just as in modern editions – but it is also possible that different passages were copied from different sources, and put together sequentially.[89]

In view of all these complications, it is difficult to form an impression of how and how often transmitters worked with multiple manuscripts.

1.4.5 Annotations by transmitters

Transmitters sometimes inserted annotations to alert readers to problems which they encountered on their exemplar.[90] They might indicate that the exemplar was damaged, or that multiple readings of a sign were possible. Annotations are surveyed in a *RlA* article by Joachim Krecher.[91]

Annotations could get transmitted in their own right, becoming part of the received text. It is not always easy to tell whether given signs originated as a transmitter's annotation or not (see § 3.4.5).

1.4.5.1 *hepi* 'it is broken' and similar

The most frequent of the annotations inserted by transmitters is *he-pí* 'it is broken',[92] used to indicate to the reader that the exemplar contained a lacuna. Usually, it was written in smaller signs and/or in superscript, to

88 E.g. the lexical tablet published by Weidner, *AfO* 7 (1931–1932) and *AfO* 11 (1936–1937); Hunger, *Kolophone* (1968) no. 231.

89 This is more likely for tablets divided into individual entries than for literary narratives.

90 Annotations about the state of the exemplar could also go in the colophon, cf. fn. 86.

91 Krecher, "Glossen. A. In sumerischen und akkadischen Texten", in Weidner, von Soden, et al. (eds), *RlA III* (1957–1971).

92 The word *hepi* 'it is broken' (stative of *hepû* 'to break') is normally spelled *he-pí*. It is sometimes followed by *eššu* 'new', and exceptionally by *labīru* 'old' (see CAD H 196a), 'new' apparently signifying that the writer is introducing the *hepi* annotation rather than copying it from the exemplar, and 'old' the opposite.

distinguish it from the transmitted text. Very occasionally, greater precision was conveyed: two Seleucid tablets give a linear measurement of how much of the exemplar was illegible.[93] A Middle Babylonian copyist indicated the point up to which the exemplar was healthy.[94]

Annotations such as *hepi* have sometimes been viewed as evidence that Akkadian transmitters aimed to reproduce the exemplar as faithfully as possible.[95] The argument runs as follows: the very existence of such annotations proves that transmitters avoided restoration,[96] and the fact that restorations were avoided even when the transmitter must have known what was missing shows that great care was taken to transmit the exemplar exactly as received.[97]

However, even if some transmitters sometimes avoided restorations, this cannot be generalised to all of them. Not only would this presumption not be compelling *a priori*,[98] it is, as we shall see, demonstrably

---

CAD and others read *hi-pí*, a noun *hīpu* meaning 'break', but this raises the problem of why the noun would always end in *-i* in this context. Some of the attestations could be sandhi spellings, cf. CAD H 196a, but this is unlikely to apply to all cases. Ditto for fossilisation. We suppose the relationship between *hepi* and *eššu* to be asyntactic ('it's broken; new'), as befits a concise annotation.

93 See Sachs, *JCS* 6/1 (1952) 71, commentary to obverse 5, on two Seleucid tablets.

94 *pānum gamir* 'the surface is complete' (see Rutz, *JCS* 58 (2006) 89b *ad* 46).

95 A different view was taken by Jacobsen, *King List* (1939) 39 for Sumerian, deeming it natural that copyists should update older spellings to conform with contemporary orthography (and grammar). See also Albright, *Stone Age to Christianity* (1957) 79: 'A principle which must never be lost sight of in dealing with documents of the Ancient Near East is that instead of leaving obvious archaisms in spelling and grammar, as later became the fashion in Greece and Rome, the scribes generally revised ancient literary and other documents periodically. This practice was followed with particular regularity by cuneiform scribes'. Owing to the absence of examples or further detail, however, this is hard to evaluate: was Albright thinking of transmission or redaction? And what archaisms?

96 West, *Helicon* (1997) 600: 'A scribe was trained to copy his exemplar faithfully and to certify at the end that he had done so; if the exemplar was damaged, he noted the fact, he did not introduce a conjectural restoration'.

97 Jursa, *Bēl-rēmanni* (1999) 21 'Die insgesamt grosse Stabilität der (sogenannten) kanonischen literarischen Überlieferung zeigt … ebenso wie die offensichtliche Zurückhaltung der Schreiber bei Ergänzungen – *hepi-eššu*-Vermerke wurden gesetzt, auch wenn der fehlende Text bekannt gewesen sein muss –, dass auf möglichst getreue Wiedergabe einer Vorlage Wert gelegt wurde'. Cf. also Glassner, *Mesopotamian Chronicles* (2005) 14 (though other interpretations seem possible there).

98 Note the interpretation proposed by Finkel, "On Late Babylonian Medical Training", in George and Finkel (eds), *Studies Lambert* (2000) 180 for *hepi* an-

false. A further problem is that we should not assume transmitters to have known as much as we would like them to (see § 3.3.4).

1.4.5.2 Other annotations

Transmitters could insert *ad hoc* annotations of their own devising, though, being less well established than *hepi*, they are not always easy to recognise.

An example occurs in a Late Babylonian medical exercise, whose likely textual history has been reconstructed by Irving Finkel:[99] a transmitter misidentified sar-*ab* (*tugallab* 'you shave') as sar-*du*, probably because it was written in slanting script, which makes AB and DU look similar. He (or she) then reproduced the ostensible sar-*du*, but added the expected *ab*, marking this as an annotation with the colon-like wedges (used for giving alternatives). This resulted in extant sar-*du* : *ab*.[100]

A possible example of an *ad hoc* annotation in an inscription of Šalmaneser III is discussed in § 3.4.3. More are provided in § 3.4.5.

1.4.6 How did transmitters deal with (perceived) obscurities?

The answer to this question has to be teased out of the extant manuscripts. This book (esp. in § 3.4; also e.g. § 3.2.2 *sub* f) will collect instances which illustrate a range of options: transmitters could reproduce obscurities as they found them (potentially adding an annotation, e.g. § 3.4.3 on UŠ SI ŠÚ), omit them,[101] or emend them.

---

notations in an advanced medical exercise: 'The careful indication of damaged spots would testify to his care and reliability in preserving and transmitting the traditional medical lore, and show how well adapted he would be to the practical task of using whatever older inscriptions he might encounter later'. In this interpretation, the attention to *hepi* annotations is dictated by the need for the writer to prove his or her abilities at a particular stage of training, and it cannot be supposed that the writer would have done like in later stages.

99 Finkel, "On Late Babylonian Medical Training", in George and Finkel (eds), *Studies Lambert* (2000) 166.

100 Another possibility is that the manuscript draws on two sources, one with sar-*du* and one with sar-*ab*, and that the colon-like wedges mark the variants as such.

101 For a possible Hittite example see Miller, *Kizzuwatna Rituals* (2004) 231. (I am grateful to Mark Weeden for drawing my attention to this work and its detailed engagement with textual change). Cf. also Gutas, *Theophrastus* (2010) 99 for Arabic translators of Greek omitting things they did not understand.

Of course, when transmitters found something obscure, the fault may have lain with them rather than with the exemplar. This situation will also be documented (see §§ 3.2.19 and 3.4).

1.4.7 Summary

Our knowledge of ancient attitudes to textual transmission, and of how they influenced transmitters in practice, is sketchy in the extreme. Clearly, we have to reckon with great diversity of knowledge and meticulousness in ancient transmitters – some who were excellent, some very poor, and no doubt many somewhere in between. Future research will hopefully add much detail to this rather vague picture.

That said, much of this book is given over to chronicling transmitters' misunderstandings and miscellaneous errors. It is therefore important to stress that they were by no means always as careless or ignorant as their worst faults suggests.

1.5 The problem of apprentices

It seems fair to suppose that both the seriousness and frequency of the errors which a transmitter committed varied with the level of experience which he or she possessed: the more experience, the fewer serious errors.[102] The question is, how experienced were the persons who wrote our extant manuscripts? It can be frustratingly hard to tell.

For some manuscripts, it is obvious that they were produced as exercises by pupils in the early stages of their education.[103] This applies especially to excerpts from poems written on 'lenticular' (lens-shaped) tab-

102 Though not necessarily the fewer trivial ones.

103 How long did training last? Most modern scholars agree on 'a prolonged period' (Oppenheim, *Ancient Mesopotamia* (1977) 238), but beyond this there is uncertainty (Charpin, *Reading and Writing* (2010) 27). Note the comment by Parpola, "The Man Without a Scribe and the Question of Literacy in the Assyrian Empire", in Pongratz-Leisten, Kühne and Xella (eds), *Fs. Röllig* (1997) 321, who argues that, while 'full mastery' of cuneiform takes and took a lifetime, 'elementary literacy' such as might have served the purposes of day to day life (cf. § 5.2.3) could have been achieved comparatively quickly.

lets.[104] However, setting aside the obvious cases (which usually stem from the earliest stages of learning), deciding whether or not a manuscript was written by a learner is a tricky issue. The further learners progressed, the harder it becomes to distinguish their work from that of people whose education was long complete.[105] Features such as careless handwriting or hasty execution have sometimes been taken as signs that a manuscript was produced in an educational context, but such ascriptions are simplistic.[106] Hence, as remarked by Irving Finkel, 'The definition of what constitutes a "school text" has always been a cloudy issue among Assyriologists',[107] and indeed the very term 'school' may be misleading.[108]

Fully-fledged manuscripts of entire Tablets (i. e. 'chapters') of compositions are generally suggestive of advanced competence. However, they were not necessarily written by expert scholars. Indeed, writing out tablets was very likely a chore, and one can imagine it being delegated to underlings.[109] This was the situation in Hellenistic Uruk as described by Laurie Pearce and Timothy Doty: 'There were two phases to a scribe's career. In the early stage, he wrote or copied tablets …; later he owned tablets and may have continued his scribal activities as well'.[110] The details

104 Of course, not all extracts need be educational exercises (and indeed an educational origin does not rule out other functions). See Finkel, "On Late Babylonian Medical Training", in George and Finkel (eds), *Studies Lambert* (2000) 145 on medical tablets. An unusual case is that of *Erra*, extracts of which had a practical use as plague amulets (see Reiner, *JNES* 19/2 (1960)).

105 See e.g. Westenholz, *AfO* 25 (1974–1977) 106: 'Obviously, we may often be unable to distinguish the more advanced specimens of such exercises [i.e. documents, letters and accounts, MW] from real-life documents'; Cavigneaux, *Textes scolaires* (1981) 39 *ad* 4: 'Une graphie aussi compliquée pourrait se justifier si la première version a bien été écrite par un maître ou par un écolier avancé'.

106 See Sommerfeld, *Tutub* (1999) 12 and Gesche, *Schulunterricht* (2001) 56. Compare Cribiore, "Education in the Papyri", in Bagnall (ed.), *Oxford Handbook of Papyrology* (2009) 329 on Greek papyri: 'The "rapid hand" is that of the older student and cannot identify [a manuscript as, MW] an exercise in the absence of other characteristics'.

107 Finkel, "On Late Babylonian Medical Training", in George and Finkel (eds), *Studies Lambert* (2000) 143.

108 See George, "In search of the é.dub.ba.a: the ancient Mesopotamian school in literature and reality", in Sefati (ed.), *Studies Klein* (2005) 131–132. Cf. Rollston, *Writing and Epigraphy* (2010) 94–95 and Charpin, *Reading and Writing* (2010) 32.

109 Cf. Brown, *Astronomy-Astrology* (2000) 48, commenting that copying was 'presumably the function of someone still lower in rank than a Scholar'.

110 Pearce and Doty, "The Activities of Anu-belšunu, Seleucid Scribe", in Marzahn and Neumann (eds), *Fs Oelsner* (2000) 341; Clancier, *Bibliothèques* (2009) 92

of this picture have been fleshed out by Eleanor Robson: manuscripts of entire Tablets were produced by young professionals in the final stages of their training (perhaps also shortly after completing it), in their late teens and early twenties; colophons state that the manuscripts were written for the writers' teachers (i. e. relatives and family friends), who presumably went on to own them.[111]

We thus need at least three terms, to identify writers in three different stages of their career: those who are very much still learners; those who are in the very final stages of their education/training or have recently completed it; those who completed their education/training long ago, and have acquired great expertise. The labels 'learners', 'apprentices' and 'experts' seem useful.

Thanks to Olof Pedersén's analysis of Kiṣir-Aššur's colophons,[112] terminology for different stages of the scribal career at Neo-Assyrian Assur is known in much more refined gradations than the three distinguished above: *šamallû ṣehru* 'young student', *šamallû* 'student', *šamallû* maš.maš *ṣehru* 'student, young exorcist', maš.maš *ṣehru* 'young exorcist', maš.maš 'exorcist', maš.maš *bīt aššur* 'exorcist of the Assur temple'.[113] However, there is at present little sense in attempting to use the ancient scale and its nomenclature, as the characteristics of the various stages are not known. Accordingly, for present purposes and in the present state of knowledge, the three-fold classification suggested above seems adequate.

Of our three types, the doings of learners are of slight importance for the purposes of this book. They will receive little attention here,[114] though they quite properly attract a large literature elsewhere.[115]

(likewise on Hellenistic Uruk): 'L'on voit très régulièrement les fils des propriétaires des bibliothèques de la maison des *āšipu* écrire pour leurs pères et ce système se transmettre de génération en génération'.

111 Robson, *Social History* (2008) 253–255. Note also the comment by Clancier, *Bibliothèques* (2009) 225: 'L'avantage qu'offrait la pratique de la copie dans le cadre de l'apprentissage est que l'élève avancé renouvelait les tablettes des bibliothèques'. Clancier (pp. 226-229) also identifies exceptions to the pattern, e. g. fathers writing tablets for their sons.

112 Pedersén, *Archives II* (1986) 45–46. Cf. already Hunger, *Kolophone* (1968) 19, reporting the sequence *šamallû ṣehru*, *šamallû* maš.maš, maš.maš, and maš.maš *bīt aššur.*

113 We reproduce Pedersén's translations. Naturally, renditions such as 'student' and 'exorcist' contain a significant element of approximation.

114 Elsewhere in cuneiform studies the doings of learners are of paramount importance. Cf. e. g. the comment apropos of Sumerian literature by Charpin, *Reading and Writing* (2010) 11: 'Sumerologists … attempting to establish the text of these

The distinction between 'apprentices' and 'experts', by contrast, is significant for our purposes. Admittedly, if it cannot be established from studying a manuscript whether it was written by an apprentice or an expert, then this very distinction may appear unreasonable: if an apprentice produces a manuscript which cannot be distinguished from the work of an expert, why, then, can he or she not claim to be as proficient as an expert? Alas, matters are not so simple, for signs correctly copied are not always signs correctly understood (see § 2.3.1). Not knowing whether a manuscript was produced by an expert or an apprentice means that it can be difficult to decide how far to give the writer the benefit of the doubt in cases of suspected error. For it seems likely that apprentices would, despite being considerably more advanced than learners, still make mistakes which experts would not.

It should be noted that an institutional origin for a manuscript does not guarantee it was produced by an 'expert'. As demonstrated by Leonhard Sassmannshausen, in Middle Babylonian administration it was standard to train employees 'on the job', giving them tasks which involved real names and data from the institutions in which they worked.[116] A similar situation was found by Michael Jursa in the Bēl-rēmanni archive from Neo-Babylonian Sippar.[117] This educational strategy may well have been widely used,[118] see e. g. § 3.4.3 for an inscription of Šal III on clay cones.

Even less clear than their role in producing extant manuscripts is the role of apprentices in the long history of textual transmission which underlies our extant manuscripts. Are our manuscripts the offshoots of a silver thread of transmission from expert to expert? Or did apprentices copy each other, perhaps with occasional bits of input from an expert in the role of supervisor? In the former case, our extant manuscripts preserve the work of experts, distorted by at most the writer of the extant

compositions ... are working from apprentices' [=learners' in our terminology, MW] copies of variable quality, some obviously produced by dullards'.

115 See refs in Visicato, *The Power and the Writing* (2000) 1 n. 1; further e. g. Gesche, *Schulunterricht* (2001), Veldhuis, *JAOS* 123/3 (2003), and Veldhuis, "How Did They Learn Cuneiform? Tribute/Word List C as an Elementary Exercise", in Michalowski and Veldhuis (eds), *Studies Vanstiphout* (2006).

116 Sassmannshausen, *BaM* 33 (2002).

117 Jursa, *Bēl-rēmanni* (1999) esp. 31: 'Das Kopieren des Familienarchivs hatte zugleich den Vorteil, die Schüler, sicherlich Kinder der Familie, in die Geschäfte einzuführen'.

118 Thus Robson, *Social History* (2008) 42: 'Doubtless many scribes were trained on the job with no pedagogically designed exercises to practice on'.'

manuscript. In the latter case, they might incorporate multiple layers of distortion by successive generations of apprentices. Regrettably, it is usually very difficult to tell.

If it be supposed that many or most of our extant literary and scholarly manuscripts were inscribed by apprentices,[119] it needs stressing that overall philological standards in ancient Mesopotamia might have been higher than those visible to us. Nonetheless, the extant manuscripts are *ipso facto* what we have, and it is important to be clear about where they are right and wrong, and how their errors came into being – regardless of whether the fault lies with apprentices, or experts, or both.

1.6 Attitudes to manuscripts among Akkadianists

Assyriologists have long been aware that Akkadian textual transmission brought about changes, and they have sometimes explored issues arising from these changes. For example, many compositions underwent redactorial intervention during transmission, and scholars have studied how different versions of the same composition relate to each other.[120] Also, by comparing duplicate manuscripts of a composition, Assyriologists have found many instances where one manuscript shows another to be in error. Nonetheless, the understanding of textual change and its mechanisms is not as advanced in Assyriology as in other fields, nor is its importance as clearly recognised.[121]

---

119 Thus e. g. George, *Gilgamesh* (2003) 37: 'Very many manuscripts of literary texts from first-millennium sites … are the products of scribes of junior rank who had progressed beyond the first two stages of the syllabus and were engaged in advanced study'. Geller, *Babylonian Medicine* (2010) 135–137 suggests that in some colophons *tāmartu* (whose general meaning is 'viewing') means 'examination'. See also Elman in fn. 41.

120 Prominent examples of such discussions are Tigay, *Evolution* (1982) and Cooper, "Gilgamesh Dreams of Enkidu: The Evolution and Dilution of Narrative", in de Jong Ellis (ed.), *Essays Finkelstein* (1977).

121 A greater degree of explicit comment has appeared for Sumerian than for Akkadian, perhaps because more manuscripts tend to be extant for Sumerian compositions than for Akkadian ones. See e. g. Wilcke, *Das Lugalbandaepos* (1969) 24–27 and Cooper, *Return of Ninurta* (1978) 44–46, surveying and classifying the changes arisen during the transmission of the compositions they edit. Exceptionally rich in insights about the mechanisms of textual change (though see § 2.4.5) is Jacobsen, *King List* (1939).

For a start, textual change has not been the subject of extended discussion in Assyriology. While brilliant insights by editors can be found for individual passages,[122] individuals have never presented their ideas on the matter as a connected system. As remarked in the Preface, it is not always easy to determine where individual scholars stand on a particular point, let alone what the consensus across the field might be (if indeed it exists).

That said, one has the impression that, on the whole, Akkadianists subscribe to the views expressed by Medievalist Joseph Bédier:

> La méthode d'édition la plus recommendable est-elle peut-être, en dernière analyse, celle que régit un esprit de défiance de soi, de prudence, d'extrême « conservatisme », un énergique vouloir, porté jusqu'au parti pris, d'ouvrir aux scribes le plus large crédit et de ne toucher au texte d'un manuscrit que l'on imprime qu'en cas d'extrême et presque évidente nécessité : toutes les corrections conjecturales devraient être reléguées en quelque appendice. « Une telle méthode d'edition, a écrit dom Quentin, risque d'être bien dommageable à la critique textuelle ». Peut-être; mais c'est, de toutes les méthodes connues, celle qui risque le moins d'être dommageable aux textes.[123]

In other words, many Assyriologists seem to be reluctant to suppose that extant manuscripts are wrong. This eventuality is accepted when extant text is senselessly garbled,[124] and/or when comparison – be it of different

---

122 Outstanding specimens are the *tours de force* by Poebel, *JNES* 2/1 (1943) 66–70 (elucidating the variants *tukul-ti*, tukul and tu.kúl in spellings of the name Ninurta-tukulti-Aššur), Lambert, *JNES* 33/3 (1974) esp. 295–297, and Wilcke (showing that the first millennium opening of *Etana* arose through misidentification of signs in the second millennium opening, see § 1.4.3). More examples will be given below.

123 Bédier, *Romania* 54 (1928) 356.

124 For example, Labat, *TDP* (1951) 124–125 n. 220 interpreted meaningless *iṣ-ṣa-na-še ina ú* as a corruption of *iṣ-ṣa-na-bu-ú* (*bu* and *še ina* being visually similar); Berger, *Königsinschriften* (1973) 6 deduced meaningless *na at ú* (Neb. Cyl. II, MS 1 ii.17-18) to be a corruption of *na-ṣi-ir*, yielding the phrase *nāṣir mê naqbi* 'the one who protects the waters of the Deep'; Grayson, *RIMA 2* (1991) 299, noted that meaningless gurun.meš.ni.e.šú (Asn II 33:26) must be a corruption of gurun^{meš} dù.a.bi. Many more examples could be cited. For the connection between senselessness and emendation note von Soden, *ZA* 71 (1981) 191 n. 44 'Die Emendation des sinnlosen BI-*ti-iš-tum*', 200 n. 80 'Die Emendation des nicht sinnvollen *ia-li*'; also Wasserman, *NABU* 2011/3, p. 57: 'Instead of … *di-du* ["(a female garment)", MW], which make little sense, I suggest to read *qú*!-*du*, resulting in *quddū*, "adzes"'. Wasserman notes that this emendation yields a convincing parallel with *pāštu* 'axe' in the previous poetic line.

manuscripts of the same passage,[125] parallel portions of the same manuscript,[126] or near-identical phrases in different compositions[127] – clearly shows an error to have occurred. If, however, some sense can be got out of a manuscript, and no duplicate is available to demonstrate corruption, then there often seems to be unease about emendation, and the manuscript is trusted as it is. (Some exceptions are cited in fn. 137).

This unease is all the stronger when a peculiarity is extant on more than one manuscript: 'Le texte semble présenter ici une cacographie: *uq-tat-tú* paraît en effet appartenir non à cette ligne, mais à la fin de la précédente. Il est toutefois troublant que la faute se retrouve dans les différents exemplaires du texte';[128] 'Perhaps *kišādīka* may be regarded as an error for *kišādīšu*; but since both extant manuscripts have *kišādī*(GÚ)-*ka* (KAR 26 rev. 36 // CTN 4, 180 obv. I 17') one would have to assume that this mistake had become part of the transmitted text'.[129]

Sometimes, reverence to an extant manuscript is felt so keenly that an oddity is allowed to stand unemended even though duplicates are available to show what the correct reading is. An example is furnished by Stefan Maul and Rita Strauß, discussing the problematic *marṣa*(^{lú}tu.ra) ŠUL-*na-a* *tulabbassu*(mu$_4^{me?}$-*su*) 'you clothe the patient with a ŠUL-*na-a*' on a Neo-Assyrian tablet of rituals. They note that a duplicate manuscript has ^{túg}*šà-ha-a* 'cloth' in place of ŠUL-*na-a*, that the expression *marṣa*

125 Scholarly examples are legion. An instance is Lambert, *Iraq* 31 (1969) 39 *ad* 57: 'A comparison of this line with the corresponding one of the other Middle Assyrian copy … shows that both halves of the same line in the late compendium are corrupt'.

126 For example, von Soden, ""Weisheitstexte" in akkadischer Sprache", in Kaiser (ed.), *TUAT 3/i* (1990) 176 emeded *ul-tu* 'from' to *ul-li* 'he lifted' in the sentence *ulli imittašu ikarraba hazanna* 'He raised his right hand, blessing the mayor' (*Poor Man of Nippur* 36), TU and LI being visually similar. His rationale for the emendation was that line 36 should match the very similar line 74, where *ullâ* 'he lifted' appears. For an example of similar thinking see George, *Literary Texts* (2009) 24 *ad* iv.6'-7' on the 'corrupt intrusion' of *ubbalu*.

127 For example, line 73 of the *Poor Man of Nippur* runs as follows on the sole extant manuscript: *ma-har-ma iššiq qaqqaru maharšu*, with meaningless *ma-har-ma*. Speiser (pers. comm. to Gurney, *AnSt* 7 (1957) 136) recognised this as a corruption of a line in *Ee*: 'The first *ma-har-šu* is probably an old scribal error for *uš-kin-ma* "he bowed down", as in *Enuma eliš* III, 69'. Hence line 73 of the *Poor Man of Nippur* should run *uš-kin-ma iššiq qaqqaru maharšu* 'He did obeisance and kissed the ground before him'. (Why this should be an 'old' error, i.e. one going far back in transmission, is unclear).

128 Labat, *TDP* (1951) 168 n. 290. See Heeßel's reply, cited in fn. 264.

129 Schwemer, *Orientalia* 79/4 (2010) 481 n. 6.

šah(*h*)*â tulabbaš* 'you clothe the patient with cloth' has ample parallels reported in CAD Š/i 96b, and that the sign ŠUL can be read *šáh* in Neo-Assyrian. But they resist emendation to *šáh-ha*!-*a* 'cloth' on the grounds that NA is clearly written ('..., scheint wegen des folgenden, deutlich geschriebenen NA die Lesung *šahhâ* ausgeschlossen'). They therefore read *dun-na-a*, positing an otherwise unattested noun *dunnû*, of idiosyncratic form and uncertain meaning.[130]

The reluctance to emend is further conspicuous in the numerous cases where errors have been suspected to occur in the published copy (i. e. scale drawing) of an Akkadian manuscript, on the grounds that a slight adjustment to the relevant wedges would give better sense. Often, inspection shows the copies to be at fault.[131] Sometimes, however, the published copy turns out to be faithful. One might expect that, for manuscripts of works with a long history of transmission,[132] the suspicion of error would shift from the modern copy to the manuscript itself. But usually this does not happen: the suspicion of error is abandoned, and the manuscript is read as it stands.

All in all, then, by the standards of fields with a long tradition of textual criticism it seems a fair assessment that Assyriology exhibits the same 'timidness' in analysing extant text which Nicholas Wyatt has remarked on for Ugaritic studies.[133] A striking example of this is the CAD entry *akla* (A/i 277a), a *hapax* word (*Gilg.* X 82, MS K) given the meaning 'apart from'. The CAD editors themselves held this *akla* to be a 'mistake

---

130 Maul and Strauß, *KAL 4* (2011) 35 *ad* Vs. 10'. They may have the notion of *lectio difficilio potior* in mind (cf. § 6.2.3). One could argue that the writer of the extant tablet *thought* he was writing a word *dun-na-a* (which he would presumably not have understood), but the possibility of *lapsus styli* and/or somnolence renders even this uncertain.

131 This was, for instance, noted by Charpin, ""Lies natürlich ..." À propos des erreurs de scribes dans les lettres de Mari", in Dietrich and Loretz (eds), *2nd Fs von Soden* (1995) 57 for many of von Soden's suggestions about Mari letters. Many further examples could be cited.

132 For documents such as letters, which were transmitted much less often, reluctance to undertake certain kinds of emendation (thus e. g. Deller, "Die Briefe des Adad-Šumu-Uṣur", in Röllig and Dietrich (eds), *1st Fs von Soden* (1969) 52 *sub* g)) is more understandable.

133 Wyatt, *UF* 39 (2007) 761. West, *Iran* 46 (2008) 124b-125a similarly notes of the Iranian *Gāthās* that some scholars 'are deeply resistant to the very idea of conjectural emendation', but comments that 'it is certain ... that the text has not reached us in a completely pure and uncorrupted state, and ... it is clearly desirable, so far as possible, to purge it of such errors as may have infected it in the course of transmission' (cf. fn. 7).

of the scribe for expected *e-la'*. Apparently, the CAD editors were reluctant to dismiss something written by an ancient writer, even if they believed it to be wrong. Presumably they reasoned that the ancient writer must have thought it to mean something,[134] but we shall see that there are complications with this reasoning.

There are, of course, exceptions to the tendency to timidness. Special mention is due to the work of Tzvi Abusch, who, in many path-breaking studies of Akkadian incantations, has long campaigned for the need to formulate hypotheses about redactional history, including conjectures about how extant text originally ran.[135] While there are differences in outlook between Abusch's work and the present discussion, and we do not always concur with his conclusions, we can only admire his wealth of insights into the mechanisms of textual change, and the methodological sophistication which he brings to bear on the sources he studies.[136] Conjectures about passages which are not senselessly garbled are also found in the writings of other scholars,[137] though very sparsely in relation to the mass of source material. The field is thus far from the provocative dictum

134 Perhaps the fact that a Kuyunjik manuscript was involved played a part. But even Kuyunjik scribes – in some respects, as argued in § 5.2.2.1, *especially* Kuyunjik scribes – were perfectly capable of writing nonsense which they cannot have understood.

135 See esp. the papers collected in Abusch, *Mesopotamian Witchcraft* (2002), also e.g. Abusch, *JAOS* 103/1 (1983) 11–12.

136 Assyriology would benefit greatly if Abusch wrote a connected exposition of the methods and principles which underpin his analyses.

137 Perhaps most prominently in the work of Wilfred Lambert, whose many acute observations on issues of textual change (e.g. those cited in this book's fnn. 10, 122, 125, 314, 320, 334) testify to his deep engagement with this subject, and to the acumen which he brought to bear on it. Some further examples: Postgate *apud* George, *Gilgamesh* (2003) 525 n. 290 proposes to alter *šum-šu* 'its name' to *šum-ma* 'if' in *Gilg.* XI 299 (both are meaningful, but the latter gives better sense); Koch-Westenholz, *Babylonian Liver Omens* (2000) 106 n. 301 notes that á 'side' could in fact be a lipographic spelling of igi-*et* 'front' (á and *et* being two readings of the same sign); Frahm, *Commentaries* (2011) 82 n. 410 suggests that túg.áb.sag.sa_5 'garment (made of) a red cow' (a motif with Biblical parallels) is a corruption of TÚG.DÙL, probably representing the more usual *nahlaptu*-garment; Borger, *JCS* 18/2 (1964) 55b argues that a transmitter swapped *eklēti* and *pētû* round in line 17 of the *Šamaš Hymn* (*BWL* p. 126). There are many valuable conjectures in the dictionaries (e.g. CAD M/i 195a *sub mamlu* lex.). See also the emendations proposed by Wasserman (*dīdu* '(a female garment)' to *quddu* 'adze'), cited in fn. 124, Biggs (*epinnu* 'plough' to *tubkinnu* 'rubbish dump'), cited in fn. 352, and West (*līrubū* 'may they enter' to *lībirū* 'may they cross'), cited in fn. 380.

which Alfred Housman attributed to Moritz Haupt: 'If the sense requires it, I am prepared to write *Constantinopolitanus* where the manuscripts have the monosyllabic interjection *o*'.

A reason for the widespread aversion to conjectural emendations ('conjectures' for short) may be an unconscious supposition that Akkadian manuscripts are less prone to corruption than those studied in other disciplines. For example, most manuscripts which form the basis of modern editions of Greek and Latin works were produced in the Middle Ages, and subject to corruption by copyists with poor command of those languages. By contrast, extant Akkadian manuscripts were written by native users of cuneiform who were also – until some point in the first millennium BC – native speakers of Akkadian. Hypothetically, then, one might argue that such textual changes as occur in Akkadian manuscripts are – excepting simple and obvious mistakes, such as the omission of a sign – simply the prerogatives of those who introduced them.

To maintain this, however, would be to stick one's head in the sand. Certainly, as one would expect, there do seem to be cases where Babylonian and Assyrian transmitters consciously altered wording which they understood (see § 3.4), but it can also be shown that they fell prey to the full battery of errors of inadvertence and misunderstanding which bedevil textual transmission cross-culturally,[138] whether it be effected by copying, dictation or writing from memory. These errors go beyond obvious cases such as the omission of a sign, and sometimes assume quite insidious (non-obvious) forms, which can be hard to recognize unless one cultivates an awareness of relevant issues. There may have been pockets of first-class transmission where serious errors did not occur,[139] but, as one would expect, this was by no means always the case.

A further reason for hesitancy to formulate conjectures may be the awareness that, at any time, a new manuscript might be found which con-

---

138 Classicists will not be surprised to hear this, since 'Very old copies such as papyri sometimes disappoint expectation by giving a worse text than the medieval tradition instead of a better one' (West, *Textual Criticism and Editorial Technique* (1973) 50). See e.g. Reynolds and Wilson, *Scribes and Scholars* (1991) 217 on Pap. Bodner 4 (Menander): 'astonishingly corrupt'.

139 Falkenstein, *Literarische Keilschrifttexte aus Uruk* (1941) 1 remarks in passing that comparison of Neo- and Late Babylonian manuscripts of the same compositions from Uruk shows the later manuscripts to have 'höchstens geringfügige Verschlechterungen'. From a scholar of Falkenstein's stature this statement is worth taking seriously, though it will only acquire full authority through detailed demonstrations.

tradicts the conjecture. Of course we should always be open to revising our ideas in the light of new evidence, but, *per se*, a new manuscript cannot disprove a conjecture (see § 6.1.4).

Finally, it is possible that, consciously or subconsciously, Assyriologists feel they can recognise errors as self-evident, so it is not worth devoting much attention to them. This attitude, if it exists, is misguided. Some errors are indeed self-evident, but for many oddities which are suspected to be errors there is a large element of doubt, irradiated by manifold complexities. Some are simply not recognised.

The picture which emerges of attitudes to manuscripts and textual change in Assyriology is thus a disconnected and contradictory one. On the one hand, it is widely recognised that transmitters made all sorts of errors. On the other hand, these errors are rarely studied in detail, and, as we shall see, the ways in which they arose are not always understood. Moreover, there is a widespread reluctance to go in search of errors arising from transmission. While obvious ones get recognised as a matter of course, non-obvious ones tend to go undetected, with injurious consequences for our understanding and appreciation of Akkadian writings.

Extreme caution of the kind advocated by Bédier was, perhaps, for a long time justified in Assyriology. But this book will argue that, with two complete dictionaries, many reliable editions, and the steady accumulation of knowledge, Akkadianists can and should become more confident in dealing with their manuscripts, and that they should grapple more closely with the vagaries of transmission.

1.7 Potential rewards deriving from the study of textual change

The study of textual change thrives on the examination of minutiae which, taken in isolation, might be dismissed as trivial. It will be one of the aims of this book to show that many such minutiae are much more important than they might seem, as they feed into far larger questions, sometimes furnishing empirical evidence where one would have imagined it was impossible to find. Compare the following remarks by Hellenist Martin West:

> When scholars argue about whether Aristophanes wrote *de* or *te* in such-and-such a passage, the debate may seem trivial to the point of absurdity, and indeed the sense may not be affected in the least. But by asking the question "which in fact did the poet write?", scholars may be led to inquire into the usage of the particles and the habits of Aristophanes more closely

> than it would ever have occurred to them to do otherwise. In the same way, by asking such questions all the way through the text, they learn all kinds of things that they did not know and never wondered about, sometimes things that were not known to anybody.[140]

In concrete terms, there are at least four benefits which the close study of textual change and its mechanisms (esp. errors of transmission) can bring to Assyriology.[141]

First, it can elucidate obscurities in extant sources. For example, an inscription of Adad-nērāri III includes the peculiar *ur-ru-uh*. The context is consistent with a derivation from *arāhu* 'to do quickly', and indeed a meaning 'quickly' would suit the passage well. For an adverb, however, one expects the ending *-iš* (*urruhiš* 'quickly'). What is an Akkadian grammarian to do with the peculiar, endingless, *ur-ru-uh*? We shall see in § 3.6.2 that it is simply a corruption of expected *urruhiš*. Another example is that a manuscript of an inscription of Assurbanipal offers 'nephew' where the other manuscripts have 'cousin' (A viii.2). The number of extant manuscripts is not always a reliable indicator of which variant is correct (see § 6.1.3). So which is the historian to believe – nephew or cousin? Again, we shall see in § 3.4.6.1.1 that considerations about textual change provide the answer.

Second, the study of variants can yield evidence for the geography of textual transmission in antiquity.

Third, the study of textual change and its mechanisms (i.e. how and why it occurred) is a rich and sorely underexploited source of information about how Akkadian transmitters thought and worked.[142] Examples of the sorts of things we can learn from it include: what words readers found obscure; what sign values they had difficulty recognising; when they copied from an exemplar, how prone they were consciously to alter-

140 West, *Textual Criticism and Editorial Technique* (1973) 8.

141 In principle, the study of textual change (in particular: errors of phonetic similarity) can also yield evidence for the pronunciation of vernacular Akkadian. However, this aspect is subject to the complications discussed in § 3.2.3, and not pursued here.

142 Note the comment by Rüster, "Materialien zu einer Fehlertypologie der hethitischen Texte", in Neu and Rüstel (eds), *2. Fs Otten* (1988) 306: 'Nicht zuletzt werfen Verschreibungen und andere Versehen Licht auf die Arbeitsweise einzelner Schreiber'. For Assyriological interest in the abilities of individual writers see already e.g. Lambert, *BWL* (1960) 152 on evidence for 'how bad a poor Assyrian scribe can be' (though why Lambert holds that the tablet in question was not written by a learner is unclear).

ing it; how thoroughly acquainted they were with the geopolitical context in which they lived; how familiar they were with the idioms of the relevant textual typology; what role literate people had in the production of stone inscriptions.

Fourth, the more we know about the working habits, methods, and degrees of competence of transmitters, this knowledge can in turn guide future scholars in formulating conjectures even where the manuscripts are not senseless.

Illustrations of all these applications will be offered in the following.

2 Some issues of method

> Eine Methodik, die todsicher zum Ziele führt, gibt es freilich nicht und wird es wohl auch niemals geben. Einige praktische Gesichtspunkte möchte ich jedoch einmal zu formulieren versuchen.
>
> Rykle Borger[143]

This chapter is devoted to background considerations which it is necessary to rehearse before analysis of textual change and its mechanisms can begin in earnest.

2.1 Problems pertaining to authors and *Urtext*s

As noted at the outset, textual criticism traditionally has the ultimate aim of reconstructing the *Urtext* (i. e. the sequence of words willed by the author). The supposition runs that all extant versions are descended from the *Urtext*, and that, insofar as they differ from it, they are inferior to it.

There are difficulties with this ambition of reconstructing an *Urtext*. One is that, even if all extant manuscripts are presumed to converge towards a single point of origin, this may not coincide exactly with the *Urtext* willed by the author. To cope with this, the notion of *Urtext* is sometimes divided into 'autograph' and 'archetype',[144] the autograph being the sequence of words willed by the author, and the archetype being the oldest version which it is possible to reconstruct. A second difficulty is that the author might have made changes over time, so that extant manuscripts could be offshoots of different stages of revision.[145] (In such

143 Borger, *Nachrichten der Akademie der Wissenschaften in Göttingen. 1. Philologisch-historische Klasse*, Jahrgang 1991/2 46.

144 Thus e. g. Maas, "Textkritik", in Gercke and Norden (eds), *Einleitung in die Altertumswissenschaften* (1927) 2.

145 In modern times this is well illustrated by the *Tintin* books, some of which were revised, with entire frames being replaced. This procedure resulted in tell-tale differences of line thickness and colouring (Thompson, *Tintin* (2011) 56). Similar things can of course happen with wording.

cases, the most recent version is usually regarded as that to be reconstructed).

A third, and perhaps the strongest criticism to the search for the *Urtext* has come from the field of Medieval Studies. Medievalists have observed that differences across manuscripts of vernacular non-sacred compositions were the norm in medieval cultures, and they argue that in consequence the aim of producing a single *Urtext*, to which all other versions of a composition are inferior, is anachronistic. One of the most vocal exponents of this stance was Bernard Cerquiglini, whose seminal work *Éloge de la variante: Histoire critique de la philologie* culminated in the much-cited assertion that 'L'écriture médiévale ne produit pas de variantes, elle est variance'.[146] In the same vein, Elizabeth Bryan comments that trying to identify what is original to the author is 'a characteristic product of print culture'.[147] Graeme Bird maintains a similar position for the Homeric poems, arguing that, in the long tradition of live performance, every performer should be understood as an 'authentic composer' in his own right.[148]

Reservations such as these have been voiced for the Ancient Near East. For example, Richard Parkinson maintains the following for the Middle Egyptian tale *Sinuhe*:

> All that survives of Sinuhe are the records of various individuals' experiences of the poem at different times and in different places, and also – un-surprisingly – in different versions. To look for an ideal Urtext is to re-

146 Cerquiglini, *Éloge de la variante* (1989) 111. Note also the provocative section title 'Monsieur Procuste, philologue' (p. 31). I first encountered Cerquiglini's book and like-minded scholarship by Medievalists in the Introduction to Fredrik Hagen's forthcoming book on *Ptahhotep*, which the author kindly sent me in draft form. I voice my thanks for this beneficial stimulus.

147 Bryan, *Collaborative Meaning* (1999) 20.

148 Bird, *Multitextuality in the Iliad* (2010). See esp. p. 45: 'We are viewing each *ἀοιδός* as an authentic composer/performer of Homer's poetry'. Bird sets out from an ultra-faithful adherence to what is often described as the Parry-Lord model of 'oral-formulaic poetry' (on p. 100 he describes Ptolemaic manuscripts of Homer as 'transcripts' of live performances), and dismisses rather than disproves the notion of a single poet (hence also that of a written *Urtext*). The contrary view is maintained equally easily, if not more so (e.g. West, *Hellenica* (2011) 176–181 (=http://bmcr.brynmawr.edu/2001/2001-09-06.html) esp. 178 and West, *The Making of the Iliad* (2011) esp. 4–7).

> move the poem from its contexts and its own complicated historicity as a composition.[149]

Parkinson (ibid.) also comments that the *Urtext* is 'arguably irrecoverable given the nature of our sources'.

In Assyriology, Jeffrey Tigay has argued for *Gilg.* that each version should be 'taken seriously as a piece of literature in its own right', with due attention to 'the aims and methods of those who produced it'.[150]

For Akkadian, these stances have much to commend them. Consider the Christmas carol entitled *The Twelve Days of Christmas.* Within a list of different types of bird, this carol features 'five gold rings'. Rings are out of place in a list of birds, and indeed originally the song ran 'five gold wrens'.[151] Nonetheless, it is rings not wrens which we besing today. If they were interested in twenty-first century culture, it would be reductive of scholars in future generations simply to emend our rings back to wrens, thereby ignoring our version and experience of the song. Similarly, when dealing with Akkadian we must not overlook how the writers of our extant manuscripts understood the compositions they transmitted, even if sometimes their understanding was flawed from the standpoint of earlier versions.

An example or two may be useful. Commenting on the sumerogram 'geštin' which appears unexpectedly on a manuscript of an Akkadian composition probably inscribed by a Hittite, Ben Foster distinguishes between geštin being 'correct' in terms of how the Hittites understood the composition (just as gold rings are 'correct' for us),[152] and at the same time being a misunderstanding of the original Mesopotamian version (just as rings are a misunderstanding of wrens).[153]

---

149 Parkinson, "The History of a Poem: Middle Kingdom Literary Manuscripts and their Reception", in Burkard (ed.), *Kon-Texte* (2004) 58. (I owe this reference to Fredrik Hagen).

150 Tigay, *Evolution* (1982) 20. Note also the observations of Clancier, *Bibliothèques* (2009) 222–223 on differences between Mesopotamian and modern notions of authenticity.

151 I owe this delightful observation to Alan Griffiths. For the earlier version (with wrens) see e.g. Gordon Carter, *Journal of American Folklore* 46/1 (1933) 47, transcribed from an informant who learned it in the 1870s 'from a woman who came from Virginia'.

152 Foster suggests that it represents the Hittite military rank gal.geštin.

153 Foster, *Before the Muses* (2005) 343, suggesting that geštin originated as a corruption of anše (the sumerogram for *imēru* 'donkey').

Martin West has argued that all extant manuscripts of *Ee* I preserve the first eight lines in a corrupted order, the original sequence (displayed by rearranging the transmitted numbers) having run 1-2-7-8 3-4-5-6 (see § 2.1). If one accepts this contention, does it follow that modern editions should give the reconstructed sequence of lines in their composite text?

This would make obvious sense for, say, Plato or Cicero: the modern reader usually wants to know what Plato and Cicero actually wrote, not what later transmitters thought they wrote. But for Akkadian matters are not so straightforward. Authors of Akkadian compositions are usually anonymous, and it is uncertain when they were alive. Moreover, since many versions (and even compositions) were redacted out of earlier ones, the concept of single authorship turns out to be problematic.

For some purposes (e. g. certain kinds of literary criticism) it makes sense to work with as original a version as possible, *à la* Plato and Cicero. But in terms of understanding *Ee*'s role in Akkadian intellectual culture and literary history, it makes sense to work with the composition as it was generally known in antiquity. In this case there is, therefore, a justification for modern editors to print the extant line sequence, even if they deem it to have arisen through corruption.

All in all, there is scope for lively debate about what the ultimate aims of Akkadian textual reconstruction should be, and there is probably no single answer. It would, therefore, be mistaken uncritically to import the ultimate aims of textual criticism from other disciplines (e. g. Classics) into Assyriology, even though Akkadianists can usefully learn a great deal from textual critics in other fields at the level of nitty gritty detail.

2.2 Problems in dealing with errors

Since a significant part of our analysis of Akkadian manuscripts will deal with oddities and errors of various kinds, it is necessary to set out some general points on method. For errors are slippery things: in corpus languages at large, it is not always easy to decide whether a particular form or spelling is erroneous. In the case of Babylonian and Assyrian, such complications are compounded by the variability which is normal even in 'good' orthography. Therefore, before embarking on analyses of oddities and errors, and what we can learn from them, it is necessary to set out the major problems one faces in dealing with them.

2.2.1 Oddities of various kinds, and problems in identifying them

One of the chief working concerns of textual critics is to identify oddities (aberrations, inconsistencies, discrepancies, exceptions, unidiomatic formulations, non-sequiturs, incongruences, etc.). Once identified, attempts can be made to account for them, and in the process they may be mined for information about the mechanisms of textual change. Paul Zumthor commented that 'une « anomalie », c'est un fait en quête d'interprétation'.[154]

Some oddities turn out to have *bona fide* justifications, and, when properly understood, not to be as odd as they first seemed; others turn out to originate through errors by transmitters. Either way, they can prove very informative on many fronts. This is as true of Babylonian and Assyrian writings as of those in other ancient languages.

Oddities of interest to textual critics fall into three main types: those of grammar and/or orthography,[155] those of style and idiom, and those of sense. These three types pose different challenges.

2.2.1.1 Oddities of grammar and orthography

Oddities of grammar and orthography are perhaps the easiest to identify. Of course, there is always the possibility that future research will vindicate Akkadian writers currently thought to be guilty of error.[156] Indeed, several such instances will appear in this book. But at least we can usually agree quite easily on what we *perceive* to be oddities.

In pointing to alleged grammatical or orthographic oddities one needs to be looking at them from the right vantage point: a form or spelling should be judged against other forms and spellings on the same manuscript, and on other manuscripts of the same period and scribal environment. Otherwise there is the danger of regarding as an oddity a feature which, in its native context, was perfectly normal.

Conversely, the fact that the language and orthography of many manuscripts has never been scrutinized in detail means that many oddi-

154 Zumthor, *La lettre et la voix* (1987) 17.

155 We group orthography together with grammar because in the present state of knowledge they can be hard to disentangle.

156 Note Finet, "Liste des erreurs de scribes", in Bottéro and Finet (eds), *Répertoire analytique* (1954) 95: 'On court … le risque de prendre pour des erreurs de simples particularités dialectales'. In his regard, matters have improved since 1954, and will presumably continue to do so.

ties have not been recognized as such. Some manuscripts, even in the first millennium, are linguistically and orthographically more consistent than is generally recognized. When this consistency is noted, departures from it become interesting. For example, if a first millennium manuscript is believed to mix case endings indiscriminately, then no particular interest attaches to an accusative singular in *-u*. But if it can be shown that a manuscript almost always exhibits accusatives in *-a*, then an isolated accusative in *-u* becomes worth examining, and might prove a starting point for interesting discoveries. We shall meet several such examples in the course of this book (e.g. § 4.4.4 on *da-la-hu*).

2.2.1.2 Oddities of style

In some disciplines, aberrations can be identified from the style of individual authors, and such instances raise the question of whether the relevant passage might be corrupt (or apochryphal).

Of course, in reconstructing an author's style, as in reconstructing other things, scholars are at the mercy of extant manuscripts, and in principle there is, as remarked by Alfred Housman in the epigraph to the Introduction, the danger of circularity. An example is provided by Jim Adams's comment on unusual *sibe* and *quase* in Livy: 'One cannot be certain what Livy's motives were in writing *sibe* and *quase* (if indeed he did: note Quintilian's uncertainty about the status of such spellings in manuscripts)'.[157]

For Babylonian and Assyrian, the study of individual style has scarcely begun, doubtless owing in part to the scantiness of the evidence.[158] More generally, our knowledge of Akkadian idiom, and of the closely related topic of lexicogrammar, is infinitely less developed than that of Akkadian grammar in the traditional sense (esp. morphology).[159] For these

157 Adams, *Diversification* (2007) 150.

158 An exception are the identifications of individual traits in the letters of particular Neo-Assyrian scholars by Deller, "Die Briefe des Adad-Šumu-Uṣur", in Röllig and Dietrich (eds), *1st Fs von Soden* (1969) 50–52 and Parpola, *LAS II* (1983) 301 *ad* 294 (esp. 'phraseology'). See also Worthington, *Iraq* 78 (2006) 69–81, esp. 80–81.

159 But see for example Nurullin, *Babel und Bibel* 6 (2012) 209, observing that, since the combination of *šumu* 'name' and *nabû* 'to call' is both intuitively natural and well attested in Akkadian, the ementation *na-bu šum-šu* 'his name has been called' to *šu*!*-pu šum-šu* 'his name is glorious' at *Gilg.* I 47 is 'scarcely appealing', even though, as observed by Wilcke, *ZA* 67 (1977) 201, only a single wedge is required to change NA into ŠU.

reasons, in our present state of knowledge Akkadian sources offer reduced scope vis-à-vis other disciplines for the identification of stylistic and idiomatic oddities.[160]

Nevertheless, the identification of oddities in style and idiom has a place in Assyriology. For, though we know little about individual authors, we are very well informed about the idioms and formulations of certain textual typologies, particularly those which tend to be highly repetitive (e.g. royal inscriptions and medical recipes). Departures from these idioms can prove useful starting points for enquiry into the mechanisms of textual change[161] (though uncertainties of various kinds can of course arise even in textual typologies whose idioms are well known).[162] Many examples will be given in §§ 3.3 and 3.4.

2.2.1.3 Oddities of sense

For the purposes of the present discussion, 'oddities of sense' include not just sentences which are semantically peculiar in their own right, but also wider problems of compositional logic and consistency.[163]

Oddities of sense, and their identification, are bedevilled by several problems. For a start, sometimes we simply do not know enough about

---

160 Jacobsen, *King List* (1939) 62–63 held that the 'author' of the *Sumerian King List* was 'a man who was fond of formulas and used them with singular precision and consistency. It is inconceivable that a man of this type should have made the purposeless and totally unnecessary change … which we find in the formula for change of dynasty'. This seems highly subjective.

161 See e.g. Schaudig, *Nabonid und Kyros* (2001) 118 commenting that *tanittu āliya u ištar(i)ya* 'praise of my city and goddess' is 'wenigstens überraschend' in view of the usual pair *ilu* – *ištaru* 'god' – 'goddess'. Being troubled by the idea that it would occur in a common phrase, and on both manuscripts, Schaudig is cautious about dubbing this an error, and envisages a fusion of city and city god, so that *ālu* would mean 'city (god)'. However, the evidence assembled in this book suggests that errors with these characteristics were possible. For an instance where *ilu* 'god' appears instead of *ālu* 'city' (Šal III 6 i.52 MS 1) see § 3.2.3.

162 For example, Labat, *TDP* (1951) 38 n. 71 commented that, of the variants ki-*ma* and di-*ma* in an entry in the *Diagnostic Handbook*, one is likely to be an error for the other – but it is hard to say which one is correct.

163 In Assyriology, the scholar who has most energetically championed the identification of oddities of sense is Tzvi Abusch (cf. § 1.6). Abusch has offered close readings of many incantations and therapeutic prescriptions, arguing that they contain oddities which can be accounted for by supposing particular redactional histories. It should further be mentioned that, in the course of pursuing his wider interests in compositional logic and structure, Abusch has also remarked on oddities of grammar, orthography and idiom.

the relevant aspect of ancient Mesopotamian life to make confident judgments about whether a statement makes good sense or not. This can be illustrated by considering an Old Akkadian seal inscription of one Aman-Aštar, servant of the *entu* priestess Tūta-napšum. The seal depicts Aman-Aštar playing a musical instrument for her mistress, and the inscription describes her as a munus.ú.húb (an obscure expression).[164] Piotr Steinkeller interpreted this in the light of the equivalence ú.húb = *sukkuku* 'deaf'.[165] Thus read, the seal would tell us that Aman-Aštar was a 'deaf woman'. Some scholars find this unlikely: Aage Westenholz holds that 'A deaf woman would hardly be playing a musical instrument to her mistress',[166] and Joan Goodnick Westenholz maintains that deafness would have rendered the unfortunate Aman-Aštar 'a poor servant for the highest clerical official in the temple hierarchy of Enlil'.[167] On the other hand, we cannot rule out that – like Beethoven, Fauré, Smetana and others – she became deaf *after* embarking on a musical career.[168] Is the concept of a deaf female musician in the service of an *entu* priestess credible? It seems fair to conclude that we simply do not know. (For a comparable quandary see fn. 352). For those who are satisfied that the sense is unacceptable, the way is open to Claudia Suter's emendation of munus 'woman' to dumu.munus 'daughter', resulting in 'daughter of Uhub'.[169] (For more on the link between poor sense and emendation see fn. 124 and § 6.2).

---

164 A further obscurity (*šat za-bi-rí-im*, not discussed here) follows munus.ú.húb as a description of Aman-Aštar. If munus.ú.húb is taken as 'deaf', *šat za-bi-rí-im* does not impinge on its interpretation.

165 Steinkeller, *NABU* 1993/1 p. 7 'Beginning with the question of sal.Ú.HUB, it is absolutely certain that we find here a female equivalent of ú-húb, Akk. *sukkuku* "deaf", "dumb"'.

166 Westenholz, *BiOr* 53 (1996) 122.

167 Goodnick Westenholz, "Who was Aman-Aštar?", in Barjamovic, Dahl, Koch, Sommerfeld and Goodnick Westenholz (eds), *Fs Westenholz* (2011) 317.

168 This hypothesis would also meet Goodnick Westenholz's objection that 'Seal owners never identify themselves by highlighting their physical abnormalities': a deaf musician might well have thought the disability worth highlighting, to celebrate the magnitude of her professional achievement.

169 Suter, "Between Human and Divine: High Priestesses in Images from the Akkad to the Isin-Larsa Period", in Cheng and Feldman (eds), *Studies Winter* (2007) 324 n. 23: 'The interpretation of Aman-Aštar's characterization in lines 3–4 is controversial. The most sensible solution [seemed to me] to emend a DUMU in front of MUNUS and understand it in terms of her origin'.

The domain of literature poses additional problems of cultural distance, in terms of how 'consistent' literary works were, and are, expected to be. Worth citing in this connection is an essay by John Smith on the *Mahābhārata*: he argues that inconsistencies are so thick on the ground there that they cannot all have arisen through corruption,[170] and should instead be viewed as naturally constitutive of the Epic. Inspired by Paul Feyerabend's comments on Ancient Greek culture,[171] Smith views the constituents of the seeming contradiction as 'paratactic aggregates', i.e. 'wholes that are made up of individual parts by a simple process of adding, with no idea that the parts might be thought to stand in some kind of relationship to each other'.[172] Thus, for Smith, the inconsistencies would not have been perceived as such by the *Mahābhārata*'s original audiences. While no such thought-provoking and far-reaching claims have been advanced for Akkadian, we must bear in mind that ancient attitudes to literature might surprise us.

A further problem in literature is that, even if we could be confident that what we perceive to be inconsistencies would have been recognised as such by ancient audiences, they should not necessarily be viewed as defects: authors might have introduced them deliberately. James O'Hara

170 Smith, *BSOAS* 72/1 (2009) 108: 'Inconsistency is piled upon inconsistency, resulting in a texture so complex that it would be very difficult to postulate any credible way of arriving at it by means of historical processes of change'.

171 See Feyerabend, *Against Method* (1975) 240–241: 'This *paratactic* feature of Homeric poetry … makes it clear why Aphrodite is called 'sweetly laughing' when in fact she complains tearfully (*Iliad*, 5.375), or why Achilles is called 'swift footed' when he is sitting talking to Priam (*Iliad*, 24.559). Just as in late geometric pottery … a dead body is a live body brought into the position of death … or an eaten kid [is, MW] a live and *peaceful* kid brought into the appropriate relation to the mouth of a ferocious lion, in the very same way Aphrodite complaining is simply Aphrodite – and that is the laughing goddess – *inserted* into the situation of complaining in which she participates only externally, without changing her nature'.

172 Smith, *BSOAS* 72/1 (2009) 112. For example, in one instance, 'Yudhiṣṭhira is simultaneously righteous (so that he remonstrates with Bhīma) and soft-hearted (so that he excuses Bhīma)'. Smith suggests that 'To read the passage aright we have to understand that there is no contradiction between the two'. Feyerabend defines the term 'paratactic aggregate' on pp. 233–234: 'the elements of such an aggregate are all given equal importance, the only relation between them is sequential, there is no hierarchy, no part is presented as being subordinate to and determined by others'.

notes of Latin epics that this could be done to indicate that characters within the story are being misled.[173]

There is also the problem wryly remarked on by Eugène Vinaver that, particularly in long compositions,[174] 'the author is liable to err, witness the story of Don Quixote ordering Sancho to dismount and tie up his ass just after it has been stolen'.[175] A similar point was made by Richard Tarrant for Roman poets:

> Ovid, Seneca, and Juvenal, though consummate masters of Latin, were not paragons of restraint, and it is quite possible that on occasion, from thoughtlessness or impetuous love of point, they produced an original with all the features of an interpolation.[176]

A likely Akkadian example of a case where it is impossible to tell whether author or transmitter is responsible for an inconsistency is provided by the first Tablet of *Gilgameš* (Standard version).[177] This instance will be expounded in the following sub-section.

Sometimes, an oddity of sense is introduced consciously but reluctantly, in deference to contextual factors which go beyond the work itself. A striking instance is found in the English translation of the Tintin book *Cigars of the Pharaoh*:

---

173 O'Hara, *Inconsistencies in Roman Epic* (2007) 2. A possible Akkadian instance of this occurs in *Gilgameš* XI, where Ea (the slipperiest of the gods) may contradict the foregoing account of his doings by the narrator (see fn. 990).

174 On short compositions, Abusch, "The Revision of Babylonian Anti-Witchcraft Incantations: The Critical Analysis of Incantations in the Ceremonial Series Maqlû", in Bohak, Harari and Shaked (eds), *Continuity and Change* (2011) 12 comments sensibly that 'Coherence of thought and congruence between its parts ... are to be expected of relatively short literary works produced by a single composer', though even here, as Abusch notes, one can envisage occasional exceptions (particularly if an assemblage of short compositions forms part of a larger whole).

175 Vinaver, "Principles of Textual Emendation", in (Anonymous) (ed.), *Studies Pope* (1939) 366.

176 Tarrant, "The Reader as Author: Collaborative Interpolation in Latin Poetry", in Grant (ed.), *Editing Greek and Latin Texts* (1989) 152. See also Tertel, *Text and Transmission* (1994) 4 (a work drawn to my attention by Kai Lämmerhirt): 'There still remains the possibility that the inconsistency was already present in the first version'.

177 Note the comment by Abusch, *History of Religions* 26/2 (1986) 162 that an unexpected feature of *Gilg.* VI might be due to 'textual omission or artistic commission'.

> The British edition got into a terrible tangle over the introduction of Rastapopulous. Because *Cigars* was one of the last books to be translated into English, Tintin's arch enemy was considered too well established in the minds of English-speaking readers to start introducing him for the first time. Hence the following absurd conversation: Rastapopulous – 'One day you'll regret having crossed my path. Just remember: my name is Rastapopulous!' Tintin – 'Rastapopulous? Rastapopulous? Ah! I've got it: the millionaire film tycoon, King of Cosmos Pictures … and it's not the first time we've met …'.[178]

Akkadian authors did not have to worry about their English-speaking readers, but the idea that inconsistency might have been consciously introduced in the service of a higher purpose is nonetheless relevant to them. Again, we shall meet a possible instance in the following sub-section.

Inevitably, a subjective element creeps into modern stances vis-à-vis what makes sense and what does not. This is well brought out by the diametrically opposed reactions of Wilfred Lambert and Eckart Frahm to the fact that Sennacherib's version of *Ee* spells the divine name 'Aššur' as *an-šár*, a spelling which the same composition also uses to represent the god Anšar, Aššur's grandfather. For Lambert, the spelling of Aššur as *an-šár* results from an 'ill-conceived attempt to put Ashur in place of Marduk', and the 'very amateurish revision … raises a conflict with a different Anšar already in the text' and puts 'the whole plot of the myth into confusion'.[179] For Frahm, by contrast, the fact that the two deities' names are spelled the same way is an indication that they 'were, in a way, regarded as the same', and that a 'sophisticated concept of divine self-creation' is in play for Aššur.[180] Both stances have arguments in their favour, and it is hard to find objective criteria to choose between them.

Notwithstanding these complications, vigilance in matters of sense seems advisable. Better to be aware of oddities and have to grapple with the issue of how they arose, than to remain unaware of them.

---

178 Thompson, *Tintin* (2011) 70.

179 Lambert, "The Assyrian Recension of Enūma eliš", in Waetzold and Hauptmann (eds), *Assyrien im Wandel der Zeiten* (1997) 79–80.

180 Frahm, *Commentaries* (2011) 350–351.

2.2.1.3.1 A two-line incongruity: *Gilgameš* I 298-299

The portion of the Epic which will concern us here comprises Gilgameš's two dreams in Tablet I. In particular, we will be interested in how they relate to what Šamhat says before she recounts them.[181]

Let us begin by reminding ourselves of the relevant background. Enkidu, initially a wild creature who lived amid a herd of gazelles, is humanised by the harlot Šamhat: as a result of six days' and seven nights' sexual delights with Šamhat, Enkidu can speak and think like a human. Šamhat suggests taking him to Uruk, *ašar gilgameš gitmālu emūqī u kī rīmi ugdaššaru eli eṭlūti* 'where Gilgameš is perfect in strength, and lords it over the menfolk like a wild bull'[182] (I 218-219). Enkidu reacts enthusiastically to this suggestion: not only does he very much want to go to Uruk, he also declares his intention to challenge Gilgameš (*lugrišum-ma* I 220) and change the order? of things (*ši-ma?-tu unakkar* I 222).[183] Upon hearing of this intention, Šamhat is still all for taking Enkidu to Uruk,[184] but she opposes Enkidu's intended challenge. For one thing, she believes Gilgameš to be stronger (*danna emūqa elika īši* I 238); for another, the gods are on his side – so much so, that to challenge him would be a mistake (*šēretka* I 240).[185] Šamaš, the sun god, 'loves him' (*irâmšu-ma* I 241), and as for the other gods:

> *anu enlil u ea urappišū uzunšu*
> *lām tallika ultu šadîm-ma*
> *gilgameš ina libbi uruk inaṭṭala šunāteka*

> 'Anu, Enlil and Ea have *alerted him*:[186]
> Even before you came from the uplands,

181 I should like here to record my indebtedness to Nunzia Invernizzi, whose intellectually coruscating exegeses of Indian myths are an inspiration for the close reading of Akkadian, and indeed all, literature.

182 Except where expressly indicated, all translations of *Gilgameš* are taken from George's masterly edition (sometimes with minor modifications).

183 Nurullin, *Babel und Bibel* 6 (2012) 203 proposes to read *ši-giš-tú* 'fight'.

184 Unless I 226 (*alik enkidu a[na uru]k supūri* 'Go, O Enkidu, to Uruk-the-sheepfold') is to be understood ironically. This possibility is incidental to the argument we will assemble.

185 On the difficulty of *šēretka*, whose basic meaning seems to be 'sin', see Nurullin, *Babel und Bibel* 6 (2012) 211 n. 41.

186 Literally, the phrase is 'they (have) broadened his ear'. The ear being synonymous with wisdom, expressions such as 'broad ear' can simply mean 'great wisdom'. Hence CAD R 158a translates our line as 'Anu, Enlil and Ea have increased his understanding', and George has 'Anu, Enlil and Ea broadened his

Gilgameš was having dreams about you in Uruk.'
(I 242-244)

Thus Šamhat's mention of the dreams comes as the climax of her argument to the effect that Enkidu should not challenge Gilgameš. The logic of what she says is that Anu, Enlil and Ea love Gilgameš so much they are sending him prophetic dreams, and it would be lunacy for Enkidu to attack one so loved by the gods. She then goes on to recount the dreams.

So where is the problem? The problem is, that the content of the dreams themselves is not such as would dissuade Enkidu from challenging Gilgameš. Far from it, they sound very encouraging. They foretell that Enkidu will be made Gilgameš's equal, thereby dispelling any worries which Šamhat might have aroused in Enkidu by telling him that Gilgameš was stronger. Also, Enkidu would hardly have been disappointed to learn from the dreams that the menfolk of Uruk would 'kiss his feet' (I 255), a gesture of submission normally reserved for gods and victorious kings (see § 6.2.4).[187] Hence, if she wants to discourage him from going to Uruk, it is surprising that Šamhat should relate the dreams to Enkidu in the way that she does: by doing so, she scuppers her own argument. She would have done better just to tell him that the gods sent Gilgameš prophetic dreams, without relating their content.

Now, in the Old Babylonian version of the Epic it seems that the dreams are recounted by the narrator rather than by Šamhat (OB II 44-45). And in the Standard version it is only two lines that follow the report of the dreams (I 298-299) which tell us that the report was spoken by Šamhat. If these lines, attested on one manuscript from Kuyunjik and two from Babylon (MSS B_1, h, o),[188] were removed, then the dreams would

---

wisdom'. However, since we hold that Šamhat is referring to the gods' having sent Gilgameš a message in the form of a dream, we have chosen a translation in which the notion of communication is more explicit.

187 If one of Enkidu's aims in challenging Gilgameš was to succour the people of Uruk from their ruler's tyranny, he would presumably have received encouragement from the dreams. However, his motivations are not explicitly stated: it is possible that he cared not a fig for the well-being of third parties, and was simply keen to measure himself against an opponent of redoubtable reputation.

188 It is possible that the Kuyunjik copyists were following a source from Babylon, so that in respect of these two lines all three manuscripts attest to the same recension of the epic, despite their stemming from two different sites. Other, lost, recensions of the Standard version may have lacked them (but even if a manu-

revert to being recounted by the narrator, as in the Old Babylonian version. The inconsistency in what Šamhat says to Enkidu would cease to be. These lines were therefore very probably inserted into a pre-existing version.

Were these crucial two lines constitutive of the Standard version from the very beginning, i. e. are they 'authorial'? Or were they inserted by a later transmitter? In the present state of knowledge, this is impossible to determine. Against their being authorial one could object that, as we have argued elsewhere,[189] the Standard version is more carefully composed than is generally recognised. On the strength of this, one might argue that the author of the Standard version would have been unlikely to insert a discrepancy. On the other hand, one can see a reason why the author of the Standard version might have thought a discrepancy worth incurring: in ancient Mesopotamia the interpretation of dreams was usually a female activity,[190] but in the Epic Gilgameš's dreams are repeatedly interpreted by Enkidu. Conceivably, the author of the Standard version wanted the audience to infer that Enkidu acquired his skill as a dream interpreter by hearing Ninsun's interpretations of Gilgameš's dreams from Šamhat. As we see it, the arguments are balanced, and the choice between them is subjective: it is hard to say for certain whether the Standard version originally included I 298-299 or not.

2.2.2 Linguistic and orthographic oddities, and problems in explaining them

While it is usually easy to determine which spellings and forms do and do not conform to our expectations of Akkadian grammar and orthography, how we should *explain* grammatical and orthographic oddities, and what we can learn from them, are thornier issues. Here we shall set out the chief complications as we see them.

---

script without the two lines were found, this would not prove that they were originally absent: they could have been excised secondarily).

189 Worthington, *JRAS* 21/4 (2011). (On names, discussed in part I section 1 of this article see also Sallaberger, *Das Gilgamesch-Epos* (2008) 116 on VII 59–63: 'Enkidu löscht mit seinem Fluch eine Form des Gedächtnisses an seinen Namen'. This contrasts with Gilgameš in Tablet VIII, who seeks to preserve Enkidu's name).

190 See Zgoll, *Traum und Welterleben* (2006) 433–437. On Enkidu's feminine attributes see fn. 692.

2.2.2.1 Orthographic conventions and the problem of normativity

Our affiliation to cultures which are permeated by a single set of orthographic[191] conventions predisposes us to expect orthographic norms and rules in antiquity, and it is indeed often convenient to speak about Akkadian spellings as if such norms existed.[192]

Yet in order to speak meaningfully of orthographic conventions as norms, it is necessary to suppose that: a) those who applied them expected others to abide by them; b) the same 'others' had been told what the conventions were; and c) knew that they were expected to abide by them. It is doubtful whether these requirements were often satisfied in the Akkadian-writing world, unless perhaps within individual scriptoria.

Of course, basic sign values (e.g. the sign LA representing /la/) must have been agreed on by all literate individuals. There are also a very few orthographic 'rules' which appear to have found near-universal acceptance. One example is use of Ú (rather than U or Ù) in word-initial position.[193] Another, specific to the first millennium, is that *u* 'and' is written

191 In this book, 'orthography' and 'orthographic' are used as synonymous with 'spelling(s)', and neutral as to whether the relevant spellings are 'correct' or not.

192 I am grateful to Eva Cancik-Kirschbaum for bringing the word 'normativity' to my notice in connection with Akkadian orthography. Though the problems are difficult, the notion of 'norm' seems to me a useful anvil upon which to hammer them.

193 I owe this observation (which discounts a few peripheral spellings) to Aage Westenholz. The cluster of three spelling of the word *ukullā'u* 'provisions' with initial u_1 in the Middle Assyrian Laws (see CAD U/W 59a) must reflect an idiosyncratic tradition. Another Middle Assyrian example is u_1-*še-piš* 'I had made' in the brick inscriptions of Etel-pī-Adad at Tell Taban (Maul, *Tall Ṭābān* (2005) 50–51 numbers 11 and 12, probably also 13-17; I thank Daisuke Shibata for alerting me to this spelling). Despite foregoing a-*šu* 'his son', it is difficult to take a-*šu* u_1-*še-piš* as an enriched sandhi spelling (§ 4.4.2) unless one supposes that it belongs to a tradition in which u_1 was used at the start of words, in which case it is no longer necessary to interpret it as a sandhi spelling. Perhaps, then, it belongs to, or was influenced by, the same tradition as the Middle Assyrian Laws. The few cases where word-initial u_1 follows a preposition may result from the entire complex preposition + noun being thought of as a single word. (On *u-kin* in a colophon see below with fn. 910). Nathan Wasserman (pers. comm.) suggests that the reason for avoiding u_1 at the start of words was to avoid ambiguity between *u-Anlaut* and *u* 'and'. For other orthographic aids to disambiguation see § 5.4. (There is also a strong tendency not to use ŠÚ at the beginning of a word, but I do not have a clear impression of the number of counter-examples, so provisionally this may best be described a strong tendency

with u_1 or *ù* (not *ú*).[194] A third is that, barring 'morpho-phonological' spellings, syllabic spelling follows the syllable divisions of the spoken word (e.g. *i-maq-qut* not *im-aq-qut*, reflecting pronunciation /i-maq-qut/). But around this very small core of (near)-universals whirl many more tricky issues.

Indeed, it is hardly possible to state 'rules' of Akkadian orthography to which one cannot find a high number of exceptions, even on tablets which have the appearance of being written by competent writers. We must reckon with the possibility that some well-educated and well-informed Akkadian writers consciously dissented from spelling conventions which other equally well-educated and well-informed writers of the same period and scribal centre subscribed to.[195]

Certain ancient Mesopotamian institutions achieved a high degree of orthographic homogeneity in their internal 'paperwork'. This had the advantage of ease of mutual comprehension: if everyone working for the institution followed the same spelling conventions, internal communications and the consultation of records would be rendered more efficient. One such institution was the Ur III state (whose documents were written in Sumerian): Claus Wilcke has observed that the spellings of this state's employees conformed to conventions which documents written by private individuals did not always respect.[196]

It is inevitable that the writings produced by institutions should loom large in modern perceptions of Mesopotamian orthography, since they account for a large proportion of extant sources. Yet to regard the conventions of institutions as 'norms'[197] seems a subjective viewpoint. It is possible that spellings which do not conform to the conventions of particular institutions, or even to a representative cross-section of Akkadian cunei-

---

rather than a 'rule'. Quantitative evaluation of a large corpus is needed to settle the matter).

194 AHw 1397a notes that *ú* is often used for 'and' in Old Assyrian, and dubs the much rarer occurrences in other varieties of Akkadian 'mistakes' (Fehler). It is my impression that there are sufficient examples in Old Babylonian letters for them to count as unusual spellings rather than true errors.

195 Cf. Adams, *Diversification* (2007) 140–141 on diversity of opinion among educated Romans of the Republican period about the pronunciation and spelling of word-final *s*.

196 Wilcke, *Wer las* (2000) esp. 40–43.

197 E.g. Wilcke, *Wer las* (2000) 40–41: 'Meines Erachtens ist der Grund für das Abweichen von der Norm nicht zur Schau gestellte Gelehrsamkeit, sondern die Unsicherheit des jeweiligen Schreibers. Er kennt das Wort, ist sich aber über die korrekte Zeichenwahl im Unklaren'.

form as a whole, were nonetheless part of small, localised networks of conventions, the evidence for which is largely lost.[198] Be that as it may, on the basis of the three criteria outlined above it is doubtful whether the conventions of institutions can truly be regarded as 'norms' outside those institutions.

It is, then, open to question whether writers of Akkadian cuneiform thought about spellings as 'right' and 'wrong' in quite the way we do today. Of course there are simple cases where spellings are obviously wrong (e.g. a missing or extraneous sign). But in very many cases it is hard to be sure whether a spelling is wrong, or consciously operated according to standards different from those which we have reconstructed for Akkadian as a whole. Therefore we should be wary of terming ancient spellings 'wrong' unless we are absolutely confident that error is beyond doubt.[199] It is salutary to draw distinctions such as that between 'deviations from classical orthography' and 'outright errors' which Roger Bagnall applies to Greek graffiti at Smyrna.[200]

This is not to say that value judgments of spellings did not occur. Presumably, first-millennium writers who took care to use the sign ŠU consistently (§ 4.8.3) regarded this practice as in some way preferable to the use of the more common, and more quickly written, sign ŠÚ. The same writers might even have gone so far as to look down on the use of ŠÚ. But this would hardly justify us in calling the use of ŠÚ a mistake. Rather than reacting to most spellings as 'right' or 'wrong', ancient writers might have thought about them in terms such as 'easy' vs 'difficult', 'modern' vs 'ancient', 'plain' vs 'sophisticated', 'plebeian' vs 'learned'.

In § 3.1, we shall see that our confidence in identifying oddities as 'outright errors' can be boosted by recourse to error typology. First, though, we need to discuss two cases in which doubts as to whether oddities are 'outright errors' or not are at their most intractable.

---

198 On orthographic variability in the Ur III period see Rubio, *ASJ* 22 (2000 [2005]) esp. 218–219.

199 Note the cautious formulation of George, *Gilgamesh* (2003) 438 about Kuyunjik manuscripts: 'spellings … that seem to me to express words and syllables in ways that deviate from the predictable orthography of Standard Babylonian literary texts at this period'.

200 Bagnall, *Everyday Writing* (2011) 13.

2.2.2.2 Error or phonetic spelling?

All students of written sources from the ancient world face this quandary:[201] spellings which look wrong may in fact be 'phonetic',[202] i.e. they may aim to record exactly how the word was spoken rather than (as traditional spellings did) how etymology would lead one to expect that it would be spoken.[203] As several Assyriologists have recognised,[204] Akkadian sources are no less riddled with this ambiguity than other languages.

Again as with other ancient languages, Akkadian presents the problem that, owing to the prevalence of traditional spelling, we know very little about vernacular pronunciation. Odd spellings can, therefore, be very difficult to evaluate: they might reflect vernacular pronunciation, or they might not; we cannot tell, without knowing more about it.

An example is *ú-pa-si-ru-in-ni*, extant on MS F2 of an Assurbanipal prism (F vi.35 // A x.69), where all other manuscripts have *upassarū'inni* 'they send me messages'.[205] It is possible that the aberrant spelling faithfully reflects an aberration in tense: preterite (*upassirū'inni*) where the other manuscripts have a (grammatically preferable?) present. If this is so, the writer of MS F2 was very probably guilty of error. But were forms of the *uPaRRaSū'inni* type pronounced as clearly as in modern Assyriological classrooms? Is it not in fact possible that the *a* before the third radical was reduced to less than a full /a/ sound? We cannot rule

201 For an example of the problem in Classics see e.g. Bagnall, *Everyday Writing* (2011) 14 (see fn. 285).

202 Some nineteenth-century Assyriologists used 'phonetic' to mean 'non-logographic, non-sumerographic' (the term 'syllabic' is now employed in this sense). It has since come to be used more specifically, in the sense 'faithful to actual pronunciation', e.g. Al-Rawi/George, cited in fn. 211.

203 For the same idea applied to the Biblical Book of Samuel see Tsumura, *Vetus Testamentum* 49/3 (1999), who argues that '*Some* of the MT [Masoretic Text, MW] spellings which have been explained as "scribal errors" can be better interpreted as "phonetic spellings"' (p. 41).

204 E.g. Finkel, "On Late Babylonian Medical Training", in George and Finkel (eds), *Studies Lambert* (2000) 177 on *nu-úr-ru-ú* for expected *nurmû* 'pomegranate': 'While this may be a simple graphic or auditory error, it is possible that it reflects contemporary pronunciation of *nurmû* as *nurwû*'; Schwemer, *Orientalia* 79/4 (2010) 497 n. 34 on *šur-ši* as 'a by-form [i.e phonetic spelling, MW] or corrupted spelling of the stative *šuršu*'. Kouwenberg, *The Akkadian Verb* (2011) 418 notes of Gtn presents with *-tna-* for expected *-ttana-* that 'some instances may simply be scribal errors' (lipography of *-ta-*).

205 Borger, *BIWA* (1996) 73.

out that the spelling *ú-pa-si-ru-in-ni* is designed to tell us that the vowel between the second and third root letters, which we would expect to be *a*, had become shewa-like.[206]

The above example involved two forms (present vs preterite) of the same word. But a phonetic spelling might even have the effect of making one word look like another. A possible example arises in line 50 of Sennacherib's Rassam cylinder: all but two manuscripts have *šu-pi-i* (*šupî* 'battering-ram'), which fits the context. The exceptions are MSS A and FF, with *su-pe-e*. Is this a phonetic spelling of *šupî*, or the different word *supê* 'prayer'? And if the latter (error of phonetic similarity, § 3.2.3), did it arise through inadvertence or misunderstanding? As noted by Frahm *ad loc.*, all this is impossible to determine.[207]

We are by no means arguing that *ú-pa-si-ru-in-ni is* a phonetic spelling, only that it *might* be. But this very possibility is a real obstacle to straightforward interpretation. Finding clear examples of an unusual phonological/morphological phenomenon which cannot be interpreted as phonetic spellings is surprisingly difficult.

Deciding how likely it is that a particular spelling be phonetic is not always easy.[208] It involves a mixture of linguistic common sense, quantification (§ 2.5), and evaluation of the orthography of the relevant manuscript. It must also be admitted that, since some genuine errors would surely look like phonetic spellings, of all the oddities which could be explained as phonetic spellings, at least some are very probably errors.

---

206 If this hypothesis were favoured, the spelling might better be transliterated with *-se-* rather than *-si-*, to show the modern reader that it does not (necessarily) represent a straightforward preterite.

207 Another example occurs in a commentary which has *ṣi-in-na-tu* for expected *ṣernettu/ṣennettu*, a disease (see Frahm, *Commentaries* (2011) 106). The spelling *ṣi-in-na-tu* looks like a form of the musical instrument *ṣinnatu*, and so it might seem that the writer misunderstood what he (or she) was supposed to be writing. But it is also possible that, in the mind of the writer, *ṣernettu* had a by-form *ṣenna(t)tu*. After all, the reason for *e*-colouring – a lost guttural, the root originally being quadriliteral (see Militarev and Kogan, *Dictionary, vol. 1* (2000) 229) – could have been long forgotten, and *a* restored (if only in scholarly circles, as a hypercorrection). It is impossible to tell for certain, but with a word which exhibits an unexpected by-form (*rn/nn*) to start with, and is quite poorly attested, perhaps our commentator deserves the benefit of the doubt.

208 Compare the comment by Wilcke, *Wer las* (2000) 39 on non-standard Sumerian orthography in the Ur-III period: 'Nicht immer lässt sich klar entscheiden, ob die bewusste Wahl silbischer Wiedergabe von Wortzeichen durch homophone Wort- oder Silbenzeichen … vorliegt oder aber eine Zeichenverwechselung aufgrund lautlicher Ähnlichkeit'.

Generally, when students of the ancient world discuss phonetic spellings, there lurks in the background an issue of competence on the part of the ancient writers, though individual stances taken on this issue differ. The disagreements can be illustrated with discussions of graffiti at Pompeii, which abound in odd spellings. One scholar deduces from the proliferation of oddities that the writers were 'semi-literates, people who could write only with some difficulty'.[209] Another replies that 'Terms like illiterate and semi-literate are used too readily to refer to people who spelled phonetically and let the syntax of oral expression enter their writing. They were literate'.[210]

For Akkadian, one encounters phonetic spellings on tablets which are sufficiently complex and well inscribed that a high level of literacy is beyond doubt. For example, sandhi spellings are a type of phonetic spelling, and they are used (though rarely and inconsistently) by writers of the highest competence (e.g. TCL III+, see § 4.4.6). Of course, if the spelling discussed above (*ú-pa-si-ru-in-ni*) is 'phonetic', the relevant writer was not following usual orthography. But he might have felt this was his prerogative, and we do not know whether the unusual spelling would have been regarded by contemporaries as orthographically wrong (see § 2.2.2.1).[211] Even less can we automatically posit misunderstanding.

In the rare instances where one can be sure that an odd spelling is phonetic, it is doubtful whether it should be classified as an error.[212]

2.2.2.3 Ignorance or inadvertence?

While there are many cases where we may feel that what a writer has written is wrong, it is not always easy to decide whether the error reflects misunderstanding or inadvertence.

This ambiguity is especially felt in connection with the substitution of similar signs (errors of sign similarity, see § 3.2.1): what do they tell us

209 Harris, *Ancient Literacy* (1989) 264.

210 Bagnall, *Everyday Writing* (2011) 26.

211 Nor do we believe it necessarily reflects dictation (for which view see fn. 25). *Dictée intérieure* seems equally possible.

212 Finet, "Liste des erreurs de scribes", in Bottéro and Finet (eds), *Répertoire analytique* (1954) 97 recognised that in *ki-ha-am* for *kī'am* (ARM V 65:13) 'le *ḫ* sert à rendre le ', but nonetheless booked the spelling as an error.

about the writers who committed them?[213] We see at least five possibilities, depending on how the error arose.

1) The writer possessed inadequate knowledge of cuneiform; perhaps, more specifically, of cuneiform as used in the relevant textual typology.

2) The writer had bad (or super-cursive) handwriting.

When the difference between two cuneiform signs is extremely small, e.g. Old Babylonian KI and DI (difference of only one wedge in a bunch of two or three), it can be difficult to disentangle inadequate knowledge of cuneiform (see previous) from bad or super-cursive handwriting. Modern editors usually transliterate a defective Old Babylonian KI as DI!, which is a convenient way to tell the reader which wedge is missing. But this notation produces the impression that the tablet has the wrong sign – whereas the writer might contend that it was his or her prerogative to skip one wedge in a bunch of three, and that it is unfair to be accused of writing a different sign (DI) even if the result is identical with it. This was noted by André Finet: 'Certains signes, comme BA et MA, KI et DI – et d'autres encore – sont souvent confondus, sans qu'il soit question, à proprement dire, d'une erreur du scribe'.[214] Probably, some Old Babylonians who wrote DI for KI (or even vice versa?) were genuinely unsure about the difference between them (see fn. 323),[215] and so fall under point 1) above; but, equally probably, others were fully aware of the difference, and should only be accused of bad or super-cursive handwriting, not of confusing sign shapes.[216]

---

213 Of course, the person who committed the error was not necessarily the same as the writer of the extant manuscript. If only for the sake of caution, we must reckon with the possibility that (some) transmitters recognised or at least suspected errors of sign identification on their exemplars, but faithfully reproduced them without correcting them, trusting to the abilities of their readers to recognise what the relevant sign or signs should be. See § 3.4.6.

214 Finet, "Liste des erreurs de scribes", in Bottéro and Finet (eds), *Répertoire analytique* (1954) 96.

215 For writers with mediocre skills, who used simplified syllabaries, getting similar-looking signs exactly right might not have seemed too important, as context would usually show which sign was meant.

216 Gelb, *Old Akkadian Writing and Grammar* (1961) 45 writes that 'One of the hitherto unobserved characteristics of cuneiform writing is the frequent interchange of signs ... As can be tested on the basis of many copies and original inscriptions, the interchange of such similar signs as HU and RI is not due to a misreading on the part of a modern copyist but forms an inherent part of the system', but one page later he calls such cases 'confusion of signs similar in form'. Presumably, then, 'inherent part of the system' means 'unavoidable' rath-

3) A writer might have intended to write a sign, but inadvertently written another sign instead (‘*lapsus styli*’, see § 3.2.1.2). In this scenario the writer is absent-minded, but this is no reason to doubt his or her ability as a reader or writer.[217] Indeed, ability and absent-mindedness often go together (cf. fn. 300).

4) The exemplar was damaged, making it hard to identify signs.

5) Even if transmitters had an excellent knowledge of cuneiform, their thoughts might well have strayed from the job in hand. In this case, they might have mechanically copied signs or groups of signs without bothering to make sense of them (§ 2.3.3), and in such cases careless misidentifications might arise.

The difficulty of determining whether an error reflects ignorance or inadvertence in the writer is not only felt for errors of sign similarity. For example, we suggest elsewhere that *Counsels of Wisdom* 129-130 runs as follows:[218]

> *ša ākil karṣī qābû lemutti*
> *ina rībāti ša šamaš uqa’’û rēssu*

> ‘One who utters slander and speaks evil
> will be called to reckoning through the repayments of Šamaš (=the god of justice)’.

The word *rībāti* ‘repayments’ is spelled in two ways on the extant manuscripts: *ri-ba-a-te* and *ri-ib-ba-a-ti* (MS g only). Probably in view of the double *bb* on MS g, other scholars have supposed the word to be the plural of *ribbatu* ‘arrears’. However, in view of the use of *râbu* ‘to repay’ with Šamaš as subject in lines 60 and 64, it seems more likely that in line 130 *ri-ba-a-te* is the plural of *rību* ‘repayment’.

If this be granted, what do we do with MS g? One possibility is to suppose that a transmitter encountered a spelling such as *ri-ba-a-ti* on the ex-

---

er than ‘deliberate’. Be that as it may, detailed palaeographic analysis of the issues raised by Gelb is desirable.

217 I therefore retract my statement (Worthington, “The lamp and the mirror, or: Some comments on the ancient understanding of Mesopotamian medical manuscripts”, in Imhausen and Pommerening (eds), *Writings of Early Scholars* (2010) 191) to the effect that the copyist who replaced é with kar on a Neo-Assyrian medical manuscript ‘clearly … mistook the former for the latter’. This is only one of two possible explanations, the other being *lapsus styli.*

218 Worthington, “Literatures in Dialogue: A Comparison of Attitudes to Speech in Babylonian and Middle Egyptian Literature”, in Enmarch and Lepper (eds), *Ancient Egyptian Literature* (forthcoming) section 2.2 with refs to other interpretations.

emplar, misunderstood it as representing *ribbāti* 'arrears', and so wrote *ri-ib-ba-a-ti*. This would be no worse a misunderstanding than many others discussed in this book. But it is also possible that the writer correctly understood the word to be *rībāti* 'repayments', but wrote *ribbāti* 'arrears' through inadvertence, in the same way that when we are tired we might type 'right' instead of 'write' (error of *dictée intérieure*, § 3.2.3).[219]

Of course, if *ri-ib-ba-a-ti* were found on multiple manuscripts, there would be a very good chance that some if not all of the writers thought it represented *ribbāti* 'arrears'.[220] But it is often the case in Akkadian literature and scholarship that (as here) only a small number of manuscripts are extant for any given word, and a variant (like *ri-ib-ba-a-ti*) is found only on one of them. Whether the writer of MS g is guilty of ignorance or inadvertence will probably never be known.

2.2.3 Problems in dealing with oddities: summary

As noted at the beginning of § 2.2, errors are slippery things. We have seen several ways in which this is so.

For a start, there are problems of identification: on the level of individual forms and spellings, what look to us like errors might in fact be phonetic spellings of vernacular forms, or operate in accordance with minoritarian orthographic conventions which we are not aware of; on the level of sense, what look to us like nonsensicalities might have had a justification in aspects of ancient culture of which we are ignorant; and even if they did not, the 'errors' might be authorial rather than due to transmitters, in which case the notion of 'error' arguably becomes problematic.

Then there are problems of interpretation: odd spellings and sign forms could have causes as varied as insufficient knowledge of cuneiform, damaged exemplar, inadvertence, and bad or super-cursive handwriting. These different possibilities have different implications for the skills and abilities of the person with whom the oddity originated.

---

219 Since purely orthographic gemination was common at morphemic boundaries, one could argue that this is such a case: *ri-ib-ba-a-ti* representing *rībāti*. But, given the existence of a word *ribbatu*, doubling the *b* for purely orthographic reasons would seem perverse, as it would be liable to lead readers into error. We therefore deem this unlikely.

220 The element of doubt arises because we must reckon with the possibility that transmitters sometimes deliberately left errors uncorrected, see § 3.4.6.

Happily, even with all these complications, it is possible to identify errors in Akkadian, and often to explain how they came about. Once this is done, information of various kinds can be extracted from them. Examples will be supplied in chapter 3.

2.3 Problems with establishing how extant manuscripts were understood by their writers

Understanding how a writer understood what he or she wrote might seem the easiest thing in the world. Unfortunately, this is by no means always so. There are two major problems, which we propose to call the 'courier effect' and the 'chameleon effect'.

It may, in the following, seem perverse on our part to suggest that transmitters had an idiosyncratic understanding of signs which are compatible with our expectations of a passage. This possibility must, however, be borne in mind. We know from their misreadings that transmitters were not always familiar with the compositions they transmitted (see § 3.3.4). We cannot assume, therefore, that they always hit on the correct understanding of the signs they reproduced. It is possible that modern composite texts conceal much greater diversity of understanding than is suspected to have existed.

2.3.1 The 'courier effect'

A courier carries documents from one person to another, without knowing what they say. Sometimes, the errors made by Akkadian transmitters are so hair-raising as to suggest a similar situation: they reproduced the passage, but without understanding it – perhaps even without attempting to. Accordingly, when they do get the signs right, this is not evidence that they understood them: accurate reproduction is not necessarily evidence of understanding.

An example is provided by *Ištar's Descent*, line 83: *illik an-hiš ina pān sîn abīšu iba*[*kki*] 'He went wearily, weeping before Sîn, his father'. A transmitter unfamiliar with the composition (or a somnolent one) would very probably, then as now, have read *an-hiš* 'wearily' as ^{d}utu (*šamaš*, the sun god).

2.3.2 Variability and the 'chameleon effect'

As is well known, the ambiguities and flexibility of cuneiform spelling mean that a given sequence of signs can sometimes be read meaningfully in more than one way.

When multiple manuscripts are available for a passage, one tends to look to unambiguous spellings for help in interpreting ambiguous ones. This procedure shows us how at least some ancient readers would have read ambiguous spellings, but at the same time it may be procrustean (cf. Bernard Cerquiglini in fn. 146), for we must reckon with disagreements (or at least variability) in antiquity.

Let us, for example, consider *Ludlul* II 119-20:

īṭi ūmu ša gimir kimtiya
ša qereb mūdê(ya?*) šamassun i*-LAGAB

The day grew dark for all my family,
The sun of *my* neighbours became dark.

The sign LAGAB can be read *kil* or *rim*, and both yield meaningful verbal forms (*īkil* 'it became dark', from *ekēlu*; *īrim* 'it covered', from *arāmu*). All manuscripts but one have LAGAB, one has *ri-im*. For one scholar, this 'settled' the question in favour of *i-rim*,[221] for another it rendered the reading *i-kil* 'untenable'.[222] It is our contention that such views give too much credit to the manuscript with *ri-im*.

For sense, syntax, and poetic structure all speak for the reading *i-kil*, which Benno Landsberger had suggested (*apud BWL* 295) before the manuscript with *i-ri-im* was found. The alternatives are simply not satisfactory. Lambert's translation 'But I know the day for my whole family / When, among my friends, the sun-god will have mercy' (relying on a reading *īdi* 'I know' in line 119) destroys the parallelism of the couplet,[223] and muddles matters by taking *ša* as 'when', while it is clearly part of a reverse genitival syntagm (*ša* ... *-šunu*). Cooper's translation 'The day has darkened for my whole family, (and) / of those among my friends, it has eclipsed their sun' lacks a subject in line 120.[224] Landsberger's read-

221 Lambert, *BWL* (1960) 344.

222 Cooper, *JCS* 27/4 (1975) 248.

223 This was observed by Cooper, *JCS* 27/4 (1975) 248. Moreover, the reading *īṭi* 'it grew dark', as opposed to *īdi* 'I know', is now supported by the appearance of the same phrase in Old Babylonian (see George, *Literary Texts* (2009) 36).

224 His contention that the subject might be 'either the general suffering of the man described throughout the tablet, or more specifically, the words of doom uttered

ing *i-kil* not only eliminates the syntactic difficulties and furnishes good sense, it also, as he himself observed, upheld the parallelism *eṭû – ekēlu* (and their derivatives) which is found elsewhere in Akkadian. Several recent editors and translators have therefore privileged the reading *i-kil.*[225]

What, then, of the manuscript with *ri-im*? Landsberger himself was undaunted by the new variant,[226] and Bill Moran adopted a similar attitude:

> I follow Moshe Held, who at the 1981 meeting of the AOS argued convincingly in favor of *īkil* in II 120 as the original reading. I would suggest that the scribe who gave us the variant *i-ri-im* was thinking of Marduk as the subject, for Marduk is referred to in the very next line (III 1, "Heavy was his hand …"). He was perhaps also thinking of *En. el.* VII 119, where Marduk is given the name Addu, "May he cover (*līrim*) the universe of the sky".[227]

Whether so much credit for intratextual agility should be given to the transmitter(s) who misread *i-*LAGAB as *i-rim* is uncertain. Be that as it may, it seems safe to conclude, as others have done, that *i-kil* is the correct reading. Obviously, *i-ri-im* arose as a corruption (error of sign interpretation). With so few manuscripts, however, it is impossible to gauge how wide a currency the variant *īrim* enjoyed. If it should prove to have had a wide diffusion, one could surmise that some of the transmitters who wrote *i-*LAGAB, which originally represented *i-kil*, actually thought they were writing *i-rim.*

Another example of how an unambiguous duplicate can be deleterious arises with the phrase *šuddû u šūšubu* 'to make desolate and to make occupied'. The attestations of *šūšubu* (Š infinitive of *(w)ašābu* 'to dwell') are written with signs in the *b*-range, which are inherently ambiguous: they could be read as representing *b* or *p*. Nonetheless, the phrase was already correctly interpreted since at least 1916.[228] In 1965, Albrecht Goetze published an early Neo-Babylonian inscription which included *ša*

---

by his countrymen in 116' is not persuasive (*pace* Annus and Lenzi, *Ludlul* (2010) xxii n. 38).

225 Foster, *Before the Muses* (2005) 401: 'For those who knew me, their sun grew dark'; Annus and Lenzi, *Ludlul* (2010) 22 (*i-kil* in the composite text) and comment on p. xxii n. 38.

226 Landsberger, *Brief des Bischofs* (1965) 370 esp. n. 143: 'Die bekannte Stelle Ludlul II 119 f. ist zu übersetzen, wie in CAD E (auch AHw) sub *eṭû* und CAD E *ekēlu* vorgeschlagen ist. … Dies gilt, obgleich inzwischen die Variante *i-ri-im* für *i-*KIL … bekannt wurde.'

227 Moran, *JAOS* 103/1 (1983) 257 n. 11.

228 See the reference to Meissner in Goetze, *JCS* 19/4 (1965) n. 54 p. 129.

šuddû u šu-šu-pi bašû ittišu 'with whom ... and ... rest'.[229] As the sign *pi* does not normally represent /bi/, Goetze (p.129) argued that the phrase had previously been misunderstood, and that it was not a form of *(w)ašābu* at all, but rather a verb *šušupu* of uncertain derivation and meaning. This is another example of allowing a manuscript to bully one into misjudgment: the original parsing made perfect sense, and it is not sensible to replace it with an obscurity. Goetze's inscription is now recognised simply to contain an unusual (perhaps erroneous, perhaps phonetic) spelling of *šūšubu* 'to make occupied' (e.g. AHw 708b *sub* 5d).

We give another example from *Ee* III 70:

a	*i-šìr*	*iz-*[	
c	[ ]*-ir*	*iz-za-az*	*i-*⸢*zak-kar*⸣*-šu-*[ ]
g	[	]*-za-az*	*i-zak-kar-šu-un*
h	*ik-mis*	*iz-*ZIZ*-ma*	*i-zak-kar-šú-un*
i	[	]*-az*	*i-zak-kar-šu-*[ ]
k	[	]	⸢*i*⸣-[ ]

The other manuscripts suggest that the correct reading of ambiguous *iz-*ZIZ*-ma* on MS h is *izziz-ma* 'he stood up', which gives good sense after *ikmis* 'he squatted down'. But from what we see of transmitters at various places in this book, we must reckon with the possibility that the same signs were sometimes (if only by somnolent transmitters) read as *iṣ-bat-ma* (lit. 'he seized'). This verb would then lack an object, but apparently in vernacular Neo-Babylonian it could be so used, with uncertain meaning (CAD Ṣ 21b *ina pānīka liṣbat-ma* 'Let him *do the work* for you!').[230]

When transmitters do not introduce spellings which unequivocally reflect a different understanding, the question of whether they had or did not have a different understanding may seem to have no practical consequences (as well as to be unanswerable). But it is useful to cultivate awareness of the possibility, so as not to allow ourselves to be conditioned by the state of our sources – nor by transliterations, which often shear ambiguous spellings of their ambiguities – into thinking that there was greater uniformity of reading and interpretation than there really was. For the overall perception of textual variability among Akkadian transmitters

229 Goetze, *JCS* 19/4 (1965) 122 line 16.

230 Perhaps cf. also *ṣabtāku umma-mi* 'I thought to myself as follows' at Old Babylonian Mari (CAD Ṣ 22a), but if this idiom originated from the passive function of the stative, it is not relevant.

which one assimilates subconsciously is likely to inform one's reactions to individual instances.

Sometimes, manuscripts which appear to offer variant forms of the same word turn out on close inspection to record radically different meanings. We shall argue this for two manuscripts of *Gilg.* VI in § 4.7.2.

In sum, the chameleon effect arises when unambiguous manuscripts influence our interpretation of ambiguous manuscripts: just as a chameleon takes on the colours of surrounding objects, so in our perception an ambiguous manuscript tends to report the readings of unambiguous manuscripts. The problem with this is, that there was evidently some variability (and perhaps uncertainty) in antiquity over how to read ambiguous spellings. This may not have been the case at the highest levels of ancient scholarship, but it might nonetheless have been the case with the writers of several of our extant manuscripts (§ 1.5).

2.3.3 The *caveat* of somnolence

When we find an instance of a transmitter misreading the signs on an exemplar, it seems fair (indeed tautologous) to say that the exemplar was misunderstood. But this might not mean that the transmitter tried to understand it, and failed: it might simply mean that the transmitter was not thinking about what he or she was doing, and not trying hard (if at all) to understand the exemplar.[231] Note the two possibilities seen by Grayson apropos of three manuscripts of an inscription of Šal III (no. 45): they were produced by someone who either 'did not understand what he was doing' or 'did not care'.[232] Similarly, Irving Finkel notes that a writer who brought sumerographic RA into the spelling of *marhaṣu* 'lotion' was 'confused or careless'.[233]

The effects of mental detachment might have been exacerbated in cases where decoding the cuneiform signs required effort (see chapter 5), but difficulties with the cuneiform script would hardly have been

231 This possibility was not taken into account by Worthington, "The lamp and the mirror, or: Some comments on the ancient understanding of Mesopotamian medical manuscripts", in Imhausen and Pommerening (eds), *Writings of Early Scholars* (2010), which therefore requires modification in places.

232 Grayson, *RIMA 3* (1996) 126.

233 Finkel, "On Late Babylonian Medical Training", in George and Finkel (eds), *Studies Lambert* (2000) 142.

the sole cause of distraction. Ralph Hanna remarks that 'pure somnolence' was sometimes exhibited by Middle English copyists.[234]

A striking instance of somnolence in modern times is reported by Salvatore Nigro in his edition of a series of lectures on Samuel Johnson by the journalist Giorgio Manganelli, originally broadcast on Italian Public Radio (RAI). Nigro writes that, in preparing his edition, he only used Manganelli's original typescripts. The recordings of the lectures as broadcast were unusable, because the RAI editors had 'polished' the prose of Manganelli's scripts, sometimes tripping up badly when the sense was not obvious.[235] Nigro cites an instance in which, owing to cursoriness in reading, a construction was misunderstood, resulting in a severe distortion of the sense.[236] This occurred in a sentence which Manganelli was quoting (in translation) from Johnson/Boswell. We give Manganelli's original:

> Ogni dolore ... non si prolunga mai per troppo tempo, a meno che non si tratti **di** follia, come quella che così blocca l'orgoglio nella mente d'un uomo, da fargli credere d'essere re; o **di** una qualche altra sregolata passione.[237]

Manganelli's construction is *di follia ...; o di ... passione* 'of madness ...; or of ... passion', both being governed by *si tratti* (*di*) 'it be a matter (of)'. A literal translation of the Italian sentence is this:

> Every pain ... never prolongs itself for too much time, unless it be a matter **of** madness, such as that which so blocks the pride in the mind of a man, as to make him believe himself a king; or **of** some other unbridled passion.

---

234 Hanna, *Middle English Manuscripts* (1996) 188.

235 Nigro in Manganelli, *Vita di Samuel Johnson* (2008) 111–112: 'La presente edizione usa come unico testo di riferimento il dattiloscritto di Manganelli. Inutilizzabili sono le registrazioni radiofoniche. Il testo Manganelliano venne sottoposto nella redazione della Rai a un sistematico riadattamento, per renderlo funzionale alla lettura (e di volta in volta si alternarono tre voci, maschili e femminili); e per tornire la prosa, spesso di ricercata asprezza. I ritocchi purtroppo andarono oltre. Là dove il testo resisteva a una immediata interpretazione, per un qualche errore di battitura, per qualche involontaria lacuna, o semplicemente per superficialità di lettura, si provvide a rifare. Malamente'.

236 Manganelli, *Vita di Samuel Johnson* (2008) 112. I am grateful to Augusto Castagnini for bringing Manganelli's book to my notice.

237 Translating 'All grief for what cannot in the course of nature be helped, soon wears away; in some sooner, indeed, in some later; but it never continues very long, unless where there is madness, such as will make a man have pride so fixed in his mind, as to imagine himself a King; or any other passion in an unreasonable way.' (Cited after Project Gutenberg, http://www.gutenberg.org/).

Since the two *di*s are quite far apart, it is not hard to see how a somnolent reader might lose track of the construction. Sure enough, the RAI editors misread the two words *re; o* 'king; or' as the single word *reo* 'guilty', and erroneously took *di … passione* 'of … passion' as dependent on this word (*reo di* 'guilty of').[238] As a result, the sentence which was broadcast translates as follows:

> Every pain … never prolongs itself for too much time, unless it be a matter **of** madness, such as that which so blocks the pride in the mind of a man, as to make him believe himself **guilty of** some other unbridled passion.

Instances such as this – there is little doubt that countless more could be cited from all modern European languages – are all the more striking as the modern editors did not face a number of obstacles which ancient transmitters often did: they were reading their own native language (as opposed to an archaising scholarly idiom, as was the case in the first millennium BC); they were using a modern typescript, rather than worn old tablets; they had recourse to lenses and electric lighting; and they were probably more practised in the skill of reading at sight than ancient transmitters (see § 5.2.1).

The *caveat* of somnolence need not apply to all errors, but it should generally be borne in mind unless there is reason to exclude it. More specifically, textual changes which can be explained away as effects of somnolence should not be used as damning evidence of total incompentence in transmitters: under different, less somnolent, circumstances, the same individuals might have performed much better.

2.4 Evidence for relations between manuscripts

At several points in this book it is argued that two or more extant versions or recensions of a composition are 'genealogically' related, i.e. one derives from the other, or they have a common ancestor. (Note: rather than 'relations between the versions or recensions to which the manuscripts bear witness', it is more practical to speak simply of 'relations between manuscripts').

The core principle is that, if a feature shared by multiple manuscripts is unlikely to have arisen independently on them, then it is suggestive of

238 Nigro's comment on their thought-processes is this: 'I redattori non capirono e, con uno slalom, si inventarono un inesistente « reo » (da « King; or »)'.

genealogical relations between them.[239] This principle is most usefully applied to certain anomalies, which we propose to call 'genealogically diagnostic'.[240]

Examination of genealogically diagnostic anomalies can sometimes pinpoint the nature of the relation, distinguishing ancestor from descendant. For example, if recension A contains all the anomalies in recension B, plus some of its own, it is likely that recension B derives from recension A. Sometimes, it can even be shown that one extant manuscript was copied directly from another extant manuscript.[241]

When a genealogically diagnostic anomaly is an error (more particularly: an error recognisable as such without consultation of additional sources), its occurrence on multiple manuscripts can be of particular interest, as it suggests that it survived multiple steps in transmission without being corrected by transmitters. Suppose, for example, that the same error occurs on three manuscripts from three different sites: at an absolute minimum, two of the three extant manuscripts are copies of the third, so the error must have been copied at least twice. Usually, however, it would be more likely that all three extant manuscripts go back to a single source, with several intermediaries. It would thus seem reasonable to posit an absolute minimum of, say, five reproductions, and the number might in fact be much larger. That the error survived all these reproductions tells us something, either about the transmitters' knowledge or at-

239 For examples of reference to this fundamental principle by Akkadianists see Grayson, *RIMA 3* (1996) 126 on Šal III no. 45; Schaudig, *Nabonid und Kyros* (2001) 116–117 on shared errors pointing to a 'gemeinsame Vorlage'; Cavigneaux, *JAOS* 113/2 (1993) 256b arguing that the use of ŠÀ for the syllable /ša/ shows an Old Babylonian tablet to have originated in Susa.

240 Classicists often use the term '*Sonderfehler*', championed by Maas, "Textkritik", in Gercke and Norden (eds), *Einleitung in die Altertumswissenschaften* (1927), to signify 'genealogically diagnostic errors'. The term was coined in an intellectual climate where all divergences from the *Urtext* were regarded as errors. Since, for reasons explained in § 2.1, we think caution on this point is necessary for Akkadian, in German we would favour the more neutral term *Sondermerkmal.* For 'diagnostic' as a text-critical term see already, in Sumerology, e. g. the comment by Gragg in Sjöberg, Bergmann and Gragg, *Temple Hymns* (1969) 157b: 'We can only hypothesize more or less impressionistically, on the basis of the writing and of certain "diagnostic" variants, that [manuscript, MW] A seems to be a representative of a slightly different tradition from that represented by the majority'.

241 Sometimes, this line of investigation produces astonishing discoveries. For example, all (strictly speaking: all but one of) the extant manuscripts of Arrian's *Indica* are descended from a single manuscript, which is itself extant. See Reynolds and Wilson, *Scribes and Scholars* (1991) 213.

tention (i.e. they failed to recognise the error as such), or about their attitudes to the process of transmission (i.e. they were happy to transmit errors even though they recognised them).

Assembling evidence of cases in which the same error appears on multiple manuscripts is also important for the purposes of formulating textual conjectures. It adds vigour to the idea that we are free to posit corruption, and formulate a conjecture, even when all extant manuscripts agree (see §§ 3.3.3 and 6.1.3).[242]

Finally, analyses of relations between manuscripts can supply information about the geography of textual transmission, showing which versions and recensions of a composition were shared by which scribal centres.[243]

Before giving examples of these uses, we need to address the question of which anomalies are genealogically significant, and which are not. This is a thorny issue, and disagreements can arise about it even in disciplines where textual criticism has a long tradition.[244]

2.4.1 Judging whether anomalies are diagnostically significant

There are at least three points of caution to be observed in deeming anomalies to be genealogically diagnostic. First, it is necessary to define the context within which the anomaly is considered such (see § 2.2.1.1). For example, Neo-Ass. *a-si-bi* for Bab. *altemi* 'I besieged' is frequent under Assurnaṣirpal II, but not attested under Sennacherib. Hence if two similar inscriptions of Sennacherib turned up, both containing *a-si-bi*, it would at least be worth asking whether they were related,

242 For skepticism on this point see Hecker, *Epik* (1974) 112 n. 3: 'Natürlich muß man immer mit Fehlern der Tafelschreiber rechnen, man wird sie aber nicht dort suchen, wo … alle zur Zeit vorliegenden Hss. [i.e. Handschriften, MW] übereinstimmen'. Unanimity across a large number of manuscripts of course tells us about how a passage was understood by many transmitters, but not whether, in historical terms, that understanding is correct (cf. § 2.1).

243 Colophons are of course another source of information about this, but they are less informative than one might wish, cf. § 5.2.2

244 See e.g. Gutas, *Theophrastus* (2010) 58, reacting to an attempt to establish a 'close connection' between MS J of Theophrastus's *On First Principles* and the manuscript which served as source for Bartholomew of Messina's Latin translation of the work.

whereas this question would not arise on the basis of *a-si-bi* for Assurnaṣirpal II.

Second, it is worth considering whether the shared anomaly might reflect a connection other than a common written source. For example, in line 17 all extant manuscripts of Sennacherib's Rassam cylinder write *dārišam* 'forever' as *dà-ri-šam.* The use of *dà* is very unusual, and *prima facie* one might well wonder whether it points to a common written source for all the manuscripts. Since they were all produced within a month, and possibly within the same scriptorium, this would by no means be implausible. Yet, precisely if they originated within a common scriptorium, we can imagine that the transmitters were told by precept (possibly during dictation), or simply agreed among themselves, to use the learned spelling *dà-ri-šam* for *dārišam* (just as they were apparently told at some point in their careers to distinguish *ša*$_1$ for the word from *šá* for the syllable, see § 5.4.4.2). This would account for the common spelling as easily as the hypothesis of a common exemplar. The unusual *dà* would still be an important connection between the manuscripts, but it would no longer prove that they are all related through one-to-one copying. This scenario is lent plausibility by the fact that, as observed by Jamie Novotny in a personal communication, the spelling of *dārišam* with *dà* prevails in Sennacherib's Ninevite inscriptions at large.

Third, it is important to distinguish between anomalies of different types, and the likelihood that transmitters would initiate them independently.[245] For example, lipographies of single signs, being probably the commonest errors in cuneiform,[246] are – in isolation – diagnostically useless: one can easily imagine two different transmitters accidentally omitting the same sign. Other types of errors have their own problems, e. g. errors of sign identification can be difficult to separate from *lapsus styli*, so the same mistake might be made by two different transmitters for two differ-

245 Jacobsen, *King List* (1939) 40 maintained the following: 'There is very little probability that two copyists should independently chance to make the same *unintentional* deviation in copying at the same place in the list. When we find the same error in two manuscripts we are therefore entitled to conclude that both inherited the error from a single original'. Jacobsen thus implies that any 'unintentional deviation in copying' can be diagnostically significant. It is possible that Jacobsen attributed a narrower meaning to this phrase than one would suppose it to have, but taken at face value the principle requires refinement.

246 See already Huehnergard, *The Akkadian of Ugarit* (1989) 95 on his corpus: 'Perhaps the most common type of error is the omission of a sign or signs'.

ent reasons. In some cases, it is hard to distinguish between intentional and unintentional variants.[247]

There are cases where even a single feature renders the hypothesis of a common origin compelling (we will meet examples below). Nonetheless, in many cases there will be doubt as to whether an anomaly (or any other feature) shared by different manuscripts possesses diagnostic significance or not.[248]

In general, *combinations* of anomalies are stronger evidence than isolated occurrences. An example is provided by Paul-Richard Berger, who notes that two manuscripts of a Neo-Babylonian royal inscription which share three corruptions must be genealogically related.[249] Another example is furnished by Jerrold Cooper, noting that an Old Babylonian and a Middle Babylonian manuscript of *An.gim* share a deviation in line order and also the spelling mè-a, which is unique among the composition's Old Babylonian manuscripts.[250] They are almost certainly related.

Particular contexts may furnish a persuasive combination of arguments in favour of an anomaly being genealogically diagnostic. For example, see Jacobsen's contention that two manuscripts of the *Sumerian King List* (MSS Su_1 and Su_{2+3}) stem from a common source:

> Considering that Su_1 and Su_{2+3} are roughly contemporaneous, that they come from the same place, Susa in Elam, where copies of the Sumerian King List to use as originals cannot have been abundant, and that both texts stop short in their account of the Agade dynasty at exactly the same point, it is an obvious conclusion that they derive from a single original.[251]

The balance of probability certainly seems to lie with Jacobsen's contention.

---

247 Gauging intentionality can of course be problematic in itself. Cooper, *Return of Ninurta* (1978) 39 wrote the following for Sumerian: 'Present knowledge of scribal practices does not permit the distinction between orthographic or grammatical features that could be considered transmitted, and those which were dependent mainly upon individual scribal preference or idiosyncrasy'. Over thirty years later, the situation for Akkadian seems somewhat rosier, though many details remain to be worked out.

248 On this problem see already Berger, *Königsinschriften* (1973) 7. The difficulty is well stated by Hanna, *Middle English Manuscripts* (1996) 86: 'No *a priori* mechanism exists for separating accidentally convergent readings from those that are the product of the vertical transmission a stemma presumes to depict'.

249 Berger, *Königsinschriften* (1973) 7.

250 Cooper, *Return of Ninurta* (1978) 37.

251 Jacobsen, *King List* (1939) 25.

2.4.2 The problem of orthographic 'convergence'

We turn now to the possibility that two manuscripts exhibit exactly (or almost exactly) the same spellings. Would this be good evidence that they are related? Alas, not necessarily: the could rather be exhibiting what we propose to term 'orthographic convergence'.

Within many groups of manuscripts,[252] many words are usually spelled in a small number of ways, sometimes only in one, as an inevitable consequence of the prevailing spelling conventions. For example, in Neo-Assyrian royal inscriptions /aš/ is usually represented with *áš*, /lu/ with *lu* and /la/ with *la*. It follows that *ašlula* 'I carried off as plunder' is usually spelled *áš-lu-la*.

Thus, two people who wrote out the same sequence of words and were both familiar with the relevant textual typology would have been likely to spell many of them in the same way – not because the two writers were copying each other, but because they were independently respecting the same set of orthographic conventions, and converging to the same result.[253]

Hence identical spellings on extant manuscripts do not prove faithfulness to a common source. This point would remain valid even if it were known for certain that two extant manuscripts were genealogically related: in theory, they could both depart from the spellings on the common source, but do so in the same way.

The possibility of orthographic convergence means that, for the purpose of deducing genealogical relations, shared anomalies are often more significant than shared 'natural' spellings.

---

252 Note 'groups of manuscripts' not 'textual typologies'. While there are orthographic habits which seem to be characteristic of certain textual typologies (defined in terms of content, structure, and linguistic style), other such habits apply to restricted groups of manuscripts *within* a textual typology. For example, the term 'textual typology' might reasonably be said to embrace all Neo-Assyrian narrative royal inscriptions, but this vast corpus is not orthographically homogeneous. A simple example of this is that the semi-logographic use of *QÉ-REB* is not attested at Khorsabad, while it is in other Neo-Assyrian narrative royal inscriptions.

253 For example, the following spellings from Sennacherib's Rassam cylinder are all the most 'natural' spelling of the relevant form in royal inscriptions of the Sargonid period, and so might well have been used independently by different writers: *kiš-šá-ti*, *la šá-na-an*, *ip-par-šid-ma*, *áš-lu-la*, *šal-la-tiš*, *ú-še-šib*, *na-ṣir ki-it-ti*, *am-hur*, *al-me*, *ú-dan-nin-ma*, *ú-še-ṣa-am-ma šal-la-tiš am-nu*, *al-lik*.

Of course, if the fact of having identical spellings is sustained over long stretches, there comes a point where it becomes good evidence for a genealogical connection. (Such a case is discussed in § 3.4.4). But over short stretches, the argument can be tenous.

Having set out these problems, we shall now offer examples of manuscripts between which we believe genealogically diagnostic anomalies to demonstrate a genealogical connection. We will first give examples where the relevant manuscripts were found at the same scribal centre, then at different scribal centres.

2.4.3 Examples of relations at the same scribal centre

It is hardly surprising that manuscripts from the same scribal centre should sometimes exhibit signs of having a common source. Here are some examples.

A passage on TP I's prism (1 v.12-14) reads differently on two different sets of manuscripts (all from Assur).[254] The first set, consisting solely in MS 1, has: *šal-lu-su-nu ù ka-mu-su-nu ina mahar šamaš bēliya apṭur* 'Plundered and bound, I untied them before Šamaš, my lord'. The second set, consisting in MSS 2, 3, 5 and 12, has *šal-la-su-nu* (*šallassunu*) 'their booty'. MS 1's *šallūssunu* 'in their plundered state', parallel to *kamûssunu* 'in their bound state', is clearly superior.[255] The second set's ungrammatical *šallassunu* 'their booty' apparently originated as an error of phonetic similarity, perhaps triggered by the fact that *šallassunu* is a much commoner word in this textual typology (and probably in the writers' vernacular). The occurrence of the error on four manuscripts strongly suggests a genealogical link between them.[256]

At Assurnaṣirpal II no. 56 (clay cone fragments from the Ištar temple at Nineveh), line 4, three manuscripts (1, 3, 7) offer *mu-kab-bi kišād ayyābīšu*, where our knowledge of the relevant idiom ('he who tramples the neck of his enemies') tells us to expect *mukabbis*. As remarked by

254 On provenance see Grayson, *RIMA 2* (1991) with ref. to Rassam, *Asshur and the Land of Nimrod* (1892) 20 ('Kalaa-Shirgat') for MSS 3 and 5.

255 When *šallūssu(nu)* next appears (v.24, in the same phrase *šallūssu u kamûssu*), MSS 2 and 3 give the expected form *šal-lu-su* (MS 5 is broken, 12 does not extend so far).

256 We cannot suppose them all to have been written at a single sitting of dictation, since we know from the colophon that MS 3 was written a day later than MS 2 (which was written on the same day as MS 1).

Grayson, it seems that 'the original from which ... the exemplars [i.e. extant manuscripts, MW] were copied ... omitted the *is*'.[257] A further sign of a genealogical relationship between MSS 1 and 3 is that in the first line they both lack the NA of *šanān* (MS 7 is broken here).

As noted in § 3.4.1, Eckart Frahm has observed MSS A and FF of Sennacherib's Rassam cylinder to share mistakes, demonstrating a genealogical link between them. As noted in § 3.4.2, at Assurbanipal B viii.10 (*BIWA* p. 113) three manuscripts have an extraneous BI, so they presumably go back to a common source.

At Assurbanipal A ii.114, a single manuscript (A2) preserves the correct spelling of the name ^{I}*pi-šá-me-il-ki* (*pīša–milkī* 'her utterance is my counsel'), while the other four manuscripts (A1, A3, A14, K16986) offer corrupted ^{I}*tu-šá-me-il-ki* (all manuscripts are probably from Kuyunjik, A2 certainly so).[258] Though in principle the error could have been committed independently by different writers, it seems likely that at least some of the four manuscripts derive it from a common source, whether this be a written exemplar or a person dictating. The diffusion of the misreading is interesting for what it tells us about the (low) level of knowledge of current affairs which circulated at the Assyrian court,[259] recalling Schaudig's observation that the failure of multiple manuscripts of Nabonidus's Ehulhul cylinder to correct BUR to ŠUR in the name of a Kassite king suggests their writers did not know the name.[260]

Shared errors can be found on duplicate manuscripts from the Kuyunjik libraries. An example is supplied by MSS K and M of *Ee* IV: in line 55, both have *lam-na* for *lam-du*. We infer that the Kuyunjik libraries contained multiple manuscripts deriving from the same source.

257 Grayson, *RIMA 2* (1991) 329.

258 On the provenance of MS A2 see Borger, *BIWA* (1996) 2–3.

259 On the latter point perhaps compare also Russell, *Palace Inscriptions* (1999) 191 on Weidner, *AfO* 8 (1932–1933) Text A, epigraph 16, which has *annanna* 'so-and-so' instead of the name Teumman (king of Elam). Here, however, though it would be unparalleled, we should perhaps also reckon with the possibility of deliberate humiliation. (Russell's suggestion that *annanna* was used because the writer knew the name but not how to spell it is less persuasive).

260 Schaudig, *Nabonid und Kyros* (2001) 119. See also Grayson, *RIMA 3* (1996) 40 *ad* iii.62 on the likelihood that, not knowing the toponym Paddira, some transmitters misread it as Šurdira (the signs PAD and ŠUR being very similar). Further instances of ancient misunderstanding arising from ignorance of geopolitical contexts are identified in Borger, *Orientalia* 26 (1957) 9. Cf. fn. 830.

Šal III 44 MSS 2 and 8 share a number of variants, suggesting that they are related. In line **2**, they are the only two manuscripts of fifteen to use min 'ditto' after the name 'Assurnaṣirpal', and (along with Šal III 45 MS 1) the only ones to write *mār* with A rather than DUMU. In line **6**, they are the only two with *e-p̊u-šu-ma* (nine have *e-pu-uš*, one has dù-*uš*). In line **7**, they are the only two to spell *sihirtišu* with *-te-* (the other 15 have *-ti-*) and to have *i-na-ha* (the others have *e-na-ah-ma*, *i-na-ah-ma*, or *e-na-hu-ma*). In line **8**, they are the only two with *uš-du* (the other 15 all have *iš-*). In line **10**, they are the only two with *arkû* 'future' – the seven other manuscripts that spell the word syllabically have the Assyrian form *urkû*. In line **14**, they are the only two with *i-ši-mu-u* 'they shall hear' – the thirteen other manuscripts have the Assyrian form *i-ša-me* or *i-ša-me-ú*, without *e*-colouring or vowel contraction. For more on MSS 2 and 8 see § 3.4.3.

See § 4.11 on the anomalously spelled *iṣ-lu-ú-ma* on all four manuscripts of Sargon's *Prunk*-inscription at Khorsabad (line 28). The inference of a common source seemes legitimate.

2.4.4 Examples of relations between different scribal centres

We now offer examples of anomalies suggestive of genealogical links between manuscripts from different sites.

In line 24 of *muššu'u* IV, the noun *labāṣu* erroneously appears as *balāṣu* (metathesis of signs) on MSS G (= BAM 338, from Assur) and H (STT 137-139, from Sultantepe). Metathesis of signs being a comparatively rare error, it is likely that the two manuscripts are related. This may reflect the role of Assur in the transmission of Mesopotamian scholarship westwards.[261] (Another textual connection between Assur and Sultantepe is perhaps that the phrase *šubulti inbi* is so far only known from colophons at these two sites, see fn. 580).

At *Gilg.* VIII 59, all three manuscripts (R and V_2, Kuyunjik; **e**, Sultantepe) have *ib-ri* 'my friend' for *ibru* 'the friend' or *ibiršu* 'his friend'

261 On this in the second millennium see George, *Gilgamesh* (2003) 27. If *muššu'u* did reach Sultantepe from Assur, it cannot be established when this happened. Manuscripts of the composition proper are not known before the first millennium, though individual incantations which form part of *muššu'u* are known in the second millennium (see Böck, *Muššu'u* (2007) 42–43).

(see § 3.2.12). The three manuscripts probably have a common source (from Assur?).

At *Diagnostic Handbook* XVII 104,[262] discussed in § 3.4.4, both extant manuscripts erroneously move a word from the end of one entry to the beginning of the next. René Labat, the first scholar to observe this, regarded it as troubling that an error should occur on multiple manuscripts,[263] but as subsequently remarked by Nils Heeßel, the diffusion of the error can simply be ascribed to transmission.[264]

At *Diagnostic Handbook* XIX/XX 114', both extant manuscripts (E, Kuyunjik; G, Uruk) give the diagnosis as *amīlu šū hi-miṭ* KA ṢAB *Ú ra a ti maruṣ*(gig) 'that man is ill with …'. After *himiṭ*, one expects the word *ṣētu* (*himiṭ ṣēti* 'sunstroke?' being a standard phrase in Akkadian medicine). The word *ṣētu* is often written sumerographically as ud.da, which is visually similar to KA ṢAB. It seems very likely, therefore, that both manuscripts preserve a corruption of original *hi-miṭ* ud.da.[265] It is hard to know which way the error travelled. MS G is later than the Kuyunjik libraries,[266] and transmission from Kuyunjik to Uruk is known to have occurred (see fn. 317), but it is also possible that the Uruk tradition found its way to Kuyunjik, or that both sites drew on a third.

The above instances are of interest for the reasons already stated: they show that reasonably obvious errors could survive copying, and travel from site to site; they can show particular manuscripts to derive from a common source; they show that extant manuscripts need not be right, even when they all agree.

---

262 For this and the following reference see the edition by Heeßel, *Babylonisch-assyrische Diagnostik* (2000).

263 See above with fn. 128.

264 Heeßel, *Diagnostik* (2000) 217: 'Da dieser Fehler sowohl in dem Niniveh-Exemplar als auch in dem Exemplar aus Philadelphia (aus Babylon?) vorhanden ist, muss er wohl schon sehr früh gemacht und dann tradiert worden sein'. However, it is not necessary to suppose that the error was made 'very early' in transmission, as the Nineveh copyists might have imported a faulty reading directly from a late source.

265 As argued in Worthington, "The lamp and the mirror, or: Some comments on the ancient understanding of Mesopotamian medical manuscripts", in Imhausen and Pommerening (eds), *Writings of Early Scholars* (2010) 194.

266 According to Falkenstein, *Literarische Keilschrifttexte aus Uruk* (1941) 1, the tablet assemblage of which MS G forms part belongs 'in die neubabylonische und die frühe persische Zeit'.

2.4.5 Stemmata

Textual critics are not only interested in the readings and idiosyncrasies of individual manuscripts, but in the history of a composition's transmission as a whole.[267] This history, whose reconstruction is chiefly founded on genealogically diagnostic anomalies, can be synthesised in a 'family tree' diagram, known as a stemma (pl. stemmata).[268] This will include both extant manuscripts and ones whose existence is inferred, and it will show how manuscripts can be grouped into families. Producing stemmata is by no means easy, not to mention the danger of its being under the influence of 'forces obscures, confinées dans les profondeurs du subconscient'.[269]

Even in disciplines where stemmata are common, it is recognised that it is not always possible or useful to reconstruct genealogical relations between extant versions. See for instance the following remarks from Alfred Housman's edition of Lucan's *Bellum Civile*:

> Lucan was popular; variant readings were present not only in the margin of books but in the memory of transcribers; and *the true line of division is between the variants themselves, not between the manuscripts which offer them* [italics MW]. The manuscripts group themselves not in families but in factions; their dissidences and agreements are temporary and transient ... and the utmost which can be done to classify them is to note the comparative frequency of their shifting alliances.[270]

This is arguably the case with most ancient Mesopotamian compositions.

Stemmata have been produced for both Akkadian and Sumerian manuscripts, but not always usefully or successfully. The most prominent and far-reaching example of stemmatic arrangement in Mesopotamian studies is Thorkild Jacobsen's edition of the *Sumerian King List*, according to which 'We can with absolute certainty draw the conclusion that our texts are related, that they ultimately descend from a common original',[271]

---

267 See e.g. West, *Abhandlungen der Akademie der Wissenschaften in Göttingen* (forthcoming).

268 The notion of producing a stemma is sometimes associated with the name of Karl Lachmann, though in fact matters are more complicated (see Timpanaro, *La genesi del metodo del Lachmann* (2010) esp. 85–88).

269 Bédier, *Romania* 54 (1928) 175. Bédier (p. 171) observed a suspicious tendency for stemmata to have two main branches, which he (reasonably) took as evidence of over-zealousness on the part of editors in simplifying the stemma in the final stages of work. This, of course, had deleterious consequences: 'Les deux bras qui restent sont munis de fortes pinces' (p. 175).

270 Housman, *Lucan, Bellum Civile* (1926) vii.

271 Jacobsen, *King List* (1939) 13–14.

a view which has since met with scepticism.[272] Though Jacobsen's work contains very many insightful observations about textual change, it seems not to take account of the possibility of 'cross-contamination' between different branches of a stemma. Still in Sumerology, Claus Wilcke reconstructed a partial stemma for five *Lugalbanda* manuscripts, while observing that 'Die übrigen Texte sollen in das Stemma nicht eingeordnet werden, da sie kein sicheres Urteil erlauben';[273] Jerrold Cooper constructed an 'intentionally simplified' stemma for *An.gim*;[274] Gene Gragg commented more generally that the Ur manuscripts of the *Lamentation over Sumer and Ur* constitute 'a relatively homogeneous group, and could be assigned to one family in a MS Stammbaum of the composition based on such criteria as line order, lexical variants, refrain forms, etc.'.[275] In none of these three cases does the reconstructed stemma seem to have great explanatory value.

The Akkadian sources which have most often been subject to stemmatic arrangement are Neo-Assyrian royal inscriptions. These are often extant in multiple versions (with verbatim overlaps), on large numbers of well-preserved manuscripts, which were produced in a short space of time. The idea that it should be possible to find 'genealogical' relations is thus inherently plausible,[276] and stemmatic arrangement concomitantly attractive. Nonetheless, some attempts at this have been criticised on the basis that they relied only on selected passages, which did not generate reliable conclusions.[277]

For other Akkadian compositions, stemmatic arrangement is usually problematic: the extant manuscripts are too short, too fragmentary, and too widely dispersed in time and space to allow detailed study of the relations between the versions to which they attest. Taking the example of *Gilgameš*, even to produce a stemma of the Standard version would be

272 Michalowski, *Lamentation over Sumer and Ur* (1989) 19–25 and Black, *Reading Sumerian Poetry* (1998) 28–38.

273 Wilcke, *Das Lugalbandaepos* (1969) 27.

274 Cooper, *Return of Ninurta* (1978) 52.

275 Gragg, *JAOS* 92 (1972) 207–208.

276 Note De Odorico, *SAAB* 8/2 (1994), who, without producing a stemma, makes many insightful observations on the relations between different versions of Tiglath-Pileser's annals.

277 See Tertel, *Text and Transmission* (1994) 72–74 on Levine, *JNES* 32/3 (1973) and pp. 97-100 on Spalinger, *JAOS* 94 (1974) 318.

hazardous;[278] to try and produce one for all versions of the Epic would be senseless.[279] Accordingly, it is not the purpose of this book to attempt stemmatic arrangement of manuscripts, or, *per se*, to recommend that Assyriologists should do this.

It has sometimes been thought that, when it is not possible to produce a stemma, it is not possible to perform the other activities of textual criticism.[280] Housman's treatment of Lucan is a good counter-example: variants still need to be evaluated, and emendations conjectured.

2.5 On the role of quantification in the study of a corpus language

As noted at the outset, a significant part of this book is taken up with lists of attestations, from which counts are derived. We here explain the reasoning behind giving what might seem superfluous detail.

Displaying the actual spellings from which counts are made allows the reader to examine them independently. This is especially important in the case of a script so full of ambiguities as cuneiform, since the reader might want to challenge some of the attestations by suggesting an alternative reading of the same sequence of signs. The reader may also want to see whether it is possible to spot sub-patterns undetected by the compiler of the list. Compare Alfred Housman's comments on an ill-fated attempt to demonstrate that the Greek aorist could be used with a future sense:

> The list of examples ... is very long indeed; but the moment you begin to sort them and examine them you are less struck by their number than by the restriction of their extent. Almost all of them are such as δέξασθαι used for δέξεσθαι, where the two forms [aorist and future, MW] differ by one letter only; a smaller number are such as ποιῆσαι for ποιήσειν, where the difference, though greater, is still slight ... Why did they say δέξασθαι for δέξεσθαι dozens of times and λαβεῖν for λήψεσθαι never? ... The phenomenon has its cause in the [ancient, MW] copyist's eye and not in the au-

278 Cf. George, *Gilgamesh* (2003) 419: 'Not all first-millennium tablets [bearing compositions of the scribal corpus, MW] were the end result of an unbroken tradition of copying from old master copies'.

279 Cf. West, *Abhandlungen der Akademie der Wissenschaften in Göttingen* (forthcoming).

280 The impossibility of reconstructing a stemma of the New Testament has sometimes led to the attitude that certain procedures characteristic of textual criticism (esp. the formulation of 'conjectures', see § 6.2) cannot be carried out for the New Testament. For references and a rebuttal see Strugnell, *Catholic Biblical Quarterly* 36/4 (1974).

> thor's mind, ... it is not a variation in grammatical usage but an error in transcription.[281]

An Assyriological example along similar lines is that of Neo-Assyrian case endings. On the basis of numerous seeming irregularities, it was long thought that Neo-Assyrian did not distinguish grammatical case in the *status rectus*. In 1965, however, Karlheinz Deller observed that the vast majority of exceptions were instances of TE for TÚ or vice versa, and proposed to regard these signs as graphic variants of each other.[282] Once these cases are filtered out, Neo-Assyrian morphology becomes much more regular.

But what about the idea of quantification *per se*? Is it necessary to be so precise? Can one not simply say 'forms/spellings of such-and-such a type are rare/common', give a few examples, and leave it at that? To counter such notions, we need to take a step back.

Quantitative analysis of a sort is inherent in most aspects of studying a corpus language (i. e. a 'dead' language). For example, an impressionistic quantification underlies even a rule so simple and basic as 'In Old Babylonian, the nominative of the *status rectus* singular of a noun ends in -*u*(*m*)'. A grammarian who asserts this is not saying that there are no counter-examples in extant sources, only that their numbers are so small that they can be dismissed as errors, and that they do not invalidate the rule. Though the frequency of aberrations has not been formally quantified in terms of a percentage, the thinking behind their being discounted is nonetheless quantitative: it is their paucity which undermines their credibility.[283]

In the example just given, formal quantification is hardly necessary. There are two reasons why not. The first is that nominative singular *status rectus* forms ending in anything other than -*u*(*m*) are so rare that this is impressionistically manifest. It is as if the rule were carried by acclama-

281 Housman, *Proceedings of the Classical Association* 18 (1921) 81–82.

282 Deller in Dahood, Deller and Köbert, *Orientalia* 34 (1965) 40: 'Apparent "exceptions" [to the norms for Neo-Assyrian case endings, MW] are mainly restricted to feminine nouns in the gen. sing. which not infrequently is spelled with the sign UD, value *tú*. In our opinion, *tú* stands here as a graphic variant of *te*'. Examples in Parpola, *LAS II* (1983) 71 n. 139 and Luukko, *Grammatical Variation* (2004) 22; also *hu-ri-ib-te a*[*ṣṣabat*] (TN II 5:44) and *ma-da-te* (AN III 7:12).

283 This is explicit in Seminara, *L'accadico di Emar* (1998) 113: 'In casi come questi, data la loro estrema rarità, vien fatto di dubitare se si tratti di omissioni involontarie di sillabogrammi e se non si debbano piuttosto ripristinare forme di tipo *uh-tal-<li>-iq.*'

tion, the overall trend being so dominant that counts are not necessary to establish it. The second reason is that grammarians know *a priori* that in some languages (e.g. Classical Arabic, a relative of Old Babylonian) one case marker suffices for all nouns in a particular grammatical form, such as nominative singular *status rectus*. The number of counter-examples being so small, Old Babylonian can clearly be assumed to be such a language. Thus the combination of linguistic knowledge and self-evidence of the trends renders formal quantification unnecessary.

There are, however, many areas of Akkadian grammar where matters are not so clear-cut. One reason for this is the ambiguous and defective nature of cuneiform spelling, which can make it difficult to distinguish between orthographic facts and linguistic ones. For example, cuneiform spellings often fail to indicate consonantal gemination where it is expected. Our normalisations cheerfully insert it in accordance with our expectations, but we cannot be sure that they are always correct.[284]

More generally, once a corpus language is quite well known, and the usual can be distinguished from the unusual, quantitative assessment plays a key role in how scholars evaluate unexpected forms or spellings: are they wrong, or should they be taken seriously, as evidence of phenomena which have gone unnoticed? We give two examples of this quandary in Classics: discussing *horithmos* for expected *ho arithmos* 'the number' in a Greek graffito at Smyrna, Roger Bagnall notes this might be 'crasis' (a linguistic phenomenon) or 'careless omission of alpha' (an orthographic phenomenon).[285] He then comments that 'There are plenty of instances in the papyri of combination of the article with the vowel at the start of a word, and I think we should give our scribbler the benefit of the doubt'.[286] Similar thinking transpires from a comment by Peter Kruschwitz apropos of *stecus* for expected *stercus* in a Latin inscription: 'Even

284 Cf. the comment by Kouwenberg, *AfO* 51 (2005/2006) 332 on consonantal gemination in Neo-Assyrian: 'Thanks to our thorough knowledge of Old Babylonian, we know that the variation between *i-pa-ra-as* and *i-pa-ar-ra-as* [in OB, MW] is orthographic and that both reflect the same 3rd p. sg. present form *iparras* "he severs, decides" … With regard to Neo-Assyrian, however, it is questionable whether our knowledge of this dialect is sufficient to make such an approach viable'.

285 Bagnall, *Everyday Writing* (2011) 147 n. 18 notes that this interpretation is corroborated by spellings of similar phrases where *arithmos* has the initial *a* (Robert and Robert, *Revue des études grecques* 77 (1964) 255 no. 618 and Robert and Robert, *Revue des études grecques* 89 (1976) 592 no. 813).

286 Bagnall, *Everyday Writing* (2011) 14.

though there are at least five more examples of omission of postvocalic R before a consonant in the Pompeian inscriptions, nobody (until now) seems to have claimed that *stecus* instead of *stercus* could possibly be anything but a mere slip'.[287] In both cases, what might have seemed a 'careless omission' or 'mere slip' when considered in isolation is taken more seriously once more attestations of equivalent spellings turn up. Again, the thinking is quantitative, whether or not the quantification is formalised.

The same principle – that once a sufficient number of examples are found, an oddity should be considered *bona fide* – is often used in Assyriology. An example is Walter Farber's work on adverbs in *-āni* (as opposed to *-āniš*):[288] isolated instances were previously deemed to be lipographic (i.e. missing *-iš* in error), and emended to *-ni-<iš>* by editors, but Farber collected a sizeable number of attestations, and the adverbial ending *-āni* is now booked in Akkadian grammars. In grammar, as in war, there is strength in numbers.

Yet it is essential to recognise that, as we have presented them so far, arguments conducted along these lines are missing something crucial. For, granted a sufficiently large corpus (such as Akkadian cuneiform), and given that omission of a letter or sign is a common error (perhaps, in Akkadian cuneiform, the most common of all), it will be possible to find a number of attestations for the omission of pretty much anything. Hence a deceptively solid argument could be made for pretty much any sort of omission being linguistically *bona fide*.

The first safeguard against this fallacy is linguistic common sense. If it were argued, without any sort of linguistic explanation, that sometimes the final syllable of *iparrasū*-forms was not pronounced, and ten instances where the syllable is missing in writing were adduced as proof, the contention would look extremely weak, for linguistic common sense suggests that it is unlikely *a priori*: much stronger proof would be needed.[289]

But what about cases where linguistic common sense supports a hypothesis? This in itself does not prove the hypothesis correct. What is

287 Kruschwitz, "Romanes eunt domus!", in Evans and Obbink (eds), *The Language of the Papyri* (2010) 162.

288 Farber, "Altbabylonische Adverbialendungen auf *-āni*", in van Driel, Krispijn, Stol and Veenhof (eds), *Studies Kraus* (1982).

289 If the ten attestations were all on the same manuscript, they might – depending on what other signs were missing on the manuscript – have a claim to be taken much more seriously (cf. Landsberger in § 3.2.6), but even then one could think of an idiosyncrasy of the manuscript's writer as opposed to a linguistic phenomenon pervading a period or variety of the language.

needed is some way of comparing the frequency of the oddities which one is arguing not to be errors to the frequency of errors in an equivalent environment. For example, in the case of Farber's adverbs in *-āni*,[290] one could ask the following question: if one divides spellings of all *-āniš* adverbs (including those with 'missing' *-iš*) into groups according to the number of signs and/or syllables which they comprise, is the omission of final *-iš* in each of these groups proportionately more common than clearly erroneous omissions of word-final signs in other words comprising the same number of signs and/or syllables? If the answer were negative, it would call the existence of forms without *-iš* into doubt.

Very likely, Robert/Bagnall, Kruschwitz and Farber rehearsed such considerations inwardly, and deemed the relevant frequencies not to require comment or formal quantification because the trends were self-evident. Nonetheless, without prejudice to the exactitude of their conclusions, it would be good practice in reasoning such as theirs to provide actual numbers. For subjective impressions of frequency are not always right.[291] When it is not practical to undertake counts, it would be desirable to state the role which estimate plays in the argument.

Finally, the history of philological investigation of various languages is littered with imprecise or wrong-headed attempts at quantification.[292] Within Assyriology, one could point to arguments along the lines of 'Everywhere else on the tablet, the sound /pi/ is represented with the sign PI, so in this word the sign BI must represent /bi/ not /pi/'. It is not informative to say 'everywhere else' on the tablet: one needs to state how many cases there are. If /pi/ were represented by PI say forty times, the argument would look strong, but even then it would not be unassailable; we shall

---

290 The form is linguistically plausible: *-ān-* is a well-known morpheme, and the additional *i* is explicable as the adverbial *ī*, which some grammarians believe to have shortened to *i*. (One could also normalise the ending as *-ānī*).

291 For example, compare Aro, *StOr* 20 (1955) 27 and Bloch, *Orientalia* 9 (1940) 337 on the frequency of *plene* spellings in contracted vowels preceding a suffix (*ilqû-šu*, *ilqû-ma*, etc.) in Middle Babylonian: Bloch held that *plene* spelling was 'in der Regel nicht geschrieben', while Aro observed it to be 'oft verwendet'. See also Worthington, "*i-ba-aš-šu-ú* vs. *i-ba-aš-šu* from Old to Neo-Babylonian", in Kogan (ed.), *Language in the Ancient Near East* (2010) 662 n. 5 (with refs) on the frequency of spellings like *i-ba-šu* (as opposed to *i-ba-šu-ú*), which are more frequent than previously realised. (Note: the sentence after Table 6 in this article should read 'not statistically significant').

292 See e.g. the comments by Adams, *Diversification* (2007) 42–43 on misguided attempts to characterise Latin genitives in *-us* of the Republican period as a 'non-urban regionalism' on the basis of numbers.

meet instances in this book of writers who follow an orthographic pattern in several dozen spellings, only to depart from it on a single occasion for no clear reason other than whim or absent-mindedness. If /pi/ were represented by PI say six times, the argument would be much weaker (unless one had special reason to think the writer highly consistent in matters of orthography). The exact threshold of persuasiveness is very hard to pinpoint, and arguably varies from case to case.

3 Mechanisms of textual change

> Mortimer Cropper's graduate students were made to transcribe passages – usually from Randolph Henry Ash – transcribe again their own transcriptions, type them up, and then scan them for errors with a severe editorial eye. There was never an error-free text, Cropper said.
>
> A. S. Byatt, *Possession: A Romance* (London: Vintage, 1991) 25.

The previous chapters set out a number of aprioristic considerations, both about the questions which we should be asking of our manuscripts, and about the difficulties which we can expect to run into when attempting to answer them. We now move to more concrete and example-driven analysis: this chapter will survey the mechanisms of Akkadian textual changes, i. e. how and why textual changes arose. We begin by establishing a typology of scribal errors.

3.1 The importance of a typology of scribal errors

An essential prelude to the study of textual change is to establish the ways in which corruptions[293] arose, i. e. to produce a typology of scribal errors.

One reason why this is necessary is that there may be cases in which the modern perception of an Akkadian form or spelling as wrong is itself erroneous, caused by our insufficient understanding of language or orthography.[294] We can safeguard against such mistakes by thinking in terms of *types* of error made by Akkadian writers:[295] if a suspected

293 For some textual critics, the term '(textual) corruption' embraces anything which differs from the reconstructed *Urtext.* We use the term in a more restricted sense, reserving it for those cases where a textual change was born of inadvertence or misunderstanding.

294 Colloquial forms are especially likely to cause problems. They are still being recognised as such (rather than errors) in a discipline with so long a philological history as Classics, see e. g. the discussion of *domi* meaning 'homewards' by Kruschwitz, "Romanes eunt domus!", in Evans and Obbink (eds), *The Language of the Papyri* (2010) 163–164.

295 This principle is already operative in disquisitions by several Assyriologists, e. g. Hallo, "Haplographic Marginalia", in de Jong Ellis (ed.), *Studies Finkelstein*

error is of a type which Akkadian writers are known to have committed, then the suspicion is strengthened; by contrast, obscurities which do not conform to a known type of error should be treated more gingerly, as they are more likely to end up being vindicated by future scholarship.

The point that, when dubbing a form or spelling erroneous, one should be able to explain how the error arose, was well made by Arno Poebel: 'The assumption that this … is a mistake remains, of course, unsatisfactory as long as one cannot show how the mistake originated'.[296] A typology of errors provides a framework within which to develop such explanations.

Typological study of Akkadian errors can usefully be informed by the writings of textual critics from other fields of research, for many types of error recur across cultures and writing systems. 'Polar errors' (e.g. 'hot' for 'cold', see below) are a good example. Their existence as a typology is recognised in Classics, but not in Assyriology. Thus an editor of a Greek or Latin composition who comes across a variant 'big' for 'small' can, thanks to his or her knowledge of error typology, simply dismiss the variant as a corruption. By contrast, an editor of an Akkadian composition who is not aware that polar errors routinely happen across scribal cultures may be left wondering how the variant arose, and how seriously it should be taken.[297]

An illustration of the importance of cultivating an awareness of error types is provided by Chaucerian scholarship. Some scholars have sought to explain the differences between extant versions of Chaucer's works as arising through revisions made by Chaucer himself. Against these attempts, Ralph Hanna has objected that in many of the cases the differences are at least as likely to have arisen in error during transmission.[298] Specifically, Hanna comments that the workings of transmission in general, and of two error types in particular, have not always been as clearly understood as they should be:

> Editors who have argued [that differences between extant versions are due to authorial revision, MW] have too easily assumed that they could recog-

---

(1977) 101: 'The hesitation no longer seems necessary in view of the large number of additional examples of the identical practice now available'. Cf. also Jacobsen, *King List* (1939) 19: an explanation involving 'a single scribal mistake of a well known type' is 'so much more simple than the others'.

296 Poebel, *JNES* 2/1 (1943) 68.

297 Editors must of course also reckon with the possibility that variants which look like polar errors are in fact deliberate. However, such cases are likely to be rare.

298 Hanna, *Middle English Manuscripts* (1996) 159–173.

nise ... scribal errors and have been unwilling to consider the potential for homographic omissions and synonymous substitutions by scribes.[299]

A further reason for cultivating an awareness of error typology is that different kinds of error tell us different things about the writers who committed them. For example, the sole extant manuscript of the report of Sargon's 8th Campaign (TCL III+), written by one Nabû–šallimšunu, contains a large number of errors: the writer often omits signs which (so we believe) he should have written. Yet, though careless, Nabû–šallimšunu was in other respects a writer of the highest order:[300] discounting omissions, what he writes is grammatically and orthographically very consistent (§§ 4.11, 5.4.6). Sure enough, in the tablet's colophon he tells us that he was the *ummânu* 'principal scholar' of Sargon. Thus his case is very different from e.g. errors which show that transmitters did not understand their exemplars. One such error would be far more suggestive of poor competence than Nabû–šallimšunu's careless omissions of signs, even though these are more numerous.[301]

3.2 A typology of Akkadian scribal errors

Typologies of Akkadian errors have, from time to time, been produced by Assyriologists:[302] note especially Richard Berger (for Late Babylonian Inscriptions),[303] André Finet (for Mari letters in ARM vols. I to V),[304] Mi-

299 Hanna, *Middle English Manuscripts* (1996) 173.

300 Cf. Parkinson, "The History of a Poem: Middle Kingdom Literary Manuscripts and their Reception", in Burkard (ed.), *Kon-Texte* (2004) 55: 'Speed and the resulting carelessness can be a sign of professional expertise'. Owing to what he regarded as erroneous morphology, the original editor of TCL III+ had a lower opinion of its writer, but the seemingly erroneous morphology can now be accounted for (see § 4.7.3).

301 Hence, though it must be warmly applauded as the first enterprise of its kind, the quantitative comparison of error frequency in different Neo-Babylonian archives by Jursa, *Bēl-rēmanni* (1999) 22 is less meaningful than it would be if it treated different types of error separately (in particular, distinguishing errors of inadvertence, such as lipography, from those which imply misunderstanding).

302 In addition to the works mentioned above, see also Huehnergard, *The Akkadian of Ugarit* (1989) 95–97 (with refs to other sections of the book) on 'errors that may be considered purely orthographic or palaeographic in nature'. Outside Assyriology, but still within the world of cuneiform, note the Hittitological studies listed by Singer, *Muwatalli's Prayer* (1996) 137 n. 309.

303 Berger, *Königsinschriften* (1973) 4–6.

chael Jursa (for Neo-Babylonian exercises)[305] and Hanspeter Schaudig (for the inscriptions of Nabonidus and Cyrus).[306] Unfortunately, perhaps because they were not integrated into broader text-critical issues, they seem to have met with limited reception. Also, being focused on particular corpora, they are not exhaustive. Sometimes their classification requires revision. Accordingly, we shall offer a fresh typological overview.

Not all the error types listed below are equally well known in Assyriology. Some are routinely identified in editions (e.g. lipography, dittography, haplography). Some are recognised to exist, but not identified as often as they could be (e.g. errors of sign similarity, errors of 'cut and paste'). Some types (polar errors, errors of attraction, errors of *dictée intérieure*) are only recognised extremely rarely.

In theory, the types of error which can arise on a manuscript depend on how the manuscript was produced: by copying, through dictation, from memory, or *ex nihilo.* In practice, however, matters are more complicated, since a manuscript produced in one way (e.g. dictation) could be reproduced in another way (e.g. copying). Thus errors associated with different manners of production can appear side by side, through a process of accumulation. Transmitters might also experience interference from their memories of the composition being transmitted (or even of other compositions), so familiarity and memory could play a part even when manuscripts were not being written from memory alone (see § 1.2.3).

We here offer a survey of the main ways (as we perceive them) in which errors arose on unilingual Akkadian manuscripts.[307] The survey is not completely exhaustive. Some individual text corpora have additional error typologies which are specific to them,[308] and we do not attempt to list all such corpus-specific error types here. Equally, we do not list phenomena which are so rare or whose applicability to Babylonian and As-

304 Finet, "Liste des erreurs de scribes", in Bottéro and Finet (eds), *Répertoire analytique* (1954).

305 Jursa, *Bēl-rēmanni* (1999) 19–22.

306 Schaudig, *Nabonid und Kyros* (2001) 116–119.

307 For terminology and many of the types we draw on West, *Textual Criticism and Editorial Technique* (1973) 15–29.

308 For example, **a)** in letters written on behalf of the interested parties by professional scribes, pronouns might erroneously get changed from second (also first?) person to third, because an individual whom the sender of the letter thought of as 'you' was 'him' or 'her' in the mind of the scribe; **b)** literary manuscripts may include errors in the division into poetic lines (see e.g. George, *Literary Texts* (2009) 58 *ad* 16-18).

syrian cuneiform is so doubtful that thinking about them typologically does not seem useful. Nor do we list instances where modern scholarship believes ancient writers to have erred, but they can in fact be vindicated (several such cases will be identified in this book).

Some of the error types listed below (e. g. errors of sign identification) occur only in reproductions of existing manuscripts, others (e. g. lipography) occur also in writings *ex nihilo*, such as letters.

Indeed, for several of the types (e. g. errors of attraction), our examples are predominantly from the Old Babylonian letter corpus. This may well be because the writers of the letters were not highly educated (see fn. 323), but that does not mean that the same types of error were not committed by better educated writers. We should be grateful to the writers of Old Babylonian letters for offering plentiful evidence, through which we can develop a typological awareness which in turn can be applied to other textual corpora.

3.2.1 Errors of sign similarity

Errors of sign similarity consist in substituting a cuneiform sign with one which is incorrect, but visually similar to the correct sign (e. g. Neo-Assyrian TU and LI).[309] A particularly charming example appears in a Middle Babylonian letter. The writer protests that he previously wrote asking for pots, but instead received straw. The explanation was found by Hugo Radau already in 1908: the sumerograms for straw and pots (in^{meš} = *tibnu* vs kan^{meš} = *diqāru*) are visually extremely similar.[310]

Not all cases in which the wrong cuneiform sign is used need be understood in terms of confusion between the wrong sign and the correct one. Some may rather be 'errors of attraction', with the confusion originating on the level of sounds rather than sign shapes (see § 3.2.12).

Boundaries between signs could be misunderstood, parts of two signs being read as one, see fn. 520; the reverse also happened, see Labat in fn. 124.

309 Some Sumerian examples are listed by Wilcke, *Wer las* (2000) 76–77 ('Zeichenverwechslung aufgrund graphischer Ähnlichkeit). Another is noted by Cooper, *Return of Ninurta* (1978) 105 *ad* lin. 4 (Assyrian transmitter misreading Babylonian script, see fn. 320).

310 Radau, *Letters to Cassite Kings* (1908) viii and 142. (I owe this reference to both James Kinnier Wilson and Christian Hess).

It is often impossible to tell how a substitution of similar signs arose: it might reflect an error in reading the exemplar (error of sign identification), or it might reflect inadvertence while writing (*lapsus styli*). This ambiguity applies to Radau's example, as to countless others.[311] 'Errors of sign similarity' therefore seems useful as a non-committal term which covers both possibilities. We now comment on the two sub-types.

3.2.1.1 Errors of sign identification

These involve failure to identify the cuneiform signs on the exemplar.[312] This need not have happened only to copyists – it might also happen to people dictating (see § 1.2.1).

In particular circumstances (e.g. when two or more consecutive signs are involved), an error of sign identification can be posited with near-certainty.[313] For example, **a)** as remarked by Wilfred Lambert, meaningless *gír gaz kin nu ú* (*Theodicy* 289, MS m) is a corruption, through errors of sign identification, of *mut-nin-nu-ú* 'pious' (extant on dupli-

311 Radau himself (p. 142) called it 'a mistake showing that even Babylonians could and actually did misread their own signs'. Though Radau's observation that the confusion was caused by sign similarity is beyond dispute, the error did not necessarily lie with the recipient of the request: we must reckon with the possibility of *lapsus styli* on the part of the sender. Another example of this ambiguity is Livingstone, *Court Poetry* (1989) 37–38 n. to 15 r.10, commenting that 'If the clear *-da-* on this well written tablet arose from a misreading of a damaged or defective *-it-* on an earlier tablet, one would have the more usual expression "a mother who gives birth"'. While one can only applaud Livingstone's editorial vigilance, and his suggestion of corruption is compelling, the way in which the corruption is hypothesised to have occurred (error of sign identification) seems unduly specific: *lapsus styli* again seems equally likely. Examples such as this could be multiplied.

312 A striking modern equivalent is that in May 2008 a nuclear-powered submarine crashed into a rock in the Red Sea after its Commander misread the depth indication of '123' metres on a navigational chart as '723' (http://www.guardian.co.uk/uk/2010/mar/15/submarine-crash-navy-court-martial).

313 When there are multiple instances of the same substitution on a manuscript, the suspicion of misidentification arises even if they are not adjacent. For example, KAR 178 twice substitutes nu (*lā* 'not') for visually similar idim (BAD = *kabtu* 'heavy'), resulting in sentences which are grammatically correct, but invert the outcome of the prediction (positive to negative), and once contradict another part of the same entry (see Labat, *Hémérologies* (1939) 59 line 33 and 85 line 36, with notes). Here the repetition of the substitution is suggestive of misunderstanding.

cates).[314] **b)** As observed by Nils Heeßel, šu.gidim.ma dingir^{meš} 'hand of ghost (and) gods' results from misidentification of the signs in *ma-dam-ma* tuk^{meš} 'he will get … much …' (preserved on other manuscripts).[315] Heeßel notes that the error of sign identification was caused by the poor state of the exemplar, as evidenced by the copyist's annotations. **c)** A likely error of sign identification is *tuk-re-ti* for expected *piš-re-ti* on a Hellenistic omen collection from Uruk (BRM 4 12:75).[316] The signs TUK and PIŠ are not particularly similar in Late Babylonian script, but they are similar in Neo-Assyrian script. Since there is evidence of transmission of Kuyunjik manuscripts to Hellenistic Uruk,[317] it is likely that this instance reflects misreading of PIŠ on a Neo-Assyrian manuscript, perhaps damaged, as TUK. **d)** Jeffrey Tigay notes that in the transmission of *Gilg.* the number 7 was misidentified as ŠÁ, and interpreted as the word *ša* 'of'.[318] Further likely examples are listed by Hanspeter Schaudig.[319]

Errors of sign identification might indicate inexpertise in the relevant textual typology, or simply somnolence (see § 2.3.3). But there might also have been extenuating circumstances such as damage to the exemplar, poor lighting (see fn. 855), poor eyesight, or unfamiliar ductus.[320] (Josef

314 Lambert, *BWL* (1960) 89.

315 Heeßel, *Diagnostik* (2000) 306 *ad* 30.

316 See the comment by Schwemer, *Abwehrzauber* (2007) 163 n. 25.

317 Farber, *WdO* 18 (1987) 35 observed that SpTU II 46, in Neo-Assyrian script, has an Assurbanipal colophon. Beaulieu, *SAAB* 11 (1997) 66–67 notes further 'signs of Assyrian influence' in the 'Iqīša library': SpTU II 31 mentions Assurbanipal, and IV 121 includes an.šár, which Beaulieu cogently argues to represent Assur. Beaulieu (p. 67) also notes that the sequence of *ummânus* in the 'Myth of the seven sages' suggests scholars of Late Babylonian Uruk thought that 'the flow of intellectual life had moved north [i.e. to Assyria, MW] during the period of the Assyrian empire, and moved south again, but mainly to Uruk, after the fall of Nineveh'.

318 Tigay, *Evolution* (1982) 68.

319 Schaudig, *Nabonid und Kyros* (2001) 118.

320 The latter eventuality might arise because the sign forms were archaic, and/or because an Assyrian was confronted with a tablet in Babylonian script or vice versa. See Landsberger, *Fauna* (1934) 101 n. 1 for an Assyrian misreading Babylonian ŠAH as DUN, and Lambert, *BWL* (1960) 85 for an Assyrian misidentifying of Neo-Babylonian DUB as RID (the two being, as noted by Lambert, 'identical in some Neo-Babylonian scripts'). Note also the suggestion by CAD A/i 101b that *a-da-an-ta-tum* 'reddish brown mouse' in place of correct *a-ša-an-ša-tum* 'dust storm' (ACh. Adad 19:27) arose through 'an ancient scribe's error in copying a Babylonian text'. Maul and Strauß, *KAL 4* (2011) 31 *ad* Vs. 6 observe that a

Delz remarks that unfamiliar ductus was the commonest source of error for transmitters of secular poetry and literature in Latin).[321] Hence though a misidentification of signs would *ipso facto* be evidence of a failure in the reader, it is not always easy to determine how poorly this reflects on his or her abilities overall.

For errors of sign identification perpetrated by illiterate stonemasons see § 3.6.

3.2.1.2 *Lapsus styli* and errors of tactile memory

It seems possible, even likely, that sometimes a writer intended to write one sign, but inadvertently wrote another instead. We propose to call this *lapsus styli*,[322] 'lapse of the stylus'.[323] From the point of view of understanding the mechanisms of textual change, the hypothesis that *lapsus styli* occurred is important: if accepted, it means that not all substitutions of signs need be evidence of misunderstanding.[324]

Neo-Assyrian tablet which contains a Babylonian RU declares itself in the colophon to derive from a Babylonian exemplar. See also fn. 309.

321 Delz, "Textkritik und Editionstechnik", in Graf (ed.), *Einleitung in die lateinische Philologie* (1993) 61: 'Die häufigste Ursache von Fehlern liegt darin, dass ein Kopist mit dem Schriftcharakter seiner Vorlage nicht vertraut war. Die Möglichkeiten für Buchstabenverwechslung sind unendlich'.

322 We deliberately avoid the phrase *lapsus calami*, current in other disciplines, as it appears to be used with several meanings or implications, which are often not defined, so that exactly what individual users of the phrase mean by it is not always clear. It seemed desirable to use a phrase which had no unwanted 'baggage'. It is noteworthy that West, *Textual Criticism and Editorial Technique* (1973) avoids the phrase altogether. Our use of *lapsus styli* to mean 'lapse of the stylus' should of course be distinguished from the use in which it means 'lapse of style'. Owing to the different contexts in which these usages are likely to appear, we doubt that confusion will arise.

323 There are many substitutions of similar signs in Old Babylonian private letters, but if – as argued by Wilcke, *Wer las* (2000) – these were written by private individuals with limited training in reading and writing (cf. Postgate, *Early Mesopotamia* (1992) 69–70, Charpin, *Comptes Rendus de l'Académie des Inscriptions et Belles-Lettres* (2004) and Charpin, *Reading and Writing* (2010) 10), they might reflect uncertainty about the shapes of the signs to be written rather than *lapsus styli.* An argument similar to Wilcke's is developed by Hackl, *NABU* 2010/1.

324 If writing cuneiform were the 'ponderously slow affair' envisaged by Crowder and Wagner, *The psychology of reading* (1992) 145, then one might in theory argue that lapses of this type would have been unlikely, as the writers would have been working under less pressure. But it is by no means certain that writing cuneiform was slow. Marduk-šākin-šumi writes to the King that he will write out

It would be nice to be able to predict what sort of substitutions *lapsus styli* might give rise to, but unfortunately this is very difficult, as we do not know whether ancient writers of cuneiform remembered signs in terms of their visual shapes, or as automated sequences of movements (or, if both, how these two methods interacted).[325]

If signs were remembered as sequences of movements, it is likely that substitutions would usually have occurred with signs whose first few strokes (in the order of inscription) were the same: the writer would begin the sign correctly, but then be led down the wrong track by faulty 'autopilot'. For such cases we propose the term 'error of tactile memory'. A good candidate for this is erroneous HUL for *ù* 'and' in a Neo-Assyrian scholarly letter – the two signs' first four strokes are identical: [m]u *ù*! (hul) *iš-di-hu* / *iš-šak-kan-šú* 'An (everlasting) name and prosperity will be his lot' (SAA X 74:22-23). Another likely instance occurs on an amulet tablet from Assur, with *lu-ud*-MEŠ-*iq* for *ludmiq* (KAR 37): the writer probably intended to write *lu-ud-me-iq*, but inadvertently wrote *meš* instead of *me* (the two signs begin with the same two strokes).[326]

3.2.2 Errors of sign interpretation

These involve correctly identifying cuneiform signs but misinterpreting them, i.e. assigning them a value which, though admissible in principle, is wrong in context (e.g. giving IŠ the value *iš* when the value *mil* is required),[327] and/or misunderstanding what they represent (e.g. taking *i-na* to represent *ina* 'in' rather than *īna* 'eye').

Here are some examples identified by previous scholars:

---

20 to 30 tablets in less than two days (SAA X 240:23-27, see Parpola, *LAS II* (1983) 176–177 for the chronology; ref. courtesy Aage Westenholz).

325 I am grateful to Mark Weeden for drawing the second possibility to my attention.

326 Maul and Strauß, *KAL 4* (2011) 54 *ad* Rs. 7 see here what we would term an error of attraction (§ 3.2.12): 'Der Fehler mag dadurch erklärt werden können, daß der Schreiber im Sinne hatte, *ūmī* ['days', MW] am Zeilenende mit der Zeichenfolge UD MEŠ zu schreiben'. However, as they acknowledge, *ūmī* at the end of this line is written ud.me not ud^{meš} (both are good spellings), so this explanation does not convince. (The spelling ud^{meš} five lines later does not seem relevant).

327 It is of course important to distinguish genuinely erroneous readings from hermeneutic 'tricks', such as commentators deliberately reading ŠÚ as *ahû* 'foreign' instead of *kiššatu* 'world' (see Frahm, *Commentaries* (2011) 63).

a) *ta-aš-li-im-tù* reflecting an error of sign interpretation by a Hittite, who misread *ta-aš-ši-tum* 'insult' as *ta-aš-lim-tum* 'final payment';[328]
b) *na-iš-tim* resulting from a misreading of *na-pi-iš-tim* as *na-wi-iš-tim*;[329]
c) níg.ba (*qīštu* 'gift') reflecting a misreading of the sign sequence KI IŠ TI as *qí-iš-ti* 'gift' instead of correct *ki-mil-ti* 'rage' (preserved on a duplicate);[330]
d) *ta pu la* for the other manuscripts' *ú-tul₅-la* / *ú-tul₅-lum*: the exemplar which gave rise to *ta pu la* ran *ú-túl-la*; *ú* was mistaken for TA (error of sign identification) and *túl* misread as *pú*;[331]
e) *ši-pir ṭu-uh-du* du on a late Urukean manuscript of an *Izbu* commentary arose from a misreading of *ši-pir irti*(gaba) *ittanallak*(du.du) as *ši-pir ṭuh-du illak*(du), with the sense 'he will enjoy constant success'.[332]
f) *ireddi*(uš)-*ši* '(a weapon) *points parallel* to it' at *Manzāzu* VI 1 turns up on a commentary as *uš-te-lì* '(a weapon) *raised* (it)', resulting from a misreading of uš-*ši* as *uš-lì* and hypercorrect insertion of the 'missing' *-te-*.[333]

Specially noteworthy is a likely instance of misinterpretation in *Malku*, identified by Wilfred Lambert: at *Malku* I 278–279 (available in the edition by Ivan Hrůša), the compiler misunderstood *iširtu* 'a group of ten

328 Sjöberg, "Some Emar Lexical Entries", in Guinan, deJ. Ellis, Ferrara, Freedman, Rutz, Sassmannshausen, Tinney and Waters (eds), *Studies Leichty* (2006) 423.
329 Albright, *JAOS* 38 (1918) 61 on OB *Gilg.* VA+BM iv.6 and 13 (the double occurrence renders lipography unlikely). Albright proposed this interpretation cautiously ('the mistake is perhaps due to the dictator's misreading of *pi* as *wi*'), and the most recent editor interprets the spelling differently (George, *Gilgamesh* (2003) 281). Nonetheless, we cite the instance in recognition of the fact that at least one Assyriologist was thinking about errors of sign interpretation already in 1918.
330 CAD K 373a. Cf. Labat, *Hémérologies* (1939) 90 *ad* 8.
331 George, *Gilgamesh* (2003) 835 *ad* VI 58.
332 Finkel, "On an Izbu VII Commentary", in Guinan, deJ. Ellis, Ferrara, Freedman, Rutz, Sassmannshausen, Tinney and Waters (eds), *Studies Leichty* (2006) 143 *ad* 16-19 (see also Frahm, *Commentaries* (2011) 102). The paraphrase as *šal-ṭiš* 'triumphantly' on the same manuscript seems to pertain to *šipir irti* (see CAD I-J 185b) rather than to the extant (and unparalleled) *šipir ṭuhdi*, so we should perhaps think of the corruption of '*irti* du' into *ṭuhdi* as something that happened in the transmission of the commentary, rather than as an error by the original commentator (cf. the *he-pí* annotations in lines 19 and 20, and igi.tab 'collated' in the colophon, line 37).
333 Koch-Westenholz, *Babylonian Liver Omens* (2000) 105 line A1 and n. 297 (this commentary is discussed in Frahm, *Commentaries* (2011) 178).

(specific) gods' as the word *iširtu* 'shrine'.[334] If this could happen to the compiler of *Malku*, who one presumes *ex officio* to be one of the best scholars of the day, one pales at the thought of what might happen to others! (See § 2.3).

3.2.3 Errors of phonetic similarity

These involve substituting a word or phrase with a similar-sounding one, e.g. *iqbû* 'he said' for *ikpud* 'he plotted'[335] (Asb A iii.117, MS A26).[336]

They could involve more than one word simultaneously. An example from Middle English is the variant 'Tis sely' for 'The sely' (line 4565 of *The Nun's Priest's Tale* by Chaucer): copyists 'contaminated the *the* ... with the initial *s*- of the subsequent adjective'.[337] An Akkadian example is *ina rēš niqê amīlv*(lú) *ul*(nu) *izziz*(gub-*iz*) 'If a man did not stand at the sacrifice'.[338] This is very probably a corruption of *ina rēš niqê amīli ilu izziz* 'at a man's sacrifice a god was present', as suggested by a commentary with *ilu ina niqê amīli izziz* 'a god was present in the man's sacrifice':[339] after crasis (§ 4.4), the pronunciation of *amīli ilu izziz* sounded like that of *amīlu ul izziz*, so the latter was substituted for the former. Some – but certainly not all – sandhi spellings (see § 4.4) may also be explicable as errors of phonetic similarity.

The substitution of phonetically similar elements can arise in two ways:[340] through misunderstanding of a person dictating (aural errors),[341]

---

334 Lambert, *NABU* 2011/2.

335 If the *b* of *iqbû* assimilated to *p* before *q*, *iqbû* and *ikpud* would have sounded even more similar than they look in modern normalisation.

336 A very striking example of an error of phonetic similarity in Sumerian might be ᵈnanna instead of the verbal prefixes na-an-na- on a manuscript of the *Instructions of Šuruppag* (see Römer, ""Weisheitstexte" und Texte mit Bezug auf den Schulbetrieb in sumerischer Sprache", in Kaiser (ed.), *TUAT 3/i* (1990) 66 *ad* 254). The possibility of a rebus writing cannot be ruled out, however.

337 Hanna, *Middle English Manuscripts* (1996) 138.

338 It is hard to determine exactly how this sentence was (mis)understood. Other translations are possible (e.g. making lú genitive).

339 These two passages were connected, and corruption hypothesised, by Koch-Westenholz, *Babylonian Liver Omens* (2000) 137 A ii 12 with n. 389 and 180 iii 12.

340 I am grateful to Lis Brack-Bernsen, Nils Heeßel and other participants in the Symposium 'Writings of Early Scholars' (Mainz, July 2009) for alerting me to the importance of this distinction.

or through inadvertence, in the writer's own head (errors of *dictée intérieure*).[342]

The existence of errors of *dictée intérieure* is hardly recognised in Assyriology,[343] but in other fields it is well known. For example, Papyrologist Peter Parsons notes that 'The process of interior dictation can lead to phonetic errors',[344] while the point is made with different emphasis and terminology by Medievalist Paul Zumthor: 'La production du manuscrit introduit ..., entre le message à transmettre et son récepteur, des filtres ... qui ... sont étroitement analogues aux bruits parasitant la communication orale'.[345] An error of *dictée intérieure* in the thirteenth century *Hystore Job* (*et* 'and' in place of *est* 'is') is expounded by Robert Champan Bates:

> Le scribe, *en copiant, se prononçait à lui-même* les mots et ainsi, en quelque sorte, écrivait comme si quelqu'un les lui dictait, en effet; il voyait *est*, il entendait le son approximatif d'*e* fermé, il écrivait *et*, les deux mots ayant, à cette époque, très probablement le même son.[346]

Some complexities of how homophony can mislead readers were unearthed in an experiment conducted by Cognitive Psychologist Guy van Orden:[347] test subjects were shown a sequence of words, and asked to assign them as quickly as possible to a particular category (e.g. 'flowers'). It transpired that they were more likely to make mistakes in the case of

---

341 On a light-hearted note, Ludwig Bayern alerts me to several websites which chronicle misunderstandings of modern song lyrics by native speakers of the relevant languages.

342 The term *dictée intérieure* is often ascribed to Dain, *Les Manuscrits* (1949) 41–46, though the concept itself had been around earlier, see e.g. Champan Bates (1937) presently, and the summary of previous scholarship in Skeat, *Proceedings of the British Academy* 42 (1956).

343 A striking exception is Seminara, *L'accadico di Emar* (1998) 113 ('sovrapposizione del "dettato mentale" ... sulla realtà morfo-fonemica'). See also Grayson, "Murmuring in Mesopotamia", in George and Finkel (eds), *Studies Lambert* (2000), though he assumes that errors of auto-dictation sprang from writers' murmuring or speaking aloud as they wrote. This – which seems also to be the view of Skeat, *Proceedings of the British Academy* 42 (1956) 186–187 – need not be the case.

344 Parsons, "Copyists of Oxyrhynchus", in Bowman, Coles, Gonis, Obbink and Parsons (eds), *Oxyrhynchus* (2007) 267a.

345 Zumthor, *La lettre et la voix* (1987) 110. See also Junack, "Abschreibpraktiken und Schreibergewohnheiten", in Epp and Fee (eds), *New Testament Textual Criticism* (1981) 290–293 (though the idea that ancient reading was done aloud is questionable, see fn. 945).

346 Champan Bates, *L'Hystore Job* (1937) 144.

347 Van Orden, *Memory and Cognition* 15/3 (1987).

words that sounded similar than in the case of those which looked similar, e.g. they would say that ROWS (homophone with ROSE) was a flower more often than they would make the same error with the visually similar word ROBS.

Returning to Assyriology, many errors of phonetic similarity have been detected by previous scholars.[348] An example is an epithet of sleep on a *Gilgameš* manuscript from Boghazköy: *rāhīt mūši* 'who seeps over the night' (or *rahīt mūši* 'which is spilled out by night')[349] for *rāhīt nišī* 'who seeps over people'.[350]

Nonetheless, errors of phonetic similarity sometimes go undetected, and this can impair understanding of the passage. For example, a statement about a temple in an inscription of Assurbanipal reads as follows: *ù ad-da-a* (= *addâ*, from *nadû*) *ši-gar-šu* 'And I sprinkled its bolt (with oil)' (Asb H1 i.21', *BIWA* p. 189). In discussing this expression, Rykle Borger cites a similar passage which instead has *ú-ad-da-a* (= *uwaddâ*, from *edû/(w)adû* D) si.gar-*šú*.[351] Borger observes that the reading and parsing in the latter passage are ensured because ú (as opposed to u or ù) is hardly used to write the conjunction *u* in Neo-Assyrian. Hence he suggests (with a question mark) that Asb H1 should also be read *ù-ad-da-a*, despite the unusual orthography. However, the sense of *uaddâ šigāršu* 'I made its bolt known' is poor, while, as observed by Borger, *šigāra nadû* 'to sprinkle a bolt (with oil)' is readily intelligible, and expected in context. It is thus very likely that the spelling with ù arose through an error of phonetic similarity: /u addâ/ 'and I sprinkled' (which could not be written with ú) was altered to /uaddâ/ 'I made known' (which could). This eliminates the doubt as to whether MS H1 should be read *ù-ad-da-a*: it should not, and the corrupt parallel should not be allowed to seduce us into thinking otherwise. Here, then, recognition of an error of phonetic similarity (coupled with common sense about what the passage is most likely to mean) helps us to recognise which of the two spellings is preferable.

---

348 In German they are dubbed 'Hörfehler', but given how the term is generally understood (i.e. mishearing of a third party) it is too narrow a designation. Either it should be changed, or its conventionally accepted meaning broadened to include *dictée intérieure*.

349 George, *Gilgamesh* (2003) 319.

350 AHw 969b sub 4a ('Hörfehler'), followed by Tigay, *Evolution* (1982) 122 n. 41.

351 Borger, *BIWA* (1996) 188. The parallel passage is from Foxvog, *RA* 72/1 (1978) 44 no. 1 i'.17'.

What can errors of phonetic similarity tell us about the pronunciation of Akkadian? In any given instance considered in isolation, caution is called for. Perhaps in the case of mis-hearings, but certainly in the case of *dictée intérieure*, the substitution can occur on the basis of very partial similarity. For example, in English one might, when tired or distracted, write 'repeat' instead of 'defeat'. In this case it would suffice to trigger the substitution that the two words have similar syllable structures, and their vowels (especially: their accented vowels) are identical.[352] Philologists of future eras would be wrong to infer from the substitution that we pronounce *p* in a way similar to *f*, let alone *d* like *r*. Nonetheless, it seems to be the case that, in *dictée intérieure*, true homophones are swapped more frequently than words which merely sound similar. When significant numbers (subject to the *caveat* expressed in § 2.5) of cases can be found which are suggestive that two sounds or words were identical, they become a force to be reckoned with.

As remarked elsewhere (§ 2.2.2.2), some seeming errors of phonetic similarity might in fact be phonetic spellings. However, sometimes this hypothesis can be excluded. For example, in the following cases the involvement of a sumerogram makes an error of phonetic similarity virtually certain:

> *aš-šur* en nun-*ú* (*rubû*) 'Assur, the lord, the prince' (Asn II 28:15 and 50:38; cf. Šal III 2 i.27 MS 1) for expected *aš-šur* en gal-*ú* (*rabû*) 'Assur, the great lord'
>
> *a-di* dingir^{meš}-*ni*(*ilāni*) 'unto the gods' (Šal III 6 i.52 MS 1) for expected *a-di* uru^{meš}-*ni*(*ālāni*) 'unto the cities' (MSS 4-5)

Admittedly, Babylonians and Assyrians sometimes chose to represent words with sumerograms which normally represented homophonous words (e.g. uru$_4$ for both *erēšu* 'to wish' and *erēšu* 'to cultivate'), but this appears to have occurred mainly with words which sounded identical or nearly so. Hence it is doubtful whether it would have been done inten-

352 It would of course be nice to know which words counted as similar in the minds of Akkadian writers, and which did not. At present, there is great uncertainty about this. Biggs, *NABU* 1993/3 intriguingly suggests that in *Ištar's Descent*, line 104, where Aṣûšu-namir is cursed with having to eat 'bread of the public ploughs', *epinnu* 'plough' is a corruption of *tubkinnu* 'rubbish dump' (the phonetic similarity being that both words end in *-innu*). It is hard to evaluate this. In terms of sense, the extant 'bread of the plough' is not impossible: Andra Mihu (pers. comm.) suggests a metaphor for 'soil'.

tionally with *rabû/rubû* or *ālu/ilu*, and the hypothesis of an error of phonetic similarity seems strong.

Similarly, a very late Astronomical Almanac (from 7-6 BC) uses AB instead of expected ÁB for *arhu* 'month' (the latter value is based on the fact that in earlier periods ÁB stood for *arhu* 'cow'). This isolated instance cannot be used as evidence of ignorance on the part of the writer: the writer might well have known that ÁB was the correct spelling, but simply written AB through inadvertence.[353]

In contexts where one has the impression that transmitters did not aspire to exact reproduction, and where two phonetically similar readings both give good sense, it is possible that one be a deliberate variant of the other rather than an error of phonetic similarity. An example is provided by two Old Babylonian spells which Andrew George has observed to make very similar statements about scorpions:[354]

uldaššu-ma asurrûm ge$_6$-eš-pa-ar pūtim 'a drain begat it, the forehead-snare'

uldaššu asurrûm na-aš-pa-ar mu-ti?-[*im*] 'a drain begat it, the envoy of death'

As noted by George, the phonetic similarity between *našpar mūtim* 'envoy of death' and *gešpar pūtim* 'forehead-snare' is great (all the more so if *gešpar* was pronounced *à la sumérienne*, as *ĝešpar*), and both phrases are meaningful in connection with scorpions. What is the relation between them? We are likely to be confronting written offshoots of lively oral happenings rather than the transmission of writings, and it seems impossible to venture beyond George's cautious statement that one probably derives from the other 'by inadvertent corruption or deliberate adaptation'.

---

353 Viewing this instance against a broader background of unusual spellings in very late astronomical writings, Brown, "Increasingly Redundant: The Growing Obsolescence of the Cuneiform Script in Babylonia from 539 BC", in Baines, Bennet and Houston (eds), *The Disappearance of Writing Systems* (2008) 90 (ref. courtesy Yoram Cohen) regards this use of AB as evidence that 'The scribe was still aware of the pronunciation of the signs, but not their Akkadian readings'. However, since an error of phonetic similarity seems perfectly possible, this unique case should be distinguished from those which are attested abundantly. Whether Brown is right that the latter reflect misunderstanding, or they should simply be regarded as abbreviations, is unclear (cf. Frahm, *Commentaries* (2011) 53 n. 229). Poor handwriting, to which Brown draws attention, is an uncertain guide to the quality of the text itself (i.e. the sequence of signs and/or words).

354 George, *NABU* 2010/1.

3.2.4 *Saut du même au même*

When a passage contained two identical elements (such as signs, words, or phrases), a transmitter might inadvertently jump from the first occurrence to the second, omitting one of the occurrences and everything between them. This is known as the *saut du même au même* ('jump from the same to the same'). A likely example is *ṭup-pí a-bi-ia* for *ṭup-pí a-na a-bi-ia* (jump from *a* to *a*, resulting in omission of *na a*; AbB II 82:26).[355]

More specific terms arise when the jump is occasioned by poetic lines with similar beginnings (*homoearchon*), similar middle phrases (*homoeomeson*), or similar ends (*homoeoteleuton*). An example of homoearchon appears on *Gilg.* XI MS J, which, as observed by Andrew George, omits lines 268 and 269 because lines 267 and 270 begin with the same word (*tēdīqu*).[356]

The *saut du même au même* is often thought to point to copying, but there is no reason to doubt that it could happen to people dictating, or indeed – though perhaps more rarely and across shorter differences – also to people writing *ex nihilo.* A possible example of this is *da-ia* for *da-ia-nu-ia* 'my judges' (AbB II 106:29; cf. line 21): having written the first *ia*, the writer's mind jumped ahead to the second *ia* in the word, and continued from that point.[357]

It is uncertain whether in Akkadian the *saut du même au même* occurred only with identical (groups of) cuneiform signs which had to be read in the same way – or whether it also occurred with identical (or similar?) words which the exemplar spelled differently, or with identical sign sequences which had to be read differently.

355 A Sumerian example is hypothesised by Jacobsen, *King List* (1939) 27: 'The phrase rîmuš dumu šarru-kîn occurs twice in close succession, so that a scribe copying such a text may easily have jumped from the first line down to the exactly similar passage in lines 4-5'.

356 George, *Gilgamesh* (2003) 894.

357 This example is from an Old Babylonian letter. So far as we know, with the possible exception of school exercises, these were not usually copied. While it cannot be ruled out that this letter is an exercise, no other copies of it are known, and there is no reason to think it was copied. (For examples of near-identical manuscripts of letters being found at different sites see Sallaberger, *"Wenn Du mein Bruder bist"* (1999) 149–154).

3.2.5 *Aberratio oculi*

We propose to use this term for cases where a transmitter jumps to the wrong part of the exemplar without this being classifiable as *saut du même au même*. Over short distances, such jumps can be hard to distinguish from lipographies.[358]

It should be noted that some editors and textual critics use '*aberratio oculi*' with a variety of other meanings, including our 'error of sign identification' and *saut du même au même*.[359]

3.2.6 Lipography

This involves omitting something which should have been written (e.g. *ma-tu* for *ma-li-tu*). We propose to reserve the term 'lipography' for the omission of an entire sign or group of signs, to distinguish it from the (much rarer) case of incomplete signs (§ 3.2.9).

Spellings which would look lipographic if considered in isolation should be evaluated against all spellings on the manuscript, as they may turn out to be susceptible of other explanations. For example, Benno Landsberger pointed out apropos of a Neo-Assyrian letter (now SAA XIII 178) that, as it includes three attestations of *li-iz-zi* for *lizziz* (lines 11, 23, 25) and one of *ul-ta-az-zi* for *ultazziz* (line 21), contrasting with expected *ú-šá-az-zi-zu* (line 20), the spellings which are missing word-final *z* cannot be blithely dismissed as lipographic, and emeded to -<*iz*>: the 'psychological' likelihood of such a cluster of lipographies is nil.[360] Earlier scholars had taken a different view,[361] prompting the thunderbolt which we cite as the epigraph of chapter 4.

Similarly, when a Late Babylonian letter thrice writes *i-dab-bu* for expected *idabbub* (PTS 2027, lines 13, 17, 21) it is difficult to dismiss this as scribal inexpertise. It presumably points to vernacular pronunciation along the lines of /idabbu/ (maybe /idabbū/ < /idabbuw/, or

358 A likely example of what we term *aberratio oculi* occurs in Borger, *JCS* 21/1 (1967) 5 line 35 MS B (see Borger's comment).

359 For Borger, *Theologische Rundschau* 52/1 (1987) 16, *aberratio oculi* comprises homoeoteleuton, homoeoarchon and dittography.

360 Landsberger, *Brief des Bischofs* (1965) 369 n. 142: '[Es muss] gesagt werden, dass die psychologische Motivierung für einen solchen Fehler gleich null ... ist'.

361 Poebel, *Studies* (1939) 175–177 and CAD E 159.

/idabbuv/).[362] Johannes Hackl's observation on the strength of other features (including an exceptional syllabic spelling of Uruk as *ú-ru-uk*) that the writer was unlikely to be a professional may explain why he or she wrote hardcore vernacular forms rather than using traditional spellings.

3.2.7 Haplography

This involves writing once what should be written twice (e.g. *ša-at-ti* for *ša ša-at-ti*, AbB II 96:13, cf. line 7). When the correct sequence would have consisted in two identical signs, it cannot always be determined whether the first was omitted or the second.

We apply the term 'haplography' also to cases where the sequence of two identical items, one of which was omitted, consists of the same sound written with two different signs rather than a repetition of the same sign. Thus we consider that the change from e.g. *ša šá-a-a-ma-nu-te* 'of purchase' to *ša-a-a-ma-nu-te* counts as haplography (for this example see § 5.4.4.2); ditto perhaps *ù nu-ti* for *ù ú-nu-ti* (AbB II 89:22, crasis also possible).

With a writing system such as cuneiform, in which many signs have multiple readings, the question arises whether haplographies could occur when the same sign should have been written twice, but with different readings. Relevant cases being few, haplography is difficult to distinguish from lipography. Nonetheless, two promising-looking instances are *be-lí di* (or *be ni-di*) for *be-lí ni-di* (AbB II 83:7), *lí* and *ni* being two readings of the same sign; and *tam-di um* (or *tam* silim-*um*) for *tam-di* silim-*um* (Šal III 2 ii.6, MS 1), *di* and silim being two readings of the same sign.

An interesting case is uku.uš *ta-ti-ma* for uku.uš *uš-ta-ti-ma* 'I met … the soldier' (AbB VI, 70:16). Here, though in a certain sense the sign UŠ was read /uš/ on both occasions, in the former case it was part of a sumerogram representing the Akkadian word *rēdûm* 'soldier', while in the latter it represented the Akkadian syllable /uš/.

362 The letter is edited by Hackl, *NABU* 2010/1, who emends to *i-dab-bu-*<*ub*>.

3.2.8 Dittography

This involves writing twice what should be written once (e.g. *lu-ša-šib-šib-bu* for *lu-ša-šib-bu*, SAA II 6:574, MS Q). The resulting two identical elements need not be directly adjacent, e.g. *qal-la-qal-la* for *qal-la-la* (CAD Q 60b).[363] For instances where the separation of the two elements needs to be underscored, we propose the term 'disconnected dittography'.

3.2.9 Incomplete signs

It would be surprising if cuneiform signs were always written perfectly, and indeed they were not. One of the faults they could exhibit (vis-à-vis their 'standard' forms)[364] was that they missed wedges. The same reasons can be distinguished as in § 2.2.2.3: inadequate knowledge of cuneiform, bad (or super-cursive) handwriting, *lapsus styli*, damage to the exemplar,[365] somnolence.[366] We propose to apply the label 'incomplete signs' only to the cases where inadvertence (i.e. *lapsus styli*, perhaps also somnolence) is responsible. Likely examples are *hi* for *im* (AbB XI 16:19)[367] and *i* for *ia* (AbB V 273:6').[368]

If cuneiform signs were written from tactile memory (§ 3.2.1.2), it would make sense for the parts of incomplete signs (in our restricted sense) which do get written to be complete signs in their own right rather than just meaningless bunches of wedges: having got to the end of what counted as a sequence of movements in its own right (e.g. HI), the 'auto-

363 For an example where a word at the end of one line is repeated at the beginning of the next see Labat, *Hémérologies* (1939) 126 lines 52-53.

364 In certain contexts, signs could have multiple 'standard' forms, with various degrees of simplification. See Sommerfeld, *Tutub* (1999) 7–10 on Old Akkadian and Jursa, *Bēl-rēmanni* (1999) 24 on Neo-Babylonian (distinguishing 'kalligraphisch' and 'eilig' as subtypes of 'Standardschrift', correlating with different writing speeds).

365 For a likely case where a transmitter could not or would not restore wedges lost on the exemplar see Worthington, *JMC* 7 (2006) 39 on iv.22 (collation on p. 27 is mis-labelled 'iv.21'; the comment should read 'part of the first half of TE').

366 Note also a Hittite instance where the reason for incompletion seems to be that the writer was writing under dictation, and had difficulty keeping up (see fn. 30).

367 Compare the copy by Ungnad, *Letters of the Hammurapi Period* (1915) plate XII, no. 16.

368 See also KU for DA and ŠU for ŠA, cited by Schaudig, *Nabonid und Kyros* (2001) 116.

pilot' might erroneously conclude that this sign had been finished and move the writer on to the next sign, even though additional wedges were needed to turn e. g. HI into IM.

Sometimes it is impossible to determine the reason for a sign's incompleteness. Such is the case with e. g. *aš-uṭ-ra* for *pu-uṭ-ra* (AbB II 170:15), AŠ being identical to the second half of PU.

It is possible that apparent instances of contraction involving the possessive suffix *-ia* – e. g. *it-ti-i* for *ittiya* 'with me' (SAA X 170 r.1); *šap-ti-i* for *šaptīya* 'my lips' (*Ee* III 64, MS g) – actually involve incomplete signs, i. e. *i* is simply incomplete *ia.* Admittedly, the occurrence of two instances within three lines renders incomplete signs unlikely as the explanation for the Sultantepe MS of *Gilg.* VIII, but here a different explanation can be found: both words are followed by a vowel (*ib-ri-i* ᵈ*en-ki-dù*, line 44, and *ši-bi-i a-ri-te*, line 47), so *-ya* might well have been pronounced /y/ (*a* lost through crasis) and written as *i.*[369] But even so, explanations in terms of sound change – whether contraction (*ittî* etc.) or apocopation (*ittiy* or similar, etc.) – cannot be ruled out even for instances followed by a consonant.

3.2.10 Polar errors

These involve unwittingly substituting a word with a word of opposite meaning (e. g. 'hot' for 'cold'). They are an error type well established in Classics,[370] but not usually recognised in Assyriology. They deserve wider recognition as a typology, as they can help us to understand how perplexing variants arose. Some likely examples:

- gal 'big' for tur 'small' (BM 134701:11')[371]
- sig_5-*TIM-ia* 'my goodness (i. e. goodness done to me)' for hul-*ti(M)-ia* 'my evil (i. e. evil done to me)' (Asb B vii.55 MS D7)

369 The orthography would be unusual, but there are possible Neo-Assyrian instances of *i* for intervocalic /y/ (e. g. SAA V 3:8 *an-ni-i-e*, see Luukko, *Grammatical Variation* (2004) 41). In any case, at Sultantepe non-standard orthography would not be too troubling.

370 See Oakley, *Commentary, vol. 2* (1998) 247–248 with n. 1 p. 248, citing *inter alia* a modern example identified by Michael Reeve: '*The Times* of 24 Nov. 1994 carries a reproduction with accompanying transcription of a ms. of a limerick by Edward Lear: the ms. has "old", the transcription "young"'. (I owe this reference to Simon Malloch).

371 See Brown and Linssen, *RA* 91 (1997) 163 *ad* 11'.

- munus.sig$_5$ 'goodness' for munus.hul 'evil' (Asb A iii.117 var)
- *šap-li-ti* 'lower' for *e-li-ti* 'upper' (TP III Summ. 4:5', Summ. 9 r.1)[372]
- 15 = *imittu* 'right' vs gab = *šumēlu* 'left' on two manuscripts of the same ritual prescription[373]
- *adi* 'up to' for *ultu* 'from' (Šal III 8:4', see Grayson *ad loc.*)
- *ana* 'to' for *ištu* 'from' (RINAP 3/1 no. 18 vii.5' MS 1d)
- ad^{meš}-*ia* 'my fathers' for dumu^{meš}-*ia* 'my sons' (RINAP 3/1 no. 15 viii.19'' MS 1)

Ambiguity of interpretation arises where the polarity results from the absence of a negation: *ša nība išû* 'which has a number' for *ša nība lā išû* 'which has no number' (Senn Rass. 26 MS BB), *hiṭītum mimma ibbašši-ma* 'Any mistake may happen' for *hiṭītum mimma lā ibbašši-ma* 'No mistake must happen'.[374] Such cases could either be polar errors or instances of lipography.

Recognition of the existence of polar errors throws light on e. g. passages in the *Diagnostic Handbook.* One entry has the prognosis úš 'he will die' on one manuscript where other manuscripts have al.ti 'he will live'.[375] Another entry reads 'If both sides of his throat (look) skinned and his flesh is healthy, he will get well / it is worrisome'.[376] In neither case need we suppose that both prognoses were *bona fide.* It is simplest to assume that one is a corruption of the other, through a polar error. In the second case the ancient transmitter or redactor (who may not have recognised polar errors) did not know how to choose between the variants, so transmitted both (cf. § 1.4.4).

372 All references to the inscriptions of TP III are taken from Tadmor, *Tiglath-Pileser III* (1994).

373 Farber, *Schlaf* (1989) 122 line 4.

374 Horowitz and Wasserman, "From Hazor to Mari and Ekallatum: A Recently Discovered Old-Babylonian Letter from Hazor", in Nicolle (ed.), *Nomades et sédentaires* (2004) 342 line 21'.

375 Tablet II line 74. See Heeßel, *AfO* 48/49 (2001/2002) 36 with note, p. 45.

376 Scurlock and Andersen, *Diagnoses* (2005) 3.51.

3.2.11 Errors of gender polarity

These involve writing a masculine form instead of its feminine equivalent – or vice versa, though masculine instead of feminine is commoner.[377] An example is ^{lú}uš.zu$_{11}$ 'sorcerer' for ^{munus}uš.zu$_{11}$ 'sorceress'.[378] Additional examples feature in the list of 'soft auto-corrections', § 4.3.

3.2.12 Errors of attraction

These involve causing a word, form or spelling to resemble another word, form or spelling in the same sentence or passage in some way which is faulty.[379] The principle has already been applied to Akkadian by several scholars.[380] We give some examples:[381]

a) *emūqīšun ittišun* 'their forces with them' for *emūqīšu ittišun* 'his forces with them' (Asb B vii.9, MS B/D20): the *-šu* 'his' of *emūqīšu* has become 'attracted' to the *-šun* 'their' of *ittišun.*
b) *i-ti-ta-a-ma* for *ittika-ma* 'with you' (AbB XI 11:11): the *k* has become 'attracted' to foregoing *t* (or /tt/), so that *ta* was written instead of *ka.*
c) *e-te-šum š*[*a*] *t*[*ē*]*p*[*ušu*] *dami*[*q*] for *epēšum ša tēpušu damiq* 'The deed you did is good' (AbB V 40:5-6): the *pē* of *epēšum* has become 'attracted' to the *tē* of *tēpušu.*

---

377 On erroneous m. for f. being more frequent than vice versa at Mari (as indeed seems to be the case in Akkadian at large) see Finet, "Liste des erreurs de scribes", in Bottéro and Finet (eds), *Répertoire analytique* (1954) 99.

378 PBS 1/1, 15:9, see Schwemer, *Abwehrzauber* (2007) 131 n. 306.

379 Some textual critics call them 'errors of assimilation', but it seems desirable to use a different term in Assyriology, to prevent confusion with the phenomenon of assimilation in the vernacular language (e.g. *inaddinšum* pronounced /inaddiššum/, with assimilation of *n* to *š*).

380 E.g. West, *Helicon* (1997) 158 n. 239, suggesting that *li-ru-bu* 'may they enter' (Ebeling, *TuL* (1931) 128 line 7*), with a river as object, is an error for *lībirū* 'may they cross', under the influence of *līrubū* in the two adjacent lines. See also Kouwenberg, *The Akkadian Verb* (2011) 416 n. 202: *li-ta-na-al-la-ak* for expected *littallak* (ARM X 54:14) may be 'caused by *attanallak* in line 12'. (Cf. further Kraus in fn. 382).

381 See also Finet, "Liste des erreurs de scribes", in Bottéro and Finet (eds), *Répertoire analytique* (1954) 102 classifying *ana pāhat ṣalmim* for *ana pāhat kaspim* as 'confusion de termes'. Since the word *ṣalmum* appears later in the sentence, we interpret it more specifically as an error of attraction.

d) *mimma ša* ME *be-lí i-qá-ab-bu* for *mimma ša bēlī iqabbû* 'whatever my lord commands' (AbB VIII 15:38-39): it is likely that the *b* of *bēlī* became 'attracted' to the prominent *m*s of *mimma*, resulting in the sign ME being written; the writer then realised the mistake and wrote *be*, leaving the faulty ME ('soft auto-correction', see § 4.3).

e) *a-nu-ma allikam* for *i-nu-ma allikam* (AbB IV 142:5) the *i* of *inūma* has been attracted into *a* under the influence of the initial (and stressed?) *a* of *allikam.*

f) *awâtum lā ilabbirā-ma ana [w]arkat šattim la i-sa-hu-ra-ma la udabba-būka* 'The matters must not drag on (lit. 'grow old'), and they (referring to people, not the matters) must not pester you again until the end of the year' (AbB IV 157:12'): *isahhurā-ma* should be *isahhurū-ma*, in hendiadys with *udabbabūka.* The masculine ending *-ū* has become attracted to the feminine ending *-ā* of *ilabbirā.*[382]

g) At *Gilg.* VIII 59 the narrator says of Gilgameš mourning Enkidu: *iktum-ma ibrī kīma* 'he covered my friend, like …' (on all three manuscripts). For obvious reasons of meaning, instead of *ib-ri* 'my friend' one expects *ibiršu* 'his friend' (or conceivably *ibru* '(his) friend'). The oddity presumably arose because a transmitter attracted the correct form (*ibiršu* or *ibru*) to the form of the same word which he or she was accustomed to writing most often in the Epic, i. e. *ibrī.* On the error's occurrence on multiple manuscripts see § 2.4.3.

h) In an anti-witchcraft incantation,[383] *šamaš mūdê rag-gi-šú-nu muhalliq raggī* 'O Šamaš, who knows their wicked ones, who destroys the wicked ones', *raggīšunu* 'their wicked ones' is corrupt for *riksīšunu* 'their poultices' (preserved on a duplicate). The corruption arose through attraction of *riksīšunu* to *raggī* later in the line.[384]

Errors of attraction can be quite insidious, since when the relevant form or spelling is considered in isolation inferior explanations may commend themselves. For example, in *umma sîn-rēmēnī-ma a-hu-ka-ni* 'Thus Sîn-rēmēnī, your brother, …' (AbB XI 44:3-4) *a-hu-ka-ni* is erroneous for *a-hu-ka-ma.* This might be interpreted as confusion of the signs NI and MA, but in our view it is more likely to be an error of attraction, induced by /ni/ at the end of *rēmēnī.*

---

382 For this explanation see already the note by Kraus, *AbB IV* (1968) 106, with different terminology (*isahharā-ma* 'in falscher Analogie zu *i-la-bi-ra-ma*').

383 Schwemer, *Rituale* (2007) 50:38'.

384 Thus also, with different terminology, Schwemer, *Rituale* (2007) 54.

CAD Ṭ 53a bottom cites what looks like a *parīs*- infinitive in Old Babylonian: *aššum ṭa-ri-di-im* 'as regards sending' (TLB 4, 15:9). In principle, there is no reason why this should not be so – the history of many languages attests to features which were originally rare going on to gain frequency in later periods.[385] That said, it is equally possible that *ṭa-ri-di-im* includes an error of attraction (RI instead of RA owing to following DI), so the spelling does not prove the existence of *parīs*- infinitives in Old Babylonian.

Some spellings which appear to record unusual phonetic assimilations may in fact conceal errors of attraction. For example, *it-ta-ab-šu* for *iltabšu* (AbB I 34:9) could genuinely reflect vernacular pronunciation /ittabšu/, with assimilation of /lt/ to /tt/; but it is also possible that, though the writer intended to write IL, the sound /l/ was attracted to the /t/ of following TA (error of attraction). Such a development would hover at the interface of language and orthography, and one might even make a case to the effect that 'assimilation' is, at some level, an appropriate term for it. But it would be assimilation in a different sense from how this term is normally used in Akkadian grammar (i. e. as in vernacular pronunciation). See also § 3.4.1 *sub* line 69 on *as-hu-ha-am-ma* for *assuham-ma*.

Similar uncertainties can arise over how to read signs. For example, in *ba-al-*TA*-ta* for *balṭāta* 'you are well' (AbB XI 95:6) is the writer consciously using TA to represent /ṭa/? Or has /ṭa/ become /ta/ through an error of attraction? In the present state of knowledge, it is difficult to tell.

3.2.13 Errors of syllable inversion

These involve writing a cuneiform sign whose reading is the reverse of what is required.[386] Likely examples are *bu-li-aṭ-an-ni* for *bu-li-ṭa-an-ni* (AbB XI 35:16), [*i*]*t-ab-lam* for *it-ba-lam* (OB *Gilg.* III 77), and *ṣu-mu-*

385 In Worthington, *ZA* 100/1 (2010) 87 n. 3 I argued this for the *-nu* form of the ventive ending. However, the three Old Babylonian attestations of this could conceivably be errors of attraction. It is difficult to tell.

386 For an example of such an error in a modern cuneiform copy, see Langdon, *Penitential Psalms* (1927) pl. xxxiv line '109' (*Ee* I 110), where the copy has *šup*-UŠ but the tablet (collated from photograph, see fn. 911) has *šup-šu*-, which agrees with duplicate manuscripts. (The sign after *šup-šu*- on Langdon's tablet can probably be read as ⸢*hu*⸣).

me-ia for *ṣu-um-me-ia* 'my thirst' (RINAP 3/1 no. 17 iv.35 MS 1);[387] perhaps also *ú-bi-ul* for *ú-bi-lu.*[388]

However, at least one CVC sign genuinely acquired the reverse of a usual syllabic value: LIŠ acquired the reading $\check{s}il_{(4)}$ (normally written with the sign TAR) in Assyrian.[389] Sporadic cases where a CVC sign appears to be reversed may be errors or they may be *bona fide*, it is hard to tell.[390]

3.2.14 Synonymous substitutions

These involve unwittingly substituting a word with a word of similar meaning (e.g. *malku* for *šarru*, both meaning 'king'). In such cases it is usually difficult to exclude the possibility of conscious modification.

3.2.15 Misremembering of words learned by heart

These are usually hard to distinguish from misrememberings of other kinds (see § 1.2.3), and also from deliberate variants.

3.2.16 Errors of sign metathesis

These involve writing two signs in reverse order (e.g. *ta-at-'i-im* for *at-ta-'i-i*, *Ee* III 83 MS g).[391] They should be distinguished from linguistic metathesis (e.g. *šahšūru*, a Neo-Assyrian form of *hašhūru* 'apple$^{?}$').

It is possible that some errors of sign metathesis arose through 'soft auto-correction' (§ 4.3): having jumped ahead to the second sign and re-

387 Following George, *Gilgamesh* (2003) 196.

388 Grayson, *RIMA 2* (1991) 132:9 in fragmentary context.

389 Reiner, *RA* 76 (1982) 93.

390 Examples in Jursa and Weszeli, *NABU* 2004 p. 56: *ú-LAM-lu-ka* and *paq-DAQ*; Nougayrol, *RA* 62 (1968) 162: ki.áĝ.ĝá // *na-MAR* (apparently followed by Renger, *ZA* 71 (1971) 38 in supposing a sign value ram_x).

391 Further examples: *šú-áš* for *aššu* 'because' (Cole, *Archive* (1996) 133 line 4, with note); $\d{t}e_4$*-ma-dam am-qá-am* (AbB XIV 112:35) for *ṭēmam damqam* 'good news'; *tu-iš* for *iš-tu* 'since' (Horowitz and Wasserman, "From Hazor to Mari and Ekallatum: A Recently Discovered Old-Babylonian Letter from Hazor", in Nicolle (ed.), *Nomades et sédentaires* (2004) 342 line 22'; cf. their translation 'Soon after …', p. 344).

alised the error, the writer might then revert to the first sign, trusting to the reader to invert the sequence.

3.2.17 Assyrianisms

These arose when Assyrians coloured the transmission of works in Babylonian with their own vernacular (see § 3.7). Not all Assyrianisms are errors.

3.2.18 Errors of 'cut and paste' and interpolation

Redactors sometimes deliberately inserted words into an existing passage (interpolation), or produced a new passage by combining passages from different sources ('cut and paste'). The wording which resulted from these procedures sometimes needed to be harmonised (e.g. making a singular verb plural), but this was not always done.[392]

Rykle Borger has identified two such instances in the Prologue to Hammurapi's laws.[393] The passages IV 11-15 and IV 38-47 are present on some early manuscripts but not on others, which suggests that they are secondary additions to a pre-existing version. The thing is, that IV 11-15 disrupts the grammar of IV 9-22, while IV 38-47 includes a suffix which lacks a referent. Thus interpolation or 'cut and paste' (it is hard to say which) led to grammatical peculiarities which were overlooked.

Another instance has been identified by Mordechai Cogan in an Assurbanipal inscription:[394] MS F_3 (i.e. Ec.Bib. B) includes both the long and short versions of the Bašimu episode. It seems logical to suppose that this overlap results from faulty amalgamation of different sources. Likely instances have also been identified by Kirk Grayson in chronicles.[395]

---

392 On the *Gilgameš* XI examples proposed by Tigay, *Evolution* (1982) 232–234, see the objections in Tertel, *Text and Transmission* (1994) 4 n. 9.

393 Borger, *Lesestücke* (2006) 7.

394 Cogan, *JCS* 29/2 (1977) 99–100.

395 E.g. Grayson, *Chronicles* (1975) 164 *ad* ii.12'-13': 'It could well be that these two lines come from a different part of the inscription from which the author of the Synch. Hist. was copying and the scribe did not bother to smooth over the sudden change in number'.

A further likely instance appears on a tablet of oracle questions. The line count given is too high for the tablet, and Wilfred Lambert suggests that the number was imported without modification from a source on which it was correct.[396]

The principle is also implicit in Grayson's comment on an inscription of AN III: 'There is considerable fluctuation in this passage between first and third person, which indicates that the author compiled the text from two different sources without bothering to blend [i.e. homogenise, MW] them grammatically'.[397]

We shall meet more examples in § 3.5.

A Hellenist states apropos of Greek papyri that 'Compositions with mistakes of morphology and syntax unmistakably belong to school contexts'.[398] The 'cut and paste' procedure is one reason why this statement does not apply to Akkadian.

3.2.18.1 Spellings as evidence for different entries' separate origins?

On tablets divided into 'entries' by horizontal lines, orthographic differences sometimes appear between entries.

When there is sufficient evidence to establish that entries are internally consistent in their orthography, orthographic differences between them may well suggest that they were gathered from different sources (for an example see § 3.5.7). The fact that they are not orthographically homogenized need not be considered an error – some transmitters might have gone out of their way to be faithful to the different sources' orthography.

When it cannot be shown that the entries are internally consistent – often they are not long enough to tell – it is difficult to exclude the possibility that the differences between them are simply due to whimsical (or elegant) variation. For an example, Nils Heeßel and Farouk Al-Rawi comment as follows on the differences in spelling between different entries on a therapeutic medical tablet:

> Originally, the thirty-eight prescriptions must have been compiled from different sources as can be deduced from numerous examples of different writ-

396 Lambert, *Oracle Questions* (2007) 155.

397 Grayson, *RIMA 3* (1996) 210. Whether the fluctuation between grammatical persons should be so explained in this particular case is debatable. Ditto, in my view, as regards Grayson, *RIMA 2* (1991) 100 (Assur-bēl-kala).

398 Cribiore, "Education in the Papyri", in Bagnall (ed.), *Oxford Handbook of Papyrology* (2009) 325.

ings for the same word, which were not harmonized during the process of compiling. Compare for instance i 26 and 35 where the logogram for *kunāšu* "flour" is written ZÍZ.ÀM and ZÍZ.AN.NA, or i 17 and 46 which give IM.KAL.GUG and IM.KAL.LI.GUG for the *kalgukku*-paste. The alum-mineral (*aban gabî*) is written IM.SAHAR.NA_4.KUR.RA in i 46 and NA_4 *gab-b[u-ú]/gab-bi-i* in ii 7 and ii 20 respectively.[399]

For the reason given above, we do not find the argument for multiple sources compelling in this case, though of course it may be the correct explanation. The problem is precisely that it seems impossible to tell.[400]

3.2.19 Hypercorrection

Hypercorrection is a 'correction' of a perceived error which is not really an error at all. It thus originates in a misunderstanding, and so is itself an error.

Instances are found across scribal cultures in general. A Latin example (Cicero, *Atticus* 1.18.8) is cited by Josef Delz.[401] The original wording ran as follows:

si ex iis quae scripsi multa etiam a me non scripta perspicis
'If among those things which I wrote you also discern many things (left) unwritten by me'

At some point, it was written on a manuscript which did not use spaces, becoming:

siexiisquaescripsimultaetiamamenonscriptaperspicis

Then, owing to a combination of erroneous word divisions and the equivalent of our 'errors of sign identification', a transmitter misread the unspaced exemplar as follows:

si ex iis quae scripsimus ta etiam …
'If among those things which we wrote *ta* also …'

399 Heeßel and Al-Rawi, *Iraq* 65 (2003) 221 (IM 132670 = Sippar 8/352).
400 Examples of cases where I believe it is possible to draw an inference of disparate sources from a medical tablet are given in Worthington, *JMC* 7 (2006), see refs in the article's introductory comments.
401 Delz, "Textkritik und Editionstechnik", in Graf (ed.), *Einleitung in die lateinische Philologie* (1993) 63.

This misreading left a free-floating (and meaningless) '*ta*' between *scripsimus* and *etiam*, which the transmitter hypercorrected to *tanta* 'many things', resulting in

> *si ex iis quae scripsimus tanta etiam a me non scripta perspicis*
> 'If among those things which we wrote you also discern so many things (left) unwritten by me'

The meaning is not so different from the original, but there is the incongruity of *scripsimus* 'we wrote' (pl.) and *a me* 'by me' (sg.). This was, in fact, the starting point for the reconstruction of the clause's textual history.

We will meet many examples of hypercorrection by Akkadian transmitters in the following.

3.2.20 Other errors

It must be recognised that it is sometimes difficult to assign a known error to any of the types listed in the present typology. For example, the writer of a Mari letter erroneously wrote Aparhâ in place of Hadurahâ.[402] Without knowledge which we currently lack (about these towns, their names, and what the writer knew or thought of them), it seems rash to speculate about how the error arose.

Anyway, having distinguished different kinds of error, we will now proceed to explore aspects of textual change about which errors can, if scrutinised with due care, prove informative.

3.3 Transmitters misunderstanding their exemplars

The ancients themselves occasionally say or imply that they found writings difficult to understand.[403] Assurbanipal boast of his skills as a reader: *aštasi kammu naklu ša šumeru ṣullulu akkadû ana šutēšuri ašṭu* 'I have

---

402 This is known from a second, explanatory, letter. See Charpin, ""Lies natürlich ..." À propos des erreurs de scribes dans les lettres de Mari", in Dietrich and Loretz (eds), *2nd Fs von Soden* (1995).

403 A Neo-Assyrian letter from the scholar Balasî (Parpola, *SAA X* (1993) no. 60) about difficulties attendant on *šumma izbu* omens is, fittingly, itself rather difficult: it may be commenting on the complexity of extracting literal sense from the cuneiform signs, or, as is the case with two other letters from Balasî (X 33 and

read *thorny* compositions (in) which the Sumerian was obscure, (and) the Akkadian was tough to get right'.[404] More generally, Esagil-kīn-aplī's statement about his editorial work on the *Diagnostic Handbook* comments on the obscurity of an entire corpus: he declares that, prior to his intervention, the relevant documents were gu^{meš} gil^{meš} *ša* gaba.ri nu tuku 'twisted threads which had no duplicates'.[405]

Unfortunately, explicit statements such as these are rare and not always credible,[406] and they tend to pertain to exceptional situations. For further information about what transmitters understood of their exemplars, we need to study the internal evidence of the manuscripts they produced, for this can sometimes reveal misunderstanding. (Though note the complications discussed in § 2.3).

This section will collect examples of such instances from medicine, literature and Neo-Assyrian royal inscriptions. In view of the interpretive difficulties noted in §§ 2.2.2.3 and 2.3 we will not list isolated substitutions of similar signs which could be explained as *lapsus styli*, e. g. *ú-šar-me-*UD for *ú-šar-me-ši* (Asb T v.32 // A vi.124, MS T1); UGU for *ù* (Asb A iii.103, MS A17); *-zēr*(numun)- vs *-šum*(mu)- (Sennacherib's Taylor (iv.53) and Chicago (iv.63) prisms);[407] *ba-*MAN*-e* for *bašê* (Asb C vii.42 // B vi.46, MS C1). More complex cases, where *lapsus styli* is conceivable but doubtful, will however be discussed.

The collection of examples is far from being comprehensive, and generalisations are correspondingly hazardous. Its principal purpose is to show the sorts of findings which the evidence can yield.

---

42), on the complexity of distilling the omens' 'true' import from their literal sense.

404 Streck, *Assurbanipal* (1916) 256.

405 Finkel, "Adad-apla-iddina, Esagil-kin-apli, and the series SA.GIG", in Leichty, de Jong Ellis and Gerardi (eds), *Studies Sachs* (1988) 148–149.

406 As remarked by Heeßel, *Diagnostik* (2000) 105 n. 36, Middle Babylonian diagnostics were not as textually distraught as Esagil-kīn-aplī's statement would have us believe. Concerning Assurbanipal, the extent of his skills in literacy have been questioned (see refs in Livingstone, *ZA* 97/1 (2007), who however adduces fascinating new evidence in the shape of tablets which he argues to have been inscribed by Assurbanipal himself), but the implication that some tablets were hard to read is not affected by this debate.

407 The difference was noted already by Ungnad, *ZA* 38 (1928–29) 198.

3.3.1 Examples of misunderstanding in medicine

We have collected samples of misunderstandings in medicine elsewhere.[408] We will re-propose the more interesting cases here.

A prescription against the ill-effects of a broken oath is extant on two manuscripts, one certainly from Assur and one probably so.[409] The two manuscripts differ notably over one instruction:

MS A *ina* udun lú.kurun.na úš-*ma*
'you enclose/heat (these ingredients) in a brewer's oven'

MS B úš-*ma* kaš lú.kurun.na úš
'you enclose/heat (these ingredients), you enclose/heat brewer's beer'

We suspect that the sequence of signs on MS B arose through corruption of the signs on MS A: *ina* udun 'in an oven' was misinterpreted as úš-*ma* 'you enclose/heat' (error of sign identification). Thus misread, version A made no sense: it now ran úš-*ma* lú.kurun.na úš 'you enclose/heat (the ingredients), you enclose/heat a brewer'. Hence a transmitter supposed the word kaš 'beer' to have been omitted, and hypercorrectly inserted it, giving rise to the sequence of signs extant on MS B.

Two manuscripts of the *Diagnostic Handbook* XVI 53' differ over a word: where MS F has meaningful igi^{ii}-*šú* 'his eyes', MS H (i.e. LKU 68c, Uruk) has obscure igi-AH-*šú*. This is almost certainly a corruption of igi$^{ii.meš}$-*šú* 'his eyes'.[410] It is difficult to explain this away as *lapsus styli*, for it involves the erroneous coalescence of two signs into one.

The two extant manuscripts of the *Diagnostic Handbook* XVII 38 respectively have sa^{meš}-*šú* 'his ligaments' (MS A, Babylon) and Ú^{meš}-*šú* (MS

408 Worthington, *JMC* 5 (2005), *JMC* 7 (2006), *Chatreššar* (2009), and "The lamp and the mirror, or: Some comments on the ancient understanding of Mesopotamian medical manuscripts", in Imhausen and Pommerening (eds), *Writings of Early Scholars* (2010). Some of the remarks made in these publications require revision (cf. fnn. 217 and 231), since they ignored the possibility of *lapsus styli* and the influence which somnolence might have exercised on competent transmitters.

409 See Worthington, *Chatreššar* (2009). MS A is BAM 165 (N4 no. 166 in Pedersén, *Archives II* (1986)), MS B was published by Herrero, *RA* 69 (1975).

410 See Worthington, "The lamp and the mirror, or: Some comments on the ancient understanding of Mesopotamian medical manuscripts", in Imhausen and Pommerening (eds), *Writings of Early Scholars* (2010) 193, noting that igi$^{ii.meš}$-*šú* as spelling of 'his eyes' (unusual on manuscripts of the *Diagnostic Handbook*) is attested on another manuscript of Tablet XVI, also from Uruk (line 91', MS B).

E, Kuyunjik), which is senseless here. As argued elsewhere,[411] ú is almost certainly a corruption of sa. Since this case involves the replacement of one sign with one similar-looking sign, *a priori* it is vulnerable to the suspicion of *lapsus styli.* However, since ú is generally a significantly larger sign than SA, we are inclined to think *lapsus styli* less likely than misidentification (perhaps induced by damage or poor lighting).

3.3.2 Examples of misunderstanding in literature

In *Gilg.* XI 149 (*illik summatu* … 'off went the dove (and) …'), two manuscripts (J and [**c**]) complete the line with *itūram-ma* 'it returned', whereas two have *iwīram-ma* 'it soared upwards' (C and [W]).[412] As seen by Andrew George, *itūram-ma* is a corruption: the sign *wi* (i.e. PI) was mis-identified as *tú*, and this hypercorrected to tu_1.[413] The spelling with tu_1 is found at both Assur and Kuyunjik, but this need not prove a link between them: the error of sign identification could have been made independently in multiple centres.

Two interesting corruptions occur on different manuscripts of *Ludlul* I. The first case involves lines 2 and 4 (which are identical on each manuscript):[414]

2				
Nim	[..	*mu-ši*]	*mu-up-pa-šìr*	[*ur-ru*]
Si	*e-ziz*	*mu-ši*	*mu-*⸢*up*⸣*-pa-šìr*	*ur-*⸢*ri*⸣
KK	[x]-*ziz*	*mu-ši*	*mu-pa-šìr*	[..]
VV	[. .]	*mu-ši*	*mu-pa-áš-š*[*ìr* ..]	
4				
Nim	[…	*mu-ši*]	*mu-up-pa-šìr*	*ur-r*[*u*]
Si	*e-ziz*	*mu-ši*	*mu-up-pa-šìr*	*ur-ri*
KK	⸢*e*⸣*-ziz*	*mu-ši*	*mu-pa-šìr*	[…]
VV	[*e-z*]*i-iz*	*mu-ši*	*mu-pa-áš-šìr*	*ur-*⸢*ru*⸣

'Who is angry by night, who is appeased by day'

411 Worthington, "The lamp and the mirror, or: Some comments on the ancient understanding of Mesopotamian medical manuscripts", in Imhausen and Pommerening (eds), *Writings of Early Scholars* (2010) 193.

412 I owe the reading *iwīram-ma* to Claus Wilcke (pers. comm.).

413 George, *Gilgamesh* (2003) 889.

414 Synoptic transliteration after Horowitz and Lambert, *Iraq* 64 (2002) 238.

Two manuscripts have *muppašir* (*pašāru* N 'to be released', 'to forgive'), one has *mupaššir* (*pašāru* D 'to release'), and one has the semi-ambiguous[415] *mu-pa-šìr*. As observed by Bill Moran, the coupling of *ezēzu* and *pašāru* N is standard in literary Akkadian.[416] The best reading is, therefore, *muppašir*.

Moran attempts to salvage *mupaššir* as a deliberate and worthwhile variant, arguing that by departing from the normal idiom it 'compels attention, and by leaving us to supply the object it also creates a rich ambiguity'.[417] This seems unduly optimistic: the symmetry of the two halves of the line is broken (we want Marduk to *be* appeased by day as he is angered by night, not to appease someone else), and the absence of a logical object for *pašāru* D is unidiomatic. There may well be cases in Akkadian literature where departures from expected idiom were deliberately introduced to compel attention and create ambiguity, but this instance does not convince. Simply, N participles being much rarer than D participles, *muppašir* was corrupted into *mupaššir*, its logical object presumably being thought to be *ūmu* 'day'.[418]

The second case from *Ludlul* I involves line 9:

ša nakbat qātišu lā inaššû šamā'ū
'The weight of whose hand the heavens cannot bear'

Three manuscripts have *nak-*BE, while one (MS AA, from Nineveh) has *nak-bi*. While the latter might suggest that *nak-*BE should be read *nak-be* or *nag-be*, these would be senseless here. The reading of *nak-*BE as *nak-bat* 'weight' gives far better sense. Hence Wolfram von Soden read *nak-bat*,[419] supposing the variant *-bi* to derive from a misinterpretation of BE as *be*. How, if at all, *nagbi/nagbe* was understood by the person who wrote *-bi* is unclear.[420]

At *Gilg.* XI 163 (MS J, the others are broken) we encounter a peculiar spelling of the word *zubbu/zumbu* 'fly': *ilū kīma zu-um-bé-e eli*(ugu) *bēl*

415 Though in principle *mu-pa-šìr* could represent *muppašir*, it would have been much more likely to have been read as *mupaššir*.

416 Moran, *JAOS* 103/1 (1983) 256b.

417 Moran, *JAOS* 103/1 (1983) 256b. See also § 6.2.3, esp. fn. 972.

418 Same conclusion in Horowitz and Lambert, *Iraq* 64 (2002) 245.

419 von Soden, ""Weisheitstexte" in akkadischer Sprache", in Kaiser (ed.), *TUAT 3/i* (1990) 115, followed by George and Al-Rawi, *Iraq* 60 (1998) 197, and Horowitz and Lambert, *Iraq* 64 (2002) 245.

420 According to von Soden, 'Die Variante *nag-bi* für *nak-bat* ist ein Schreibfehler, der keinen Sinn ergibt'. One wonders exactly what he meant by 'Schreibfehler' (*lapsus styli*?).

niqî iptahrū 'The gods gathered like flies round the man making the sacrifice'. Why *plene e*? There is no reason to think that *zumbu* terminated in a contracted vowel: the Neo-Babylonian spelling *zu-um-ba-a*, cited CAD Z 155b, represents hypochoristic *zumbāya*; and the *Gilgameš*-like narrative edited by Thompson, *Gilgamish* (1930) plate 59 and p. 91 (K 3200, cited CAD Z 155a) could easily have imported the spelling from a manuscript of *Gilg.* XI, along with the image of the gods as flies. Hence it cannot be presumed to constitute independent evidence. We suspect that *zu-um-bé-e* originated through corruption of a manuscript with *zu-um-be e-li.* Probably the LI was damaged, and the transmitter presumed the exemplar to run *zu-um-bé-e* [ugu] rather than correct *zu-um-bi e-*[*li*], the transmitted spelling resulting from this misperception. Another possibility is that *e-li* turned into *e e-li* through dittography, the first *e* being misunderstood as belonging to *zumbī* when *e-li* was converted into ugu.

Further likely examples of misunderstanding in literature are cited in §§ 1.4.3 (Claus Wilcke on SB *Etana*) and 2.3.2 (*i-*LAGAB misread as *i-rim*). Many more could be listed,[421] though care should always be taken to exclude cases which could equally be due to inadvertence.

3.3.3 Examples of misunderstanding in Neo-Assyrian royal inscriptions

Most extant manuscripts of Neo-Assyrian royal inscriptions are generally believed to have been produced in the reign of the king whose deeds they record, so that the people who inscribed them were writing about recent events, and would often have had opportunities to consult with each other. Many manuscripts were produced *en masse.* The script employed was usually contemporary Neo-Assyrian. For all these reasons, one might imagine that the exemplars were very well understood by the people who wrote and reproduced them. The reality was sometimes rather different, however. We shall give some examples.

In an inscription of Assurbanipal (A iv.69, *BIWA* p. 44), the phrase *lišānšunu* (eme-*šú-nu*) *ašluq* 'I cut off their tongue' appears on one manuscript as *pīšunu ašluq* 'I cut off their mouth' (spelled *pi-i-šú-nu*). The explanation was spotted by Hugo Winckler already in 1897: a copyist mis-

421 E.g. George, *Gilgamesh* (2003) 887 on the variants in XI 126 and their relationship to *Ah* III iv.15.

took eme 'tongue' for ka 'mouth'.[422] This is all the more striking as the copyist had the option of reading the putative KA as *appu* 'nose', which would have given a better sense. Apparently this did not occur to the copyist because *pû* is a commoner reading of the sign KA than *appu.*

At Assurbanipal A ii.129, MS A1 reads *qerub māt mannāya ērub it-ta-lak šalṭiš* for the other manuscripts' *qereb māt mannāya ērub-ma at-tallak šalṭiš* 'I entered the land of the Mannaeans, and marched through it triumphantly'.[423] The third person form *ittallak* is unexpected here. Most likely, the wedges making up the two signs MA AT were mistaken for the single sign IT.

It is standard in royal inscriptions for kings to say that they renovated or constructed a building 'from top to bottom', employing the words *ištu* ... *adi* 'from ... to'. We meet peculiar variants of this phrase in Šalmaneser III 44 (an inscription attested on clay cones at Assur), line 8:

> *iš-tu* (varr. *iš-du, iš-di, uš-du*) *uššīšu adi šaptišu*
> 'from its foundations to its rim'

Here the expected word *ištu* seems to be spelled in unexpected ways: ten manuscripts (MSS 1, 4, 5, 6, 7, 9, 12, 14, 19, 24) have *iš-du*, one has *iš-di*, and two (MSS 2 and 8, which are related, see § 2.4.3) have *uš-du.*[424] Only MS 15 has expected *iš-tu.* Kirk Grayson noted the oddity, and attributed it to the influence of Neo-Assyrian vernacular, but this does not convince.[425] Rather, we must suppose that the writers of all the extant manuscripts except MS 15 understood the line to contain the word *išdu* 'base' (which has a by-form *ušdu*). This is confirmed by the fact that MSS 1 and 3 of the very similar inscription Šal III 45 have suhuš,[426] which is a sumerogram for *išdu.* The spelling *iš-du~uššīšu* should be understood as a 'split' sandhi spelling for /išduššīšu/ (cf. § 4.4.1), this in turn resulting from *išid uššīšu* 'the base of its foundations'; ditto, *mutatis mutandis*, for *uš-du uššīšu.*

422 Winckler, *Forschungen* (1897) 248 *ad* 69. Borger *ad loc* appears sceptical of Winckler's explanation.

423 MS A6 has *qerub* like MS A1, but this does not affect the argument above.

424 MS 10 is broken: *iš*-[xx].

425 Grayson, *RIMA 3* (1996) 125. The normal Neo-Assyrian equivalent of *ištu* 'from' is *issu.* (A spelling *iš-du* is however found in Old Babylonian, see AbB XIV 220:14).

426 As noted by Grayson, Šal III 45 (attested on three manuscripts, which are related to each other) is not really a different composition from Šal III 44, but rather a badly a garbled version of it.

The spelling *iš-di uššīšu* on MS 3 suggests the writer was thinking of a dual (*išdī*), which *išdu* often stands in.

Now, the wording 'the base of the foundations' is suspect: it looks like an error for the usual *ištu uššīšu* 'from its foundations'. But dare we correct so many manuscripts, when only one preserves the reading we deem true? Encouragement is forthcoming from Šal III 43 (written in 836 BC), which is almost identical to Šal III 44 (written later, in 834 BC). The corresponding line of no. 43 has 'ta', the sumerogram for the expected word *ištu* 'from'. This strongly suggests that *ištu* was the correct word all along, and that *išdu* is corrupt. It is striking that so simple an expression which is used so frequently could be corrupted, and (with the possible exception of the writer of MS 15) not corrected by transmitters. There could hardly be a better illustration of the principle that counting manuscripts is not a reliable way of choosing between variants (§ 6.1.3).

In line 89 of Sennacherib's Rassam cylinder, MSS A and FF have *ú-šá-na-*AŠ*-ma* where the other manuscripts have *ú-šá-an-dil-ma* 'I broadened'. We explain this by supposing that a transmitter misread *dil* as *aš*, the latter being a commoner reading of the sign than the former, and so hypercorrected the spelling, changing perceived *ú-šá-an-aš-ma* to better-looking *ú-ša-na-aš-ma.*[427] In this interpretation, the transmitter guilty of the misreading was making at least some effort to read the signs, but failed to do so correctly. Whether full concentration was employed, however, we cannot be sure.[428] The fact that the mistake appears on both A and FF is a nice example of how, once introduced, an error could be transmitted (§§ 2.4 and 6.1.3) – it presumably went unrecognised.

The phenomenon of a sign (in this case NA) causing a reader to misread an adjacent sign (in this case AŠ/DIL) is one which we shall meet again in § 5.4, where we shall observe strategies used by ancient writers to prevent such misreadings.

As observed by Eckart Frahm, MS Z is the most error-prone manuscript of the Rassam cylinder.[429] The writer seems quite absent-minded,

427 In principle, of course, an error of syllable inversion (§ 3.2.13) is possible, but these are (in my perception) so rare in Neo-Assyrian royal inscriptions that a misreading of *dil* as *aš* seems more likely.

428 It is uncertain whether the writer was thinking about the meaning (see § 2.3.3 on somnolence). If so, he or she probably derived the form from *sanāšu* 'to drive in' (a Neo-Assyrian would not have been troubled by *š* for *s*), though what meaning this would have been thought to have with a town square as object is unclear.

429 On this manuscript's Assyrianisms see § 3.7.

probably as a result of time pressure: lipographies and dittographies are both considerably more common than usual, and there are two errors of sign metathesis.[430] Some of the errors are interesting for what they tell us about the sort of difficulties the writer encountered in understanding the exemplar.

In line 15, MS Z erroneously gives the word *musukkannu* (a tree) the person determinative lú. This is presumably because it was misunderstood as a by-form of *muškēnu* or *mussuku* 'wretched'. In line 84 of the same manuscript, the correct determinative appears, as if the writer had realised, or been apprised of, the mistake.

In line 85, MS Z has *qereb māt kaldi* 'the middle of the land of Kaldu' instead of *māt kaldi qerebšu* 'the land of Kaldu, its middle'. The paraphrase shows that the *-šu* 'its' of *qerebšu* 'its middle' was erroneously understood to refer to *māt kaldi* 'land of Kaldu'. In fact, however, the referent is completely different.[431] The syntax of the line was obviously badly misunderstood.

At Asb F ii.70, MS F33 offers ^{I}*tu-ma-ri-tu* for ^{I}*tam-ma-ri-tú*, almost certainly owing to a misreading of UD on an exemplar as *tú* (instead of correct *tam*):[432] the misreader then decided to change the spelling, writing /tu/ as *tu* not *tú*, as the latter is unusual in word-initial position.

Similarly, at Asb A ii.114 the name ^{I}*pi-šá-me-il-ki* also appears in the variant ^{I}*tu-šá-me-il-ki* (see § 2.4.3). Apparently, at some point PI was mistaken for UD,[433] which in turn was read as *tú*, giving rise to a variant spelling *tu* on the grounds (as above) that *tú-* is unusual in word-initial position.

Further likely examples of misunderstanding in Neo-Assyrian royal inscriptions are found in § 5.4.4.2.

---

430 MAR.URU-*ú-biš-ti* for ^{uru}*mar-ú-biš-ti* (line 26) and ^{anše}MAL.GAM^{meš} for ^{anše}gam.mal^{meš} (line 51).

431 The line runs as follows: *kirimahhu tamšīl hamani ša gimir riqqī inib ṣippāti iṣṣī tuklat šadî u māt kaldi qerebšu hurrušū itâša azqup* 'I planted at its (the palace's) side a garden, the equal of the Hamanus mountain, in whose middle all herbs, orchard fruits, trees, sustenance of the mountains and Chaldea are *collected*'. The *-šu* of *qerebšu* refers to *kirimahhu* 'garden' (or conceivably to *hamani*).

432 A colleague suggests another explanation, i.e. that the difference between *tu-* and *tam-* is due to attempts to render foreign sounds (e.g. *o*). This is, however, not convincing: the explanation would commend itself if there were variation on many manuscripts, but for the name Tammaritu we have numerous attestations with *tam-*, and only one with *tu-*.

433 For a similar case see § 3.3.2. Note also the comment in George, *Topographical Texts* (1992) 275 *ad* 25.

3.3.4 How well did transmitters know the compositions?

What knowledge of literature did transmitters carry around in their head? This is a very difficult question to answer. It is well established that, perhaps excepting Assurbanipal's libraries,[434] more first millennium manuscripts of literary and lexical works survive for the first Tablet of a composition than for later ones.[435] This may reflect the use of these compositions in scribal education.[436] But whether this be the case or not, is it an indication that, in a given scribal context, compositions were not always known or owned in their entirety? While indications to this effect can occasionally be found,[437] generalisations are hazardous. In the long term, the best source of information about what compositions transmitters did and did not know may well prove to be the mistakes they made, in particular mistakes which they would have been very unlikely to make if they knew passage in question.

Several misinterpretations in literature can only have happened in the mind of someone who had little or no previous knowledge of the composition,[438] at least in the relevant version (though of course the erroneous variant might subsequently have gained currency, and entered peoples' memories in its own right). This applies to *īrim* for *īkil* in *Ludlul* II (§ 2.3.2), *itūram-ma* for *iwīram-ma* in *Gilg.* XI 149, *nakbi* for *nakbat* in *Ludlul* I (both in § 3.3.2), and to the beginning of first-millennium *Etana* (§

434 In general, Reade, "Ninive (Nineveh)", in Edzard et al. (eds), *RlA IX* (1998–2001) 423 holds that the pattern applies also at Kuyunjik, but according to the computation by George, *Gilgamesh* (2003) 38, Kuyunjik *Gilgameš* manuscripts do not follow it.

435 This seems to have been first observed by Chiera, *They Wrote on Clay* (1939) 171. See also Veldhuis, *JCS* 50 (1998) 78 and George, *Gilgamesh* (2003) 38.

436 Thus e. g. Chiera, *They Wrote on Clay* (1939) 171, followed by Driver, *Writing* (1976) 69; George, *Gilgamesh* (2003) 38. That teachers started at the beginning of compositions is also thought to be the case with Greek papyri (see Cribiore, "Education in the Papyri", in Bagnall (ed.), *Oxford Handbook of Papyrology* (2009) 329).

437 See e. g. Worthington, *BSOAS* 72/1 (2009) on the fact that manuscripts of *muššu'u* VI are not currently known outside Kuyunjik. (There, I suggested that this was because Tablet VI was not needed. Eleanor Robson suggests in a personal communication it was because copies of Tablet VI were hard to come by). Cf. also Clancier, *Bibliothèques* (2009) 95 on the *āšipu* house in Late Babylonian Uruk: 'Les séries ne semblent pas complètes'.

438 See already Cavigneaux, *JAOS* 113/2 (1993) 253b, commenting on errors in bilingual lamentations which show that their transmission was 'non seulement orale, mais aussi littéraire et même écrite!'.

1.4.3). In all these cases, the written tradition appears to dominate over the oral tradition,[439] in the sense that transmitters made mistakes which they would have been unlikely to make if they had known the correct formulation. The same situation sometimes emerges from commentaries.[440]

First-millennium commentaries quoting from the 'stream of tradition' rarely specify their source. Eckart Frahm suggests that this is 'because it was assumed that scholars would know the relevant texts well enough to recognise them immediately'.[441] While this may well be the explanation, owing to the vast gulf between recognition and active recall, it is of limited help in establishing what knowledge transmitters carried around in their head.

Another feature of quotations in commentaries is that they often depart from the versions of the compositions as we know them from other sources. These 'inexact' quotations were copied in their own right, without being corrected.[442] What we should make of this is uncertain, however. For a start, we cannot be sure the commentators knew the compositions in the same version as we do. For most compositions we have very few manuscripts, and it is possible that there were more oral versions current than written ones. Also, it is one of the contentions of this book that close analysis of manuscripts can uncover greater variability between them than previously realised (see esp. §§ 2.3.2 and 4.7.2). Thus the commentators' quotations might be perfectly accurate in terms of the versions they were drawing on. But even if it were presumed that the commentators knew the versions we know, and misquoted them, this would not be hard evidence of misremembering, for the misquotations might be deliberate.[443] As for the transmitters of the commentaries, they might have rec-

439 This eventuality would be especially likely to arise when transmitters were faced with completely unfamiliar manuscripts (see § 5.2.2).

440 See Durand, *RA* 73/2 (1979) 155 esp. n. 10 on a commentary which gives two alternative (*šanîš*) interpretations of the obscure ki.ud.bi: 'Il est … vraisemblable que les sens de l'idéogramme était perdu (inattesté dans les listes lexicales à disposition des scribes) et qu'on ne se fondait pour l'équivalence que sur les souvenirs d'interprétations précédentes'. One should note, however, that explanations of this kind are not automatically required when commentators give alternatives, see (Frahm, *Commentaries* (2011) 70–76).

441 Frahm, *Commentaries* (2011) 103.

442 Frahm, *Commentaries* (2011) 107.

443 See e.g. Frahm, *Commentaries* (2011) 103 on the possibility of deliberate suppression of Marduk at Uruk. (Also Frahm's p. 107 n. 558).

ognised the misquotations as such, but deliberately have refrained from correcting them, out of respect for the tradition.[444]

Moving on to Neo-Assyrian royal inscriptions, misunderstandings which show that their writers did not know them by heart are not particularly interesting. For narratives of royal achievements were very fast-moving, subject to constant revision (see fn. 447), and one would hardly expect the royal scribes to have learned them by heart. At the same time, instances which reveal ignorance of the *idiom* of this textual typology are worth noting. Perhaps the most striking example is the corruption of *ištu* 'from' to *išdu* 'base' under Šalmaneser III (§ 3.4.3), but we saw that it by no means stands alone.

3.4 Transmitters making conscious changes

Basic to the understanding of textual change is the issue of transmitters *consciously* altering the signs and words on their exemplars (see § 1.4.3, with several examples of restorations by transmitters). We have already met some instances (hypercorrections) in the previous section.

Here we will give more examples. Our procedure for finding them will be to compare manuscripts for which a common source is beyond doubt, and monitor differences between them: when they differ, at least one of the manuscripts must witness to a textual change vis-à-vis the common source.[445] While some of the differences thus found are clearly the result of unintentional lapses (e.g. lipography), for others one can construct an argument in favour of conscious change (to wording, or spelling, or both).[446]

It should be noted that we will not be concerned with redaction of a fresh version of a composition, such as the *Diagnostic Handbook* or the Standard version of *Gilgameš*. Nor are we concerned with the special case of Neo-Assyrian annals, where new versions constantly compressed

---

444 Frahm, *Commentaries* (2011) 107.

445 For a different procedure see Tigay, *Evolution* (1982) 67: he compares the vocabulary used in different versions of *Gilg.*, and deduces that transmission involved 'a measure of linguistic and stylistic updating', e.g. *leqû* vs *našû* as the older and younger verbs for 'to take (a weapon) in hand'.

446 Note however that such an argument can only be constructed in a minority of cases. Usually, variants which look as if they might have been introduced deliberately could equally be due to inadvertence.

and modified previous ones.[447] In all these situations, many sorts of changes were made.[448] Rather, we are concerned with the transmission of a given version (or even recension) of a composition.[449]

3.4.1 Sennacherib Rassam, MSS A and FF

Two manuscripts of Sennacherib's Rassam cylinder (A and FF) share a number of anomalies (most of which are mistakes) vis-à-vis the other manuscripts, showing that there is a genealogical link between them.[450] The most persuasive of these cases are as follows (arranged by line number): A and FF are **28** the only two manuscripts (of five) with ^uru^*ku-um-ah-lum* for ^uru^*ku-um-ma-ah-lum* (FF initially had *-ma-*, but it was erased); **32** the only two of eight with *ishupūšunūti-ma* for *ishupūšu-ma* 'they overwhelmed him' (A additionally has an extraneous HU, disconnected dittography); **45** the only two of five with *ik-šu-du qā-tāya* for *ik-šu-da qātāya* 'my hands reached'; **48** the only two of eight with ^uru^*ur-sa-li-im-mu* for ^uru^*ur-sa-li-im-ma* 'Jerusalem' (though A omits *-li-*); **55** the only two of four with ^uru^*ur-sa-lim-mu-ú* for ^uru^*ur-sa-li-im-mu* 'Jerusalem' (though *-ú* on A is erased); **57** the only two of five with *as-sa-ma-re-e* for *as-ma-re-e* 'lances' (A had *-sa-*, but it was erased); **57** the only two of five to use *šá* for *ša* 'which' (in contravention of an orthographic pattern, see § 5.4.4.2); **65** the only two of six to omit *lā* 'not'; **69** the only two of five with *as-hu-ha-am-ma*, error of attraction for *as-su-ha-am-ma* 'I removed' (see § 3.2.12); **78** the only two of eight with *ziq-rat* for *ziq-qur-rat* 'ziggurrat'; **87** the only two of seven to omit AN.BAR 'iron'; **88** the only two of four with *ú-šar-ši-da-a* 'I established

---

447 This procedure was discovered by Olmstead, *Assyrian Historiography* (1916). Many more detailed studies have been undertaken since, e.g. De Odorico, *SAAB* 8/2 (1994).

448 Equally, we are not concerned with the change of Marduk to Aššur on manuscripts of *Ee* from Assur (see Labat, *Création* (1935) 22).

449 It may well be that there were many instances which fell between the two extremes of simple transmission on the one hand and high-intervention redaction on the other. If this could be shown, it would in itself be a useful addition to knowledge.

450 See Frahm, *Einleitung* (1997) 50b. Either they have a common source, or A is a copy of FF (very unlikely to be vice versa, owing to A's erasures in lines 28 and 55 of signs which are present on FF). On the basis of 'dem Schriftduktus und der äusseren Form der Tonfässchen', Frahm deems it probable that they were inscribed by the same person.

firmly' for *ú-šar-da-a* 'I made flow' (see § 3.4.6.1); **89** the only two of four with *ú-šá-na-*AŠ*-ma* for *ú-šá-an-dil-ma* 'I broadened' (see § 3.3.3).[451]

Given that a genealogical link between the two manuscripts is beyond doubt, we now proceed to monitoring differences between them. Several of these simply reflect distraction, and do not constitute evidence of conscious textual change. For example, sometimes one manuscript exhibits lipography while the other has the correct spelling: **29** FF *ge-e* A *na-ge-e* **48** A ^{uru}*ur-sa-im-mu* FF ^{uru}*ur-sa-li-im-mu* **62** A *it* FF *it-ti* (followed by consonant, so a 'truncated' spelling, see § 4.4.3, is excluded) **37** FF ^{uru}*as-da-a-a* A ^{uru}*as-du-da-a-a* **61** FF omits A uru. Further, MS A is once guilty of inserting an extraneous HU (**32** A *is-hu-pu-*HU*-šu-nu-ti-ma* FF *is-hu-pu-šu-nu-ti-ma*), once of writing 6 instead of 8 (line **14**),[452] once of what we suspect to be an unusual error of phonetic origin (**14** A *ka-bit-tú* A *áš-lu-la* FF *ka-bit-tú áš-lu-la*, see § 4.3), and once of sign metathesis (**58** A munus.dumu^{meš}-*šú* FF dumu.munus^{meš}-*šú*). FF is once guilty of dittography (**43** FF kur.kur *mu-uṣ-ri* A kur *mu-uṣ-ri*).

Other differences between A and FF do not involve errors, but are simply a matter of spelling:

Ci vs *Ce*

Line	A	FF
6	*ú-maš-ši-ru*	*ú-maš-še-ru*
50	*kal-ba-na-ti*	*kal-ba-na-te*
53	*ha-zi-ti*	*ha-zi-te*
63	*ni-ṣir-te*	*ni-ṣir-ti*
83	*mah-ri-ti*	*mah-ri-te*

tú vs *tu*

15	*ka-bit-tú*	*ka-bit-tu*

451 It should be noted of lines 88 and 89 that numerically 'the only two of four' may not seem very impressive, and indeed *per se* it is not. However, in both these cases the error committed (insertion of *ši*, *na* for *an*) is of a type which occurs so rarely that for two manuscripts to share it is significant.

452 It is of course possible that the correct figure is 6, and that all manuscripts except A (which might then be correcting its source) are wrong. We remark elsewhere (§ 6.1.3) that counting manuscripts is not an infallible criterion for deciding which variant is superior.

šu vs *šú*

55	*is-hu-pu-šú-ma*	*is-hu-pu-šu-ma*
62	*ṣi-in-du-šu*	*ṣi-in-du-šú*
63	*qé-reb-šu*	*qé-reb-šú*
92	*qé-reb-šu*	*qé-reb-šú*

u vs *ú*

31	*iš-mu-ú*	*iš-mu-u*
44	^{uru}*al-ta-qu-u*	^{uru}*al-ta-qu-ú*
46	*ú-šab-šu-ú*	*ú-šab-šu-u*
55	*ir-šu-u*	*ir-šu-ú*
61	*ba-šu-u*	*ba-šu-ú*
93	*i-nam-bu-u*	*i-nam-bu-ú*

Plene vs non-*plene*

16	*ba-hu-la-te*	*ba-hu-la-a-te*
76	*šap-la-a-nu*	*šap-la-nu*
82	*ar-ka-nu*	*ar-ka-a-nu*
89	*su-qa-a-ni*	*su-qa-ni*

CVC vs CV-VC

27	*áš-lu-lam-ma*	*aš-lu-la-am-ma* (sole MS of seven)
55	*pu-ul-hi*	*pul-hi*

Different sumerograms

68	^{md}en.zu.šeš^{meš}-*eri-ba*	^{md}en.zu.pap^{meš}-*eri-ba*

Miscellaneous other differences

19	*i-na*	*ina*
20	^{uru}*ha-ar-diš-pi*	^{uru}*har*^{ar}*-diš-pi*
24	*qé-reb*	*qe-reb*
24	*li-i-tú*	*li-i-tum*$^{?}$

80	*ina*	*i-na*
40	*e-me-su-ma*	*e-mid-su-nu-ma*[453]

In all these cases, at least one of the two manuscripts must be differing from their common source. What should we make of these differences *vis-à-vis* the source? In principle, it is impossible to gainsay the notion that they would all have been regarded as outright errors. However, even if the spellings did contravene some principle current in antiquity, their numbers strongly suggest that it was a principle which the writer(s) of MSS A and FF was/were not committed to upholding. It would not, therefore, have been a universal principle.

One might be tempted to set against the numbers of different spellings the larger numbers of identical spellings, but here the possibility of orthographic convergence (§ 2.4.2) comes into play: identical spellings do not prove faithful reproduction, even on manuscripts known to be related.[454]

For practical purposes, we infer from all this that, at least some of the time, our writer(s) felt at liberty to vary the spelling of words.

It is, therefore, all the more interesting that in some cases care has been taken to be faithful to the exemplar. In three cases, the writer of MS FF wrote but then erased signs which are absent from MS A:

	A	FF
9	é.bàd^{meš}	é.bàd^{meš}-*ni* (*ni* partly erased)
28	^{uru}*ku-um-ah-lum*	^{uru}*ku-um-ma-ah-lum* (*-ma-* erased)
88	*ul-tu*	ta *ul-tu* (ta erased)

It is hard to escape the conclusion that, in these three cases, MS FF's exemplar (which, as remarked in fn. 450, was probably not MS A itself) ran

453 In the case of *e-me-su-ma* vs *e-mid-su-nu-ma* (line 40), the purely orthographic difference is between *-me-* and *-mid-*. The difference between *-su* and *-su-nu* is linguistic (*-nu* is extraneous).

454 In the case of our two manuscripts there is the additional consideration that they were probably written by the same person (see fn. 450). Though we know that he was not always consistent, it nonetheless seems possible that, given a spelling on his exemplar, he might have converted this into a different spelling, doing this the same way on both MSS A and FF. Again, agreement between the two daughter manuscripts does not prove that they are faithful to their common source.

as MS A runs. When inscribing MS FF, the writer first used the spelling which felt most natural, then realised this was unfaithful to the exemplar, and corrected it.

Line 88 is particularly interesting: apparently, in the case of a simple sumerogram such as 'ta' for *ultu*, the two spellings (sumerographic and syllabic) were so interchangeable that the writer swapped one for the other, even though, as we know from the correction, this was subsequently regretted. This shows how easy it could be for variant spellings to arise.

It is interesting that there are also likely instances of unfaithfulness to the exemplar which went uncorrected. In the two cases besides line 9 where MSS A and FF disagree over the use of the plural phonetic complement *-ni*, it is again FF that has *-ni* and A that lacks it (20: A é.bàd^{meš} FF é.bàd^{meš}-*ni*, 21: A uru^{meš}-*šú-nu* FF uru^{meš}-*ni-šú-nu*). It is likely that the writer of MS FF added *-ni* to the signs on the exemplar. Whether it is not erased because the writer did not become aware of the difference, or because the ambition of faithfulness waxed and waned with the mood and circumstances of the moment, is uncertain.

The above features suggest that MSS A and FF of the Rassam cylinder were produced through copying. If correct, this would be noteworthy: they were inscribed at a time when there was urgency to produce a large number of manuscripts of the inscription quickly, and this would have been done more efficiently through dictation.[455]

3.4.2 Assurbanipal B/D VIII

An exercise similar to that just undertaken with MSS A and FF of the Rassam cylinder can be undertaken (albeit on a smaller scale) with column VIII of Assurbanipal's prism B/D, where three manuscripts have an extraneous BI in the same place in line 10.[456] As there is no discernible reason for its presence, and transmitters would have been very unlikely to introduce it independently, we take it as evidence for a common source.

455 On dictation's ability to produce more manuscripts in less time see e.g. Skeat, *Proceedings of the British Academy* 42 (1956) 189 and 197.

456 Composite text (and indication that these three manuscripts have the 'BI') in *BIWA* p. 113. MSS B9 and BM 128053 can be read in *BIWA*'s microfiches (slide 7, p. 19 and slide 8, p. 164), while the relevant portion of MS D3 is available in the copy by Thompson, *Iraq* 7 (1940) fig. 8 (Asb B viii.10 corresponds to line viii.3 of this manuscript).

On this assumption, we can compare the manuscripts (all three are fragmentary), and tabulate their differences as follows:

Line number (Asb B/D VIII)	B9	D3	BM 128053
7	edin-*uš-šu*	[...]	*ṣe-ru-*[...]
8	un^{meš}	un$^{hi.a}$	un^{meš}
8	[...]	*áš-kun*	*iš-*(x)*-ku-nu*
10	*mu-ša-bi-šu-nu*	*mu-šá-bi-šú-nu*	[...]
14	*si-hir-ti-šu*	[*s*]*i-hir-ti-šá*	[...]

Even in the small number of lines where we are able to compare them, no two manuscripts agree completely. The differences are of the same kinds as those which we found between MSS A and FF of the Rassam cylinder: sumerogram vs syllabic spelling (line 7), equivalent sumerograms (line 8), and *šú* vs *šu* (line 10). In line 14 we get two different suffixes referring back to *mātu* 'land', *-ša* and *-šu*. Whether this is a linguistic or purely orthographic difference cannot be decided. In line 8 we find confusion between a first and third person verb form. This is no great sin in royal inscriptions, and indeed the same variation occurs on manuscripts of the Rassam cylinder (though not between A and FF).

The same considerations voiced above for Rassam A and FF apply here: the transmitters seem to have regarded themselves as free to vary spellings, at least some of the time.

3.4.3 Šalmaneser III 44 (and 45)

All manuscripts of this inscription except MS 15 have the surprising corruption *ištu* 'from' to *išdu* 'base' (see § 3.3.3). It is likely, therefore, that they are genealogically related.

In line 4, in the phrase *ana balāṭišu* (*u*) *šalām ālišu* 'for his life and the well-being of his city', the vast majority of manuscripts (seventeen out of twenty-three) spell *balāṭišu* syllabically, using the sign LÁ: this is found on MSS 1, 3-7, 9-15, 17, 19-20, 26; MS 18 and MSS 1 and 2 of Šal III 45 have sumerographic ti-*šu* (see fn. 426); MSS 2 and 8 (which have a common source, see § 2.4.3), have LA.

Though the spelling with LÁ has parallels,[457] it is nonetheless a rarity, and it is inconceivable that its occurrence on so many manuscripts should be the result of independent choices. Since we already suspect the manuscripts to have a common source on the strength of corrupt *išdu* 'base', it seems probable that the spelling with LÁ also goes back to a common source. Apparently it was reproduced faithfully by a large number of transmitters.

It is, then, all the more interesting that, in many other respects, spellings on the same the manuscripts diverge. For example, still in line 4, the word *ālišu* is spelled in at least three ways: uru-*šú* (MSS 2, 3, 5, 8, 13), *a-li-šu* (MSS 1, 4, 6, 7, -*š*[*u*] 10), *a-li-šú* (MSS 9, 16);[458] and *šalām* is spelled with LÁ on MSS 1, 6-7, 9-10, 11 (*l*[*á*]), 14, 15 (*l*[*á*]) and 17, but with LAM on MSS 2, 3, 5, 8, 13, 18.[459] In line 5, MS 5 has different wording (bad ká.gal *e-li šá ina* igi man-*ni*), but in line 4 this manuscript too uses LÁ. We see that transmitters could privilege some spellings over others in the matter of fidelity: the unusual LÁ was carefully transmitted, while more commonplace items were susceptible of variation.

Interestingly, the two manuscripts which spell *balāṭišu* with LA (MSS 2 and 8) are those which offer the grammatically most correct recension: in line 6 they have *e-pu-šu-ma*, whereas other manuscripts have *e-pu-uš* or (once) dù-*uš*; as this is a subordinate clause, the form with -*šu*- is grammatically more 'correct'. In line 15, MSS 2 and 8 (also MS 3 of Šal III 45)[460] have *ašrišina* 'their place' referring to *ziqqāte* 'foundation cones', where the other preserved manuscripts have *ašrišu* 'its place' (nine occurrences) or just *ašri* 'place' (one occurrence). Again, *ašrišina* is grammatically preferable. If the person who generated the sequence of signs extant on MSS 2 and 8 (they are related, see § 2.4.3) changed LÁ to LA, it is not surprising that he or she felt at liberty to do so when others did not: on the evidence of *ašrišina* and *īpušu-ma*, it would make sense for this person to be more confident in his or her own abilities.

It is further instructive to see what MSS 2 and 8 do with line 8, which contains the peculiar *ušdu* 'base' (corruption of *ištu/ultu* 'from'):

ušdu uššīšu adi šaptišu ēpuš

---

457 To judge from the CAD entry *balāṭu*, it is chiefly known from prayers and incantations.

458 MSS 11 and 14 have *a*-[…]. MSS 12, 15, 17 and 18-27 are broken here.

459 MS 4 omits the word.

460 Conceivably also MS 23 of Šal III 44, which is broken. On Šal III 45 see fn. 426.

MS 8, if the reading PU is correct, has expected ⸢*e-pu*?⸣-*uš*. MS 2 uniquely has UŠ UŠ UŠ SI ŠÚ at the end of the line, and lacks *ēpuš*. Since we know this line to contain a corruption before the word *uššīšu*, it is tempting to suppose that the unexpected sign sequence is an annotation alerting the reader to a textual problem (§ 1.4.5). If this were so, the final three signs in the annotation (UŠ SI ŠÚ) would be a syllabic spelling of *uššīšu*. As for the first two (UŠ UŠ), perhaps the writer, rightly suspicious of *uš-du*, conjectured that the correct sequence was 'uš uš', i.e. 120 (as a measure of depth to which the foundations were built). If an interpretation along these lines were correct, the absence of *ēpuš* on MS 2 could be explained: inserting the annotation might have caused the writer to overlook it.

Finally, though related, MSS 2 and 8 are not identical. In line 10 MS 2 has nun-*ú*, while MS 8 has *ru*-[*bu*]-*ú* (see fn. 538), these being spellings of the same word *rubû* 'prince'. At least one of these must represent an alteration from the common source, though whether conscious or not is hard to say.

In line 12, MSS 2 and 8 have *e-nu-hu-ma*; other manuscripts have *e-nu-hu-ú* (MSS 1, 6, 10, 14, 24), *e-na-hu-ú* (MS 9), *e-na-ah-ma* (MSS 3, 5) or *e-nu-uh* (MSS 4, 7).[461] The unexpected *plene* spellings probably originate through a misreading of *-ma* as *-ú*. It is striking that they were transmitted so often without emendation. The fact that connective *-ma* did not exist in the writers' vernacular may have played a role. (Or did this same fact lead *-ma* to be corrupted independently by several transmitters?)

The high concentration of oddities in the manuscripts of Šal III 44 (and 45) is suggestive of inexpertise.[462] This may reflect 'on-the-job training' (cf. § 1.5).

3.4.4 Two manuscripts of the *Diagnostic Handbook* XVII

Tablet XVII of the *Diagnostic Handbook* is extant on eight more or less fragmentary manuscripts, but two – MSS A (perhaps from Babylon) and B (from Kuyunjik) – are especially interesting. In line **104** they both misplace the same word in the same way (the other manuscripts are broken

461 MS 12 has [...-*h*]*u-ú*.

462 The low quality of these manuscripts was noted already by Delitzsch, *MDOG* 32 (1906) 26, commenting that they are 'zumeist nachlässig, zum Teil ... geradezu liederlich geschrieben'.

here). This is strong evidence for a genealogical connection between them. A further hint of this comes from their both having the obscure and perhaps corrupt sequence ‘u tu me šú’ in line **20** (the other manuscripts are again broken).

If compared on the strength of their likely genealogical connection, it is striking how similar the two manuscripts’ spellings are. Over an impressively large number of lines they are absolutely identical. This does not just apply to ‘obvious’ spellings, which could be argued away as manifestations of orthographic convergence (see § 2.4.2), but to the less-obvious *i-ṣa-ád* (line **21**) and *li-lá-a-ti* (lines **90**, **91**, **93**, and **100**). They also both have accusative *buhbuhtu* ending in *-ta* in line **1**, and in line **103** they both have the uncontracted *mi-ni-a-ti-šú*. In view of all this, one can infer that both writers, and also the transmitters who preceded them, took care to reproduce their sources exactly as they found them. Contrasted with the evidence of the previous two sections, this reminds us that we must reckon with great diversity of practice among transmitters.

In view of the near-identicalness of the two manuscripts, their few differences are worth examining.[463] Different spellings of the same word (**10** A *la* B nu **45** A lú B na **75** A ti-*ma* B tin-*ma*) probably betoken inadvertence, a transmitter unwittingly writing down his or her own preferred spelling instead of that on the exemplar (as happened to the writer of Senn Rass. MS FF, e.g. with ‘ta’ instead of *ul-tu*, § 3.4.1).

Thrice A has a phonetic complement which B lacks, and once the opposite occurs: **13** A nag-*ú* B nag **20** A bal-*it* B bal **24** A huluh.huluh-*ut* B huluh.huluh **105** A ki.ta B ki.ta-*nu*. With transmitters so attentive to exact reproduction, it seems easier to imagine phonetic complements being inserted than omitted – unless inadvertently, and it is hard to imagine this happening in all four cases. Very likely, then, in at least some of these four cases the phonetic complement was added secondarily, for added clarity. This would have been especially useful in line 13, where ‘*ina* a nag nag’ (*ina mê ištû išatti* ‘he drinks from the water he drank’) could be misread as ‘*ina* a nag.nag’ (*ina mê ištanatti* ‘he constantly drinks … in water’).[464]

---

463 An obvious lipography (**24** A *qé* B *il-qé*) and several likely ones (**8** B *u* A omits **27** A 1-*šú* B 1 **29** A *i*[*rm*]*û u* B *irmû* **72** A *u* B omits **105** A : B omits) are not particularly noteworthy. At **23** A du_{10}.gam-*is* B gam.gam-*is*, A displays an error of sign similarity. At **95** A šub? B ta[g_4] the reading of MS A is not clear, though Heeßel comments that it is not tag_4.

464 On spellings chosen to prevent readers misreading signs see § 5.4 and its subsections.

In lines **78** and **79**, which belong to two different entries, B links two clauses in the protasis with *-ma*, while A omits it. The entries seem to read better with *-ma* (so that it is hard to imagine the absence of *-ma* being original), but it is unlikely that a single person would omit both in error. Possibly at some point in transmission one of the two *-ma*s was omitted, and subsequently a transmitter decided to homogenise the two entries, but plumped the wrong way.

In line **31**, A has *ul mi-šit-tu*$_4$, B has *ul mi-šit-ti*. This rare expression seems to mean 'It is not a blow'.[465] The variants here may reflect different understandings of the grammar: for those who wrote *-tu*$_4$, *mišittu* was nominative *status rectus*; for those who wrote *-ti*, *mišitti* may have been in the *status predicativus*.[466] It is perhaps not surprising to find the latter, more *recherché* construction at Kuyunjik.

Line **97** (for which we also draw on the other extant manuscript, E) is especially interesting: A en bar en.nun B en en.nun E en pa en.nun. The first 'en' = *adi* 'until'. The problem arises with the other signs. The most recent editor interprets MS A as bar.en.nun = *bārārītu* 'first night watch', but no corroboration for this can be found in the dictionaries, and it leaves PA on MS E (also from Kuyunjik) and corresponding zero on MS B unaccounted for. We suggest the following solution, which seems to be the most economical. As is well known, en.nun = *maṣṣartu* 'watch'. We propose that the common source of the three manuscripts[467] had the difficult sequence 'pa en.nun', itself probably a corruption of original 'bar en.nun' (*mišil maṣṣarti* 'middle of the watch', a well-known phrase). The three extant manuscripts show three different transmitters dealing with 'pa' as best they could: one (MS E) transmitted 'pa en.nun' faithfully, probably without understanding it; another (MS B) simply omitted 'pa', reasoning that the resulting sign sequence was clearer (cf. fn. 101); thirdly, MS A emended PA to BAR, and was probably quite right to do so. If this reconstruction is correct, it shows how even transmit-

---

465 So understood (*pace* Heeßel, *Diagnostik* (2000) 213), *ul* – as opposed to *lā* – is unproblematic, since an entire clause is being negated (even if it is only one word long).

466 Grammatically, this would be possible if the Akkadian for 'he is a queen' (*sic*!) were *šarrat* (stem ending in *t*, plus zero ending for the 3rd m. sg. subject): *mišitti* would represent **mišitt*, with *i* being a (written or spoken) approximation of zero after a double consonant.

467 Above, a common source was argued for MSS A and B. MS E is so textually similar to MS B that the idea of a common source is attractive – all the more so since they are both from Assurbanipal's libraries.

ters who went to great lengths to be faithful to their exemplars could consciously alter them when they found them obscure.

In line **72** (A *kap-pi-šú u* eme-*šú* B *kap-pi-šú* ka-*šú* : eme-*šú*), MS B gives the two (visually very similar) variants ka-*šú* 'his mouth' and eme-*šú* 'his tongue'. It is possible that they were imported from separate sources. If that were the case, since MS B is generally so careful to preserve the signs in the same tradition witnessed to by MS A, we suppose that the writer would have been unlikely to accept a variant from a manuscript which departed drastically from the same tradition. Hence we have to imagine two almost identical manuscripts, but one with ka-*šú* and one with eme-*šú*. This scenario would suggest that one arose as an error of sign similarity for the other (cf. Winckler in § 3.3.3). The other possibility is that the writer of MS B was working from a slightly damaged exemplar and, not being sure whether the sign was ka or eme, supplied both.

3.4.5 Glosses?

When transmitters deemed their exemplar wrong or obscure (either to themselves or to future readers), instead of altering the words in question they had the option of reproducing the signs as seen but adding an explanatory annotation, known as a gloss (see § 1.4.5).[468]

Adel Nemirovskaya argues persuasively that a gloss is found at *Gilg.* I 17 (*ša šarru arkû lā umaššalu* lú *mam-ma*).[469] She holds that lú *mam-ma* does not represent *amīlu mamma* 'any man' but simply *mamma*, with lú as a sumerogram for *mamma* (for which there is lexical support): 'Which no later king can replicate, none whatsoever'.[470] The arguments advanced in support are that: disposing of *amīlu* improves the rhythm, and removes the second, grammatically awkward, subject of *umaššalu.* The second argument seems especially weighty. To these one can add that a nice parallel to line 14 (which also ends in *mamma*) results. Together, they seem strong enough to compensate for the fact that the spelling

468 According to Delz, "Textkritik und Editionstechnik", in Graf (ed.), *Einleitung in die lateinische Philologie* (1993) 69–70, glosses (along with interpolations of other kinds) are one of the most controversial areas of textual criticism in Classics.

469 Fully preserved only on MS h, from Babylon.

470 Nemirovskaya, *NABU* 2008/4.

would be unusual in *Gilgameš*[471] (and indeed anywhere outside lexical lists).

A gloss was further envisaged by Wolfram von Soden at *Agušāya* A i.3-4: *bukrat ningal dunnaša lulli šumša* 'Daughter of Ningal, I shall extol her might, her name'.[472] While metrical considerations are not probative here (for, as von Soden himself acknowledged in his subsequent footnote, not all poetic lines in the composition have three or four 'beats'), the construction reads oddly. Whether or not a secondary interpolation (i.e. gloss) is at issue is hard to decide here.[473]

Another example of this situation is provided by Martin West, in his study of the Nanāya hymn for king Samsuiluna.[474] West suggests that line 34 is exceptionally long, in having fourteen syllables (other lines have twelve at most). This difficult line runs as follows:

> *šar-ri tu-ud-di-<i?> samsuiluna zi-bu-ki li-qú-ud*
> 'May Samsuiluna, the king you *know*, *burn food-offerings for you*'.

West suspects 'that Samsuiluna is a gloss, added in the written version of the hymn to identify the king for future readers'. Regardless of whether or not one agrees with West's interpretation of this particular instance,[475]

---

471 Nemirovskaya also suggests that lú should be read *mamma* at *Gilg.* XI 176. I find this less persuasive. Here lú is attested, without gloss, on both extant manuscripts (J, Nineveh; **c**, Assur). It is scarcely credible that the writers would have expected readers to recognise unglossed lú as *mamma*, so one would have to suppose misunderstanding on their part. This seems unnecessary, however. Nemirovskaya holds that 'the idea here is undoubtedly that no creature (and not just human beings) had been intended to survive the Flood', but in *Atra-hasīs* I 358 it is precisely the *rigim awīlūtim* which angers the gods, and in *Gilg.* XI 176 the speaker (Enlil) knows from seeing a man-made artefact (the Ark) that a human being has survived. Furthermore, it is doubtful whether *mamma* would refer to non-humans (just as English 'nobody' does not).

472 See von Soden, *ZA* 71 (1981) 193 n. 49: 'Das auf *lu-ul-li* folgende *šu-um-ša* stellt wohl eine Alternativlesung zu *du-un-na-ša* dar, obwohl solche Zusätze sehr ungewöhnlich sind'.

473 Von Soden's interpretation appears not to be followed by Streck, *JAOS* 130/4 (2010) 561.

474 West, *Iraq* 59 (1997) 179.

475 If the second syllable of *šarri* were discounted on the grounds that it might simply be a sophisticated spelling of the more common form *šar* (or that the *i* of the *status constructus* was probably not a full vowel), /sui/ in samsuiluna were counted as a diphthong, and the verbal form *tu-ud-di-<i?>* were supposed to be bisyllabic, then the line would have twelve syllables. Also, Mesopotamian kings liked to throw their names around. As remarked by Radner, *Macht des Namens* (2005) 130, the king's name is *conditio sine qua non* of a royal inscription.

his contention is a salutary reminder that we should be on the lookout for glosses in Akkadian sources.

3.4.6 Correction of (supposed) errors ?

The significance which we attribute to errors on extant manuscripts varies with how we think transmitters dealt with errors they found on their exemplars. If we could be certain that they corrected errors which they recognised, then when they transmit errors we could be certain that they were not recognised. Errors of transmission would thus serve as indicators of ignorance or somnolence in the transmitters.

If on the other hand we are to envisage transmitters faithfully reproducing their exemplars as seen, errors and all, even though they recognised the errors as such,[476] then the errors no longer attest to incompetence.[477]

Be that as it may, we here present cases where transmitters can be shown to have or (much more rarely) not to have consciously corrected their exemplars. (See also the examples of hypercorrection in § 3.3).

3.4.6.1 Examples of correction

As argued in § 3.5.1, a building inscription of Adad-nērārī II (1 r.10'-16') was produced through a 'cut and paste' procedure. In the process, a passage about a grammatically masculine building was inserted into an inscription which dealt with a *kisirtu* 'bitumen coating', which is grammatically feminine. On MS 1 of the inscription, this is reflected in a puzzling mixture of masculine and feminine suffixes referring to the *kisirtu.* On MS 2, however, all suffixes are feminine. We infer that the sequence of signs preserved on MS 1 is older than that preserved on MS 2, and that the person responsible for the sequence of signs extant on MS 2 consciously corrected the suffixes found on the exemplar.[478] Interestingly, however, the person who generated the sequence of signs extant on MS

476 This possibility is envisaged by Frahm apropos of the transmission of wrong-looking quotations in commentaries, see above with fn. 444.

477 An error might still tell us something about the person who introduced it (not necessarily identical with the writer of the extant manuscript), but in many cases it is difficult to distinguish low skill from inadvertence.

478 By contrast, *mahrê* was left to stand (i.e. not changed to grammatically preferable *mahrīti*): u[gu *mah-r*]*e-e.* See § 3.5.6.

2 did not venture beyond grammatical harmonisation. The composite inscription was semantically odd because the referent of the imported passage had very different physical attributes from a *kisirtu* (see § 3.5.1), but this oddity was left to stand, perhaps because it was not noticed, or perhaps because tackling it would have required much more substantial changes.

Rykle Borger observed that, in Assurbanipal's T prism (at A vi.111), a sentence which originally had only one, feminine singular, subject (verb = Ass. 3rd f. sg. *tabbû*) was changed to include more subjects. All extant manuscripts with the intrusion preserve the original (but now ungrammatical) singular verb *tabbû*, except for one (MS T1), which changes it to grammatically more correct *ibbû* (though the construction as a whole is still odd):

Original version: (several MSS)	*ša … ina ūmešu tabbû šumī* 'who … at that time spoke my name'
After interpolation: (several MSS)	*ša … ina ūmešu šī u ilū abbûša tabbû šumī* 'who … at that time she and the gods her fathers she-spoke[479] my name'
After improvement: (only MS T1)	*ša … ina ūmešu šī u ilū abbûša ibbû šumī* 'who … at that time, she and the gods her fathers spoke my name'

Again, we see a transmitter correcting the worst feature, without attempting to eliminate all the problems.

Two interesting examples of *hyper*correction (§ 3.2.19) are provided by manuscripts A and FF of Senn's Rassam cylinder. These two manuscripts have a common source (see § 3.4.1), so in both these cases the hypercorrection was presumably found on this source. The first example (*ú-šá-na-*AŠ*-ma* vs *ú-šá-an-dil-ma*, line 89) was discussed in § 3.3.3. The second example occurs in line 88. MSS A and FF are the only two of four (cf. fn. 451) to offer *ú-šar-ši-da-a* 'I established solidly' for *ú-šar-da-a* 'I made flow'. Here it seems that a transmitter did not keep track of the sentence. He or she may have misunderstood the rare form/spelling *ma-a-me* 'water' as representing a solid object, or considered *ašarša ú-šar-da-a* 'I caused its place to flow' in isolation from the rest of the sentence, as the writer of MS Z did with *māt kaldi qerebšu* (see § 3.3.3). Either way, the guilty transmitter inserted *-ši-* to produce a verb form which

479 The ugly 'she-spoke' is our attempt to render the faulty Akkadian syntax into English, *tabbû* being feminine singular.

seemed more fitting.[480] The now extraneous *plene* spelling *-a* (appropriate for *ušardâ* but not *ušaršida*) was retained, confirming that the whole thing was badly executed.

A comparison of the same two manuscripts provides evidence of justified corrections (as opposed to hypercorrections): in line 55, MSS A and FF are the only two manuscripts of four to write ^{uru}*ur-sa-lim-mu-ú* with the extraneous *-ú*. On MS A, the *-ú* is erased: the spelling was reproduced as seen, but then realised to be faulty. The same happened in line 57, where MSS A and FF are the only two of five to write *as-sa-ma-re-e* for *asmarê*. The writer of MS A reproduced, but then erased, the extraneous *-sa-*. In both these cases the writer of MS A noticed too late that the spelling on the exemplar was faulty. In other words, he or she was not a careful reader.

It deserves note that some instances of seeming (hyper)correction could actually be misrememberings. For example, the first line of the Gula Hymn runs as follows: *iltu le'ât gimir ilāni āšib parakkī* 'The goddess, the ablest of all the gods who dwell on the dais'.[481] MS 'a' instead has *a-ši-bat* 'who dwells', referring to the goddess rather than the gods (for more on this manuscript see § 1.4.2). It is possible that at some point a transmitter saw *āšib*, misunderstood which of the deities it was supposed to refer to, and consciously hypercorrected it to *āšibat*. But it is also possible that at some point in transmission the line was simply misremembered (cf. § 1.2.3). The two processes are very similar, except that one is conscious and the other unconscious.

3.4.6.1.1 Hypercorrections on Assurbanipal MS A21

We here examine a manuscript of Assurbanipal's prism A (MS A21), for which we are dependent on the edition of Rykle Borger.[482] Comparison with parallel manuscripts reveals that MS A21 is rich in substitutions of similar signs – so much so, that once their high incidence has been established on the basis of clear instances, it is possible to scrutinise what might *prima facie* seem like deliberate variants, and explain these too as errors of sign similarity. We will encounter several hypercorrections.

480 We cannot prove that this is what happened, but no other reason for the presence of *ši* seems plausible.

481 The hymn is edited by Lambert, *Orientalia* 36 (1967).

482 Borger, *BIWA* (1996).

We begin with instances which we believe to be clear.[483] Three times there was difficulty in distinguishing between the exemplar's MA and ŠU. **a)** At A ii.13, *ad-din-šú // a-din-šú* appears on MS A21 as *a-di-ma*, which results from a misreading of *a-din-šu*, perhaps with damaged DIN. **b)** A few lines later (A ii.17), MS A21 presents *a-na maš-kan-i-ma* for expected *ana maškanišu.* Here too the exemplar probably had ŠU which was misidentified as MA. **c)** At A v.97-8, the sentence *ištar āšibat arba-ilī ina šāt mūši ana ummānātiya šuttu ú-šab-ri-ma* 'Ištar who dwells in Arbela showed a dream to my armies in the middle of the night' appears on MS A21 with the highly ungrammatical verb *ú-šab-ri-šú-ma* 'showed him'. It is hard to envisage a copyist introducing *šú* on his own initiative. More likely, the exemplar ran *ú-šab-ri-ma*, which was misread as *ú-šab-ri-šu* and hypercorrected to *ú-šab-ri-šú-ma*, with addition of *-ma* and the change of spelling from *šu* to *šú*.

Further, at A iv.99, MS A21 has ud-*me* 'day' for *pi-i* 'mouth'. Misreading of PI as UD is attested elsewhere (see §§ 3.3.2 and 3.3.3), and is very likely the origin of the variant on MS A21. At A i.27, MS A21 is the only manuscript to offer *im-al-du* for *i'-al-du* 'was born'. Both *immaldu* and *i''aldu* are good N preterites of *walādu* 'to be born', but the spelling *im-al-du* is non-standard for *immaldu* (one expects *im-ma-al-du*). Given the similarity of the signs IM and I' (= A'), *im-al-du* very likely originated with a misidentification.[484]

In view of all these cases, which add up to strong evidence that the writer of MS A21 (or of an ancestor manuscript) was working from a written exemplar, we may advance similar explanations for other difficult forms and spellings on MS A21 which considered in isolation would be puzzling.[485]

At A viii.12, MS A21 has *ar-ku-us-šu-u-GIŠ* for expected *arkussu-ma.* On another manuscript one might be tempted to explain this as *lapsus styli*, but here one suspects that an original *-ma* was misread as GIŠ, perhaps owing to damage.

483 Taken in isolation, most of these instances could be taken as reflecting *lapsus styli*, but in combination they look like hypercorrections.

484 Cf. [*m*]*a*-IM-*du* for *ma-a'-du* 'they are numerous' in Lambert, *JNES* 33/3 (1974) 29 MS K (*lapsus styli*?).

485 MS A21 also offers variants which cannot be explained as misreadings, e.g. *ṣēr* (edin) for *eli*(ugu) at A ii.126 (probably an Assyrianism).

At A v.100, MS A21 has *al-lik* for *al-lak*. The signs *lik*(UR) and *lak* (ŠID) are sufficiently similar in Neo-Assyrian ductus for *lik* to derive from a misidentification of (damaged?) *lak*.

Twice there is a problem involving the sign AD as a sumerogram for *abu* 'father': at A ii.124, MS A21 offers the nonsensical *at-tu-u-a* 'belonging to me' instead of the other manuscripts' ad-*u-a* (*abūya*) 'my father'; at A viii.2, MS A21 offers the unique variant dumu šeš-*šú* 'son of his brother (i.e. nephew)' for dumu šeš ad 'son of the brother of (his) father (i.e. cousin)'. We infer that in both cases the writer failed to recognise AD as a sumerogram: the signs AD U A were interpreted as a defective spelling of *attūya*,[486] and hypercorrected;[487] dumu šeš ad was misread as dumu šeš-*šu* (we have already seen that there was confusion with the shape of ŠU on the exemplar), and hypercorrected into dumu šeš-*šú*, changing putative *šu* to *šú* as with *ušabrišu-ma*.[488]

This array of examples opens a window onto the mind of the writer of MS A21 (or an ancestor manuscript), who occasionally had difficulty reading or understanding the exemplar, sometimes attempted to improve it (with disastrous results), sometimes slavishly reproduced it as (mis-) read, even if it made little sense.

3.4.6.2 An example of non-correction

For the purposes of gauging what we can about transmitters' competence from their extant writings, it would be very useful to know: did they always correct errors which they recognised (or thought they recognised) as such, or did they sometimes consciously leave them to stand, out of fidelity to the exemplar? There are many cases where this *might* be happening (most any example will serve), but the number of cases where one can be sure is very small. We could only find one (though future research may well uncover more).

486 *attūya* 'my' may have been a specifically Babylonian (not pan-Akkadian, not Assyrian) word, but, if so, Assyrians engaged in the transmission of works in Babylonian might well have been taught it.

487 One might be inclined to attribute the substitution of ad-*u-a* with *at-tu-u-ia* to an error of phonetic similarity, but this would presuppose pronunciation /at/. Further, there are so many serious errors on this manuscript, almost certainly including another involving 'ad', that a misreading seems likely.

488 Thus the person responsible for the sequence of signs extant on MS A21 deliberately departed from the spelling on the exemplar at least twice. The unusual use of limmu(NÍG) for standard límmu(TAB.TAB) in writing the name of Arbela (*arba-ilī*) at A x.63 can probably be ascribed to this person.

Why only one? Because we do not know how confident writers of extant manuscripts were in their own abilities. Consider the case of extraneous BI present on three Assurbanipal manuscripts (§ 3.4.2): today, this really looks like it must be an error. But, though the writers of the three manuscripts in question would surely have been puzzled by it (if they thought about it at all), they might not have had the confidence to decide it was an error. They would probably have been used to encountering things they did not fully understand, and so might have transmitted the BI with vague doubts rather than serious misgivings.

Similarly, we saw in the previous section that MSS A and FF of the Rassam cylinder have *ú-šar-ši-da-a*, which is a corruption of *ú-šar-da-a*. The final *plene* spelling is expected in *ú-šar-da-a*, but not in *ú-šar-ši-da-a*. In view of the difficulties with fitting cuneiform spelling into the straight-jacket of normativity (§ 2.2.2.1), it may be going too far to say that *ú-šar-ši-da-a* involves a spelling 'error'. But at least it seems fair to suppose that most readers encountering this spelling would have been mightily puzzled by it. It is curious that the same person who inserted ŠI did not remove the *plene a*, and that at least one transmitter who encountered *ú-šar-ši-da-a* did not remove it either. Why not? It may be that the oddity was allowed to stand, reluctantly, in deference to the exemplar; or that the transmitter felt it best not to tamper with something he or she did not understand.

The one case which stands out involves the Neo-Assyrian chief scribe Issar-šumu-ēreš, for one can presume a chief scribe to have had confidence in his own abililities as reader. In two astrological reports, Issar-šumu-ēreš quotes an omen protasis (SAA VIII 23:5, 24:6). The expected formulation is as follows:

šumma sîn šamaš lā ūqi-ma irbi
'If the moon does not wait for the sun, and sets'

This is how the protasis is quoted by Nabû-ahhē-iddin and Šumāya (SAA VIII 481:4 f, 499:1). Issar-šumu-ēreš, however, inserts what appears to be an extraneous *u* 'and' between *sîn* and *šamaš*.

As we suggested elsewhere,[489] this is probably due to a badly written (or poorly preserved) exemplar, on which 30 looked like 30 *u*. But a chief scribe would surely have spotted the peculiarity as such (particularly since the omen is not rare, and he probably knew it from elsewhere), and should have been capable of suppressing it. If this assumption be granted,

489 Worthington, *Iraq* 78 (2006) 64.

it would appear that Issar-šumu-ēreš deliberately left the *u*, even though he realised it was problematic. Perhaps, in the atmosphere of intellectual competition and aggression which prevailed at the Neo-Assyrian court,[490] Issar-šumu-ēreš wanted to make a point of quoting his source exactly as it was written, reserving corrections to it for oral commentary.

3.5 The effects of 'cut and paste' redaction

New documents were not always created *ex nihilo*: sometimes a pre-existing passage or passages were modified, or multiple passages were amalgamated. This was probably done more often than is easily visible, but sometimes the procedure left traces, for amalgamating sources or otherwise tampering with them offered much scope for errors and inconsistencies of various kinds (§ 3.2.18).

Here, we will be concerned with cases in which the differently sourced passages were not harmonised, resulting in an inscription which consists of morphologically and/or orthographically inconsistent chunks. We will offer five examples.

3.5.1 Adad-nērārī II's *kisirtu*

Here we examine the building report on a manuscript of the annals of AN II (1 r.10'-16' MS 1, see § 3.5.1). The building work recounted is that of a *kisirtu* 'bitumen facing (of a wall)', an unequivocally feminine noun ($\sqrt{}$*ksr* + feminine *-t*). Suffixes referring back to it should accordingly be feminine (*-ša*) rather than masculine (*-šu*), but our source wavers between the two. We reproduce the relevant passage, dividing it into four portions for convenience of reference:

a) r.10'-12' *enūma* ***ki-sir-tu*** *ša sippi āli šapla bīt aššur / ša adad-nērārī iššak aššur mār arik-dēn-ili iššak aššur rubû / ālik pānīya ēpušu ēnah-ma i''abit* 'At that time the bitumen facing (of the wall) at the entrance to the city below the temple of Assur, which Adad-nērārī (I), viceroy of Assur, son of Arik-dēn-ili, viceroy of Assur, prince my predecessor, had built, became dilapidated and fell in.'

490 Brown, *Astronomy-Astrology* (2000) e.g. 51 and 240.

b) r.13' *an-hu-***su***~uddiš dan-na-***sa** *umessi* 'I restored it where weak, I delineated its foundations.'
c) r.13'b-16' *ištu uš-še-***šu** / *adi gaba-dib-bi-***šu** *arṣip ušeklil eli* **mah-re-e** / *ussim narêya alṭur ina qer-bi-***šu** / *aškun* 'I built it up and completed it from its foundations to its parapet. I made it more ornate than the previous one. I wrote my stelae (and) installed (them) inside it.'
d) r.16'b *rubû arkû an-hu-***sa** *luddiš* 'May a future prince renew it when dilapidated.'

A gender incongruence in addition to the pronouns is m. *mahrê* for expected f. *mahrīti* at r.15' (see § 3.5.6).

We reconstruct the history of the passage as follows: its redactor imported (c) from an inscription about a building denoted by a masculine word, but failed to change the gender of the masculine pronouns as required by the new referent. This notion is supported by the fact that the content of passage (c) does not work well for a bitumen wall coating, which has neither foundations nor parapet. The apparent gender incongruence in (b) can be explained orthographically, as a sandhi spelling (for a parallel see § 4.4.2 on AD II 3:9 MS 1). On the other extant manuscript of this inscription (MS 2), where grammatical harmonisation was undertaken, see § 3.4.6.1.

3.5.2 Sennacherib's 'Walters' inscription

Our second example of the 'cut and paste' procedure resulting in grammatical incongruities is Sennacherib's 'Walters' inscription.[491] In his *editio princeps*, Kirk Grayson noted that, with the exception of *e-ki-mu* (line 20), which is governed by *ša* 'which', all verbs in lines 16-41 (and perhaps 43) are governed by *kī* 'when' (line 16), but that not all of them have the expected subordinative ending *-u.*[492] The verbs in these lines are spelled as follows (all are 1st sg.):

16 *ú-ri-du-ma*
18 *ak-šu-du-ma … áš-lu-la ap-pu-lu*$_4$ *aq-qu-ru*
19 *[a]q-mu-ú … al-li-ku-ma*
(20 *ša šar māt elamti e-ki-mu*)

491 That the sole extant manuscript is made of stone does not concern us here: we presume that the stonemason faithfully reproduced the incongruities found on the exemplar.
492 Grayson, *AfO* 20 (1963) 84 with n. 7.

21 *al-me akšud*(kur-*ud*) *áš-lu-la*
22 *ú-še-rib* ... *ú-ter-ram-ma*
23 *am-nu*
35 [*ap-pu*]-*lu aq-qu-ru* ... [*aq-m*]*u-ú áš-pu-ka*
36 *iš-mu-ú* ... *im-qu-t*[*u-šú*]
37 *ú-še-lu-ú*
39 *aq-bu-ú*
40 [*i*]*m-da-ha-ru*
41 [*aṣ-ba*]-*tu*
43 *ú-še-ri-da*[*m-ma*]

In Grayson's analysis, the verbs missing the subordinative ending are those in lines 21 and 22. To these, *am-nu* in line 23 should be added.[493]

The clause with *am-nu* ('I delivered (these two cities) into the hand of the fortress commander of Dēr') shares its grammatical object with the preceding clauses. What we have, then, is a cluster of syntactically connected clauses, extending from line 19b to line 23a, whose verbs lack the subordinative ending, and which together make up a self-contained piece of narrative about the fate of two particular cities (whereas the narrative which precedes and follows refers to other cities):

> uru*bīt-ha'iri* / [uru]*raṣa ālāni ša miṣir māt aššur ša ina tarṣi abīya šar elamti ēkimu* / [*da*]*nāniš ina* [*m*]*ēteq girriya al-me* kur-*ud áš-lu-la šallassun* lú*ṣābē qašti* giš*arī*[*te*] / *qerebšun ú-še-rib ana miṣir māt aššur uterramma qātē rab* HAL-ṢU / *dēr am-nu* ... (lines 19b-23a)

> 'Bīt-ha'iri (and) Raṣa, cities at the border of the land of Assur, which in the time of my father the king of Elam stole by force: as I passed by in my chariot I re-conquered them by siege, plundered their booty, sent archers and shieldsmen into them, re-annexed them to the land of Assur, (and) delivered them into the hand of the governor of Dēr.'

Grayson's explanation of the absence of the subordinative marker in lines 21 and 22 was that the writer 'forgot for a moment that the whole description was governed by *kī*'. However, with the addition of *am-nu* to the forms lacking the subordinative marker, another explanation suggests itself: the redactor of the Walters inscription took the passage about Bīt-ha'iri and Raṣa from a source on which the narrative was

---

493 Although *am-nu* could stand for *amnû*, on this manuscript all other III-weak verbs with the subordinative ending are spelled *plene*: lines 19 (especially relevant, since *aqmu*, like *amnu*, ends in *u*), 35, 36, 37, 39. This confirms that *am-nu*, without *plene* spelling, does not exhibit the subordinative ending (had this been present, we would expect the spelling *am-nu-ú*).

non-subordinative,[494] and inserted it into the string of clauses governed by *kī* without the necessary addition of subordinative markers. (The failure to add them may have been facilitated by the demise of the subordinative ending in the vernacular).[495]

3.5.3 Assurnaṣirpal II 17

Our third example of grammatical incongruity arising from the 'cut and paste' technique of redaction stems from a monolith of Asn II (no. 17). The concluding portion of the inscription (v.24b – end) includes a number of features which are unusual for Asn II:[496] *man-ma* for *mamma* (v.65); numerous *plene* spellings (e.g. v.62 *bu-ú-li*, v.65 *ki-i*, v.65 *la-ma-a-ri*, etc.); perhaps most tellingly, accusatives in *-a* (v.68*2, v.69, v.91, v.92, v.94*2, v.95, v.102, v.103*2). The combination of these features allows us to posit that this, the concluding portion of no. 17, was borrowed from another source,[497] probably one which was considerably older.

This hypothesis explains the problematic plural *li-du-ú* (*liddû*, v.96), which in the version transmitted to us has only Aššur as subject, and so should be singular (*liddi*). Obsession with Aššur is a feature of Neo-Assyrian times. The original (pre-Neo-Assyrian) formulation included more than one deity, which Asn II's (or an intermediate) transmitter has removed *ad maiorem gloriam dei sui*, but without making the verb singular.[498]

---

494 Cf. e.g. Chicago prism vii.55-60, which has the passage almost word for word, non-subordinative.

495 See discussion of said demise in Worthington, "*i-ba-aš-šu-ú* vs. *i-ba-aš-šu* from Old to Neo-Babylonian", in Kogan (ed.), *Language in the Ancient Near East* (2010) 684–689.

496 If the reading is secure, the spelling [*a-i*]*a-a-ba* (rather than *a-a-ba*) at v. 68 should be added to these.

497 It is striking that the only spelling *man-ma* under Šal III, whose style is very similar to Asn II's, also occurs in a sentence which includes an accusative in *-a*: *arhī pašqūte <ša?> šadê dannūti / ša kīma šēlut patri ana šamê zi-qip-ta šaknū ina šarrāni abbēya / man-ma lā ētiqu qerbīšunu ina akkullāti ša erî aqqur* 'With copper picks I hewed narrow paths (through) mighty mountains which rose upwards to the heavens like the points of daggers, (and through whose) midst none among the kings my fathers had ever passed' (1:19-21, translation based on Grayson's). Perhaps this sentence too was imported from, or modelled on, an old source.

498 Two verbs in parallel constructions in preceding lines are singular: v.90 *li-ru-ur*, v.93 *li-it-ta-ás-qar*. Perhaps these curses were interpolated into the formulation of

For a similar case see Andrew George's comment on *Gilg.* I 94:

> The publication of the fragment MB Nippur$_1$ shows that the Standard Babylonian text is telescoped: there, and no doubt in other versions of the epic, before instructions were directly put to Aruru, some figure – unidentified as the text now stands but presumably Ea – made the suggestion to the gods that she be given the task of creating a match for Gilgameš. The sometime mention of these gods leaves its trace in the plural *issû.*[499]

3.5.4 Assurnaṣirpal II 19

Our fourth example comes from another stele of Asn II, the 'Kurkh monolith' (no. 19). The oddity here are three occurrences of the spelling AK KUR (lines 44, 53, 77), all of which are followed by the phrase (*n*) *ṣābī tidūkišu ina kakkē ušamqit* 'I felled (a number) of his combat troops with the sword'. Twice elsewhere in the inscription, the same phrase or a very similar one (with *muddahhiṣīšunu* instead of *tidūkišu*) is preceded by *ak-ta-šad* (lines 74, 102). For this reason and for reasons of idiom, it is very tempting to emend AK KUR to *ak-<ta>-šad* (KUR and *šad* being the same sign), as indeed is done in the RIMA edition.

The complication is, that this can hardly be simple lipography. For the likelihood of this happening three times with the same sign in the same word in the same inscription is extremely slight. Accordingly, while admitting that AK KUR ultimately is a corruption of *aktašad*, we need to envisage an intermediate step, in which someone thought that the faulty spelling was *bona fide.* The simplest solution would seem to be that of a not-too-competent person redacting the inscription using multiple sources, one with the correct spelling *ak-ta-šad*, and another with the defective spelling *ak-<ta>-šad.* The faulty redactor interpreted the latter as *aq-qúr* 'I destroyed', and used it several times in redacting the new inscription, without realising this involved propagating an error.[500]

---

the older source, or, through oversight, their plural endings were removed while that on *liddû* (singular *liddi*) was not. But it is also possible that they had a singular subject already on the source.

499 George, *Gilgamesh* (2003) 449–450.

500 The fact that *aqqur* also occurs in the spelling *aq-qur* (e.g. lines 61, 76, 79, 84) is not an obstacle to the suggested interpretation. Cf. *appul* 'I destroyed' spelled *ap-púl* (lines 69, 76, 79, 99) and *ap-pùl* (lines 66, 84).

3.5.5 *Gilgameš* X 151, *idnī*

An error similar to those we have been discussing occurs at *Gilg.* X 151, where the f. sg. imperative *id-ni* 'give me!' (MS K_1) is addressed to Ur-šanabi. Line X 151 is one of a group of lines which appeared verbatim earlier in the epic, addressed to the ale-wife Šiduri. A transmitter simply imported the Šiduri lines into the Ur-šanabi passage, neglecting to change the verb to match the new (masculine) referent. Thus, though this is not an error of cut-and-paste in composition or redaction, it is an error of cut-and-paste in transmission.

3.5.6 *eli mahrê* and *eli ša mahri* 'than the previous one'

We will discover a further likely instance of cut-and-paste redaction if we examine the phrases *eli mahrê* and *eli ša mahri*,[501] which appear frequently in building sections of Neo-Assyrian royal inscriptions.

These phrases, which context shows to be more or less synonymous, are usually translated as adverbial phrases with temporal meaning: 'than before', 'than ever', 'than ever before' (passim in *RIMA* 2 and 3), 'als zuvor' (Borger, *BIWA*, 252), 'than earlier' (CAD M 114a). While these translations obviously capture the overall sense, the grammatical analysis can be refined.

Considering only *eli mahrê* and its counterpart with insertion of *ša*, the inscriptions present a clear distinction between phrases with *ša* but without the *plene* spelling (*eli ša mahri*), and phrases with the *plene* spelling but without *ša* (*eli mahrê*).[502] Thus the former phrase simply uses the noun *mahru* 'previous time', while the latter uses an adjective 'previous'

---

501 We disagree with CAD M/i 113b-114a (which normalises *eli ša mahrê*). Similar phrases include *eli ša pāna* 'than the previous one' (Sar Ann. 71, Ann. 269), *eli ša ūmē pānī* 'than the one of former days' (Asb A i.115, B viii.72, C x.97, D viii.75, T ii.45), *eli ša ūmē ullûti* 'than the one of days of yore' (Asb T iii.48), *eli ša abi bānîya* 'than the one of my bodily father' (Asb A ii.19), *eli ša šarrāni abbīya* 'than the one of the kings my fathers' (Asb T iv.25).

502 ***eli mahrê***: TP I 1 vii.86, 10:87, 11:6'; AN II 2:130; TN II 3:11'; Asn II 40:36, 56:16, 57:3; Šal III 10 iv.49, 27:11 (*mah-ri-i*); ***eli ša mahri*** Asb A vii.46, E St.11.50, D viii.72, A ii.9, A x.97, NL 56. Hence a case such as [...] *mah-re-e* (e.g. Sar Ann. 410) should be restored [*eli*], not (Fuchs, *Khorsabad* (1993) 179) [*eli ša*].

formed from *mahru* with the *nisbe*-morpheme -*ī*-.[503] In the case of *ša mahri*, *ša* is pronominal ('that of previous time', i. e. 'the previous one'), while in the case of *mahrê* the adjective is substantivised ('the previous one'). Thus, at least in 'good' Akkadian, both *eli ša mahri* and *eli mahrê* mean 'than the previous one' as opposed to 'than before'.

The equivalence of the phrases *eli mahrê* and *eli ša mahri* offers an interesting window onto ancient *Sprachgefühl*: *ša* was felt to perform the same function as a *nisbe* morpheme. Indeed, one can find this principle in the phrase *ša šarrūti* 'of kingship': as many translators have recognised, this effectively does service as an adjective 'royal' (which Akkadian lacks).[504]

When the referent of the phrase *eli mahrê* is feminine, we expect *eli mahrīti* (correctly e. g. AD II 3:12).[505] In two places, however, we find *eli mahrî* referring to a feminine noun. One instance is the example above (AN II's *kisirtu*, § 3.5.1), which we have argued to be a cut-and-paste affair: the phrase was imported unchanged from an inscription where its referent was masculine. We therefore suggest this explanation also for the other instance (Šal III 46:10), though here suffixes referring to the feminine referent (a ceremonial gate) are correctly feminine.

It would be interesting to know whether in the Šal III inscription *mahrî* was left unaltered through oversight, or because the redactor did not understand the grammar, and took *eli mahrî* as a set phrase. The latter possibility (which receives support from MS II of AN's *kisirtu* passage) is what prompted mention of the possible restriction to 'good' Akkadian above.

3.5.7 Spelling patterns in a compendium of oracle questions

An interesting set of orthographic patterns occurs on a well preserved Neo-Assyrian tablet from Kalhu bearing oracle questions.[506] The distribution of spellings of *ālu* 'town', *ina* 'in' and *ša* 'of/which' on the tablet suggests that different oracle questions were gathered from different exem-

503 CAD M/i recognises the adjectival construction with the preposition *ana* (p. 114 sub f), it is unclear why it does not recognise it with *eli*.

504 A similar phenomenon comes into view through comparison of the phrases 'scribal errors' and 'erreurs de scribes'.

505 Cf. also *eli ma(n)dattišu mah-ri-ti* 'than his previous tribute' (Sar *Prunk* 29; Asb A iii.25, H1 iii.8').

506 ND 5492, no. 1 in Lambert, *Oracle Questions* (2007).

plars which possessed separate orthographic conventions, and reproduced as seen, without orthographic homogenisation. The distribution is as follows (slightly simplified):

	Query			
	3	4	5	1, 2, 6
ālu	uru^{ki} (and *an-ni-im*)	uru	uru	uru
ina	*i-na* (but 1 * *ina*)	*i-na*	*ina*	*ina*
ša (as word/as syllable)	*ša*	*šá*	*ša/šá*	*šá*

We will first consider the distribution of ŠA and ŠÁ. There are three different traits. **a)** The fifth query (lines 184-231) uses ŠA for the word *ša* 'of/which' (four attestations), and ŠÁ for the syllable *ša* within a larger word (four attestations),[507] a pattern found elsewhere (see § 5.4.4.2). **b)** Three queries use only one of these two signs: the third query (lines 96-160) uses only ŠA,[508] four times for the word *ša* and four times syllabically;[509] the fourth and sixth queries (lines 161-183 and 232-345) use only ŠÁ, to a total of nine and twenty-three attestations.[510] **c)** The first two queries (lines 1-95) similarly use only ŠÁ (twenty-six attestations),[511] except for two uses ŠA, the switch apparently being motivated by concerns of readibility: *ša-lim* (line 29) probably aims to prevent a reading 4 *lim* 'four thousand' (ŠÁ = 4); more tentatively, we suggest that *ša it-ti* (line 42) was used to prevent a reading gar-*it-ti* (*šikitti*; ŠÁ = GAR). Further examples of this type will be given in § 5.4.

These different spellings of *ša* tally with two other differences across different queries. The third query, which uses only ŠA, spells *ālu* 'city' as uru^{ki} (seven attestations),[512] whereas everywhere else on the tablet it is written just uru, without ki (28 attestations).[513] These are both older spellings, which coheres with mimated *an-ni-im* 'this' after uru^{ki}.[514]

507 ŠA as word: 215, 218, 219, 220; ŠÁ as syllable: 191, 206, 210, 221.

508 As already indicated by Lambert, the reading [*š*]*á* at the end of line 98 is doubtful.

509 As word: 100, 103, 108, 122; as syllable: 109, 133 (*2), 154.

510 **a)** 4th query: ŠÁ as word: 162, 167, 173, 176, 177, 178, 179, 182; ŠÁ as syllable: 178. **b)** 6th query: ŠÁ as word: 233, 236, 237, 239, 248, 267, 268, 273, 275, 277, 301, 306, 310, 314, 315, 319, 328, 331; ŠÁ as syllable: 287, 314, 322, 333, 334.

511 ŠÁ as word: 5, 10, 12, 21, 25, 33, 34, 36, 37, 40, 62, 69, 78, 81, 82, 85 (*2), 88; ŠÁ as syllable: 44, 47, 52, 70 (*sic*!), 74, 76, 79, 89.

512 101, 108, 110, 116, 126, 128, 149.

513 First query: 18, 20; second query: 29, 47, 48, 62, 69, 75, 78 (*2), 84, 88, 89 (and catch-line: 95); fourth query: 174; fifth query: 186, 194, 212, 213, 215, 220 (*2),

A further difference between our queries is the spelling of *ina* 'in': in the first, second, fifth, and sixth queries this is spelled with the AŠ sign (i. e. *ina*);[515] in the third and fourth it is (except in line 159, third query) spelled with the two signs *i-na*.[516]

Thus the tablet incorporates parts from at least four sources: one which used uru^ki^, *i-na* and only ŠA (third query); one which used uru, *i-na*, and only ŠÁ (fourth query); one which used uru, *ina* and ŠA for the word but ŠÁ for the syllable (fifth query); and one or more which used uru, *ina* and only ŠÁ (first, second and sixth queries).

3.6 Errors of sign similarity by stonemasons

Cuneiform was not only inscribed on clay (tablets, prisms, cylinders, etc.) but also carved onto stone (slabs, stelae, statues, vases, tablets, beads, rocks, etc.). No ancient source tells us who carved inscriptions onto these objects, or what sort of training they had. It seems fair to suppose that they would usually have been trained in the technique of carving, and in forming correctly proportioned cuneiform signs. But there is the additional question of whether they were actually readers of cuneiform, in other words whether they understood what they were carving.

The notion that the people who carved cuneiform onto stone possessed limited or even zero literacy can be found, if only by implication, in Assyriological writings since at least the year 1912, usually in *ad hoc* comments to isolated errors.[517] Nonetheless, for whatever reason, it has

---

223, 226; sixth query: 288, 289, 306. Interestingly, the summary label to the third query (line 160) spells it as uru, suggesting (though not proving) that the summary label was not original to the source.

514 Lines as per fn. 512, plus 140 and 157 (where uru^ki^ is lost). Exception: *an-ni-i*, line 146.

515 First query: 11, 15, 16; second query: 27, 33, 48, 49 (*2), 50 (*2), 51 (*3), 52 (*2), 53 (*2), 54 (*3), 55 (*2), 56 (*2), 57 (*2), 58 (*2), 59 (*2), 60, 69, 75, 78, 90, 92, 94; fifth query: 185, 210, 211, 221, 224; sixth query: 235, 237, 238, 239, 240, 241, 243, 245, 249, 251, 252, 253, 261, 262, 264, 266, 267, 272, 273, 274, 275, 276, 277, 280, 281, 285, 286, 287 (*2), 288 (*2), 290, 294, 295, 297, 299, 302, 305, 307, 313, 316, 328, 329, 330, 332, 343.

516 Third query: 103, 108, 113, 115, 117, 119, 122, 125, 130, 139, 150 (*2), 155; fourth query: 173, 174, 175 (*2).

517 King, *Boundary-Stones* (1912), note to no. 5 iii.44 'The engraver has written DA, for IŠ, by mistake' (King gives the actual cuneiform signs rather than 'DA' and 'IŠ'). See also King's p. 6 n. 7 ('carelessness or want of skill on the part of the

failed to gain currency. This is despite a large body of evidence which suggests that, though the stonemasons knew (or at least could correctly inscribe) the shapes of a wide range of cuneiform signs, they did not understand them. The result is that certain forms and spellings, including even the odd much-discussed one, have failed to be explained as stonemason's errors when they clearly should be.

With the intention of raising the profile of errors of sign identification by stonemasons, we will first offer a number of fairly trivial examples from Neo-Assyrian royal inscriptions (arranged by king), then consider two cases where recognition of a stonemason's error can solve a crux. Finally, the evidence assembled will enable us to deduce something of how stonemasons worked.

In any one of the instances we shall cite, the stonemason(s) could of course be faithfully transmitting an error by the person who provided the sequence of signs to be carved. Indeed, two errors which we shall attribute to stonemasons have direct parallels on clay tablets. Overall, however, confusion of signs with similar shapes is so common in so many stone inscriptions that one can only conclude that stonemasons were especially prone to them. Accordingly, when an error of sign similarity arises on a stone inscription, it most likely originated with the stonemason – '*Habent sua fata etiam inscriptiones*'.[518]

3.6.1 Some simple examples of stonemasons' errors

An Old Babylonian example is *aš-lu-un* for *aš-ku-un* (RIME 4 p. 341 line 33). Many more examples appear on the Hammurapi stele in the Louvre, which was apparently inscribed by one or more stonemasons who did not understand what they were writing.[519]

From the Neo-Assyrian royal inscriptions we can cite the following:

TP I: A.LU for íd(=A.ENGUR) (TP I 4:41 MS 15, stone tablet).
Abk: 7 iii.17 *gu-la-ta* for *šal-la-ta.*

---

engraver'), p. 6 n. 10 ('carelessness of engraving'), p. 7 nn. 1, 3 and 4, etc. More recently see Grayson, *RIMA 3* (1996) 97 on 'engraving errors' on a stone statue of Šal III (no. 25). (By contrast, the commentary to Asn II no. 19 (*RIMA* 2, p. 257) speaks of 'the scribe who engraved the text on the stele').

518 Weißbach, *ZDMG* 72 (1918) 177 (though the phrase is older).

519 See e.g NI for GAG in paragraph 111, line 46, and many more instances noted by Borger, *Lesestücke* (2006).

Asn II: **1)** *i-pa-li-šu* for *i-pa-ša-šu* (50:45 MS 1); LI and ŠA correctly written elsewhere (*li* lines 23, 40; *ša* lines 4, 5, 6 etc.). **2)** MAN (i.e. U U) for U (50:2 MS 2); MAN twice correctly written in the very same line. **3)** *a-*[*h*]*a-ta* for *a-ha-iš* (17 ii.80). **4)** The stonemason who carved *ki-dúr-ru* (1 ii.50 var.) failed to realise that KI on his exemplar consisted in U and KU written too close together;[520] **5)** stonemasons are the likely culprits of the errors in IA-*ba-te* for *ṣi-ba-te*, *e-*IA*-di* for *e-ṣi-di* (1 iii.32 var.), *at-ti-*IA*-a* for *at-ti-ṣi-a* (1 iii.104 var.), NA_4-*su* for *kib-su* (1 iii.110), BAR *a-nim* for ^{d}*a-nim* (2:1 MS 6), *gim-ri-šú-*AŠ for *gim-ri-šú-nu* (2:18 MS 1), ZA-*ši* for *ía-ši* (2:23 MS 7), *mat-*IA*-Ú-te* for *mat-te-ia-te* (17 iv.8, cf. ibid. and lines 18-19), *kib-*MAR for *kib-rat* (17 v.51), NI for dù (26:54 MS 2), and TA-*tu* for *iš-tu* (32:4).

Šal III: **1)** a stone monolith from Nimrud has *IR-šit* for *ni-šit* (2 i.6 MS 2) and U-*ti-ia* for man-*ti-ia* (2 i.14 MS 2); **2)** the 'Kurkh Monolith' has *g*[*íl*]*-za-na-a-*KUR for *gíl-za-na-a-a* (2 i.28 MS 1);[521] **3)** a stone statue (12)[522] has KUR for AN (line 22), A' for KUN (23), BÚR for BAL (30), ZU for SU (40).

ŠA V: a stone stele from Nimrud has *PI-ṣi* for *mar-ṣi* (1 iii.31) and uru^{meš}-*IR* for uru^{meš}-*ni* (iv.15).

AN III: a stone stele has *ina qereb* [*t*]*am-ha-ru*, with the ending *-u* for expected *-i* (2011:17'). Given the similarity of certain forms of the signs RI and RU and the rarity of faulty genitive endings before the Sargonid period, a misidentification by the stonemason may be supposed.

TP III: ^{MAŠ}*šar-rat* for ^{d}*šar-rat* (Ann. 17:16', MS A), anše.kur.ra^{meš}-DIŠ for anše.kur.ra^{meš}-*šú* (Ann. 17:13' MS A).

Senn: **1)** on ^{uru}*ban-ba-KAB-na* for ^{uru}*ban-ba-ri-na* in the Bavian inscription (122:8) see Weissert *apud* Frahm, *Sanherib*, p. 153b top. Note also KAL for UN in line 45 and AT for I in line 42 of the same inscription. **2)** As copied by Arthur Ungnad, an alabaster tablet of Sennacherib exhibits *as-ma-*MIN*-ti* for *as-ma-a-ti* and [*ru*]*-uk-*LU*-sa* for [*ru*]*-uk-ku-sa* in two successive lines (62:48'-49').

3.6.2 Two *cruces*

The first crux we shall present which can be resolved through awareness of stonemason's errors is the Šamšī-ilu inscription from the Orontes, dating to the reign of AN III (no. 2). The relevant lines run thus (a translation will be given after discussion):

---

520 For examples of this very mistake on clay tablets see *JMC* 5 (2005), 24 *ad* 44' and Deller, *Orientalia* 26 (1957) 152 n. 7.

521 See Yamada, *Construction* (2000) 350 and 380.

522 The edition in Grayson, *RIMA 3* (1996) 58–61 relies on the copy by Kinnier Wilson, *Iraq* 24 (1962), without collation.

8b-10 *mi-ṣir* NAM A *adad-nērārī šar māt aššur šamšī-ilu / [tar]tannu uzakkiū-ma ana atar-šumki mār adramu ana mārīšu / mārī-mārīšu kī rīmūti irīmū*

14b-15 (*ša*) *mi-ṣir an-na-a ištu qāt atar-šumki / [mār]īšu u mārī-mārīšu ina danāni ekkimu*

The problem is NAM A in line 8.[523] Grayson suggests ana_x-*a* and *a:nam* (both for *annâ* 'this') as solutions, and translates *mi-ṣir* NAM A as '*this is* the boundary'.[524] However, the spelling would be very odd, one would expect *annû* (nom.) rather than *annâ* (acc.), and (though this is less probative, cf. § 4.7.2) one might expect *-ma* to mark the predicate.

We suggest that NAM A is a corruption of *an-na-a*. The sign NAM is sufficiently similar to AN NA for it to originate with an error of sign identification by a stonemason. This conjecture has the merit of rendering the constructions in lines 8-10 and 14-15 pleasingly parallel, with *mi-ṣir an*!-*na*!-*a*(NAM-A) as object of *irīmū* 'gave' in line 10, and *mi-ṣir an-na-a* as object of *ekkimu* 'steals' in line 15.

The translation of lines 8-10 thus runs:

'Adad-nērārī, king of Assyria, and Šamšī-ilu the field-marshal have exempted this boundary (from tax) and given it as a gift to Atar-šumki son of Adramu, to his sons and sons' sons'.

The second crux we shall consider occurs in a curse formula on a stone stele from the reign of Šal IV (no. 1). The relevant sentence runs thus:

*māssu kī libitti lu-šá?-bi?-ru? ur-ru-*UH
'May they (the gods) *smash* his land like a brick, *ur-ru-*UH' (line 18).

The problem which concerns us here is *ur-ru-*UH. Previous discussants plausibly derive this from the verb *urruhu* 'to do quickly',[525] but, as they observe, one would expect *urruhiš* 'quickly', with the adverbial ending *-iš*. The form with zero ending is grammatically odd.

---

523 By contrast, the spelling MI-ṢIR for expected *miṣru* in the same line is unproblematic: it can be interpreted as semi-logographic, with parallels in the inscriptions of Sargon (*e-ke-me* MI-ṢIR-*ia*, Ann. 200; cf. ND-D v.23 *e-ke-mi me-iṣ-ri-ia // e-ke-me mi-iṣ-ri-ia*, *Prunk* 31; *a-na* MI-ṢIR-[*ia*], Ann. 301) and perhaps Assurnaṣirpal II (62:3': *me-ṣIR-ri*, i. e. ME-ṢIR^{ri} for /miṣri/?). Thus the form is not a *status absolutus.*

524 Grayson, *RIMA 3* (1996) 203.

525 Donbaz, *ARRIM* 8 (1990) 10, Zaccagnini, *SAAB* 7/1 (1993) 56 n. 9, Grayson, *RIMA 3* (1996) 240.

The form can be explained by positing a stonemason's error. The sign UH is composed of two parts, one identical to HI and one similar to IŠ. The exemplar had *ur-ru-hi-iš*, which the stonemason misidentified as *ur-ru-UH.*

Another case of this type (i.e. confusion of similar signs resulting in loss of the adverbial ending *-iš*) occurs on MS dd of *Gilg.* V, line 100: with George *ad loc.*, *pis-nu-uq* represents a corruption of *pis-nu-qiš* (the signs UG and KIŠ are similar in Neo-Babylonian). Here a literate person was responsible (§ 3.2.1.1).

3.6.3 How were stone inscriptions produced?

What do the errors discussed above tell us about the working methods of the stonemasons who produced the inscriptions in which the errors appear?[526] In the first place, we can deduce that the sequence of signs to be carved was supplied to the stonemasons in written form. Secondly, for the errors to occur, the stonemasons must have found the written sources which they were using moderately hard to read (in the sense that cuneiform signs were difficult to identify). Hence it is unlikely that the signs were drawn directly onto the stone, for on most stone inscriptions the signs are large enough that errors of sign identification should not occur. The likeliest scenario is that the stonemasons had to read directly from clay tablets.

Thirdly, though stonemasons were obviously well acquainted with the shapes of individual cuneiform signs (as shown *inter alia* by the fact that they never write nonsensical assemblages of wedges, only proper signs), their errors suggest that they possessed no or very limited literacy – otherwise they could have identified the correct sign from the context.

526 In connection with how stone inscriptions were produced we note a comment by Wilcke, "Die Inschrift "Tukultī-Ninurtas I 1" – Tukultī-Ninurtas I. von Assyrien Feldzug gegen Gutäer und andere, nordöstliche und nordwestliche Feinde und der erste Bericht über den Bau seines neuen Palastes", in Fincke (ed.), *Fs Wilhelm* (2010) 432 n. 104: 'Von hier [Anfang Z. 115 = iv.5, MW] bis Zum Zeilenende von Z. 119 (iv.9) sind die Zeichen (mit Ausnahme der Winkelhaken / schrägen Keile von KUR in Z. 116 [iv 6], TI in Z. 117 [iv 7], EŠ und BE in Z. 118 [iv 8], ŠAL, SU, NAM und den beiden NU in Z. 119 [iv 9], sowie dem Zeichen ŠUD am Ende von Z. 117 [iv 7]) nur schwach eingeschnitten, gleichsam angerissen'. At least in this instance, then, the stonemason was not carving signs sequentially, but began by carving the *Winkelhaken* and diagonal wedges for several signs at a time.

Fourthly, they were not working under the supervision of a literate individual, who would have put them right.

The sources from which these inferences were made are sufficiently numerous and widely distributed over time to suggest that the inferences apply to the working habits of large numbers of stonemasons. But they need not apply to all cases. In her edition of Darius's Babylonian inscription at Bisitun, Elizabeth von Voigtlander argues that the inscription falls into portions which differ from each other in both calligraphy (sign shapes) and orthography (spellings).[527] From this she infers that eight different stonemasons were involved, who chose their own spellings (i.e. were literate). Interesting as this possibility is, we reserve judgment.[528]

It also deserves mention that substitutions of similar signs are rare on the numerous stone inscriptions of Sargon's palace at Khorsabad. This supports Grant Frame's view that at Khorsabad the signs were drawn directly onto stone.[529] Sargon thus followed a different practice from e.g. Assurnaṣirpal II. The reason may be precisely that he wanted to avoid an epidemic of stonemason's errors.

527 See the chart in von Voigtlander, *Bisitun* (1978) 73. (I owe this reference to Walther Sallaberger).

528 The divisions are not as neat as von Voigtlander suggests. For example, according to her chart, in lines 46-60 '*tu*$_4$ replaces *tú* in final position in nouns and adjectives', but there are many counter-examples: *ṣe-el-tú* (line 46), *ṣa-al-tú* (52 and 54), *ni-ik-ru-tú* (passim), *bal-ṭu-tú* (passim). Note also the sceptical remarks of Saggs, *JRAS* 113/1 (1981) on the calligraphic dimension: 'So far as [the] conclusion depends upon minor variations in signs rather than technical aspects of engraving, it needs to be treated with caution; variants of the same sign, or alternations between homophones, often occur even in a single cuneiform letter where without question only one scribe was involved'. The orthography of the inscription requires detailed study which cannot be undertaken here. Whether von Voigtlander's overall findings be confirmed or not, we can only applaud the spirit of her enquiry.

529 Frame, "The Order of the Wall Slabs with the Annals of Sargon II in Room V of the Palace at Khorsabad", in Frame (ed.), *Studies Grayson* (2004) 93: 'While the inscription was probably cut by illiterate stonecutters, scribes would probably have drawn the signs lightly upon the stone slabs as a guide'.

3.7 Assyrians transmitting Babylonian

As is well known, manuscripts in Babylonian language but Neo-Assyrian script sometimes include Assyrianisms. One's first instinct might be to view these cases as errors. Certainly it would be plausible for errors of this type to arise – compare the comment by Medievalist Henry Chaytor: 'If a scribe was copying a text composed in a dialect not native to himself, he was likely to substitute his own auditory memory of the text for his visual impression of it'.[530] Nevertheless, it cannot be assumed that all Assyrianisms are born of inadvertence. Some Assyrians might have regarded it as their prerogative to make conscious acculturations of wording in Babylonian compositions to their own taste. As the matter cannot be resolved *a priori*, it is necessary to study individual instances.

In undertaking such studies, it would be advantageous to have some idea of how natural or unnatural it felt for Assyrians to write (and speak) Babylonian. This is in turn related to the tricky issue of ease of mutual intelligibility. In modern normalisations of cuneiform spelling Babylonian and Assyrian are very similar, but Mark Geller observes that similarity in writing is no guarantee of mutual intelligibility,[531] and there is the problem of how what was written related to what was spoken.[532] Since they diverged over time, mutual intelligibility was probably more extensive in the second millennium than in the first,[533] though some scholars suppose full mutual intelligibility even in the first.[534]

What we can do is observe users of Neo-Assyrian script (whom we presume usually to have been Assyrians) who there is special reason to think were supposed to be writing Babylonian, and see how they got on.

We begin with the Rassam cylinder of Sennacherib. This king's inscriptions are generally noteworthy for their pure Babylonian style, and concomitant abandonment of Assyrianisms which his predecessors used for stylistic purposes. Since the vast majority of manuscripts of the Rassam cylinder are in good Babylonian, and this tallies with what we know of Sennacherib's inscriptions generally, it seems fair to infer that Assyrianisms in the Rassam cylinder were unwarranted. Sure enough, As-

530 Chaytor, *Bulletin of the John Rylands Library* 26 (1941–1942) 55.
531 Geller, *BSOAS* 65/3 (2003) 563.
532 Kouwenberg, *The Akkadian Verb* (2011) 10.
533 Kouwenberg, *The Akkadian Verb* (2011) 10.
534 This appears to be the view of Parpola, "Proto-Assyrian", in Waetzoldt and Hauptmann (eds), *Wirtschaft und Gesellschaft von Ebla* (1988) 294, commenting simply that Babylonian and Assyrian were 'mutually understandable'.

syrianisms are found on the most error-prone of the Rassam manuscripts, namely MS Z (which we already met in § 3.3.3).

Two cases on MS Z are doubtful, in that they may be Assyrianisms or lipographies. In line **47**, *a-ra-an-šú-nu* 'their crime' (on 4 manuscripts) appears as *a-ra-šú-nu*, perhaps representing /araššunu/, with vernacular assimilation *nš*>*šš*.[535] In line **55**, *ša a-na dun-nu-un* (on 6 manuscripts) appears as *ša dun-nu-un*. In vernacular Neo-Assyrian, *ana* was probably often assimilated to a following consonant, which was not necessarily spelled double.[536] Hence this may be a sandhi spelling (*ša~dun-nu-un*) representing the result of assimilation and crasis: /ša ana dunnun/ > /ša addunnun/ > /ša(d)dunnun/. Uncertainty similarly surrounds *ú-te-šir* for *ú-še-šir* in line **75**, with TE as *lapsus styli* for ŠE or pronunciation /uþēšir/.

Much more interesting are lines 29 and 66. In line **29**, Babylonian *mahrâ* (on 4 manuscripts) appears as *mah-ri-a-a*, representing vernacular Assyrian /mahrī^{y}a/. In line **66**, *lib-bu-uš ul ih-su-us* (on 4 manuscripts) appears as *lib-bu-uš li~ih-su-us.* Frahm has identified the latter case as a sandhi spelling, and interestingly the spelling is more likely to reflect crasis of *lā ihsus* than *ul ihsus*: the writer translated the Babylonian negation *ul* into its vernacular Assyrian equivalent *lā*.[537]

Another interesting case is Šal III 44, discussed in (§ 3.4.3). A shared corruption suggests that all manuscripts with the possible exception of MS 15 go back to a common source. All manuscripts except 2 and 8 exhibit Assyrianisms in line 10 (*urkû* vs Bab. *arkû*) and 14 (*išamme* or *išam-*

---

535 This assimilation was not exclusive to Assyrian, but here (unless lipography of *-an-* be supposed) it almost certainly represents an intrusion of the writer's own vernacular as opposed to a conscious choice of a different Babylonian form.

536 Thus frequent *a-dan-niš* for *ana+danniš*, see Luukko, *Grammatical Variation* (2004) n. 344. Cf. Parpola, "The Man Without a Scribe and the Question of Literacy in the Assyrian Empire", in Pongratz-Leisten, Kühne and Xella (eds), *Fs. Röllig* (1997) 317 n. 6 on frequent spellings of *issi* with *i-* (not *is-*) when followed by a suffix, suggesting reduction of /ss/ to /s/. See also fn. 906.

537 Crasis of *lā* with following vocalic *Anlaut* also occurred in vernacular Neo-Babylonian. An example is *le~gu-ú* for *lā egû* 'not to shirk' on a Neo-Babylonian medical commentary (Frahm, *Commentaries* (2011) 237). See also an exercise tablet published by Gesche, *Schulunterricht* (2001) 247, with *la ub-lu* for expected precative *lubla.* Here, accustomed to *l* at the start of vernacular verbal forms being a reduced form of the negation *lā* (or *la*?), the writer misinterpreted /lublu/ 'may I bring' as *lā ublu* 'I did not bring', and wrote this. However, on MS Z it seems more likely that vernacular Assyrian was responsible for the introduction of *lā* (see fn. 535).

meū vs Bab. *išemmû*).[538] Perhaps the absence of subordinative marker in line 8 on all manuscripts except 2 and 8 (see § 2.4.3) also reflects Assyrian vernacular. Be that as it may, it seems likely that the person responsible for the recension on MSS 2 and 8, which in several respects is the best, 'tidied up' the language of the source, de-Assyrianising it. This in turn encourages the suspicion that in the first place the Assyrianisation occurred through accident rather than policy.

These manuscripts reflect the phenomenon described by Chaytor: Assyrianisms could indeed creep in unwanted. As more evidence for this is found, it will contribute to our understanding of how different Babylonian and Assyrian were perceived to be by their native speakers.

3.8 Conclusions

The mechanisms of Akkadian textual change were varied and complex. Some arose through inadvertence, some through misunderstanding, some through the particular type of misunderstanding involved in hypercorrection. (To these should be added the group, not studied here, of conscious changes founded on correct undestanding of the exemplar).

We suggested that a typology of errors was a prerequisite for studying textual change, and duly offered such a typology. We then showed how even quite simple text-critical considerations, informed by an awareness of how corruptions arose, can help us make better sense of transmitted text. Sometimes this results in new translations.

It was shown that errors can be informative about transmitters' knowledge of the compositions they transmitted, but also of their understanding of written Akkadian. We saw how one transmitter was mislead by preceding *na* into reading AŠ as *aš* instead of *dil*, even though the resulting form was meaningless in context; and how another read KA as *pû* 'mouth' instead of *appu* 'nose'. Evidently, even among sign values which Assyriologists today do not think of as particularly rare, some were less at the forefront of transmitters' minds than others.

Comparison of manuscripts which are shown by genealogically diagnostic anomalies to have a common origin revealed an interesting diversity of attitudes to transmission. In the *Diagnostic Handbook* XVII, we saw transmitters keen on preserving the smallest details of their sources, but giving up on this when they proved obscure. In Senn Rassam MSS A

538 It is therefore likely that in line 10 MS 8 ran *ru*-[*bu*]-*ú* rather than *ru*-[*ba*]-*ú*.

and FF we encountered a transmitter who was sometimes keen to preserve details of the exemplar, and sometimes not so. It is clear that in some cases transmitters were happy to change the spellings on their exemplars. As for whether transmitters undertook restorations of damaged exemplars, the answer is that they sometimes did.

The extent to which transmitters understood their exemplars was of course variable, and generalisations are impossible on the basis of the very limited sample of manuscripts studied here. Nonetheless, our sources showed that understanding could be surprisingly slight, even among manuscripts which do not seem to be learners' exercises. Misunderstanding of course went hand in hand with hypercorrection.

In several cases it is clear that the written tradition gained the upper hand over the oral tradition. The simple fact of being native speakers did not safeguard first millennium transmitters of Akkadian from linguistic misunderstandings.[539] There is all the more reason, then, to posit variability in the ancient understanding of passages, even when to modern editors it is clear that one meaning is correct.

Some manuscripts (and some compositions) were put together by a 'cut and paste' procedure, resulting in incongruities of several kinds. Even transmitters who corrected some of these incongruities did not do so with all of them (e.g. a *kisirtu* having foundations and a parapet).

Something which emerges forcibly is how fallible our extant manuscripts, even those not obviously written by learners, can be. The implications of this will be discussed in § 6.2.

539 Weeden, *WdO* 39/1 (2009) 83 observes that the sign ésag was misunderstood at Boghazköy when it appeared in a lexical list, even though Hittites were accustomed to using it in utilitarian contexts. He comments (p. 84) that 'This furnishes a neat illustration of how distant the relationship between "everyday" writing-practices and scholastic writing can be'. It is likely that this principle is very relevant to Akkadian transmitters faced with sources not written in their vernacular.

4 Some patterns in orthography–phonology–morphology

Unser Beispiel mag … denjenigen zur Warnung dienen, die leichter Hand und ohne psychologisches Verständnis die alten Schreiber Regeln unterwerfen, die sie nach 2000 oder mehr Jahren am Schreibtische ausspinnen.

Benno Landsberger[540]

4.1 Introduction

In order to analyse extant manuscripts in terms of things such as scribal errors and wider issues of textual change, we need a detailed understanding of the orthographic and other conventions according to which the writers operated. Hence, for the foreseeable future, the practice of Akkadian textual criticism and the study of Akkadian orthography will be mutually supportive, and indeed inextricable.

This chapter will argue that Babylonian and Assyrian orthography – and morphology and phonology, which are often hard to disentangle from it – should be studied in more ways, and in more detail, than is currently the case. We shall see that several orthographic conventions have gone unnoticed or been imperfectly understood. Also, while it has long been known that orthography is a valuable source of information about the pronunciation of Akkadian,[541] its value as a source of information on other topics is less widely recognised.[542] We shall see that, if given due at-

540 Landsberger, *Brief des Bischofs* (1965) 369 n. 142, apropos of SAA XIII 178 (see § 3.2.6).

541 Notable discoveries along these lines include: Poebel, *Studies* (1939) 116–117 showing that, in lexical lists from Old Babylonian Nippur, U and Ú represent separate sounds; and the demonstration by Kouwenberg, *JCS* 55 (2003) that in (Old) Assyrian ṣ and ṭ were post-glottalised rather than pharyngeal.

542 This was remarked on by Rüster, "Materialien zu einer Fehlertypologie der hethitischen Texte", in Neu and Rüstel (eds), *2. Fs Otten* (1988) 306 n. 66: 'Auch durch die Feststellung von Schreib(er)gewohnheiten können sich wichtige Hinweise zur Textüberlieferung ergeben (vgl. StBoT 21, 1975, 13)'.

tention, spellings can shed light on issues such as procedures of redaction, ancient *Sprachgefühl*, and how cuneiform was sight-read.

It should be stressed that, whereas chapter 3 aimed to provide a survey of its topic as whole (however preliminary), this chapter has no such ambition: it consists in a series of case studies.[543] The observations made here arise simply from the author's observations while reading, and many more presumably await discovery.

Especially rewarding for the identification of orthographic patterns is the study of spelling conventions on individual manuscripts. Many Akkadianists have recognised the value of this activity. Thus Aage Westenholz discerns different orthographic habits in individual lexical manuscripts from Nippur.[544] Eckart Frahm notes that the 'Marduk Ordeal' spells the divine name 'Aššur' as *an-šár* only in a passage paraphrased from *Ee*, elsewhere spelling it ^{d}*aš-šur.*[545] Andrew George writes that 'An orthography *ka-bar* for the *status rectus* of the adjective *kabru*, "fat", would be acceptable in a later copy, but on this tablet with its impeccably regular morphology one would have to propose that the sign group is a pseudo-logogram'.[546] Similarly, Alasdair Livingstone draws attention to the problem of interpreting *ana ea ma-ši-šu* as 'to Ea, the one who wipes' (as opposed to 'to Ea, her twin') on a manuscript which is otherwise 'diptote, though not absolutely consistently so'.[547] Detailed orthographic analysis is also the foundation of James Kinnier Wilson's proposal to identify 'desonance' in Akkadian.[548] In recent years, comments on orthography have become a standard part of editions,[549] which frequently

543 We will not explore the extremely interesting issue of how orthography interacts with calligraphy, which has been raised by Sommerfeld, *Tutub* (1999) 10–11. This will surely prove to be an area of major importance in future research.

544 Westenholz, *ZA* 81 (1991) 12. See § 4.12.

545 Frahm, *Commentaries* (2011) 353.

546 George, *Iraq* 55 (1993) 68.

547 Livingstone, *NABU* 1988 p. 46.

548 E.g. a single manuscript having *a-na a-ma-ti ša-a-ti*, *ana a-mat ša-a-ti*, and *ana a-ma-ti ša-a-at* in four successive lines (Kinnier Wilson, *Iraq* 18 (1956) 146). See also Kinnier Wilson, *JSS* 13 (1968) and – on Sumerian – Kinnier Wilson, *ZA* 54 (1961) 75–77. Whether the explanation of the variation in spelling which Kinnier Wilson so acutely observes is phonetic ('desonance', i. e. the purposeful avoidance of assonance) or purely orthographic (elegant variation) is disputable.

549 See e. g. Millard, *Eponyms* (1994) 17–21 (esp. MS B10, p. 21), Goodnick Westenholz, *Legends* (1997), George, *Literary Texts* (2009), Streck and Wasserman, *Iraq* 73 (2011).

remark on 'Northern' vs 'Southern' features (see fn. 9) and the presence or absence of mimation, whether geminate consonants are so spelled, and whether word-final contracted vowels are spelled *plene*. Unfortunately, however, the orthographic-morphological analysis of individual manuscripts is still vastly under-practised. This is clear from the many fruitful patterns which have gone unrecognised (as others doubtless still do).

Also important, though it will receive less attention here, is the orthographic-morphological analysis of manuscripts that – because they were inscribed by the same person, or in the same environment – belong together as a group. More work has been done on this front than for individual manuscripts,[550] sometimes with remarkable results,[551] but here too, much probably remains to be discovered. In particular, it will be interesting to reconsider groups once the habits of individual manuscripts are better understood.

550 See for example Seminara, *L'accadico di Emar* (1998) 76 on Mašru-hamis's exceptional use of *sà* in word-initial position at Emar; Wilhelm, *UF* 3 (1971) 288 on the absence of spellings like *i-ik-ka-al* from the archive of Abdu (Ugarit); Huehnergard, *The Akkadian of Ugarit* (1989) 58 on *la* vs *la-a* at Ugarit ('It is interesting to note that individual scribes apparently preferred one writing over the other, since the two do not co-occur within the same text [i.e. manuscript, MW] or even within a set of texts written by the same scribe; the only exception I have noted is the lit. Ug. 5 162, with *la-a* in line 26', *la* in 32"); and many comments in Parpola, *LAS II* (1983) on the orthography of individual Neo-Assyrian letter writers. Note also Nurullin, *Babel und Bibel* 6 (2012) 199 with n. 33, observing that NIM is not used with sign value *ni*$_7$ or *nù* on manuscripts of the Standard version of *Gilgameš*. Wagensonner, "A Scribal Family and its Orthographic Peculiarities", in Selz and Wagensonner (eds.), *The Empirical Dimension* (2011) studies unusual spellings of Sumerian used by three closely related Middle Assyrians.

551 Gooseens, *Le Muséon* 55 (1942) 81–84 argued that, in contracts from Seleucid Uruk, it is possible to identify orthographic traits which are characteristic of individual writers, and others which are characteristic of families. This paper should have had a revolutionary impact on the study of Akkadian orthography, but despite the approving comment by von Soden, *ZA* NF 14 (1944) 239 ('In einigen Fällen konnte G. sogar besondere Schreibgewohnheiten bestimmter Schreiberfamilien feststellen') it has enjoyed a very limited reception.

4.2 Issues of orthographic consistency and convention

As is well known, the cuneiform script allowed writers many more choices than those enjoyed by users of modern European scripts. For a start, one could spell words syllabically or sumerographically, and these two possibilities in turn raised choices of their own. With syllabic spellings, CVC syllables could be split into CV-VC or left whole; a given syllable could usually be written with different signs; double consonants could be written double or single; some environments presented the choice of whether or not to use a *plene* spelling; the writer could also choose whether to prioritise etymology ('morpho-phonemic' spellings, e.g. *iškunma* for /iškumma/) and/or the word's morphological structure ('morpho-phonological' spellings, e.g. *i-par-ras-u* for /i-par-ra-sū/) over pronunciation ('phonetic' spellings).[552] With sumerographic spellings, different sumerograms might be available for writing the same word, and phonetic complements could be added or omitted.

It is equally well known that, within this enormous array of possibilites, writers did not usually choose spellings at random.[553] In the end, it is of course likely that there was an element of whim – which, it should be noted, needs distinguishing from elegant variation[554] – in orthographic choices.[555] This does not, however, absolve us of the responsibility of de-

552 Reiner, *JCS* 25/1 (1973) 25 helpfully explains the label 'morpho-phonemic' as indicating that 'the spelling preserves the phoneme known from the morphology'.

553 Sometimes, the conventions were extremely narrow. See e.g. Leichty, *šumma izbu* (1970) 27 on consistent use of igi-*mar* over igi-*ar*$_{(2)}$ and kur-*ád* over kur-*ad* or kur-*šad*. With Leichty, this consistency was probably intended as an aid to reading (see § 5.4), though in the case of scholarly writings (such as *šumma izbu* omens) the intent might have been to facilitate rapid scanning, which was probably less necessary for literature. In other words, an even higher level of disambiguation than normal might have been necessary in certain branches of scholarship, as readers might have wanted to plough through them more quickly.

554 For examples of elegant variation see Luukko, *Grammatical Variation* (2004) 170 on 'how important it was for some writers to avoid writing a word always the same way' and George, *Iraq* 55 (1993) 64 on 'variation in orthography for its own sake'. Cf. Streck, "Orthographie. B", in Edzard, Streck, et al. (eds), *RlA X* (2003).

555 For modern examples of whim in spelling and its history see Gelb, *A Study of Writing* (1963) 224–225 (including the non-representative but colourful instance of T. E. Lawrence 'Who, when asked by his perplexed publisher to try to spell his foreign words and names more uniformly, answered "I spell my names anyhow, to show what rot the systems are"').

termining how far whim extended, and how far instead orthography was governed by conventions (or the desire for elegant variation). As will be shown in this chapter, spelling conventions could extend further than is generally recognised.

So, what orthographic conventions were there for writers to respect or ignore? Why were they introduced? How wide a diffusion did they enjoy? Can they be correlated with geographical location, or the writer's educational level, or specific textual typologies? What periods did they emerge in? How long did they survive? When were they not followed, and why not, and by whom?

The more research is undertaken on such questions, the better we will understand how the ancients thought about spelling, and how choice (and whim) interacted with convention in the minds of ancient writers; and the more we will understand about the aesthetic side of orthography, about linguistic self-awareness, and about scribal education. We will also become more precise analysts of individal manuscripts, of the proclivities of individual writers and scribal centres, and of the mechanisms of textual transmission.

This chapter will undertake several case studies which shed light on the issue of orthographic consistency, both within individual manuscripts and across them. Examples of orthographic consistency within manuscripts are also provided in chapter 5.

4.3 'Soft' auto-corrections

Babylonians and Assyrians could, like all writers, become aware that they had made a mistake – or, less specifically, that (for whatever reason) something else was preferable to what they had just written. When such realisations dawned, at least sometimes the writers altered what they had written. Such alterations could take the form of, or include, erasures.[556] When an erasure is clearly present, the intent to self-correct is usually obvious.

More insidious are cases in which the writer corrected the faulty spelling by adding cuneiform signs, but without erasing or modifying the cu-

556 On these see e.g. Charpin, "Corrections, ratures et annulation: la pratique des scribes mésopotamiens", in Laufer (ed.), *Le texte et son inscription* (1989).

neiform signs already written.[557] We propose to call these 'soft' auto-corrections.[558] While in principle one could suppose that in all these cases the writer forgot to erase the superseded signs, it seems at least as likely that the writer decided to allow them to stand, for reasons of aesthetics (erasure would be ugly)[559] or laziness. Here are some instances:[560]

1) *at-ta-ti-ma* for *atti-ma* 'you (f. sg.)':[561] the writer began with the masculine pronoun *atta* (error of gender polarity, see § 3.2.11), then corrected it to feminine *atti*, but without erasing the erroneous *ta*.
2) *a-wa-bu-wa-qar-ma* for the personal name 'Abu–waqar'-*ma* (AbB II 109:3): after writing *a* the writer jumped ahead to the *wa* of *waqar*, but upon completion of *wa* became aware of the mistake and returned to *bu* – without, however, erasing the extraneous *wa*.
3) *an-ni-im-tim* for *annītim* (AbB XIV 177:18): the writer began with the masculine form *annîm* (error of gender polarity) then changed it to the feminine form *annītim*, without deleting the now extraneous IM.

557 For this principle see already e.g. AbB IV p. 32 note to 49 on *i-ta-ar-ru-ma* 'they shall return' (for expected *iturrū-ma*): 'Nach der Verteilung der Zeichen auf die Zeile zu urteilen, hat der Schreiber zunächst versehentlich den Singular *i-ta-ar-ma* geschrieben und sich dann damit begnügt, zwischen AR und MA das Zeichen RU einzufügen'. This case differs from those we shall discuss, however, inasmuch as the writer did not realise the mistake straight away.

558 For a Hittite example see Miller, *Kizzuwatna Rituals* (2004) 301 *ad* 46. Of course, spellings of this type are not confined to cuneiform. Luiselli, "Authorial Revision of Linguistic Style in Greek Papyrus Letters and Petitions (AD i-iv)", in Evans and Obbink (eds), *The Language of the Papyri* (2010) 85–86 considers that occurrences of *hapasin hapa-* on Greek literary papyri of the Roman period may *inter alia* be 'unemended lapses' or 'errors made by scribes in copying'. The first of these two possibilities, perhaps also the second, appears to be tantamount to our 'soft auto-corrections'.

559 AbB V 161:23 is a case where the writer first wrote *ša-al-ma-am*, but then realised this left an unsightly gap at the end of the line, and so repeated *-ma-am*, to fill the line. So much has been ingeniously established by Kraus *ad loc.* (p. 76). Kraus goes on to assert that the first (and now redundant) *-ma-am* is extant because the writer forgot to erase it, but since erasure would have resulted in an ugly gap, defeating the very purpose of the correction, it seems at least as plausible to suppose that the erasure was deliberately avoided.

560 In giving the examples, it needs stressing that we rely on modern editors for the absence of an erasure. Some of the cases above may be eliminated by collation, but this is very unlikely to happen to all of them.

561 Dalley, Walker and Hawkins, *OBTR* (1976) no. 28 line 29.

4) *wa-aš-ba-bu* for *wašbū* (AbB I 27:33): why *ba* was first written for *bu* is uncertain (f. pl.? m. sg. ventive? f. sg.?), but it nonetheless seems self-evident that *bu* is a correction of non-erased *ba*.
5) *ṣú-ha-re-ra-tim* for *ṣuhārātim* 'girls' (AbB I 31:11): the writer began by writing the masculine form *ṣuhārê* 'boys' (error of gender polarity), then switched to the feminine equivalent without deleting *re*.
6) *šu-ku-un-ni-ma* for *šuknī-ma* (AbB XIV 45:16): the writer began with the masculine imperative *šukun* (error of gender polarity), then realised that in fact the feminine equivalent *šuknī* was required, and so added *-ni*, but without altering the signs already written.
7) *šu-bi-bu-li-im* for *šūbulim* (AbB XII 163:8): perhaps under the influence of following /li/ (error of attraction), or perhaps owing to confusion with the imperative (*šūbil*), the writer wrote *bi* instead of *bu*, then corrected this to *bu* without erasing *bi*.
8) *is-qí-šu-im* for *is-qí-im* (AbB IV 138:9): the writer first wrote *isqišu*, which was not wrong *per se*, but then decided that *isqim* was better in the context of the sentence, so added *im* without deleting *šu*.[562]
9) *i-na mu-úh-hi-i ta-ri-bu* 'to Tarību' (AbB XI 91: r.5'): it would be very odd for the vowel of the *status constructus* to be spelled *plene*. Probably the writer first intended to write *ina muhhišu* 'to him' (for which a *plene* spelling of *i* would not be unsual), referring to Tarību (mentioned two lines earlier) with the pronoun *-šu*; but, just before writing *-šu*, decided to refer to Tarību explicitly. The (now otiose) *plene* spelling was left to stand.
10) *i-na* giš *pa-an* for *ina pān* (TP I 1 ii.2 MS 3): as seen already by Grayson, 'The GIŠ is a badly formed PA … corrected by inscribing a proper PA'.[563]
11) *ih-ru-ṣu-uṣ* for *ihruṣ* (AN II 2:55): the writer first wrote plural *ihruṣū* where singular *ihruṣ* was required, then amended it by writing *uṣ*. It is curious that this should have been thought necessary, since the spelling *ih-ru-ṣu* could also have stood for the singular (cv-cv- for /cvc/, as often in the first millennium).
12) *hur-ru-ri* for *hurrī* 'gulleys' (Asn II 19:82): the writer first wrote the singular form *hurru*, then corrected it to plural *hurrī*, which is stan-

---

562 The AbB editor describes this as a 'Kontamination' of *isqišu* and *isqim*, but soft auto-correction seems a simpler explanation.

563 Grayson, *RIMA 2* (1991) 399.

dard (hence idiomatically preferable) in the inscriptions of Assurnaṣirpal II.[564] On *ú-ut-te-ra* in line 94 of the same inscription see below.

13) *mur-tap-raš-pi-du* for *mur-tap-pi-du* 'roaming' (*BWL* 144:22 MS **a**): while writing *murtappidu* the writer got confused with the (semantically and formally) similar word *muttaprašsidu* 'fleeting' in the previous line (error of attraction, § 3.2.12), and so erroneously wrote an extraneous *raš*. On realising the mistake, the writer continued the original spelling, but left *raš*.
14) *ina nu-ru-ú-ri-šu* for *ina nūrišu* 'with his light' (*Ee* VI 128, MS a):[565] the writer began by writing something other than *ina nūrišu* (exactly what is uncertain; *ina nūruššu* 'by his light'?), but switched to *ina nūrišu* after writing RU.
15) *a-lit-ti-a-ni* for *ālittani* 'she who bore us' (*Ee* II MS a 11): the writer began with *ālittī* 'she who bore me', perhaps an error of attraction induced by *abī* 'my father' (lost, but of virtually certain restoration) at the start of the line. After writing TI the writer became aware of the mistake, and since a sign in the *t*-range was already written, simply added *-a-ni*, trusting to the reader to understand that the *i* of TI could be ignored.
16) é.gal.zag.nu.di.nu.tuku.a for é.gal.zag.di.nu.tuku.a (Senn Rass. 84, MSS A and FF): these two manuscripts share a common source (or one is a copy of the other),[566] so the error presumably goes back to the source. The writer of the source jumped ahead to NU after writing ZAG, realised the mistake, and resumed at DI, but without erasing the extraneous NU.
17) giš^{meš} kur *tuk-lat* kur-*i* for giš^{meš} *tuk-lat* kur-*i* (Senn Rass. 84, MS Z): the writer jumped ahead to KUR after writing MEŠ, realised the mistake, and resumed at TUK, but without erasing the extraneous KUR.

564 This inscription is on a stone stele (the 'Kurkh monolith'). The 'softly' corrected spelling could be interpreted as an indication that the inscription was carved onto the stele by a literate individual, but it is possible that the mistake already featured on the exemplar from which the inscription was copied.

565 The manuscript is written in Babylonian script, and therefore, following Labat, *Création* (1935) 120, we give it a lowercase siglum.

566 As observed by Frahm, see fn. 450.

18) *id-di-da-a* for *iddâ* (Senn Rass. 66, MS Z): the writer first wrote non-ventive *iddi*, then altered it to ventive *iddâ*, without erasing the extraneous DI.[567]
19) *da-a-a-nu a-na* ᶠ*i-la-ta i-ša-al-ma* 'the judge asked to (*sic*!) Ilatu' (UET VII 8:11, Middle Babylonian): Claus Wilcke suggests that the writer originally intended to write *dayyānu ana ilati iqbi* 'the judge said to Ilatu', but after writing *ana* decided instead to use *šâlu* 'to ask'.[568] Since *šâlu* takes a direct object (whereas *qabû* 'to say' takes *ana* + genitive), this seems more plausible than the hypothesis of a faulty case ending (which would be surprising in Middle Babylonian).[569]

For more examples see § 3.2.12 on ME *be-lí* and § 5.4.6 on *ma-'-at-ta-tu.*

Likely examples of soft auto-corrections also include a number of odd spellings of feminine plural nouns: *pu-ul-hi-a-tim* for *pulhātim* 'terrors', *um-me-a-tim* for *ummātim* 'summer', *ma-ti-a-ti* for *mātāti* 'lands', etc. It has been argued that such spellings are *bona fide*, i. e. that they reflect unusual spoken forms, and should not be emended away.[570] However, they would be unparalleled (and phonologically surprising) in Akkadian. Since they are readily understandable as soft auto-corrections, they are best regarded as such: the writer initially wrote (or was half-way through writing) singular or masculine plural forms (*pulhī*, *ummim*, *mātim*), then decided or remembered they should instead be feminine plural,[571] and added *āti* without correcting the signs already written. The thinking be-

567 It is interesting that the writer did not simply add *a* to *id-di* (as other writers did in *a-lit-ti-a-ni* and other examples). Is this because the resulting *id-di-a* would have looked like a vernacular Assyrian form?

568 Wilcke, *ZA* 70/1 (1981) 140.

569 This was the view of Oelsner, *ZA* 65 (1976) 291, followed by Gurney, *Texts from Ur* (1983) 127.

570 Lambert *apud* George, *Gilgamesh* (2003) 210–211. Some such instances could also be interpreted as wrong attempts at archaism (a suggestion I owe to Aage Westenholz), though this seems unlikely for *mātāti.*

571 On certain late tablets, where signs seem to be used vowel-indifferently, one could interpret a spelling such as *pu-ul-hi-a-tim* as one which aims to indicate the morpheme boundary between *pulh-* and *-ātim*, so that the *i* of HI would be purely graphic. This is, however, unlikely to apply to the examples discussed above, as the relevant sources do not display vowel-indifferent spellings (except in certain cases at the end of words, but that is a different story: here the vowels were pronounced indistinctly, and writers simply represented them as they preferred).

hind the resulting, non-erased spellings was presumably that an erasure would be ugly, and that the reader would have enough information not to be confused (cf. *a-lit-ti-a-ni* in no. 15 above).

The same principle can be invoked to explain forms other than feminine plurals, e.g. *si-qi-a-ni-šú* 'his thighs' (SAA XIII 34 r.5): perhaps the writer started to write dual *sīqīšu*, but decided to change to plural *sīqānišu* half way through. The same may apply to *bir-ki-a-šú* (*Gilg.* I 200 MS n), though on a Late Babylonian manuscript this spelling could aim to indicate the morpheme boundary, *birk–āšu* (cf. fn. 571).

The principle of soft auto-correction may also explain spellings which begin v-vc- where one expects vc-. Though one could interpret this as a way of marking initial aleph,[572] it is neither clear that initial aleph was present,[573] nor why it should be marked so sporadically. It is likely that in at least some of these cases the writer erroneously began by writing down the initial sound of the word (i.e. just the vowel) rather than its initial syllable (i.e. vc-), and then, upon realising the mistake, wrote the correct sign, but without deleting the extraneous v sign. Old Babylonian examples include *a-ab-bu-ut-ka* (AbB II 159: r.10', preceded by *annītim*), and *i-iq-bu-ku-nu-ši-im* (AbB II 120:8), though here there is the possibility of confusion with spellings of first-weak verbs. First millennium examples include *ú-ut-te-ra* (Asn II 19:94) and *a-áš-lu-la* (Senn Rass. 7, MS A).[574]

As several of the above examples show, when they are considered in isolation it is not always obvious that soft auto-corrections are such. If not recognised, the resulting sequences of signs may seem to reflect anomalies requiring linguistic explanations, when they are in fact purely graphic

---

572 That vowel signs could be so used within a word is beyond doubt, e.g. *šu-ta-i-im* and *iq-bi-a-am-ma* (AbB IV 53:16 and 19; *š.* also 55:6 and passim), *ra-i-im-ka* (AbB XI 85:7; if here *-i-* stood for a glide *y*, one would expect to find spellings such as *ra-IA-im-ka*, as *i* is unusual for /y/ in Old Babylonian). See also Veenhof, *Old Assyrian Trade* (1972) 227–228: from the fact that, in Old Assyrian, *plene* spellings are common in the *status constructus* of *dātum* '(a tax)' but not attested for its *status rectus*, Veenhof deduces that spellings of the *status constructus* such as *da-a-at* represent /da'at/. This agrees with spellings such as *da-ha-at* in Old Babylonian.

573 Sandhi spellings show it was not the rule (cf. e.g. Weeden, *BSOAS* 74/1 (2011) 62–66). Several of our examples follow consonantal *Auslaut*, so that it is impossible to suppose the written representation of a hiatus between vowels (whereas in principle this could be argued for a case such as *ù e-er-re-ši-im* representing *u errēšim* 'and the farmer', AbB XI 33:13).

574 See Frahm, *Einleitung* (1997) 51–52. No other manuscript has the extraneous *a-*.

phenomena. Accordingly, when encountering peculiar forms Akkadianists should be live to the possibility that they include soft auto-corrections.

4.4 Sounds and spellings at word boundaries

Like many writing systems, including that of Modern English, Akkadian cuneiform usually wrote words as they would appear in pausal form. Occasionally,[575] however, ancient writers recorded in writing the phonetic changes which resulted from the interaction of the *Auslaut* of one word with the *Anlaut* of the next. Such instances are the subject of the present discussion. We will be particularly concerned with two sound phenomena which can occur at Akkadian word boundaries,[576] and with their orthographic manifestations.

The first phenomenon is that conjunction of vocalic *Auslaut* and vocalic *Anlaut* results in one of these two disappearing. It is debatable whether this should be described as vocalic 'contraction'.[577] Given this uncertainty, we shall use 'crasis' as a neutral term for vowel loss through col-

575 In Ur III Akkadian, such instances are so far attested only in the spellings of personal names (Hilgert, *Akk. Ur III* (2002) 65), but as these make up the lion's share of the Ur III evidence, it is not clear whether this reflects the original distribution. Oddities in the spelling of personal names are known also from other cultures, see e.g. Clanchy, *From Memory to Written Record* (1993) 128 on Medieval England.

576 Many others doubtless occurred too. Just as in English the word 'in' is pronounced differently before 'Ghana' and 'Tibet' (before 'Tibet' the sound /n/ remains such, but the /g/-*Anlaut* of 'Ghana' causes it to assimilate to /ŋ/), so in fast speech *šikin kāri* was surely pronounced /šikiŋkāri/ (if not /šikikkāri/).

577 Hilgert, *Akk. Ur III* (2002) 65 n. 82 observes that 'contractions' in Akkadian normally result in the loss of the first vowel, whereas conjunction of vocalic *Aus-* and *Anlaut* can result in loss of the second. He therefore holds that different phonological explanations (and terminology) should be applied to the two situations. However, Hilgert derives the general principle that vocalic contractions result in the loss of the first vowel from occurrences of contraction within words. It is unclear whether one should expect the principle to apply also to contractions across words. It is noteworthy that *luprus* (from **lū aprus*), an exception noted by Hilgert, comes from what were originally two words. A different view of vowel loss was advanced by Finet, *L'accadien* (1956) § 7d, who thought that assimilation was at issue: 'Il arrive que la voyelle de la dernière syllabe d'un mot, si cette syllabe est ouverte et non accentuée, prenne la couleur de la voyelle "d'attaque" du mot qui suit'.

lision of vocalic *An-* and *Auslaut*, without committing ourselves as to whether the vowel was lost through contraction or through elision.

When crasis occurred, the norm in Akkadian seems to have been victory by *Anlaut* over *Auslaut*, though there are exceptions. One is the Assyrian word *issu*, which elided vocalic *Anlaut* in Neo-Assyrian,[578] and probably already did so in Middle Assyrian.[579]

The second phenomenon which will occupy us is re-syllabification across word boundaries. This happens very frequently in spoken speech in many of the world's languages. For example, English 'an elephant' is often pronounced in such a way that the *n* of 'an' becomes syllable-initial: /a-nelephant/. Similarly, it is well known that a spelling of *bābiš atmanī* 'to the gates of the sanctuaries' as *ba-bi-ša-at-ma-ni* (as opposed to *ba-bi-iš at-ma-ni*) in *Ah* I 69 reflects pronunciation /bābišatmanī/, syllabified /bā-bi–šat–ma–nī/.

Crasis and resyllabification could co-occur (examples below). Indeed, it is likely that in spoken Akkadian resyllabification was the norm after crasis.

The orthographic manifestations of these simple sound changes are diverse, and not all of them have always been correctly understood. Some of them are well known; some have been recognized sporadically, but not achieved wide recognition; others seem not to have been recognized at all.

When orthographic manifestations of crasis and/or resyllabification are not recognised as such, one is left with wrong-looking forms which unfairly lower one's estimation of the linguistic abilities of the relevant writer. Hence, in turn, they can have adverse repercussions on the interpretation of other parts of the relevant manuscript, and ultimately on the understanding of many aspects of Akkadian grammar and linguistic history. It is therefore important that the orthographic manifestations of crasis and resyllabification should be understood.

Resyllabification could give rise to what Assyriologists call 'sandhi'-spellings, i. e. spellings in which a single cuneiform sign straddles two words. An example is the above-cited *ba-bi-ša-at-ma-ni*, where the

578 Hämeen-Anttila, *Sketch* (2000) 37 citing [T]A-*un-na-ka* and *su-na-ka* for (*is*)*su*-(*a*)*nnaka*.

579 *iš-tu-ber-ta-an* (TP I 1 vi.40 MS 1) and ta-*ber-ta-an* (TN II 6:2), i. e. /ištubertān/, for *ištu ebertān* 'from the other side of'. Since the phenomenon is known to happen in later Assyrian and there are two examples with the same phrase, it seems sensible to posit elision rather than lipography here.

sign ŠA straddles the two words *bābiš* and *atmanī*. This basic idea needs several refinements, which we will offer in the following sections.

In the process of making these, we will introduce terms to distinguish between different types of sandhi spelling: 'simple', 'split' and 'enriched'. A '**simple**' sandhi spelling is one where the syllable which includes bits of both words is represented in writing by a single cuneiform sign (CV or CVC), e.g. *bi-ta~wi-li* for *bīt awīli* 'the house of the man' or *bi-tum-mi* for *bīt ummi* 'the house of the mother';[580] a '**split**' sandhi spelling is one where the syllable which includes bits of both words is of the type CVC, and split in writing into two cuneiform signs (CV-VC), e.g. *bi-tu~um-mi* for *bīt ummi* 'the house of the mother';[581] an '**enriched**' sandhi spelling is one where the syllable which includes bits of both words is of the type CV, but written CV-V, with an apparently redundant V sign, e.g. *bi-ta~a-wi-li* for *bīt awīli* (explanation suggested below).

Sandhi spellings have sometimes been regarded as errors, born of inadvertence or misunderstanding of words dictated.[582] As a blanket view, this presupposes an excessively normative perception of Akkadian orthography and an excessive degree of orthographic consistency in ancient writers. Clearly, writers did not employ sandhi spellings systematically,

---

580 The above examples are made up to suit the needs of the exposition. Real instances with a CV sign are numerous, e.g. *ú-li-le-qè* for *ul ileqqe* 'he will not get', *ú-li-šu* for *ul īšu* 'I do not have' (AbB XI 27:13, 28; interpretation with Stol). Real instances with a CVC sign (as in *bi-tum-mi*) are rare. An example (identified by Reiner and Civil, *JNES* 26/3 (1967) 199) is *šu-bul-tin*$_{(2)}$*-bi* for *šubulti inbi*, a term for a young scribe used in colophons at Assur and Sultantepe (Hunger, *Kolophone* (1968) nos. 225, 372 and 361) and equated lexically with *ṣehru* 'small/young' (see now Hrůša, *malku* = *šarru* (2010) 40 I 143).

581 Real example: *ma-ti~ib-la* for *māt ebla* 'land of Ebla' (OB *Gilg*. Sch.$_2$ 26; interpretation with George).

582 For example, Gurney, *JCS* 8/3 (1954) 90 argues apropos of the Sultantepe manuscript of *Gilgameš* VII that 'In two instances [*ši-ma-NA~a-a-ši* for *šimā'inni yaši* and *lu-ba-ri~ši-na-TA-a* for *lubār isinnātiya*, MW] words are run together in a way which suggests that the scribe was working from dictation, without understanding what he was writing'. A view of sandhi spellings as errors also appears to underlie Grayson, "Murmuring in Mesopotamia", in George and Finkel (eds), *Studies Lambert* (2000) 303; Edzard, *ZA* 53 (1959) 304 n. 1: 'Sog. Sandhi-Schreibungen, in denen die Wortgrenze durch ein Silbenzeichen hindurchgeht, lassen glauben, dass nach Gehör geschrieben wurde' (cf. Edzard, "Keilschrift", in Edzard et al. (eds), *RlA V* (1976–1980) 560, though the example cited there, ARM IV 65:14, is phantom, see Durand, *NABU* 1988 p. 66). Seminara, *L'accadico di Emar* (1998) 113 notes apropos of sandhi spellings in his corpus that they might be errors.

and we can see no way of predicting where they do and do not appear. Nonetheless, it is clear that at least sometimes they arose from conscious choices by writers – TCL III+ has a dense cluster of sandhi spellings, and it is impossible to suppose they are all the result of inadvertence (see § 4.4.6). That said, some instances of sandhi spelling may have been born through inadvertence.

To tell the reader that a sandhi spelling is at hand, we use the symbol ~ in transliteration: *bi-ta~wi-li*, *bi-tu~um-mi*, *bi-ta~a-wi-li*, etc.

4.4.1 'Split' sandhi spellings

If a 'split' sandhi spelling is not recognised as such, the first word may seem to end in a 'wrong' vowel. For instance, when 'days and nights' is spelled *mu-šu~ur-ri* (AbB XI 178:31), removing the ~ would give the two words heterogenous case endings (*mu-šu ur-ri*). But in fact they were almost certainly pronounced as one, after crasis and resyllabification: /mūšurrī/ for *mūšī* (*u*) *urrī*.[583]

Here are examples of how the recognition of sandhi spellings can eliminate ostensible grammatical oddities (see also fn. 695):

> *ana šu-ul-mi-ka~aš-pu-ra-am*
> 'I wrote (about) your (f. sg.) well-being' (AbB X 170:10)

The problem with interpreting this as *ana šulmika ašpuram* is that, since the addressee is female, one expects feminine *-ki* rather than masculine *-ka*. It is true that erroneous *-ka* for *-ki* is well attested in Old Babylonian letters (cf. fn. 377), but these attestations usually occur in greetings formulae, where the set phrase was inadvertently written with the (more frequently occurring) masculine suffix. Accordingly, the case above is different. Since it is sandwiched between a number of correct *-ki*s in the same letter (lines 5, 8, 11, etc.), it is simplest to posit crasis: /šulmikašpuram/ for *šulmiki ašpuram*.

> *an-hu-su~ud-diš*
> 'I restored its (f. sg.) dilapidation' (AN II 1 r.13' MS 1; Šal III 47:7 MS 4)

This phrase occurs in the inscriptions of two Neo-Assyrian kings. Under AN II, the referent is the feminine noun *kisirtu* 'bitumen facing'. Exclud-

583 Interpretation with Stol *ad loc.*, who refers to two more examples in an unpublished Susa letter, cited CAD M/ii 295.

ing some lines which represent an interpolation (§ 3.5.1), the two other suffixes referring back to *kisirtu* on MS 1 are *-sa* (i.e. *-ša*). Under Šal III, the referent is the unequivocally feminine abul.tibira *mah-ri-tú* 'ancient Tibira gate'. The other manuscripts (1-3) have the expected *-sa* in line 7, and all manuscripts, including MS 4, have *-sa* in line 10: *an-hu-sa / luddiš* 'May he restore its dilapidation'.[584] In both cases, it seems advisable to suppose crasis: /anhūssuddiš/ for *anhūssa uddiš*.[585]

When vocalic *Aus-* and *Anlaut* have the same vowel (e.g. *ša aššuri* 'of Assur') it is usually impossible to determine whether crasis and resyllabification have taken place or not. For example, on the face of things it seems hopeless to ask whether *šá(~)áš-šu-ri* represents /ša aššuri/ or (through a split sandhi spelling) /šaššuri/. Sometimes, however, the question can be decided by close study of spelling (see § 5.4.4.2 on the use of *ša* vs *šá*).

4.4.2 'Enriched' sandhi spellings

Where resyllabification impinges on vocalic *Anlaut* that originally formed a syllable by itself and turns it into part of a CV syllable, the orthographic manifestation of this can be CV-V, i.e. CV (sandhi spelling) followed by an apparently redundant V sign, e.g. *bi-ta~a-wi-lim*.[586] As noted above, we propose to call such spellings 'enriched sandhi spellings'.

We interpret enriched sandhi spellings as a means of maintaining the orthographic integrity of the second word's beginning, to help the reader recognise the word. This would have been especially important in a script which did not put spaces between words.[587] The same principle of main-

584 Vernacular pronunciation is also reflected on MS 4 in the Assyrianising form *i-šá-mu-ú* (Ass *išamme'ū*, Bab *išemmû*) in line 13.

585 Another likely example is *a-šá-re-tú~um-ma-ni-šu* 'the best troops in his army' (TCL III+ 289), as a *status constructus* in *-u* would be unexpected on this manuscript (except in epithets). See also *a-ha~am-ba-si* 'the side of the *game park*' (RINAP 3/1 no. 17 viii.19).

586 Scholars who have previously recognised spellings of this type include Streck, *Onomastikon* (2000) §§ 2.20 and 23.67, with examples from Amorite and Akkadian personal names, and W. Mayer, *GMA* (1971) § 23 on *e-mi-it-ta~a-na* (*KAR* 139:2).

587 On the importance of recognising the beginning of words in unspaced script see e.g. Hunger, *Schreiben und Lesen in Byzanz* (1989) 128: 'Die sehr oft klein gehaltenen Akzente (besonders der Zirkumflex) genügten, in Kombination mit den Spiritus in halbierter Eta-Form, durchaus zur übersichtlichen Kennzeich-

taining the orthographic integrity of word beginnings probably explains the rarity of vc for cv, or vice versa, at the beginning of words in corpora which effect the switch in other positions.[588]

Some examples of enriched sandhi spellings:

ta-ki-it-ta~a-wa-tim for *takītt(i)*[589] *awâtim*
'the confirmation of the things' (ARM II 26:11)

ni-da~a-hi for *nīd* (or *nidi*, or *nīdi*?) *ahi*
'negligence' (MDP II 17 iii.29)[590]

a-hi-i~ina for *ahû ina* (BAM 471 ii.28')[591]

an-hu-su~ú-né-kir$_6$ for *anhūssa unekkir*
'I cleared away its (f. sg.) ruined parts' (AD II 3:9 MS 1).[592]
Compare the phonetically equivalent (though orthographically different) case of *an-hu-su~ud-diš* for *anhūssa uddiš* under AN II and Šal III, in the previous section.

qut-ra~ana for *qutru ana* '…smoke to…' (BAM 480 i.38)[593]

šub-su~ú-sa-tu for *šubsi usātu* 'bring aid into being!' (*BWL* 102:65)[594]

šu-bat ne-eh-tu~ú-še-šib for *šubat nēhti ušēšib*
'I caused (them) to dwell (in) a dwelling of peace' (Sar XIV 9).
Similar phrases in Sargon's annals confirm that the construction is genitival,[595] so we know to expect *šubat nēhti* 'a dwelling of peace'.

---

nung der Wörter und *vor allem der Wortanfänge*' (italics MW). On Seminara's suggestion about marking word *ends* in Emar lexical lists see fn. 799.

588 Among the examples of cv for vc and vc for cv cited by Deller, *Orientalia* 31 (1962) 188–193, the paper which introduced the concept of these inverse spellings, only one, and a dubious one at that, appears in word-initial position: *as-a-ta* (ND 2079:1, published by Parker, *Iraq* 16/1 (1954) 33 and 54). Deller, p. 188, interprets this as a spelling of *sartu* 'fine, compensation'. If this is correct (but what about the missing *r*?), we could envisage an error of syllable inversion (§ 3.2.13) rather than conscious use of vc for cv.

589 On the elision of the *status constructus* shewa vowel see *GAG* § 64e.

590 See Aro, *StOr* 20 (1955) 66.

591 Edited by Scurlock, *Ghosts* (2006) 225. Note the spelling *a-hu-ú* on the duplicate BAM 323:67.

592 The referent of the pronoun is the feminine word *abullu* 'gate'. Subsequent words in the same passage referring back to *abullu* have feminine *-ša/-sa* on all manuscripts: line 10 *a-šèr-ša u-me*($_2$)*-si dan-na-sa ak-šu-da* (MSS 1 and 2); 11 *ištu uššī-ša* (MSS 1, 2 and 3) *adi gabadibbî-ša arṣip* (MSS 1 and 2); 16 *an-hu-sa uddiš* (MSS 1, 2 and 3).

593 See Worthington, *JMC* 5 (2005) 35.

594 See Lambert's note on his p. 314.

595 Sar Ann. 216 *šu-bat né-eh-ti* 'dwelling of peace', 289 *šu-bat ru-uq-ti* 'dwelling of farawayness'; for the phrase already in Old Babylonian see Frayne, *RIME 4*

re-še-e-ta~a-na (Asb A vii.1 MS A 8053). Other manuscripts have the expected *re-še-e-ti a-na.*

ki-ma ši-ṭir bu-ru-mu~ú-nam-mir for *kīma šiṭir burumme unammir*
'I made (it) as bright as the heavenly writing' (RIMB 6.32.1:16)

(*ša* ...) *šu-mu šaṭ-ri~i-pa-ši-ṭa* for (*ša* ...) *šumu šaṭru ipaššiṭa*
'(the one who) ... effaces (my) written name' (AN III 2:16, 6:28).

rēhāt bēl zar-pa-ni-ti [*nabû*] [*taš*]*-me-ta~a-na* for *rēhāt bēl zarpānīti nabû* [*taš*]*mēti ana*
'The remaining offerings of Bēl, Zarpanītu, Nabû (and) Tašmētu, to ...' (Sar Ann. 312, room II).

ú-ša-pa~a-na (Šal III 2 i.49 MS 1) for *ušāpi ana.* A preterite is expected from context, and indeed appears on MS 2 (*ú-ša-pi a-na*).[596] Cf. *kab-ta u // kab-tu* (§ 4.4.4), and note that in both cases MS 1 displays crasis while MS 2 does not.

When enriched sandhi spellings are not recognised, the first word looks as if it ends in a wrong vowel. This can create the impression that a manuscript exhibits 'wrong' morphology where it does not.

Enriched sandhi spellings could also disguise a *status absolutus* as an ungrammatical *status rectus*:

(*ša* ...) *ṣalma šu'ātu hulliq ša pîšu / la* ***e-pa-še~i-qa-ab-ba-aš-šú***
'(one who ...) says to him "Destroy this statue! Its dictates are not to be observed"' (Asn II 17 v.78-79)

šattišam lā ***ba-aṭ-lu~ú-kin*** *ṣēruššu*
'... I imposed on him on a yearly basis' (Senn Rass. 35 and Chic. ii.49)

In both these cases, failure to understand the orthography results in the ostensible forms **epāše* and **baṭlu*, which are difficult to parse.[597] The difficulties evaporate if it is recognised that the forms are both *status abso-*

(1990) 341 line 36. (Other sources, e. g. *Gilg.* VII 142 MS L_1, feature non-genitival *šubtu nēhtu* 'peaceful dwelling', but at XIV 9 the spelling *šu-bat* and the double occurrence of *šubat nēhti* in the Annals argue for a genitival construction).

596 Score in Yamada, *Construction* (2000) 356 line 127.

597 Both dictionaries were forced to postulate an expression *lā baṭlu* meaning 'unceasingly'. In recognition of the grammatical difficulties, CAD B 178a went so far as to give the phrase its own entry. I do not deem my interpretation to be invalidated by cases where *baṭlu* and *ukīn* are separated by a line break (e. g. Grayson and Novotny, RINAP 3/1 no. 15 iii.18–19 and no. 17 ii.73–74). *Status absolutus* forms were rare, and transmitters could easily have misunderstood the spellings, or reproduced them unthinkingly.

lutus,[598] and that the spellings refect their having been pronounced as one with the following word: /epāšiqabbâššu/ and /baṭlukīn/.[599]

For another example with the *status absolutus* (treated separately because the conjunction *u* is involved) see below, section § 4.4.4, on *zik-ru~u sin-niš*.

4.4.3 'Truncated' spellings

Sometimes, when resyllabification occurred after crasis, writers prioritised morphology over pronunciation: they kept the two words separate in writing (i. e. avoided a sandhi spelling), even though they were run together in pronunciation. We propose to call these 'truncated' spellings. They presumably represent a compromise between orthographic integrity of the second word and pronunciation of the first.[600]

We again use ~ in transliteration, to tell the reader that not all is as it seems.

Here are two examples of truncated spellings:

ba-aš~dingir, i. e. /bašilum/ for *baši ilum*
'the god is present'[601] (personal name; AbB IX 107:1 and XIV 157:3)

Here the writer wrote the word *baši* as it appeared after its *i-Auslaut* was swallowed by the *i-Anlaut* of *ilum*, i. e. as *baš*. The spoken form contained a syllable /ši/, but the word boundary was prioritised over pronunciation.

ba-la-aṭ / *iš-tu*, i. e. /balāṭištu/ for *balāṭī ištu*
'... my health since ...' (Old Babylonian; MS3057:4-5)[602]

---

598 The *status absolutus* is standard after *lā*: see Kienast, *JCS* 29 (1977).

599 The *status absolutus* of *baṭlu* in pausal form is *baṭal*. In the case of /baṭlukīn/, one can either think of the second *a* in *baṭal* as having been elided after the words were run together, or suppose that the *status absolutus* before a vowel was in fact *baṭl*.

600 The nature of truncated spellings was recognised by Knudsen, *BiOr* 43 (1986) 723–724, commenting that three spellings cited above exhibit 'sandhi'. While this seems an awkward and potentially misleading label, and the possibility of lipography is perhaps not given sufficient weight for the examples he cites, it is nonetheless clear that Knudsen understood how what we call truncated spellings work.

601 Also spelled *ba-ši*(~)dingir (AbB X 73:12).

602 I am grateful to Andrew George for permission to quote this tablet (available to me in George's copy and transliteration) in advance of publication. It will appear in his volume *Babylonian Divinatory Texts Chiefly in the Schøyen Collection*.

In line 18 of the same manuscript one finds *<ba>-l[a]-aṭ-ia*, but this probably spells a by-form of *balāṭiya*,[603] and does not impinge on the interpretation of *ba-la-aṭ iš-tu*. The sign DI is correctly written in line 11 (*še-di* 'protective spirit').

Cases as clear as these are hard to find. The following, for instance, is somewhat murkier:

li-ta-am(~)*u_4-me-šam*
'May he decree every day' (Šal III 12:40)[604]

The expected form of the verb *awû* is *lītamu* (Gt) or *lītammu* (Gtn). The adverb in *-išam* speaks in favour of Gtn *lītammu*, but the Gtn of *awû* is otherwise attested only in Old Assyrian. If one deems this sufficient reason to exclude a Gtn here, then the case is analogous to *ba-aš* dingir above, as *li-ta-am* cannot be explained as a lipographic variant of *lītamu*. If however one favoured the Gtn parsing, this could be reconciled with the expected form by positing lipography (*li-ta-am-<mu>*), and it would be difficult to determine which explanation is correct.

This ambiguity of interpretation extends to other cases:

inūma eqelšina ina bīt / ni-ik-ka-as(~)*um-ta-al-lu-ú*
'When their field was assigned at the accounts office, ...' (AbB II 158:6-7).

ši-bir(~)*ú-nu-ut tāhāzišu*
'the sceptre, his tool of battle' (AN II 2:70).
There are two definite lipographies on the same manuscript (42 *e-<mu>-qa-a-ia*, 121 *ṣi-im-<da>-at*).

šum-ma–li-ib(~)*ì-lí*, i.e. /libbilī/ for *libbi ilī*
'If (it agrees with) the heart of the gods' (OB personal name; CT 33, 47:16)[605]

---

603 Cf. *aš-šum-ia* (AbB IV 72:12, 145:4 and passim), *ina qibīt be-el-ia / ašpurakkum* 'I wrote to you at my lord's command' (AbB IV 113:10-11), *ana ni-ir-ia* 'to my yoke' (Senn Rass. 69, MSS A and FF), *kala kimtiya u sa-lat-ia* 'all my kith and kin' (*Gilg.* XI 85, courtesy Aage Westenholz), *ālik pa-an-ia* 'my predecessors' (Šal III 44:6, MS 9). (Unless they are morpho-phonological, and/or to be read as *-iya*, these spellings suggest that the genitive *i* was not stressed in the forms which they represent). Cf. also *šá-nin e-muq-ia* 'who rivals my strength' (TCL III+ 109), but here *emūqīya* is probably dual.

604 Kinnier Wilson, *Iraq* 24 (1962) proposes another interpretation (*līta*^{ww}*âm*, with the glide not marked in writing), noting however that interpreting *m* as the verb's second radical 'is perhaps preferable'. I thank Marten Stol for drawing my attention to this form.

605 Knudsen, *BiOr* 43 (1986) 723.

mu-úh(~)agurri, i.e. /muhhagurri/ for *muhhi agurri* 'on a burned brick' (Neo-Babylonian, Nabonidus year 8; Hunger (1968: n. 443) line 1)[606]

In principle, the concept of truncated spellings could be extended to the countless cases where consonantal *Auslaut* is followed by vocalic *Anlaut*, but no sandhi spelling ensues (e.g. *ba-bi-iš at-ma-ni* for *bābiš atmanī*). In the absence of crasis, however, the notion of pausal form is arguably more potent.

Some truncated spellings cause the first word to look as if it ends in a vowel. This happens when a syllable of the type CVC is spelled CV-CV:

ša-ma-ma~ú-ṣa-al-lil
'he roofed over the heavens' (*Ee* IV 138, MS a)

As the writer of so high quality a manuscript (see §§ 5.4.4.3 and 5.4.5) would surely have known, *šamû* (of which *šamāmū*, probably representing /šamāwū/, is a by-form) occurs only in the plural, so the ending *-a* is out of place. We suppose a crasis of *šamāmī uṣallil* resulting in /šamāwuṣallil/ written *ša-ma-ma~ú-ṣa-al-lil*, where *ša-ma-ma* represents /šamāw/, using the first-millennium principle that CV-CV can represent CVC.[607] For comparable spellings see *ana šá-la-la* níg.ga^{meš} (*ana šalāl makkūrī* 'to plunder goods') in § 4.4.7 and *nap-ša-ta~i-še-'u-ú* etc. in § 5.4.6.

4.4.4 Spellings involving the conjunction *u*

The points made above apply to the conjunction *u* 'and/or': resyllabification (whether or not accompanied by crasis) can lead *u* to form a spoken syllable with the foregoing word. When this happens, a sandhi spelling (simple or enriched) or even a truncated spelling may arise. We offer examples:[608]

606 Knudsen, *BiOr* 43 (1986) 724. Knudsen also cited *ka-ak* ⸢*i*⸣-[*lim*], i.e. /kakkilim/ for *kakki ilim* 'weapon of the god' ('Proto-Diri 162'), after CAD K 51a, but the edition by Civil, *The Series DIRI = (w)atru* (2004) 21 *ad* lin. 228 disposed of this spelling.

607 Another likely instance of CV-CV for /CVC/ on this manuscript is *nu-nu maš-ṭe-e* for *nūn mašṭê* 'dried fish' (line 137): *nu-nu* probably represents /nūn/.

608 Another possible case is *a-na šu-zu-ub / ù né-ra-ru-ut-te ša* … 'for the deliverance and assistance of …' (TP I 1 ii.17-18; *šu-zu-ub* is preserved on MSS 1, 3, 4; MS 5 has […-*u*]*b / ù né-ra-ru-ut-ti*; MS 2 is broken here). According to our modern textbooks, *šūzub* (*status constructus*) would be grammatically faulty here, so we should either suppose an unskilled interpolation (see § 3.5), or a truncated

ina ... / *su-un-qu bu-bu-ti* (Asb A iii.134-135 MS 1).[609] On this manuscript, genitives regularly end in *-i/e*, so we suppose *su-un-qu* to represent *sunqi u.*

ina qab-lu~ù ta-ha-zi (Esar Uruk B.19). Genitives ending in *-u* are rare under Esarhaddon, so crasis of *qabli* and *u* seems more likely.

zik-ru~u sin-niš (and similar spellings) 'male and female' (Senn, Asb).[610] The phrase *zikar u sinniš* (*status absolutus*, zero ending)[611] was pronounced as one word, *a* then being elided because of the standard rules of vowel elision: /zikar u/ > /zikaru/ > /zikru/. The new spoken syllable /ru/ was represented with an enriched sandhi spelling.

da-la-hu~ù šá-ta-a tal-ti-miš-šu 'You (f. sg.) have allotted to him muddy water to drink (lit. 'muddiness and drinking')' (*Gilg.* VI 56, MS A_1 ii.12). Elsewhere on this manuscript singular accusatives overwhelmingly end in *-a*,[612] so the final *u* on *da-la-hu* almost certainly results from crasis of *dalāha u*.

---

spelling (for *šūzubi u*). It is, however, just possible that this was a *bona fide* construction in vernacular Akkadian, evolved to cope with the fact that one could not say 'X and Y of Z' putting both X and Y in the the *status constructus.*

609 Though MS A1 of prism A has many occurrences of *-u* in place of expected genitive endings, we shall argue in § 4.5 that these should be explained as 'honorific nominatives'. If spellings belonging to this category are excluded, then genitive endings on this manuscript are usually regular.

610 *zik-ru~ù/u* munus (Senn Chic. i.51 etc.); *zik-ru~u sin-niš* (etc.) (Asb A ii.40, A ix.42, Gbr. i.54); [*zik*]*-ru~ù sin-n*[*iš*] (Asb K 2656+ 22").

611 Spellings of the phrase with *zikar* (pausal form) include e.g. Senn Chic. ii.19, Chic. iii.24, Rass. 51.

612 Line numbers after *Gilg.* VI: *a-gu-u*[*h-h*]*a* (4), *i-na* (6 and 67), *šá-ni-na* (21), *zi-i-qa* (34), *šat-ta* (47), *bi-tak-ka-a* (47 and 57), *a-la-lá bit-ru-ma* (48), *iš-tuh-ha* (54), *dir-ra-ta* (54), *la-sa-ma* (55), corrupt TA-BU-*la* (58, see § 3.2.2 sub *d*), *šu-gu-ra-a* (65), *mi-*⌜*na*⌝*-a* (71), *an-na-a* (75, 80 and 154), *a-la-a* (147), *hu-up-pa* (152), *bi-ki-ta* (159), *su-qa* (169), *šu-na-ta* (181 and 182); probably also [... *a*] *k-la* (27), [...]*-x-a* (28), and – unless construct /ummān/, cf. end § 4.4.3 – *um-ma-na* (160); maybe *kiš-šu-ta* (68; see fn. 708) and *mi-ih-ha* (78; *GAG* § 148c*?). The apparent exceptions can be explained: *i-šu-ul-la-nu* (64) and *an-tum* (genitive, line 83) are honorific nominatives (see § 4.5); *bil-tu* becomes regular if one translates 'may ... be brought to you as tribute'; *la-sa-m*[*u*] (20) and *na-ah-lap-tu* (31, line frag.) could be locatives – though, as George comments on p. 884 *ad* XI 101, locatives are unexpected in *Gilg.* as a whole, we cannot presume the Kuyunjik copyists to have been aware of this. A morphological oddity on the manuscript is *ku-da-nu* for *kudānī* (12), but as a plural this does not impinge on accusative singulars.

[p]i-riš-ti šá-ma-mu~ù eš-m[ah-(hi)] 'secret of the heavens and the underw[orld]' (Senn 182: 'Text B' line 4).[613]

ša kip-lu~ù (TCL III+ 387) for *ša kipli u* 'of rope and …'. Genitive *-u* is unexpected on this manuscript.

Perhaps also:

šu-me kab-tu siq-ri ṣi-i-ra // *šu-me kab-ta u siq-ri ṣi-ra* 'My important name and exhalted command' (Šal III 2 i.9 MS 1 // MS 2):[614] *kabta u* may have become /kabtu/, spelled *kab-tu* on MS 1. Cf. the comment to *ú-ša-pi a-na* // *ú-ša-pa a-na* (§ 4.4.2 above).

ur-ru mu-šu akpud (Sar *Stier* 48; 8 MSS). In every other occurrence of the phrase at Khorsabad (there are five),[615] the conjunction *u* is written separately, suggesting that it was a regular part of the phrase. Accordingly, there has probably been crasis: *urru u mūšu* > /urrumūšu/. Lipography is possible, however. Either way, the absence of *u* on all manuscripts suggests a common origin (see § 2.4).

4.4.5 Sandhi spellings across determinatives

Enriched sandhi spellings (perhaps also split ones, but probably not simple ones) were compatible with the second word's beginning with a determinative.

ì.giš dùg.ga-*be*~^{giš}*e-re-nu* (Asn II 1 i.87), i.e. /šamnu ṭāberēnu/ for *šamnu ṭābu erēnu* 'good oil, cedar'. All three words are accusatives, and it would be very odd under Asn II for a singular accusative to end in *e*.

a-šib-ti~^{uru}*i-ši-in*, i.e. /āšibtišin/ for *āšibat išin* 'who lives in Isin' (MB; *GAG* § 64 h*)[616]

It seems safe to infer that, in such instances, the determinatives were not pronounced.

613 George, *Iraq* 48 (1986) 133. Though the tablet is inscribed in Neo-Babylonian script, its case endings generally conform to 'good' grammar (exception: *[ṣ]er-re-e-ti šamê rabûti* 'nose-rope of the great heavens'; purely graphic?).

614 See the score in Yamada, *Construction* (2000) 343 line 9.

615 Zyl. 49 *ur-ra u mu-šá ak-pu-ud*; Zyl. 43 *ur-ru ù mu-šu … akpud*; XIV 73 f *im-mu ù mu-šu*; Ann. 403 *mu-šu ù ur-ru*; Ann. 455 *i[m-m]u ù mu-[šá/u]*.

616 See already Aro, *StOr* 20 (1955) 66.

4.4.6 Sandhi spellings mingling with sumerograms

As several scholars have recognised, sandhi spellings could arise even if one of the two words (usually the second) was spelled sumerographically.[617] When the second word is spelled sumerographically, the first can look as if it ends in a 'wrong' vowel.[618]

This principle sheds light on the seemingly irregular morphology of TCL III+, lines 357-395, where we meet a number of feminine plural construct forms. One expects these to end in *-āt*, but spellings in *-āte* and *-āti* also occur:

-ātv: 362 *nàr-ma-ka-a-te*~urudu(*erî*), *a-sa-al-la-te*~urudu, *qu-li-a-te*~urudu
363 *hu-ru-pa-a-te*~urudu
394 *a-za-na-te*~urudu
395 *nàr-ma-ka-a-ti*~urudu, *a-sa-la-a-te*~urudu, *qu-li-a-te*~urudu

-āt: 357 *t*[*e*]-*r*[*in*]-*nat* kù.GI(*hurāṣi*)
361 *a-za-na-at* kù.babbar(*kaspi*), *mu-qa-te-rat* kù.babbar(*kaspi*)
370 ⌜*a*⌝-*ri-at* kù.GI
374 *sik-kàt* kù.GI
379 *a-ri-at* kù.babbar
382 *a-ri-at* kù.babbar, *ṣip-rat* kù.babbar
384 *qar-nat* am(*rīmi*)

The principle which underpins the above spellings is as follows: when the second word begins with a vowel (e.g. *erû* 'copper') the *t Auslaut* of the *-āt* morpheme forms a syllable with following vocalic *Anlaut*,[619] resulting in spellings with a *tv* sign; when the following word begins with a consonant (e.g. *kaspu* 'silver'), resyllabification does not take place, so no sandhi spelling occurs. The three exceptions in line 392 do not vitiate the pattern.[620]

Examples from other sources:[621]

---

617 Examples from the West are given in Huehnergard, *The Akkadian of Ugarit* (1989) 109 and Seminara, *L'accadico di Emar* (1998) 114.

618 For an unusual case of the first word being spelled sumerographically see fnn. 578 and 579.

619 The question of whether written *t* in the feminine plural ending was pronounced in the vernacular (for refs see Luukko, *Grammatical Variation* (2004) 137 n. 403 and *GAG* § 64 m*) cannot be pursued here.

620 *a-ri-at* urudu(*erî*), *ṣip-rat* urudu, *gul-gul-lat* urudu.

621 Woods, *JCS* 56 (2004) 36 notes a further likely case in *a-šib-bé*~é.babbar.ra for *āšib ebabbar* 'who dwells in the Ebabbar'.

re-ṣí~dingir, i.e. /*rēṣili*/, for *rēṣū*[622] *ilim* 'help of the god' (OB omen)[623]

šèr-ti~dingir, i.e. /šērtili/ for *šēret ili* 'sin against a god' (MDP VI 10 vi.14, MB)[624]

a-ra-ku~ud^{meš}/*-mu*, i.e. /arākūmē/, for *arāk ūmē* 'length of days' (letters of Bēl-ibni, six attestations)[625]

qa-na~uru^{meš}*-ni-šú*, i.e. /qannālānišu/, for *qanni ālānišu* 'the environs of his cities' (Šal III 10 iv.29). Note *qa-ni* uru^{meš}*-ni-šú*, with *qanni* in pausal form, on the same manuscript (iv.32).

ú-šal-la~uru, i.e. /ušallāli/ for *ušalli āli* 'meadow land around the city' (Sar Ann. 337)

ultu ^{uru}*kal-ha*~uru *šarrūtiya*, i.e. /kalhāl/, for *ultu kalhi āl šarrūtiya* 'from Kalhu, my royal city' (TCL III+ 8)

ṭa-a-bé~ugu ^{d}utu, i.e. /ṭābeli/ for *ṭāb eli šamaš* 'it is pleasing to Šamaš' (*BWL* 132:100, 106 and 119 MS A)

šim-ma-ti~tuku.tuku*-ši*, i.e. /šimmatirtanašši/, for *šimmatu irtanašši* 'he will get paralysis' (BAM 323:90)[626]

ár-ni~dab*-su*, i.e. /arniṣabbassu/, for *arnu iṣabbassu* 'the sin will seize him' (KAR 384+385:9)[627]

sa-am-ma-ti~^{giš}eren, i.e. /sammâterēni/, for *sammât erēni* '*scents* of cedar' (*Gilg.* VI 13)

ka-a-re~é.zi.da, i.e. /kārezida/, for *kār ezida* 'quay of the Ezida temple' (SAA X 364:15)[628]

ša-ak-ni~^{d}bel, i.e. /šaknillil/, for *šakin illil* 'appointee of Enlil' (*passim* in the inscriptions of Šalmaneser I)

[*qú-u*]*r-di*~ištar, i.e. /qurdištar/, for *qurud ištar* 'heroism of Ištar (= a personal name)' (AbB XIV 39:29)

---

622 This is unlikely to be one of those cases in which a *status constructus* singular does service for the plural (W. R. Mayer, *Orientalia* (1990) 452–453), because this usually happens when the genitive is also plural.

623 Jeyes, *Extispicy* (1989) 1:23'.

624 See Aro, *StOr* 20 (1955) 66.

625 Attestations: de Vaan, *Bēl-ibni* (1995) 97–99. For the interpretation as sandhi spellings see already Schaudig, *Nabonid und Kyros* (2001) 137.

626 Edited by Scurlock, *Ghosts* (2006) 305. The duplicates (BAM 228:25 and 229:19') have *šim-ma-tu*$_4$ and *šim-ma-tú.*

627 Edited by Heeßel, *Divinatorische Texte I* (2007) 53.

628 Recognition that this is a sandhi spelling explains the *plene* spelling *-a-*, which one would otherwise not expect here, cf. Worthington, *JNES* 69/2 (2010) 185 n. 28.

ri-ig-ma~^{d}adad, i.e. /rigmadad/, *rigim adad* 'shout of Adad' (YOS 10 18:47; see CAD A/i 106b).

pu-uh-ri~dingir!^{meš}, i.e. /puhrilī/ for *puhur ilī* 'assembly of the gods' (KAR 74 r.13)

Note how in several cases the spellings give rise to seemingly irregular construct forms.[629]

A similar case occurs in Ur III personal names: *BE-LÍ-la*~*ri*$_{(2)}$*-ik*, i.e. /bēlarik/ for *bēlī arik* 'my lord is long'.[630] Here it is difficult to suppose pronunciation /lil/, as it would run counter to linguistic common sense. Hence we interpret *BE-LÍ* as a fossilised spelling of *bēlī*,[631] with LA showing how the word was actually pronounced.

4.4.7 A 'trap'

It is worth drawing attention here to a 'trap' which one encounters when hypothesizing sandhi spellings in the first millennium.

What look like sandhi spellings can arise through the orthographic trait of representing CVC by CV-CV. For example, *si-ta-ta* uru^{meš}*-ni* (Šal III 6 i.53), i.e. *sītāt ālāni* 'the remainder of the cities', could be interpreted as a sandhi spelling indicating resyllabification: /sītātālāni/. But it is also possible that *ta-ta* represents /tat/, as in the genitival phrases used by AN II: *ana šá-la-la* níg.ga^{meš} (*ana šalāl makkūrī* 'to plunder goods', 2:13 MS 1) and *a-bu-bu na-às-pan-te* (*abūb naspante* 'a destructive deluge', 2:67 MS 1), where a sandhi spelling is impossible. If this were so, the phrase would probably still have been pronounced with resyllabification, but the writer would have been matching speech to writing in a different way. The same ambiguity of interpretation arises e.g. with [*mit-hu-ṣ*]*u*

629 Unexpected construct forms of the type (c)vcc*i* are found in Neo-Assyrian (e.g. *re-eh-te* un^{meš} 'the rest of the people', SAA I 128: r.1), and a likely instance occurs in the very late Graeco-Babyloniaca (αρδιβηλτειος, which – with Westenholz, *ZA* 97/2 (2007) 287 – points to underlying *ardi bēltiya* 'slave of my lady'). However, this *i* is – with Knudsen *apud* Westenholz – most likely 'an epenthetic vowel in consonantal clusters across the word boundary of a construct chain', and so does not apply to the cases above, where the second word begins with a vowel.

630 The attestations are collected by Hilgert, *Akk. Ur III* (2002) 76.

631 In principle one could also suppose a 'soft' auto-correction (§ 4.3) and emend LÍ away, but this hypothesis loses plausibility in the face of the high number of attestations of this spelling.

erim$^{\text{hi.a}}$-*ia* (Asb F iii.16 // A iv.7, MS F1) for *mithuṣ ummānātiya* 'a fight with my troops' and *še-ṭu-tu* ^{m}*ul-lu-su-nu* for *šēṭūt ullussunu* 'contempt for Ullussunu' (Sargon, TCL III+ 80).

4.4.8 Glides between *i-Auslaut* and vocalic *Anlaut*

The conjunction of vocalic *Auslaut* and vocalic *Anlaut* did not always result in crasis. When the vowels coexisted, a semiconsonantal glide (*y*, *w*) could arise between them.[632] This probably happened in speech with both *i* and *u Auslaut*, but we can document the phenomenon only for *i*.

> *ku-nu-uk-ki~ia-an-n*[*i*]*-a-am*, i.e /kunukkī^{y}anni'am/ for *kunikkī anni'am* 'this sealed document of mine' (AbB IX 22:4)
>
> *nādinat a-gi~ia-a-na šarrī*, i.e. /agî^{y}ana/, for *nādinat agî ana šarrī* 'the one who gives sceptres to kings' (Ištar 3:4).[633] Here and in the following case an enriched spelling is used, to preserve the orthographic integrity of *a-na*.
>
> *šāpikat im-ri~ia-a-na alpī*, i.e. /imrî^{y}ana/ for *imrî ana* 'who pours fodder for the oxen' (Gula Hymn 38)[634]
>
> arad-*ti~ia-al-qa-a*, i.e. /ardūtī^{y}alqâ/ for *ardūtī alqâ* '... my serfdom I took' (Asb F v.39 // A vi.56-57, MS F1)
>
> lugal-*ti~iu*(IA)*-u*, i.e. /*šarrūtī^{y}u*/ for *šarrūtī u* 'my kingship and ...' (Asb F vi.30-31, BM127880; *BIWA* p. 72)[635]

It is possible that in some such cases transmitters thought they were writing the possessive ending *-ia*. For example, in the Ištar prayer above the writer might have misunderstood the spelling as *nādinat agîya ana šarrī* 'who gives my sceptre to kings' (cf. § 2.3).

---

632 It is also possible that the first vowel directly turned into the corresponding semivowel, i.e. /kunukk^{y}anni'am/ as opposed to /kunukkī^{y}anni'am/. Such a development was envisaged by von Soden, *ZA* 71 (1981) 167, suggesting that *baniat* was sometimes pronounced as /banyat/ and *ilu ul* as /ilwul/. The spellings listed above are compatible with such a hypothesis. (I regard possible triple consonant cluster as unproblematic in such contexts, though others may differ).

633 See Zgoll, *Kunst* (2004) 150 with note.

634 Lambert, *Orientalia* 36 (1967) 118. CAD Š/i 418a normalises *imrīya ana*. (I thank Charlie Draper for drawing my attention to this spelling).

635 This interpretation seems preferable to a faulty genitive form (*šarrūtiya*).

4.4.9 Summary

We have surveyed the interaction of orthography and morphology at word boundaries, identifying several orthographic principles (including 'sandhi' spellings of different kinds) applicable to these situations. Some are well known, some are not. Appropriate invocation of these principles can explain many odd-looking spellings, and absolve numerous writers of error. We have provided examples of the various principles from several varieties of Akkadian, and we see no reason to doubt that they occurred in all varieties.

4.5 The 'honorific nominative'

Titles, epithets, and divine names standing in a case other than the nominative occasionally nonetheless display the nominative ending *-u*. These instances contrast with 'correctly' written endings elsewhere on the same manuscripts, so that there seems to be a conscious drive to use the nominative ending *-u* for titles etc. regardless of their grammatical case as determined by syntax.[636] The intention seems to be to confer an absolute and unvarying quality to the epithet or title, and accordingly we propose to call this the 'honorific' use of the nominative.[637] Owing to the idioms in which titles and epithets appear, it most frequently affects what should be genitives, but a small number of cases can be found where it affects what should be accusatives.

The origin of this usage almost certainly lies in the behaviour of personal names. As is known, though rarely remarked on, a name which consists in a single declinable noun is, already in Old Babylonian, often left in the nominative whatever its syntactic role in the sentence.[638] We suppose

636 Titles and epithets of course usually appear in apposition to a name, but this in itself is no explanation of why the nominative ending should appear, as Akkadian normally maintains case concord for appositions (cf. *GAG* § 134a).

637 An instance was insightfully noted by Maul and Strauß, *KAL 4* (2011) 57: [*i*]*t-ti ellil ma-lik* kur-*ú igigī* 'with Enlil, the counsellor, the mountain of the Igigi-gods' (IV R^2 55/2 obv. 27), who viewed it an 'erstarrten Nominativ innerhalb dieses Epithetons des Enlil'. Given the multiplicity of examples (and their temporal distribution), however, we interpret such cases as common reflexes of an overarching linguistic-stylistic principle rather than as individual fossils.

638 Old Babylonian examples of nominative instead of **genitive**: *a-na ta-ri-bu* 'to Taribu' (AbB II 82:21), *ša ib-ba-tum* 'of Ibbatum' (II 98:2), *a-na*

that this habit, which has parallels in other languages,[639] was extended to epithets and titles. One could, then, apply the same term ('honorific nominative') to both personal names and epithets/titles, with the proviso that with names it is a very common phenomenon, while with epithets and titles it is rarer. If separate terms were thought necessary, for names one could use 'onomastic nominative'.

We will first give some examples of honorific nominatives (excluding personal names) from the Old Babylonian period. From the first millennium, where case endings are less regular, we will begin by citing examples where a manuscript includes non-honorific *status rectus* singular genitives in *-i/e* which provide a contrast with honorific ones in *-u*. Subsequently we will consider manuscripts on which a contrast cannot be drawn (owing to the lack of *status rectus* singular genitives in *-i/e*), but on which genitives in *-u* are nonetheless likely to be honorific nominatives. Finally, we will offer further discussion of the phenomenon.

Apparent instances of honorific nominatives can admit of other explanations.[640] For example, a possible honorific nominative features in a string of epithets of Adad (AN III 7:1): *ana adad bēli šur-bé-e etelli ilāni mug-dáš-ri bukur anim e-diš-šú-ú ra-šub-bi* 'To Adad, the greatest lord, the noblest of the gods, the powerful one, the scion of Anu, ...'. The problem is *e-diš-šú-ú*: while it could be a honorific nominative of the adjective *eddešû* 'self-renewing' (in which case *rašubbi* would mean 'terrifying'),[641] on present knowledge it would be unparalleled for a string

---

^{munus}*hu-un-na-tum* 'to Hunnatum' (II 100:22), *ša i-ba-tum* 'of Ibbatum' (II 114:23), *mēreš ta-ri-bu-um* 'the cultivated land of Taribum' (II 149:8), *a-na ri-ša-tum* 'to Rīšatum' (II 172:18), *a-na be-le-sú-nu* 'to Bēlessunu' (II 157:1), *mār sa-bu-*[*u*]*m* 'son of Sabum' (VI 168:9). Examples of nominative instead of **accusative**: ^{m}*ib-ba-tum šu'āti / ana mahrika aṭṭardam* 'I herewith send this Ibbatum to you' (AbB II 98:14-15), *anumma ša-pí-kum aṭṭardakkum* 'Now I herewith send you Šapikum' (interpretation as a personal name follows CAD Š/ii 451b; vowel length unclear). Note also *aš-šum si-ru-ú-um ù z*[*i*]*-ni-i* 'about Sirûm and Zinû' (AbB II 146:5), where the second name is inflected but the first is not. A Middle Babylonian genitive example is *ina tarbaṣ / ^{m}si-ia-tum* in Gurney, *Texts from Ur* (1983) no. 45:2-3 (Gurney, p. 127, calls it a 'rare example of false case-ending'; on ^{f}*i-la-ta* for expected ^{f}*ilati* at UET VII 8:11, which Gurney refers to, see Wilcke in § 4.3).

639 See J. N. Adam's forthcoming *Social Variation and the Latin Language*, chapter 12, esp. section 3.3 for Latin and Greek.

640 In addition to the cases discussed above, a source of spellings which look like honorific nominatives but are not is the destabilisation of case concord (§ 4.6).

641 It seems difficult to connect *e-diš-šú-ú* with the stem *ēdiššī-*, since this is normally followed by pronominal suffixes (e.g. *-šu*) rather than nominal case markers

of epithets to switch from genitive endings (*šurbê* 'greatest', *mugdašri* 'powerful') to a honorific nominative (*eddeššû*?) back to a genitive ending (*rašubbi*?). Hence we tentatively raise the possibility that ostensible *e-diš-šú-ú ra-šub-bi* should in fact be read *e-diš(i)-šú šam-ra ru-bi*, i. e. *ēdiššīšu šamra rūbi* 'solely furious of rage (i. e. who alone is truly furious)'. For this we would presume a use of the *damqa(m) īni* construction, attested in a private inscription from the same reign (*rap-šá uzni* 'broad of understanding', AN III 2002:4). Our passage may be atypical for this construction, but not, we think, implausibly so.[642] In the first millennium the construction was both rare and archaising, and might well have been poorly understood (just as it is today). Until the plausibility of a 'switch' back and forth between case endings can be assessed objectively, we find it hard to choose between the two interpretations.

Another ambiguous instance is *awâtim ša tašpuram kīma abūka anāku lulammidka* (AbB IX 250:10-13). If this is interpreted as 'I want to inform you myself, as your father, *about* the matters of which you wrote to me',[643] then *abūka* looks like a honorific nominative (which would fit the context). But another possibility is that *kīma* is a subordinator rather than a preposition (*kīma abūka anāku* 'as if I were your father'): 'I shall inform you *about* the matters of which you wrote to me as if I were your father'.[644]

Scrutiny of potential honorific nominatives is required from case to case.

(e. g. *-u*). The ingenious suggestion by Schwemer, *Wettergottgestalten* (2001) 610 n. 4926 that the locative ending *-u(m)* is in play lacks parallels. We are unlikely to be confronting the rare word *ēdiššu* known only from lexical lists, which in any case is usually spelled without *plene u* (*e-diš-šu*, *e-de-šú*, *e-di-iš-šú*, see CAD E 33b). Hence we cannot follow RIMA 2, which translates 'unique, awesome', nor CAD R 213a, which has *ēdiššu ra-šub-bi* 'who alone is awesome' (grammar?).

642 Atypical in that it does not conform to the features listed by Reiner, *StOr* 55 (1984) 179, but cf. the 'type 1' exceptions she notes on her p. 181. See also Wasserman, *Style and Form* (2003) 45–60, for detailed discussion of Old Babylonian examples.

643 Thus Stol, *AbB IX* (1981) 155.

644 A similar construction may feature in an Old Babylonian baby incantation: *kīma ša-tu-ú karānim / kīma mār sābītim / limqutaššum šittum* 'May sleep fall on him as if *he were* a wine drinker, as if *he were* a pub regular' (Farber, *Schlaf* (1989) 34–35 lines 9–11, with different interpretation: 'Wie auf Weintrinker, wie auf Stammtischhocker, möge Schlaf sich auf es senken!').

4.5.1 Old Babylonian examples

ki-ma … a-na ***šar-rum*** *ta-aq-bu-ú eš-me-e-ma* 'I heard that … you spoke to the king' (AbB XII 172:12'-14').

a-na ***ra-bi-a-nu-um*** *šu-up-ri-im-ma* 'Write to the mayor!' (AbB VII 53:23 and 54:24-25).

a-na ᵈen.ki *ù* ᵈ*dam-gal-nun-na* ***mu-šar-bu-ú*** *šar-ru-ti-šu* 'to Ea and Damgalnunna, who make his kingship great' (*Codex Hammurapi*, Prologue iv.17-20, MS B and Louvre stele; MS A has the singular, case-neutral, form *mu-šar-bi*).[645]

A letter containing three genitive feminines in *-tum* may also belong here:

a-na é *ù* ***mu-ut-ta-al-li-tum*** 'to the household and to the *muttallītum*' (twice) and *a-na* ***ṣú-ha-ra-[t]um*** 'for the young women' (AbB VII 91:6, 8, 27).

Note also *ana* ⌜*narām-s*⌝*în* ***šar-ra-šu*** 'to Narām-Sîn, his king',[646] different from the other examples (*status possessivus* rather than *status rectus*).

4.5.2 Clear examples in Assyrian royal inscriptions

In the following cases, individual manuscripts include sufficient genitives in *-i/e* to provide a clear contrast with the honorific use of *-u*.

4.5.2.1 Assurnaṣirpal II 26

An inscription preserved on several stone tablets uses honorific nominatives for the titles of the king's ancestors:

mār tukultī-ninurta šarru **gal-*ú*** *šarru* ***dan-nu*** *… mār adad-nērārī / šarru* **gal-*ú*** *šarru* ***dan-nu*** 'son of Tukultī-Ninurta, great king, strong king, … son of Adad-nērārī, great king, strong king' (Asn II 26:2-3).

Elsewhere in the inscription, all genitives end in *-i/e.* Examples include *šākin / li-i-te* 'achiever of victory' (13-14), *qereb tam-ha-ri* 'the midst of battle' (17), *le'û qab-li* 'able in battle' (42), *ina lìb-bi* 'inside' (52), *ana muš-pa-li* 'to the bottom'. The contrast between genitives which have become honorific nominatives and other genitives obtains on all published manuscripts.

645 Manuscripts cited after Borger, *Lesestücke* (2006).
646 Goodnick Westenholz, *Legends* (1997) 194 line 19.

4.5.2.2 Adad-nērāri III 1 and 2

Three stone pavement slabs bear an inscription which begins thus:

> *ēkal adad-nērārī šarru rabû šarru* ***dan-nu*** 'palace of Adad-narari, great king, strong king' (AN III 1:1)

After 'palace of' one expects the genitive, but the king's title is given a honorific nominative. The same happens some lines later with the epithets of the ancestors, for whom syntax would also have us expect the genitive:

> *mār šamšī-adad / šarru rabû šarru* ***dan-nu*** *...* 14 *mār māri ša aššur-nāṣir-apli zikru* ***qar-du*** *...* 15b *pír-'v / adad-nērārī rubû* ***na-'-du*** *...* 21 *līp-līpi ša šulmānu-ašarēdu šarru rabû šarru* ***dan-nu*** 'son of Šamšī-Adad, (who was a) great king, strong king, grandson of Assurnaṣirpal, (who was a) valiant man ... offspring of Adad-nērārī, (who was a) reverent prince, ... descendant of Šalmaneser, (who was a) great king, strong king' (AN III 1:9-21).

By contrast, *status rectus* singular genitives in the rest of the inscription end in *-i/e*, as expected:[647] dù *gim-ri* 'the totality of everything' (9), man *pa-ni* 'previous king' (24), *a-lik mah-ri* 'predecessor' (25); also ta *TAM-TIM* gal-*ti* 'from the great sea' (5) and *a-di TAM-TIM* / gal-*ti* 'to the great sea' (6-7).[648]

A stone stele almost certainly begins with [*ana*] *adad* '[to] (the god) Adad' (AN III 6:1). After the preposition *ana* one would expect Adad's epithets to stand in the genitive, but he is given honorific nominatives: ***qar-du šar-hu*** (line 1), [***gí***]***t-ma-lu*** (2). The same is true of the epithet of an ancestor: *šarru* ***dan-nu*** 'great king' (9). By contrast, other *status rectus* singular genitives on the stele display the expected case marker *-i/e*: [*na-a*]-⌜*ši*⌝ *qí-na-an-zi* kù-*te* 'bearer of the pure whip' (5), *a-na* ^íd^*pu-rat-te* 'to the Euphrates' (13).

Another stone stele of Adad-nērārī calls him *mār šamšī-adad šarru* ***dan-nu*** 'son of Šamšī-Adad, (who was a) great king' (AN III 2:2), with a honorific nominative in the epithet of Šamšī-Adad. A further honorific nominative appears later: *šum*(mu) ... *ber ellil* ***AŠ-ŠUR-ú*** '(in) the name of ... Ber, the Assyrian Enlil' (line 11). The two honorific nominatives contrast with three non-honorific genitives in *-i/e*: *kī ri-mu-ti* 'as a gift' (10),

647 *ul-tú ul-la-a* (lines 26-27) is a special case, as the phrase appears with the ending *-a* even in the second millennium.

648 In the last example, only gal-*ti* is significant; the spelling *TAM-TIM* is fossilised.

āšib uru kaskal-*ni* 'who dwells in Harrān' (12), *ina dan-na-ni* 'by brute force' (15).[649]

4.5.2.3 Sargon

In room V of Sargon's palace at Khorsabad, where, as numerous examples show, genitive endings are normally regular, the honorific nominative ending attaches to two divine names standing in the genitive, to a total of three attestations:

> *rēhāt* … [***zar***]***-pa-ni-tum*** … ***taš-me-tum*** 'the offerings of … [Zar]panītum (and) … Tašmētum' (Ann. 312)[650]
>
> *ana* … [***taš-me***]***-tum*** 'To … [Tašmē]tum' (Ann. 325)

The inscription in Khorsabad's room XIV begins like the pavement slabs of Adad-nērārī III (AN III 1), discussed above: *ēkal šarru-ukīn šarru* **gal-*ú*** *šarru* ***dan-nu*** 'palace of Sargon, great king, strong king' (Sar XIV 1); the same considerations apply. In the rest of the inscription, genitives are regularly spelled with the expected ending *-i/e*, e. g. *kiš-šá-ti* (line 1), *nam-ri* (36), *ni-i-ri* (67), *el-li* (72).[651]

4.5.2.4 Esarhaddon

> *ēkal aššur-ahu-iddina šarru* **gal-*ú*** *šarru* ***dan-nu*** … / ***re-é-um ke-e-nu*** 'Palace of Esarhaddon, great king, strong king … firm shepherd' (Nin. i.1-4). In the rest of the inscription genitives are regular, with many examples.
>
> *mār sîn-ahhē-erība / šarru* **gal-*ú*** *šarru* ***dan-nu*** */ šar kiššati šar māt aššur / šá-ak-nu ellil* (Ass. i.5-8). Other genitives in the inscription end in -i/e.

4.5.2.5 Assurbanipal

A sizeable crop of likely honorific nominatives occurs on a large, very well preserved clay prism bearing an inscription of Asb (MS A1):

> *ina bīt ridûti /* ***áš-ru nak-lu*** 'in the house of succession, the artful place' (i.23-24)

---

649 Line 18 also has [*ina*] *narê an-né-e* 'on this stele', but since the endings of nouns ending in a contracted vowel evolved differently from those of other nouns (a matter I intend to discuss elsewhere), this is not directly comparable.

650 The parallel passage in room II has the genitive ending for Zarpanītu (*zar-pa-ni-ti*), while the case marker on Tašmētu has been lost through crasis with following *ana* (*taš-me-ta~a-na*, see § 4.4.2).

651 The seemingly aberrant *ne-eh-tu* in line 9 reflects crasis (*ne-eh-tu~ú-še-šib*), see § 4.4.2.

guggu šar māt luddi ***na-gu-u*** *ša ina nēberti tâmti /* ***áš-ru ru-u-qu*** 'Gyges, king of Lydia, a region which at the crossing of the sea, a distant place, ...' (ii.95-96)

qaqqad teumman šarrv̄šunu / ***mul-tar-hu*** 'the head of Teumman, their arrogant king' (iii.36-37)

ina simāni arah sîn bēl purussê / māru ***reš-tu-u a-šá-re-du*** 'In Sivan, the month of Sîn, lord of resolutions, firstborn (and) foremost son' (iv.110-111)

ana tammaritu ekṣu ***ba-ra-nu-u*** 'to Tammaritu, the insolent rebel' (v.31)

ṣalam tammaritu **egir-*ú*** 'a statue of the later Tammaritu' (vi.55)

ina simāni arah sîn / māru ***reš-tu-u a-šá-re-du*** 'In Sivan, the month of Sîn, firstborn (and) foremost son' (viii.96-97)

ina mad-bar ***áš-ru ru-u-qu*** 'In the desert, a faraway place ...' (viii.108)

ina ābi arah qašti / mārat sîn ***qa-rit-tu*** 'In Ab, the month of the Bow (constellation), the heroic daughter of Sîn' (ix.9-10)

ina ^{kur}*hukrina* **kur-*ú mar-ṣu*** 'in Hukrina, a tough mountain' (ix.15)

narām libbi ... / mullissu ri-im-tú ^{d}en.líl.lá-*i-tu* 'heart's desire of ... Mullissu, the Enliline wild cow' (ix.74-75)

mahar mullissu ummi ilāni [rabûti] / ***hi-ir-tu*** *narāmti [aššur]* 'before Mullissu, mother of the [great] gods, spouse beloved of [Assur]' (x.26-27)

qé-reb ninua / ālu ***ṣi-i-ru*** 'in Nineveh, the great city' (x.51-52)

mušarû šumiya abīya / abi-abīya zēru ***da-ru-ú*** *ša šarrūti* 'the inscriptions bearing the name(s) of myself, my father, my grandfather, eternal kingly offspring' (x.111-112)

This manuscript uses honorific nominatives more freely than other manuscripts, and indeed some cases do not look particularly 'honorific'. Just as the writer of this manuscript was confused about where to put the *plene* spelling in suffixed feminine plural nouns (§ 4.10.3), we suspect that he or she misunderstood the principle of honorific nominatives, and thought that the ending *-u* applied to all appositions.

4.5.3 Likely examples in the Assyrian royal inscriptions

In the following cases, forms which are syntactically genitive but end in *-u* are – owing to context (titulary) and to the fact that genitives in most Neo-Assyrian royal inscriptions have 'correct' endings – very likely to be honorific nominatives. Since, however, these inscriptions are so short that there are not sufficient other genitives with which to draw a clear contrast, we list them separately from the examples above.

ēkal aššur-dān šarru ***dan-nu*** 'palace of Assur-dān, strong king' (AD II 5:1, three bricks)

mār RN *šarru* ***dan-nu*** *mār* RN *šarru* ***dan-nu*** 'son of (royal name), strong king, son of (royal name), strong king' (AD II 5:2,3,4 = three bricks)

ša šamaš-ilu ***tar-ta-nu*** 'of Šamaš-ilu, the field marshal' (AN III 2014:1, label on golden bowl)

ana ištar-dūrī ša-rēši / ša nergal-ilāya / ***tur-ta-nu*** 'To Ištar-dūrī, eunuch of Nergal-ilāya the field marshal' (AN III 2009:1-3, cylinder seal)

4.5.4 Other examples from the first millennium

4.5.4.1 Neo-Assyrian

[*a-na*] dumu lugal **gal-*u*** '[To] the son of the great king' (SAA X 195:1, Adad-šumu-uṣur)

4.5.4.2 Standard Babylonian

gimil-ninurta ana ēkal ***mal-ku*** *iltakan pānīšu* 'Gimil-Ninurta directed himself towards the palace of the king' (*Poor Man of Nippur*, line 70)[652]

gimil-ninurta ana mahar ***mal-ku*** *ina erēbišu* 'When Gimil-Ninurta entered into the presence of the king' (*Poor Man of Nippur*, line 72)

The signs KU and KI being similar in Neo-Assyrian script, one could emend *mal-ku* to *mal-ki*! (supposing an error of sign similarity). However, in view of both the double occurrence and the word involved ('king'), the interpretation of the spellings as honorific nominatives seems preferable. Other genitives on this manuscript have the 'correct' ending.

4.5.5 Further discussion

Use of the honorific nominative seems to be optional: some manuscripts do not use it at all, even though opportunities present themselves. Other manuscripts use it, but not consistently. A good example of inconsistency

652 The original edition of this composition by Gurney, *AnSt* 6 (1956) is out-dated in many respects. See the improvements in Gurney, *AnSt* 7 (1957) 135–136 and several other works cited by Foster, *Before the Muses* (2005) 936.

occurs at the beginning of an inscription extant on two stone statues from the reign of Adad-nērāri III:

> *ana nabû* ***da-pi-ni šá-qé-e*** *mār esaggil igigallu* ***šit-ra-hu*** */ rubû* ***kaš-ka-šu*** *… /* ***re-me-nu-ú*** *muš-ta-lu … /* ***re-me-nu-ú ta-ia-a-ru*** 'To Nabû, exalted hero, wise (and) splendid son of Esagil, mighty prince, …, merciful and relenting' (AN III 2002:1-7).

Here the expected genitive marker is used in the first epithet (*dapīni šaqê* 'exalted hero'), but later in the string there was a switch to the honorific nominative. This was used in all other epithets on which case markings are visible, over a further six lines. There are several ways to account for this heterogeneity: one is to suppose that the list of epithets was compiled from several sources (cf. § 3.5); another is to suppose a conscious stylistic device (e.g. perhaps the honorific nominative was more arresting if used after a normal genitive ending). Another possibility still is that what we propose to term the 'destabilisation of case concord' has occurred.

4.6 The destabilisation of case concord

Honorific nominatives are not the only reason why some manuscripts whose case endings conform to particular patterns sometimes display aberrations. This could also happen owing to the 'destabilisation of case concord'. We will suggest that this could be induced by distance, or by agreement with 'logical' case as opposed to 'grammatical' case.

A stele of Šamšī-Adad V (no. 1) begins [*a*]*na ninurta* 'To (the god) Ninurta', and a string of epithets of Ninurta follows. From lines 1 to 8, all epithets on which case marking is visible are in the genitive (1 *ga-áš-ri*, 2 [*šá-g*]*a-pi-ri šur-bi-i e-tel-li*, 5 *ma-am-li*, 6 *šit-ra-hi*, 8 *šu-pi-i*), while from line 17 to 23 only nominative markers appear (17 *šit-lu-ṭu*, 18 *gis-gal-lum*, 20 *dan-dan-nu ṣi-ru šur-bu-ú*, 22 *ṣur-ru šum-du-lu*, 23 *e-tel-lu*). We suppose that here the words ending in *-u* were so far removed from 'Ninurta' that case concord was abandoned because the original case was forgotten.

Similarly, the report of Sargon's 8th Campaign (TCL III+) contains a long passage about the mountain Uauš. This begins thus: *ina uauš* kur-*i* gal-*i* 'In Uauš, the great mountain …' (line 96). Here the epithet of Uauš, which stands in the genitive, displays the expected genitive marker *-i/e*. By contrast, after two and a half lines of relative clauses, another epithet in apposition to Uauš has a nominative case marker: kur-*ú zaq-ru* 'sharp-peaked mountain' (line 99).

In addition to distance, a factor which may have triggered the change in case marking here is the presence of the relative clauses: Uauš being their logical subject, the (nominative) case of *šadû zaqru* 'pointed mountain' may have been determined by agreement with this.

A similar explanation may fit the difficult line 132: *itti narkabat šēpīya ēdēnīti u sīsê ālikūt idiya ša ašar nakri u salmi lā ipparakkû ki-tul-lum pe-er-ra-<ni> sîn-ah-uṣur* 'With my single personal chariot and the cavalry who ride at my side, who neither falter in enemy or friend(ly) territory, the *kitullu*,[653] *p.* of Sîn-ah-uṣur'. The same ambiguity exists in Akkadian as in English: the *kitullu* and the *perrā<ni>* of Sîn-ah-uṣur could either stand in apposition to the cavalry, or be listed alongside them as separate items. We here adopt the former view, as this enables an explanation of the forms: the cavalry are the logical subject of the relative clause, and *kitullu*, in apposition, exhibits concord with what has now become the cavalry's logical case (nominative).[654] As for *pe-er-ra*, this would be morphologically aberrant on this manuscript,[655] so the emendation *pe-er-ra-<ni>* is almost certain.

Under Assurnaṣirpal II genitives regularly end in *-i/e*. The following sentence is, therefore, odd: *ana* ^{uru}*išpilipria āl dannūtišunu u* **kur-*ú* *mar-ṣu*** / *ittaklū-ma* 'They trusted (for safety) to Išpilipria, their fortified city, and (to) the impassable mountain' (1 ii.16-7). Since here there is no great interval between the endings *-i* and *-u*, distance is unlikely to be the reason for the discrepancy. In our view it was more likely the intervention of *āl šarrūtišu*: as this lacked an overall case marker, and

653 The word *kitullu/kidullu* is *hapax* and difficult; CAD K 476a followed by CAD P 411b notes that in similar formulations the place of *kitullu* is taken by *idāya*, and accordingly translates it as '(my) side(?)', as an object of the verb *ipparakkû*. AHw 495b proposes instead that *kitullum* might be a troop formation.

654 On another manuscript, one might simply take *ki-tul-lum* as a hypercorrect form, or posit vocalic indifference in the sign LUM (i.e. = /li(m)/), but these would be the only such instances on TCL III+. Excepting *a-bu* in line 1 (a likely honorific nominative) and kur-*ú zaq-ru* in line 99 (discussed above), *ki-tul-lum* and *pe-er-ra* in line 132 are both unique (*ki-tul-lum* contrasts with about 300 other forms in the genitive singular *status rectus* on the tablet which all end in *-(t)i/e*). Thus they invite special discussion.

655 There are four other singular construct forms of nouns (incl. verbal infinitives) with CVCC- stems on the manuscript, and all of them end in *-i*: *tu-ur-ri* (32) and *tur-ri* (55, 57, 61), *kun-ni* (54), *kap-pi* (98, unless dual), *lìb-bi* (4).

was therefore isomorphic with the nominative/accusative, it facilitated the shift to nominative/accusative *-u*.[656]

When studying a manuscript's use of case endings, instances which could reflect destabilisation of case concord should be analysed as a group in their own right, without prejudice to the behaviour of other groups.

4.7 Analyses of case markers on individual manuscripts

Here we will study the use of *status rectus* case endings on individual manuscripts.[657] In particular, we will be interested in first millennium manuscripts whose use of case endings is sufficiently consistent that exceptions can be meaningfully identified, and principles distilled from them.[658]

As noted in § 4.5, we need to take into account the possibility of honorific nominatives. Another complication is that certain spellings are semi-logographic, i. e. they are fossilised, and do not represent the form which was read aloud.[659]

Understanding apparent oddities in case-marking is important: it can raise our esteem of writers, causing us to reconsider whether other oddities on their manuscripts might in fact have a justification. Of course, showing that a manuscript is morphologically 'correct' does not necessarily mean that, morphology aside, its readings are better than those on a

656 If correct, this explanation hovers at the interface of errors and *bona fide* linguistic phenomena, and it is hard to classify exclusively in terms of one of these two categories.

657 As noted above, orthography and morphology are sometimes hard to disentangle. Here, however, parallels from other languages (and linguistic common sense) suggest that we are confronting truly linguistic phenomena rather than ones confined to the realm of spelling.

658 In the second millennium, case endings on nouns and adjectives were – give or take the odd archaism or peculiarity (including honorific nominatives, § 4.5), and ignoring mimation – simply dictated by the rules of vernacular grammar. In the first millennium, matters were different: as is well know, around 1000 BC case marking collapsed in the vernacular Babylonian *status rectus*, while in vernacular Assyrian it survived but with modification. Accordingly, first millennium manuscripts display great variability in how they spell case endings.

659 See e. g. § 4.4.6 on *BE-LÍ-la-ri*$_{(2)}$*-ik*, § 5.4.5 on *TAM-TIM* and § 5.4.8 on *-TIM* as a fossilised complement to sumerograms.

manuscript whose morphology is poor.[660] But if it is known that the morphology is good, this can help in understanding details. Indeed, we shall see that sometimes the analysis of case endings (whether one regards it as an orthographic or morphological exercise) leads to different translations.

4.7.1 *Gilgameš* I MS B

In relating his first dream to his mother Ninsun, Gilgameš says the following:

> *ib-šu-nim-ma kakkabū*(mul^{meš}) *šamê*(an-*e*)
> *kīma*(gim) *ki-iṣ-ru ša* ^{d}*a-nim im-ta-naq-qu-tú e-lu ṣēri*(edin)*-ia*
> *áš-ši-šu-ma da-an e-li-ia*
> (I 247-249)

The translation in the most recent edition reads as follows:[661]

> The stars of the heavens appeared before me,
> Like lumps of rock from the sky they kept falling towards me.
> I picked one [lit. *-šu* 'it', MW] up but it was too much for me.

This interpretation was followed e.g. by Stefan Maul and Wolfgang Röllig:

> Da erschienen mir Sterne des Himmels.
> Wie Brocken des Anu fallen sie immer wieder auf mich hernieder.
> Ich hob einen an, doch er war zu stark über mir.[662]

> (...) erschienen mir die Sterne des Himmels,
> wie Meteoriten stürzten sie ständig auf mich nieder.
> Ich wollte (einen) heben, da war er mir zu schwer.[663]

There are two linguistic difficulties with this interpretation. One is syntactic: there is no antecedent for *-šu* 'it' in line 249. The other is morphological: for 'like meteors' one would expect *kīma ki-iṣ-ri(kiṣrī) ša anim* rather than *kīma ki-iṣ-ru ša anim.*

The unexpected *ki-iṣ-ru* is preserved only on MS B_1. There may well be first millennium manuscripts on which *-ū* for expected *-ī* would not be

660 This is well known among Classicists, see e.g. Dain, *Les Manuscrits* (1949) 155: 'L'idée qu'on se fait, à tort ou à raison, de la qualité d'un manuscrit, ne doit pas, en principe, entrer en ligne de compte dans le choix d'une leçon'.

661 A survey of earlier translations of *kīma ki-iṣ-ru ša anim* is given by Streck, *Bildersprache* (1999) 88. Streck himself translates as 'Etwas wie ein Meteor Anus'.

662 Maul, *Das Gilgamesch-Epos* (2008) 54.

663 Röllig, *Das Gilgamesch-Epos* (2009) 43–44.

surprising, but this does not apply to MS B, which displays extremely 'good' grammar. In particular, singular accusatives on MS B regularly end in *-a* (24 examples).[664]

That is not to say that the manuscript is faultless: at I 231 the thinking behind the spelling *ri-šá-tu*[*m*] (nominative) seems to be that it is a substantivised feminine plural adjective, subject of the two statives (i. e. 'the happy ones were graced with, and full of, charm'), whereas *ri-šá-*(*a*)*-ti* (accusative, found on two manuscripts) yields a better construction; and at I 239 *lā ṣālilu ša ur-ra ù* gi$_6$ involves an odd relative clause (or perhaps lipography of *-āte*).[665]

Other scholars ascribe a further linguistic fault to MS B, but here we think it can be vindicated. At I 188 the dictionaries interpret *di-da-šá* as an accusative dual form, for which *dīdīša* would be expected. CAD D 135b maintains that this word only appears in the plural and dual, but in view of the small number of attestations this seems unduly categorical, and indeed AHw 169a recognises the existence of the singular. It seems feasible to suppose that the writer of *di-da-šá* regarded it as a singular form with a literary anaptyctic vowel. The writer of MS x, who wrote *di-da-a-šú*, may well have had a dual in mind, but that does not impinge on the interpretation of MS B.[666]

The overall impression one derives from MS B is that the writer was highly proficient in morphology, and it would be odd for such a writer to write 'like meteors' as *kīma ki-iṣ-ru*. Indeed, when it is clear that 'like meteors / like a meteor' is intended, we find *ki-ma ki-iṣ-ri* (line 152).

664 *ka-ti-im-t*[*i~ipte*] in line 7 is almost certainly a split sandhi spelling. Otherwise: [*n*]*ag-ba*, line 3; [*ni*]*-ṣir-ta*, 7; *ṭè-e-ma*, 8; [*u*]*r-ha ru-uq-ta*, 9; *maš-qa-a*, 111; *u*$_4$*-ma 2-a*, 115; *ur-ha*, 148; *nam-maš-š*[*á-a* …], 159; *ha-rim-tam*/*ta*$_5$, 162; *lul-la-a*, 185 and 192; *ba-la-ṭ*[*a*], 233; *eṭ-lu-ta* … *bal-ta*, 236; *k*[*u-u*]*z-ba*, 237; *dan-na e-mu-qa*, 238; *šu-na-ta*, 245; [*k*]*a-la*, 260; *šá-ni-ta šu-ut-ta*, 276; [*ma-l*]*i-ka*, 297. Perhaps also *bi-nu-ᴜ*[ᴅ] in line 230 ([*har-ma*]*-a-ti* [*-m*]*a*? *bi-nu-ᴜ*[ᴅ]).

665 At I 240, MS B has *še-ret-su* 'his sin', referring to Gilgameš, for *še-ret-ka* 'your sin', referring to Enkidu (on two other manuscripts). If not a deliberate variant, it is evidence of inadvertence rather than morphological incompetence.

666 At I 199 MS B has *ul-tah-hi-iᴅ* 'he jumped back' for *ul-tah-hi* 'he was defiled' (attested on two other manuscripts). Though *ultahhi* may well be poetically superior to *ultahhiᴅ* (thus George), this does not prove it is original – transmitters could improve as well as corrupt. Be that as it may, this is not a morphological error, and so, like *še-ret-su* in the previous footnote, does not impinge on the interpretation of *ki-iṣ-ru*.

Given this, the simplest way to interpret MS B is to take *kīma* at I 248 not as a preposition but as a subordinating conjunction: 'When (*kīma*) a meteor fell down on me, I picked it (*-šu*) up but it was too much for me'.

The suggested interpretation brings the Standard version closer to earlier ones, where the lines corresponding to I 248 of the Standard version contain no comparison.[667] It also removes the necessity of the emendation of [*ki*]-*ṣir* to [*ki*]-<*ma ki*>-*ṣir* at I 262 on MS h: *kīma* 'when' on MS B is otiose in terms of the overall meaning, and MS h dispensed with it: 'A meteor fell down on me, I picked it up but it was too much for me'.

Our suggested interpretation is not undermined by the use of the Gtn stem, for the Gtn stem in this line need not necessarily imply the fall of multiple meteors. It can render the idea of a single meteor's gradual fall to earth,[668] and *maqātu* Gtn is several times so used for other celestial phenomena (see CAD M/i 244a, N/ii 279b, AHw 607a). The present tense (replaced by a preterite at I 262) most likely has a durative nuance.

Everything we have written so far about this manuscript may seem to pertain to trivial matters of detail. In fact, however, the change in meaning alters the symbolism in the dream (which portends the arrival of Enkidu). According to the translations by other scholars cited above, the passage would say that Gilgameš picked up a star which had fallen to earth like a meteor. Thus Enkidu would be represented in the dream not *by* a meteor, but by a star which fell to earth *like* a meteor. In our interpretation, by contrast, the meteor ceases to function as a *tertium comparationis,* and symbolises Enkidu directly. This in turn opens the way to a new interpretation of the two dreams of Tablet I. Since this interpretation is not directly relevant to the primary aims of this chapter, we put it in an independent subsection, but it should not be forgotten that it hinges on the orthographic-morphological analysis conducted above, and serves as an illustration of the finds which such analyses can yield.

---

667 See OB II 7 x (x)-*rum ša anim imqutam ana ṣēriya* 'A … of Anum fell onto me (or: before me)' and the (probably Middle Babylonian) tablet recently edited by George, *RA* 101 (2007) 64 line 9: *kiṣru ša ani imquta ana ṣēriya* 'A meteor fell down onto me (or: before me)'.

668 Similarly Landsberger, *JNES* 17/1 (1958) 58, translating *zunnāni kīma kakkabi mitaqqu*[*tā*]*ni kīma nabli* in a medical prayer/incantation as 'Rain down like star-shoots, fall down and down like meteors!'. A different interpretation of the *Gilg.* passage is proposed by Streck, *Bildersprache* (1999) 89, who sees in the Gtn an indication that the dream is a recurring one.

4.7.1.1 Enkidu as an axe of meteoric iron

In the first of his two dreams in Tablet I (lines 246-258), Gilgameš sees a meteor (*kiṣru ša anim*, lit. 'lump of rock of the sky-god') fall down to earth; in the second (I 276-285), he sees an axe (*haṣṣinnu*). Both objects, the meteor and the axe, attract an enthusiastic crowd. Gilgameš 'loves' (*râmu*) the objects 'like a wife' (*kīma aššati*),[669] and his mother makes them his equal (*šutamhuru*). Ninsun explains these dreams as signs that Gilgameš will acquire a 'mighty companion who will save (his) friend' (*dannu tappû mušēzib ibri* I 268 and 291).

All scholars are agreed that the two dreams symbolise Enkidu's coming. The question is, how does the symbolism work? Why two dreams? Why is there no mention of Enkidu's remarkable transformation from wild animal to human being? Or of the unusual way in which he was created (from a pinch of clay, by the goddess Aruru)? And above all, why a meteor and an axe?[670]

Before suggesting an answer to these questions, we need to introduce an existing interpretation which, much as we respect its ingenuity, we find wanting. In a paper in the Festschrift for Fritz Kraus,[671] Anne Kilmer (building on an idea of Turan Tuman) suggested that *kiṣru* 'lump' and *haṣṣinnu* 'axe' are veiled allusions to the words *kezru* and *assinnu*, two terms pertaining to male prostitution in the cult of Ištar.[672] The Tuman/Kilmer

669 Building on an observation by Wilcke, *Acta Sumerologica* 20 (1976) 210 about Sumerian, Streck, *Bildersprache* (1999) 41–42 made the exciting discovery that in Babylonian figurative language the verb is usually chosen to match the term of comparison, not vice versa. Thus e.g. 'they flew like birds' does not imply that they actually flew – rather, that they moved as straight and as fast as birds fly: the use of the verb 'to fly' is simply induced by the comparison with birds. Hence 'to love like a wife' (whether the simile matches the subject or object) does not necessarily imply sexual contact between Enkidu and Gilgameš. The implication could simply be 'You will be as fond of him as a husband is of his wife'. (Is it possible that *kīma* here means 'instead of?' Depending on how one understood the idea of 'love' here, this too could be compatible with a platonic friendship).

670 Ninsun herself gives us a pointer, telling us that 'his strength is as mighty as a meteor' (*kīma kiṣri ša anim dunnunā emūqāšu* I 293): part of the function of the meteor is to represent strength. We shall see that this is not the whole story.

671 Kilmer, "A Note on an Overlooked Word-Play in the Akkadian Gilgamesh", in van Driel, Krispijn, Stol and Veenhof (eds), *Studies Kraus* (1982).

672 On the *assinnu* and *kulu'u* see Maul, "*kurgarrû* und *assinnu* und ihr Stand in der babylonischen Gesellschaft", in Haas (ed.), *Außenseiter* (1992) and George, "Babylonian Texts from the Folios of Sidney Smith, Part Three", in Guinan,

view has proved influential,[673] even beyond the confines of Assyriology.[674] To anyone who accepts it, it becomes self-evident that the relationship between Gilgameš and Enkidu was sexual.

What originally led Tuman to the idea of connecting *haṣṣinnu* 'axe' with *assinnu* 'male cultic prostitute' was the idea that an axe in Gilgameš's second dream was hard to account for – it lacked a 'rationale'. Rather than providing such a rationale, the Tuman/Kilmer interpretation circumvents it: the axe was never important *qua* axe, rather it only served as spring-board for the sexual allusion. Read thus, the second dream ends up looking rather weak: it has no sensible surface meaning, only an oblique allusive sense. Another difficulty is that the word *assinnu* was closely connected to the word *kulu'u* (another term related to male prostitution), which was used as a term of abuse.[675] We think it unlikely that the poet would have used such a word of Enkidu, or had Ninsun do so.

If no other explanation of the dreams were forthcoming, then the Tuman/Kilmer interpretation could perhaps be left to stand, and its problems overlooked. Another interpretation can, however, be proposed.

The rationale behind the meteor in Gilgameš's first dream is clear: it represents the pinch of clay which Aruru threw down to earth from the heavens, to create Enkidu in the wild (I 102-103).[676] What, then, about the similarity between *kiṣru* and *kezru*? The hypothesis of allusion is unnecessary. Long before we hear of Gilgameš's dreams, Enkidu is described as *kiṣir ninurta* 'knit strong by Ninurta' (I 104),[677] and his animal strength is twice compared to the strength of meteoric iron: *kīma kiṣri ša* *ᵈanim dunnunā emūqāšu*, lit. 'His strength is as mighty as a lump of

de Jong Ellis, Ferrara, Freedman, Rutz, Sassmannshausen, Tinney and Waters (eds), *Studies Leichty* (2006) 175–177.

673 E.g. Walls, *Approaches* (2001) 56; George, *Gilgamesh* (2003) 452–454, esp. 454. Streck, *Bildersprache* (1999) 89 is cautious: 'Möglicherweise handelt es sich um ein Wortspiel mit *kezru*'.

674 E.g. Conner, Sparks, Sparks and Anzaldúa, *Cassell's encyclopedia of queer myth, symbol, and spirit: gay, lesbian, bisexual, and transgender lore* (1997) s.v. 'Gilgamesh'.

675 See Llop and George, *AfO* 48/49 (2001/2002) 5 line 63'.

676 Once it is accepted that the meteor directly symbolises Enkidu, it becomes understandable why the meteor is said to have 'feet', and the emendation proposed in § 6.2.4 becomes plausible.

677 Thus George's elegant paraphrase, lit. 'lump of Ninurta'. The root √*kṣr* is applied to the creation of bodily beings in the phrase *dāma kaṣāru* 'to knot the blood-vessels', attested in a Mari letter and at *Ee* VI 5. See most recently Ziegler, *JMC* 5 (2005) 4–5.

rock of the sky god' ([I 125], I 152; repeated by the shepherds at II 43). Thus, when it appears in Gilgameš's dreams, the relevance of the word *kiṣru* to Enkidu is already well established in a way which is semantically plausible, and there is no need to suppose the word was introduced for the sake of a pun with *kezru*.

As for the axe in the second dream, we propose that its symbolic function becomes apparent if one supposes it to be made of a metal of meteoric origin (probably iron). Just as the axe was made from 'raw' meteorite, so the humanised Enkidu whom Gilgameš is to meet will have arisen from a much wilder 'raw' version: he will be made out of the clay which, like the meteor which supplied the iron for the axe, fell from the sky.[678] Thus, although Ninsun's interpretations of Gilgameš's dreams make no overt reference to Enkidu's creation or transformation,[679] these are inherent in the symbolism: the first dream symbolises Enkidu in his pre-human state, the second symbolises him in his humanised state.

This interpretation coheres with the fact that at I 288 Ninsun says the axe represents a man (*haṣṣinnu ša tāmuru* lú 'The axe you saw is a man', on the likely absence of *-ma* see § 4.7.2). She does not say this about the meteor, despite the many verbatim overlaps between the two dreams and their interpretations (though admittedly this point is not probative, see fn. 690).

A few words are necessary on the plausibility of our passage alluding to meteoric iron.[680] Roger Moorey expressed scepticism that this material was in use in Mesopotamia in the early second millennium BC, when Gilgameš's dreams are first attested.[681] Be that as it may, for our purposes it is sufficient that awareness of it existed.[682] Perhaps the strongest evidence

678 An interpretation similar to this was arrived at independently by Peter De Ville.

679 Perhaps we should understand Ninsun's report to be 'telescoped' (cf. Worthington, *JRAS* 21/4 (2011) 409). If so, this reminds us of the complexity of the Epic: not everything is explained. (Cf. Sallaberger, *Das Gilgamesch-Epos* (2008) 38: 'Vom erzählerischen Standpunkt aus bietet ein Traum … die Chance, eine weitere Bedeutungsebene zu schaffen').

680 The problems with supposing a reference to meteoric iron were pointed to by Streck, *Bildersprache* (1999) 89: 'Wusste man im Alten Orient, dass Meteore nicht immer in der Atmosphäre verglühten? Kannte man die Herkunft des Meteoreisens?'

681 Moorey, *Materials and Industries* (1994) 178–179.

682 Such awareness is attested in Hittite Anatolia (see e.g. refs in Valério and Yakubovich, "Semitic word for "Iron" as Anatolian Loan-word", in Nikolaev (ed.), *Fs Ivanov* (2010) esp. 112; they argue that the Akkadian word *parzillu*, attested

for such awareness is an Old Babylonian hymn to Papulegarra: *mi-qì-it pa-ar-zi-il-li-im ša qaqqara irassu* 'fall of (meteoric) iron which crushes the soil'[683] – even if one wanted to dispute the translation of *parzillu* as 'iron', it would still be clear that awareness existed that metal of some kind came from the heavens, and this suffices for the purposes of our argument. Axes of meteoric iron are also very probably mentioned in the Sumerian poems *Lugalbanda in the Mountain Cave*,[684] *Šulgi D* 160,[685] and *An axe for Nergal* line 4,[686] for all of these are subject to Andrew George's observation that an.na 'can hardly be tin, which is useless for an axe-head'.[687]

In connection with the symbolism of the axe, mention is due to Tablet VIII, where Gilgameš is mourning Enkidu.[688] He calls him

haṣṣin ahiy[a tukl]at idiya
namṣar šībiya arītu ša pānīya

Axe at m[y] side, [tru]st of my arm,
sword at my belt, shield afore me.
(VIII 46-47)

Its proximity to 'sword of my belt, shield afore me' suggests that 'axe at my side' is no empty phrase used for the sake of a pun with *assinnu.*[689]

---

from Old Assyrian onwards, is an Anatolian loanword deriving from a putative Luvian root *parza-*). For iron in Hittite writings generally see Friedrich and Kammenhuber, *Wörterbuch, vol. III fasc. 13* (1998) 206–214 (*hapalki*) and Weeden, *Logograms* (2010) 152–154.

683 CAD (P 213 and earlier volumes) cites this passage after the copy by Pinches, "Hymns to Pap-due-garra", in Anonymous (ed.), *JRAS Centenary Supplement* (1924) Plate VIII, line v.21. It has been more recently edited by Streck and Wasserman, *Orientalia* 77/4 (2008), after collation. Their translation 'the iron meteorite that smashed the ground' (p. 344; also SEAL, number 2.1.14) is free: *miqtu* is not 'meteorite', but 'fall (of a meteorite)'.

684 George, *Gilgamesh* (2003) 793.

685 ETCSL reads nagga but translates 'meteoric iron'.

686 ETCSL t.5.7.3, ha.zi.in an.na.

687 George, *Gilgamesh* (2003) 793. It is also worth noting that *Lugalbanda* and *An Axe for Nergal* use the Sumerian word ha.zi.in, equivalent to the Akkadian word *haṣṣinnu* which appears in Gilgameš's dream.

688 That *haṣṣinnu* 'axe' in VIII 46 alludes to the second dream was noted already by Streck, *Bildersprache* (1999) 117: ('spielt … auf die Enkidu symbolisierende Axt im Traum des Gilgameš an').

689 There is, however, a different pun in the Old Babylonian version (II 35-36): *aštakanšu ana ahiya* can mean both 'I placed him at my side' and 'I made him my brother'. That the sentence could be read in two ways was first pointed out by Ungnad, *ZA* 34 (1922) 17, while Schott, *ZA* 42 (NF 8) (1934) 103 was the first

Rather, the idea of Enkidu as an axe is intended to be taken seriously, and probably, like the other items of military gear, symbolises Enkidu's role as protector of Gilgameš. This, in turn, should inform our interpretation of the axe in the dream, to which the same notion applies: the axe not only symbolises Enkidu's transformation from beast to human, but also his future role as Gilgameš's fellow warrior and protector.

Admittedly, on the basis of the interpretation of the dreams here proposed, one might expect the kissing of feet to occur in the second dream (which in our view represents the humanised Enkidu) rather than the first (which in our view represents the pre-human Enkidu). Foot kissing is absent from the second dream also in the Old Babylonian version. This does not seem an insuperable difficulty, however: though we understand the dreams to symbolize sequential stages of Enkidu's existence, it is obvious that not *all* the content of the two dreams is supposed to be understood in sequential fashion.[690] For example, they both (I 258 and 285) refer to Ninsun making Enkidu Gilgameš's equal, though in the waking world this only happened once. We suppose that the first dream would lead interpreters to envisage foot kissing as some point in the prophesised events, regardless of its absence from the second dream.

All in all, then, *haṣṣinnu* 'axe' and *kiṣru ša anim* 'meteor' make good sense in Gilgameš's dreams: they are integrated into the narrative which precedes and follows, and they are well explicable in terms of oneiric symbolism. Since the hypothesis of word-play with *assinnu* and *kezru* **a)** introduces probably offensive language which one would not expect to be applied to Enkidu and **b)** is unnecessary, it seems better not to suppose that a word play *haṣṣinnu–kiṣru–assinnu–kezru* was deliberately worked into the Epic.[691] Also, it no longer seems justified to use word-play as evidence for the relation between Gilgameš and Enkidu being sexual.[692]

to realise that the two meanings could be in play simultaneously ('Statt mit Ungnad … mich für eine der beiden möglichen Übersetzungen gegen die andere zu entscheiden, nehme ich ein Wortspiel an'). Subsequent responses have included hesitation (e.g. Tigay, *Evolution* (1982) 83 n. 36 'a double entendre may be intended here') and full acceptance of the pun (e.g. Westenholz and Westenholz, *Gilgamesh – Enuma Elish* (1997) 9–10, 'Dobbelttydigheden er utvivlsomt bevidst'). The double meaning of *ahu* as 'side' and 'brother' presumably carries into line VIII 46 of the Standard version (see George, *Gilgamesh* (2003) 183).

690 This is why above we deemed the fact that Ninsun says that the axe represents a man, but does not say this of the meteor, to be non-probative.

691 The possibility of secondary interpretations in antiquity must however be allowed for, and we cannot rule out that some ancient audiences understood the Epic precisely *à la* Tuman/Kilmer.

In sum, morphological analysis of *Gilg.* I MS B suggests that in Gilgameš's first dream Enkidu is symbolised directly by a meteor, not by a star compared to meteor. This in turn makes it possible to suggest that Gilgameš's two dreams in Tablet I of the Epic symbolise Enkidu in his pre-human state (raw meteorite) and after humanisation (axe, made from the meteorite). We offer this as an example of how, in the study of individual manuscripts, the smallest and most trivial-looking detail can have surprisingly wide-ranging implications.

4.7.2 *Gilgameš* VI MS **a**

As we know from its colophon,[693] MS **a** of *Gilg.* VI, from Assur, was produced through copying (gim libir.ra.bi *šá-ṭir*[!]) by a *šamallû ṣehru* 'junior apprentice'. This manuscript (consisting of the two fragments $\mathbf{a}_1$ and $\mathbf{a}_2$) exhibits a number of oddities. In isolation they might suggest incompetence on the part of the writer, but if the manuscript is analysed *in toto*, a different picture emerges, with some interesting results.

Unusually for the first millennium, the manuscript uses the old accusative singular ending *-a* (at least 22 examples),[694] and a number of instances where the ending *-a* seems not to occur are susceptible of straightforward explanations.[695] Hence the polyvalent UD sign at the end of singular

692 Other indications of homoeroticism are doubtful – note the observation of Foster, "Akkadian Literature", in Ehrlich (ed.), *From an Antique Land* (2009) 178–179: 'A more plausible interpretation [than homoerotic love, MW] is that the poet feminized Gilgamesh's feelings because in Akkadian literature women were considered to have deeper and more accessible emotions than men'. We see much wisdom in the summary of the matter by Ziegler, "Gilgameš : le roi héroïque et son ami", in Durand, Römer and Langlois (eds), *Le jeune héros* (2011) 298: 'La question de savoir si c'est une amitié homoérotique ou au contraire platonique qui reliait les deux hommes n'est pas cruciale pour le narrateur. Il laisse la question volontairement sans réponse évidente, même si des éléments sont donnés'. (I owe this reference to Gonzalo Rubio).

693 Hunger, *Kolophone* (1968) no. 255, George, *Gilgamesh* (2003) 739.

694 Line numbers after *Gilg.* VI: *a-gu-ha* (4), *la-sa-ma* (20), *šat-ta* (47), *bi-tak-ka-a* (47), *bit-ru-ma* (48), ⸢*iš*⸣*-t*[*uh*]*-ha zi-iq-ta dir-ra-ta* (54), *la-sa-ma* (55), [*da-l*]*a-ha ù šá-ta-a* (56), *bi-tak-ka-a* (57), *re-'-a na-qid-da* (58), ⸢*tu*⸣-[*u*]*m-ra* (59), ⸢*mi-na-a*⸣ (71), *ak-*[*l*]*a* (73), *a-la-a* (94 and 103), *an-na-a* (also *qa-ba-a*, if *ša* 'of' should be added) (113), *a-pa* (117), *a-l*[*a-a*] (147), [*a-r*]*u-ra-ta* (152). Perhaps also *š*[*á-ni-n*]*a* (21, though the signs are very fragmentary).

695 At $\mathbf{a}_2$ v.19' (*Gilg.* VI 152), [*hup-p*]*i~it-ta-di* is almost certainly a split sandhi spelling (§ 4.4.1) reflecting crasis of *huppa ittadi.* At $\mathbf{a}_{1+2}$ v.27'-28' (159), the manu-

accusatives should probably be read *-ta₅* or *-tam* (not *-tú*).[696] It is true that on at least one Neo-Assyrian manuscript (TCL III+, see § 5.4.6) nouns with stems ending in *-t* did not display the same variation in case endings as other nouns, but this manifestly does not apply to MS **a**: *šat-ta*, *dir-ra-ta*, etc.

We are left with a small number of morphological oddities in the manuscript,[697] most of which can be explained easily. The peculiar *annâ qabâ ištar* 'this speech of Ištar's' (**a₂** iv.5', *Gilg.* VI 113) probably simply involves lipography of *ša* 'of'. Given the similarity of KU and KI, genitive *nap-la-ku* at **a₂** v.3' (140) is probably a *lapsus styli* – when the same words occur again (at **a₂** v.11', *Gilg.* VI 146), one meets the expected spelling *nap-la-ki*. Where other manuscripts have *elmēšu qarnāša* 'its horns are *elmēšu*-wood', **a₁** i.12 (*Gilg.* VI 11) reads *el-me-še qarnāši*. The ending on *el-me-še* can be explained by interpreting the form as a plural (or perhaps even dual):[698] 'its horns are *elmēšu*-trees'.[699] At **a₂** iii.14' (89), *tag-ge-ri-i* looks like an N form (thus George), but then it would be problematic for it to take a direct object. We interpret it as a phonetic spelling.[700]

script is fragmentary: *bi-[ki-]x iš-ku-nu*. Though the broken sign can be interpreted as *-t]u*, *-t]a* looks at least as likely from the copy. At **a₂** ii.29' (64) *i-šu-ul-la-n[u]* is a personal name, and so not subject to ordinary morphological rules (cf. the introduction to § 4.5).

696 Thus *šu-na-*UD at **a₁** vi.4' (*Gilg.* VI 182) and *an-ni-*U[D] at **a₂** iii.3' (*Gilg.* VI 80). The reading of *q[iš-*U]D at **a₂** iv.10' (117) is uncertain, as there could be crasis with following *u*.

697 At **a₂** iv.4' (112), it is more likely that *a-[n]a uz-z[u(-)...]* is incomplete than that it exhibits genitive ending *-u*. Perhaps restore *ana uzzuz* 'to make ... furious' / 'at the utter fury of ...'. Genitive *an-tum* at **a₂** iii.7'-8' (83) is not surprising in a name (see introduction to § 4.5). Where other manuscripts have the obscure *a-ba*, **a₂** iii.14' (*Gilg.* VI 89) has *a-bu*. Without knowing more about *a-ba*, we cannot establish if *a-bu* is an error or not.

698 If *erēnu* 'cedar' could be plural in Neo-Assyrian, *elmēšu* probably could too.

699 While we cannot absolve the writer of error in using accusative *-ši* instead of possessive *-ša*, this may well be an error of attraction (§ 3.2.12) under the influence of *el-me-še* rather than a reflection of morphological incompetence.

700 When resyllabification in fast speech created syllable-initial consonant clusters, Akkadian speakers might well have heard a mini-vowel, i. e. /ta–grî/ might have been heard as /ta–g^{e}rî/, since there is evidence that what speakers of a language hear is determined by that language's sound ('phonotactic') constraints. In Dutch, glide stops between nasals and following obstruents (such as /^{k}/ in the English word 'youngster' /yun^{k}stə/) are more likely to be heard in clusters in medial position, where they do not violate sound constraints, than in final position, where they do (see Warner and Weber, *Journal of Phonetics* 29 (2002)). More

The masculine suffix in *pâšu* 'his mouth' (**a$_2$** iii.18', *Gilg.* VI 92) is very odd referring to Ištar (one expects *pâša* 'her mouth'), but interestingly the two Kuyunjik manuscripts also have it. If it is an error, at least we may suppose that our writer transmitted rather than initiated it, but thinking also of another grammatically masculine form used of Ištar in *Ištar's Descent*,[701] one wonders whether her association with cross-dressing and gender ambiguity sometimes caused Ištar to be referred to as a man (or whether certain transmitters thought this to be the case).

The phrase *na'id qab-lum* 'expert in battle' (ii.18', *Gilg.* VI 53) appears as *na'id qabli* on other manuscripts. One could explain *na'id qablum* as a different (and in fact grammatically easier) construction (stative + locative), but it is also possible that we should connect it with accusative *ú-tul$_5$-lum* a few lines later (**a$_2$** ii.23', *Gilg.* VI 58) and suppose an orthographic habit in the writer, whereby LUM was used generically to represent the ends of words with stem-final *l* (compare the use of *-tum* on *Ee* IV MS a, § 5.4.5).

We cannot account for *ug*-UGU-*ma* instead of *uggugat* (**a$_2$** iii.4', *Gilg.* VI 81). Frankena suggested an error of sign similarity (UGU for *gu-gat*).[702] Be that as it may, this single instance need not lower out esteem of the writer too badly.

So far, then, we have a manuscript which once has *-ši* for possessive *-ša* (but plausibly as an error of attraction), once has *ug*-UGU-*ma* for *uggugat-ma*, once has *pâšu* instead of *pâša* (but other manuscripts have

---

spellings which can be interpreted in this way are [*ni*]-*im-me-ra-ni* for *nimrāni* 'leopards' (Šal III 16:347') and *na-da-ba-ku* for *natbāku* 'terrace' (attestations in AHw 766). (In the latter case, von Soden, *AfO* 18 (1957–1958) 122 sought to explain the voicing of *t* to *d* independently of *b*, but with Streck, "Keilschrift und Alphabet", in Borchers, Kammerzell and Weninger (eds), *Hieroglyphen, Alphabete, Schriftreformen* (2001) 78 it seems simplest to suppose that *d* and *b* are in contact, and that this is the cause of the voicing. This was probably also the reasoning of Thureau-Dangin, *Huitième Campagne* (1912) 6:21, transliterating *na-ad-ba-ak*). The much later Graeco-Babyloniaca contain vowels of this type: σαφαλις for *šapliš* 'below' and ασανω for *asnû* 'Dilmun date' (Sollberger, *Iraq* 24/1 (1962) 65, A3 rev. 2 and 66, A4 rev. 3).

701 *lā tanaddâšši* for expected *lā tanaddîšši* 'Don't knock it down!', line 23 (MS A). Or is *lā tanaddâšši* for *lā tanaddīšši* an error of attraction (§ 3.2.12), triggered by the foregoing string of syllables containing *a*?

702 Frankena, "Nouveaux fragments de la sixième tablette de l'Épopée de Gilgameš", in Garelli (ed.), *Gilgameš et sa légende* (1960) 117.

this too), may once have *utullu* instead of *utulla.* Otherwise, its morphology is excellent,[703] and its ostensible oddities can be vindicated.

It is against this background that we approach the final two, and most interesting, oddities:

> **a**$_2$ ii.33' (*Gilg.* VI 68)
> *[i-š]u-ul-la-na kiš-šu-⸢ta⸣-ki i na kul*
> 'O Išullānu, … your power'
>
> MS A (Kuyunjik) has *ī nīkul* 'let's eat'.
>
> **a**$_2$ ii.34'-35' (*Gilg.* VI 69)
> *⸢ù⸣ qa-at-ka ⸢šu-ṣa⸣-am-ma / [l]u-pu-⸢ut hur⸣-d[a]*-x-*na*
> 'So put out your hand and touch …!'
>
> MS A has *hurdatni* 'our vulva'.

These two cases belong together, both because each of them involves MS **a**'s NA for MS A's NI for, and because on MS A the words have the same plural referent ('us', used rhetorically by Ištar).

From our examination of MS **a**, it seems very unlikely that the writer would consciously spell *ī nīkul* 'let's eat' as *i na-kul* in the same way that first-millennium manuscripts which are vowel-indifferent might.[704] It does not look like a phonetic spelling,[705] an explanation which would also implausibly leave *-na* at the end of the following line unexplained.[706] One

703 The variant *indennâ* (Gtn) for *umtannâ* (Dtn) in line 85 may be intentional or inadvertent, but it hardly detracts from our estimate of the writer's proficiency in morphology.

704 As observed by Lambert, Sultantepe manuscripts have a preference for signs in the *a*-range regardless of the spoken vowel. The curious mè^{meš}*-na-ṭu-lu* for *tāhāz-ni iṭṭulū* 'they saw our might' on MS **e** of *Gilg.* VIII 22 may reflect this preference: if, with George, *Gilgamesh* (2003) 854, crasis has occurred, it is hard to envisage verbal *Anlaut* being elided by an accusative ending, so the spelling would (despite the use of the sign normally read as *na*) represent /tāhazniṭṭulū/. But lipography of *i-* or *iṭ-* is also possible.

705 Long *a* sometimes changed to long *e* – e. g. *ma-ha-za-ni-ia // ma-ha-ze-ni-ia* (Senn Rassam 60 MS FF), *ma-ha-za-a-ni-ia // ma-ha-ze-ni-ia* (Asb F vi.20), *bīt hi-la-ni-šú // bīt hi-le-ni-šú* (Asb A x.102) – so it is likely that written *ā* was sometimes pronounced as vernacular /ē/ (as often in Arabic, where the phenomenon is known as *imaala*). Hence if one were to suppose that *nīkul* was pronounced /nēkul/ (which seems esp. possible for Assyrians), one could perhaps just about imagine *nīkul* being written with an *a*-vowel. (We mention this idea for completeness's sake, but do not favour it; as noted above, it would leave *hurdat-na* unexplained).

706 Frankena, "Nouveaux fragments de la sixième tablette de l'Épopée de Gilgameš", in Garelli (ed.), *Gilgameš et sa légende* (1960) 117 reports a suggestion

might wonder whether Ištar is being made to speak hardcore vernacular Akkadian to render her advances to Išullānu more vulgar, but: a) such a use of distinctly vernacular forms would be without parallel in *Gilgameš*; b) there is no evidence that /nākul/ and /hurdatna/ were vernacular forms; c) the vernacular equivalent of *ī nīkul* would in first millennium Babylonian probably have dispensed with *ī*.[707] On present knowledge, therefore, this does not convince.

We therefore propose that MS **a** transmits the following tradition:

išullāna kiš-šu-ta-ki~i-na numun
u qātka šūṣâm-ma luput hur-da-ta-na

Išullānu, your[708] power is in seed(s),
so stretch out your hand and touch, (you) *hurdatānu*!

We interpret the spellings *i-šu-ul-la-na* and *hur-da-ta-na* as morphologically 'correct' vocatives (i.e. *išullān* and *hurdatān*, with zero ending), cv-cv spelling /cvc/.

In this interpretation, the passage contains two double-entendres: 'seed' refers both to the domain of gardening and to sperm; the very rare word *hurdatānu*[709] (only attested once elsewhere) denotes a type of date-palm, but, whatever its true etymology, for an Akkadian speaker it would have borne an obvious relation to *hurdatu* 'vulva', and would in fact furnish a good parallel to the vulgar Italian word *ficaiolo*. Here again a single word would simultaneously encapsulate the domains of gardens and sex.

---

by von Soden that the spelling is 'neu-spät-babylonisch' (i.e. it is a purely graphic variant of *hurdatni*), but as shown above this is radically at odds with the orthography elsewhere on the manuscript.

707 *GAG* § 81 g (examples in W. R. Mayer, *Orientalia* 56 (1987) 58 *ad* 8' and 9'; Borger, *BIWA* (1996) 22 *ad* A i.125).

708 Addressed to a man, we would expect 'your' to appear as *-ka* rather than *-ki*. Crasis of *ka* with following *i-Anlaut* resulting in an enriched sandhi spelling is likely, but it is possible that some readers (and transmitters) understood the signs on MS A as *kiššūta kī nīkul* 'how were we able to taste strength?' (see § 2.3). (Or is Ištar deliberately addressing Išullānu as if he were female?)

709 AHw 358b does not question the reading; CAD H 99a notes the polyvalency of the sign HUR, and books the word under *ḫardatānu*, observing that it might also be read *murdatānu*. However, nouns in *-ānu* are usually derived from pre-existing nouns, and neither *hardatu* nor *murdatu* is attested as a noun in its own right. The reading *hurdatānu* therefore seems likeliest. CAD notes that the underlying noun might be *hurdatu* 'pole of a chariot' rather than *hurdatu* 'vulva', but for the purposes of our interpretation this is immaterial.

In the first line one might expect *-ma* after numun, but we do not deem its absence a serious obstacle to the suggested interpretation. Compare I 288 *haṣinnu ša tāmuru* lú 'the axe which you saw is a man', which likewise lacks *-ma.*[710] Three possibilities are: a) lú in fact represents *awīlum-ma*, with *-ma* included in the logogram; b) *-ma* was not thought necessary; c) its absence is lipographic. All these explanations can apply to numun at VI 68.

Whether MS **a** itself had *hur-d*[*a-a*]*t-na* or *hur-d*[*a-t*]*a-na* in line 69 is uncertain (both seem possible from the published copy). The spelling *hur-da-at-na* is found in a quotation of this line on a medical commentary from Nippur of uncertain date.[711] In our intepretation this results from a misunderstanding of *hur-da-ta-na*. If the date-palm-related word *hurdatānu* was as rare in spoken Akkadian as it is in our extant sources,[712] it might well have been misunderstood and emended to *hurdatna* (as in the Nippur commentary), particularly if the person who undertook the emendation was familiar with a recension with *hurdatni* 'our vulva', as on MS A. The change of *ina zēri* to a plural verb *ī nīkul* would then become possible.

There is a case for arguing that the version which we find on MS **a** is original, and that on MS A a modification of it. On the other hand, Alexa Bartelmus observes in a personal communication that *hurdatni* produces an elegant chiasmus (acc. verb, verb acc.). We therefore leave the question open of which version is earlier and which derivative.

---

710 In theory, lú could represent the stative *awīl* 'it is a man', but this would be an odd formulation in *Gilgameš.*

711 Frahm, *Commentaries* (2011) 104 and 230-231.

712 This is admittedly very uncertain. As John Tait pointed out to me many years ago, future scholars could read a great many of our novels and newspapers without seeing the flower name 'pansy', and conclude that it was extremely rare. Indeed, in one sense it is. Yet it is a simple enough word which we all know, and its occurrence would not surprise people in the way that 'iwis' or 'sesquipedalian' might. Compare the comment by Bagnall, *Everyday Writing* (2011) 128 that a Greek ostracon from Smyrna 'seems – as is also often the case with letters from Egypt – to contain some rare words, a reminder that even now, after hundreds of years of philological work, we do not know all of the Greek vocabulary that … not-very-well-educated people used in their everyday communications'.

4.7.3 TCL III+

Line 4 of the sole extant manuscript of Sargon's 8th Campaign (TCL III+) reads as follows:

ana āli u nišīšu lū šulmu ana ēkalli āšib libbiša lū šulmu

In his ever-astonishing edition of 1912, François Thureau-Dangin rendered the line as follows:[713]

'A la ville et à sa population, salut ! Au palais qui y est situé, salut !'

By contrast, Ben Foster translates it thus:[714]

'Hail to the city and its people, to the palace and the dweller therein'.

For Thureau-Dangin, *āšib libbiša* is an epithet of *ēkallu* 'palace', with *-ša* referring to *ālu* 'city'. For Foster *āšib libbiša* refers to a person (Sargon himself), and *-ša* refers to *ēkallu* 'palace'.

Thureau-Dangin was a brilliant scholar, and even after a century his voice carries authority.[715] How did he reach his interpretation? Foster's reading, which Thureau-Dangin can be presumed to have considered and rejected, has two advantages: it creates a pleasing symmetry between the two halves of the line (place, its occupant; place, its occupant), and it has feminine *-ša* refer to a feminine noun (*ēkallu*). Thureau-Dangin probably objected that **a)** for the symmetry to be complete, *u* is necessary between *ēkalli* and *āšib libbiša*; and **b)** *-ša* referring to a masculine noun (*ālu*) is not problematic on this tablet, which exhibits some odd morphology: he would have pointed to genitive *kalha* in line 8, to many feminine plurals in the *status constructus* which end in *-āte* rather than *-āt*, to the odd *itaplussa ana īnī* in line 21, perhaps also to the fact that the tablet wavers between *-a* and *-u* for the accusative singular ending.

Thus far, the positions are equally balanced. However, orthographic–morphological analysis of the manuscript tilts the scales in Foster's favour. First, the writer committed a large number of lipographies, so inserting *u* between *ēkalli* and *āšib libbiša* is a painless emendation. Second, the endings on *kalha* and the feminine plurals can be explained as sandhi spellings (see § 4.4.6). Third, the signs making up *itaplussa ana īnī* are now read *itaplus niṭil īnī*, which is morphologically regular.[716] Fourth, the dis-

713 Thureau-Dangin, *Huitième Campagne* (1912) 3.
714 Foster, *Before the Muses* (2005) 791.
715 His interpretation was followed by W. Mayer, *MDOG* 115 (1983) 69.
716 See e.g. CAD I/J 156b.

tribution of the accusative endings *-a* and *-u* is not random: nouns with stem-final *t* have accusatives in *-u*, other nouns have them in *-a* (see § 5.4.6). Once all these facts are taken into account, the objections to Foster's interpretation evaporate.

4.8 The distribution of pairs of interchangeable signs

It is a basic feature of the cuneiform script that writers could choose between several signs to represent a given syllable. Sometimes, the conventions of a particular period or scribal setting weighed heavily in the choice. For example, it would be very unusual in the first millennium to use u_4 except in forms or derivatives of *ūmu* 'day'. Thus although in theory any first millennium writer was free to use u_4 wherever an /u/ sound was required, in practice this was very rarely done.

There are, however, cases of genuine interchangeability. Two of these are *ša* vs *šá* and *šu* vs *šú*: with the proviso that *šú* is rarely used at the beginning of a word (fn. 193), the fact that many manuscripts seem to switch between the two signs more or less at random encourages the suspicion that many writers regarded them as true equivalents of each other (though *šá* and *šú* were quicker to write).

Precisely in cases where one knows that some writers regarded pairs of signs as interchangeable, it is all the more interesting if other writers did not: in these cases it is rewarding to search for their rationales. One possibility is that a manuscript only ever uses one sign of a pair (e.g. always *šá*, never $ša_1$). In such cases the question arises of how the choice was made. Another possibility is that a manuscript uses both signs, but according to a particular criterion (e.g. *ša* for /ša/ as an independent word, and *šá* for /ša/ as a syllable within a word). In these cases the criterion must be explicated.

The three factors which seem to us to have been uppermost in determining writers' choices between interchangeable signs (when they were not used at random) are: **a)** one sign being quicker to write than the other;[717] **b)** one sign being in some way more highly regarded than the

717 Cf. the comment by Wilcke, *Wer las* (2000) 35 on the spelling áb amar nu.a instead of áb amar.nú.a (NU instead of NÚ) in Ur III economic documents: 'Ein deutlicher Akt von Schreibfaulheit, da das Zeichen [NU] in der Ur III-Zeit mit drei Keilen, das [NÚ] dagegen mit ca. 24 Keilen geschrieben wird'. See also Aro on *šú* being 'bequem zu schreiben' in fn. 732. Non-standard spellings are

other; **c)** one sign avoiding ambiguity of reading where the other would be ambiguous.[718] The first two are related: highly regarded signs were harder to write. In the following and in § 5.4.4 we will offer illustrations of these three principles.

4.8.1 Orthographic flourishes: MAN VS LUGAL

We are here concerned with the sumerographic spelling of *šarru* 'king' (and its derivative *šarrūtu* 'kingship') in Neo-Assyrian royal inscriptions: whether MAN or LUGAL is used. (Phonetic spellings of the word are rare in these sources, and not studied here).

Most manuscripts of Neo-Assyrian royal inscriptions use MAN throughout. Of the two signs, MAN is more recent and very easy to write (a mere two wedges), while LUGAL originated earlier and is much more complicated. Though writers of cuneiform did not always choose the easiest sign to write,[719] in some instances they do seem to have preferred it (see fn. 717), and we regard the ascendancy of MAN over LUGAL as motivated by convenience (though the fact that MAN was the sumerogram for Šamaš, god of justice, may have plaid a part too).

A minority of manuscripts make consistent use of LUGAL. In particular, there is a renaissance of LUGAL over MAN under Šamšī-Adad V, whose inscriptions strive for grammatical correctness and use old ductus: his scribes recognised the antiquity of LUGAL, and regarded it as preferable to MAN.

In a small number of cases, both signs are used on one and the same manuscript. This can be seen already on several manuscripts of TP I's prism inscription (no. 1): MSS 4-5 have LUGAL at i.2 but MAN at i.3 and

sometimes employed in Chinese for the sake of writing a simpler character. Ingulsrud and Allen, *Learning to read in China* (1999) report that, according to an article published in the *China Daily* in 1991, 'Between 1989 and 1990 the Beijing Language Commission found more than 27.000 cases of non-standard characters used on signs in the capital' (though preference for a simpler character need not be the explanation in all these cases).

718 Inger Jentoft suggests that the position of the writer's hand on completing the previous sign may also have played a part.

719 See Wilcke, *Wer las* (2000) 40 on Ur III Sumerian: 'Keinesfalls liesse sich behaupten, das einfachere Zeichen werde bevorzugt. Das zeigt schon die Verwendung von [ne, bí] (12 Keile) für [ni, né] (4 Keile) oder [bi, bé] (6-8 Keile).' See also Akkadian manuscripts consistently using *šu*$_1$ instead of *šú* (§ 4.8.3).

i.21. On Šal III 14, LUGAL appears in lines 1-31 (twelve attestations), while MAN follows in lines 43-172 (25 attestations).[720] On ŠA V 1, LUGAL appears in lines i.26 to iii.21 (9 attestations), while MAN follows in lines iii.35-iv.44 (7 attestations).[721]

In the cases just listed, the distribution of the two signs is not random, but rather reveals a pattern: LUGAL appears first, while MAN takes over later. This pattern suggests that the writers decided to start off with an orthographic flourish, using the more spectacular LUGAL at the beginning of the inscription, but then grew tired, or perhaps even supposed that nobody would read much further, and switched from LUGAL to the aesthetically less rewarding but more conveniently written MAN.

In an inscription of AN III (no. 1) preserved on three pavement slabs, the opposite happens. The inscription includes 18 MAN signs. All three manuscripts have MAN throughout (MS 1 has lines 1-27, MS 2 lines 1-25, MS 3 lines 1-21), except MS 2, which in its last line (25) has LUGAL-*ti* instead of MAN-*ti* for *šarrūti* 'kingship'. The writer apparently decided to conclude with a recherché sign as a gesture of orthographic sophistication.

In the use of MAN and LUGAL in royal inscriptions we thus discern the desire for an orthographic flourish as a reason for forsaking consistency.

4.8.2 Consistent use of *šá*

Some manuscripts always use *šá*, never *ša* (probably because *šá* was quicker to write).[722] Examples include the 'Broken Obelisk' of Aššur-bēl-kāla,[723] a stone slab of Assurnaṣirpal II (Asn II 3),[724] the Nim-

---

720 LUGAL: 1, 2, 5, 6, 11, 14, 15 (*2), 16, 22, 23, 31; MAN: 43, 58, 60, 71, 73, 84, 86, 88, 91, 93, 106, 109, 112, 119, 124, 127, 131, 139, 148, 150, 154, 156, 166, 169, 172.

721 LUGAL: i.26(*2), i.29, i.34, i.51, ii.3, ii.33, iii.14, iii.21; MAN: iii.35, iii.64, iv.10, iv.24, iv.31(*2), iv.44.

722 We refer of course to manuscripts on which there are sufficient attestations for the consistency to be manifest. A manuscript with e. g. three occurrences of ŠÁ cannot usefully be said to be consistent (cf. § 2.5).

723 As word (61 occurrences): ii.2, ii.21, iii.1 (*3), iii.2, iii.3, iii.6, iii.8, iii.9, iii.10, iii.11, iii.12 (*2), iii.13, iii.14 (*3), iii.15, iii.16 (*2), iii.18 (*2), iii.20, iii.21 (*2), iii.22, iii.30, iv.1, iv.2, iv.5, iv.6, iv.15, iv.17, iv.18, iv.29, iv.38, [iv.39], v.1 (*2), v.2, v.4, v.5 (*2), v.7 (*2), v.12, v.17, v.18 (*2), v.20, v.24 (*2), v.25, v.28 (*2), v.29, v.32 (*2), v.34 (*2); within word (15 or 16 occurrences): ii.17 (?), iii.7, iii.16, iv.2, iv.12 (*2), iv.21, iv.27, iv.31, iv.37, v.4, v.21 (*2), v.22, v.23, v.26.

rud stele of AN III (no. 1),[725] the Tell Abta stele of Šalmaneser IV (Šal IV 2),[726] the cylinder of Marduk-apla-iddina,[727] the Sippar manuscript of *Ludlul* I,[728] MS J of *Gilg.* XI,[729] and Sargon's Uruk cylinder (RIMB pp. 147-149, no. 2.66.3).[730]

Since Neo-Assyrians usually use *ša*$_1$ to write the word '*ša*', but the corpus of haruspical queries uses *šá*, it has been argued that a Neo-Assyrian historical document which uses *šá* for the word '*ša*' was written by a haruspex.[731] The above examples suggest that this argument is not probative, as there are a sizeable number of exceptions outside the extispicy corpus.

The letters of Rašil in SAA XIII always use *šá*; accordingly, it is doubtful whether the small fragment no. 180, which uses *ša*$_1$ for *ša* 'of' in lines r.10 and r.12', is by the same writer.

Manuscripts which use ŠÁ and ŠA for different purposes are discussed in §§ 5.4.4.2 and 5.4.4.3; a sample of manuscripts which switch between them at whim is provided in fn. 884.

---

724 As word (24 occurrences): 2, 6, 7, 8, 10, 11, 12, 13, 15, 16, 20, 21, 22, 23, 24, 26, 32, 34, 38, 39, 41, 43, 44, 45; within word (10 occurrences): 2, 17, 22, 27, 28, 32, 36, 37, 41, 42 .

725 As word (10 occurrences): 2, 6, 7, 12, 14, 16, 21, 24, 26 (*2); within word (3 occurrences): 4, 11, 23.

726 As word (7 occurrences): 6, 7, 9, 17, 18, 19, 26; within word (8 occurrences): 7, 13, 19, 20, 22, 24 (*2), 27.

727 RIMB, pp. 136-138. Hence at the start of line 35 the reading [*qí*?-*š*]*a*?-*at*-⌜*su*⌝-[*nu*] is even more doubtful.

728 George and Al-Rawi, *Iraq* 60 (1998) 187–201. As word (11 occurrences): 5, 9, 11, 13, 16, 37, 45, 71, 77, 96, 97; within word (17 or 18 occurrences): 9, 11, 36, 43, 46, 68, 72 (*2), 73, 83, 91, 94, 101, 103, 108, 114, 115 (?), 119. Given this consistency, the reading of the second sign in line 69, which the editors give as *ša*?, becomes even more doubtful.

729 As word (15 occurrences): 10, [68], [69], 115, [120], 132, 155, 165, 174, 179, 208, 213, 222, [224], 257; within word (34 occurrences): 3, 4, 8, [10], 57, 58, 59, 76, 88 (*2), 91 (*2), 125, 128, 129, 130, 134, 137, 145, 146, 147, 156, 161, 164, 172, 193, 207, 209, 212, 215, 219, 236, 249, [283].

730 As word: i.12, 18, 31, 35, ii.5, 28, 30; within word: i.15, 40, ii.5, 7, 11, 14, 19, 23, 35, 41. (Also line 9, in fragmentary context).

731 Tadmor, Landsberger and Parpola, *SAAB* 3/1 (1989) 51 n. 32.

4.8.3 Consistent use of *šu*$_1$

Some manuscripts always use *šu*, never *šú*. Of these signs, *šú* is quicker to write (two wedges as opposed to five).[732] Probably, manuscripts which exclude *šú* in favour of *šu* do so for the sake of enhanced orthographic sophistication.[733]

MS 'a' of *Ee* IV does not use the sign *šú*; there are many occurrences of *šu*$_1$, both in suffixes (*-šu*, *-šunu*) and the word stem (in initial, medial and final position). As is evident also from other features (see §§ 5.4.4.3 and 5.4.5), the sequence of signs extant on this tablet was determined by a person who worked to an impressive degree of orthographic consistency. The use of *šu* over *šú* was most likely driven by an ambition of orthographic sophistication. The same manuscript consistently uses *i-na* and *a-na*, not *ina* and *ana.* The same reason presumably applies.

It is interesting that here orthographic sophistication was prioritised over helping the reader. As argued in § 5.4.4.3, the distribution of *ša* and *šá* on the same tablet is intended to help the reader, and a similar effect could have been achieved by the appropriate distribution of *šu* and *šú*, helping the reader to spot suffixes, but this was not done.

4.9 Orthography as evidence for pseudepigraphy

From time to time, pseudepigraphic inscriptions were produced. How often this happened, we do not know – for obvious reasons, we can only identify cases where the attempt was unsuccessful. Clues to pseudepigraphy can be of various kinds, including linguistic and orthographic. A well known example is the 'cruciform monument', which purports to date to the Old Akkadian period but was shown by Ignace Gelb to be a later forgery.[734]

---

732 Cf. Aro, *StOr* 20 (1955) 25 on Middle Babylonian: '*šú* neben dem aB allein verwendeten *šu* wird immer häufiger, vermutlich weil es bequem zu schreiben war'.

733 Being the much narrower sign, *šú* was arguably more liable to corruption during transmission, as transmitters might have failed to see it. Some highly skilled writers might have avoided using it for this reason, but *šu* could also be corrupted (see e.g. § 3.3.3).

734 Gelb, *JNES* 8/4 (1949) attributed it to the Old Babylonian period, but Sollberger, *JEOL* 20 (1968) (a reference I owe to Aage Westenholz) showed it to be Neo-Babylonian.

There is a likely case also among the Assyrian royal inscriptions, namely a rock inscription ostensibly of TP I (no. 15), inscribed near the source of the Tigris:

1. *ina re-ṣu-te šá aš-šur*
2. [d]utu [d]iškur dingir[meš]
3. gal[meš] en[meš]*-a*
4. *ana-ku* [m]*tukul-ti-*A*-é-šár-ra*
5. man kur aš a [m]aš-sag*-i-ši*
6. man kur aš a [m]*mu-tàk-kil-*[d]*nus*[*ku*]
7. man kur aš*-ma ka-šid*[735]
8. *tam-di* gal*-te šá* kur *a-mur-ri*
9. *u tam-di šá* kur *na-i-ri*
10. 3*-šú ana* kur *na-i-ri* du

In several respects the orthography of the inscription is at odds with other inscriptions of TP I. The possessive suffix spelled *-a* (as opposed to *-ia*) in line 3 and the sequence of signs man kur aš would be exceptional under TP I. Furthermore, TP I overwhelmingly writes /šu/ as *-šu*₁ not *-šú*; prefers to write *ša* 'of/which' as *ša*₁ not *šá* in narrative inscriptions; prefers kur.kur *na-i-ri* to kur *na-i-ri*;[736] and overwhelmingly prefers to write *tâmtu* sumerographically rather than syllabically.[737] Thus the inscription has two exceptional orthographic features, and four unusual ones.

Two explanations can be envisaged for these aberrations. The first is that the orthographic differences between the rock inscription and other inscriptions of TP I should be attributed to differences in the contexts in which they originated. With the exception of nos. 15 and 16 (also a rock inscription, from the Malazgirt region, north of Lake Van), all preserved manuscripts of TP I's inscriptions are small objects (tablets, prisms) from Assur and Nineveh. The Ninevite manuscripts either duplicate Assur

735 'Despite the way the text is transliterated e.g. in *RIMA* [i.e. *ka-šid i*[*š-tu*], MW], the rock is not damaged in this place, and the two horizontals are part of the sign šɪᴅ' (Karen Radner, pers. comm.).

736 kur.kur([meš]) *na-i-ri* is attested fourteen times in five different inscriptions: 1 iv.49, 1 iv.83, 1 iv.96, 1 v.9, 1 v.29, 1 viii.13, 3:9, 3:10, 3:12, 4:15, 10:7, 10:17 (*2), 16:4. The only attestations of kur *na-i-ri* appear at 4:7 and 1 viii.13 (MSS 3 and 8), but given that elsewhere the writer of MS 3 habitually wrote kur.kur[meš] *na-i-ri*, the latter instance may be lipographic.

737 ᴀʙ[meš]*-ti*: 1 i.10; a.ab.ba: 1 iv.50, 1 iv.99, 2:26, 3:7, 3:23, 3:25, 4:6, 4:7, 4:68, 5:12', 5:14', 10:7, 16:7, 17:3(*2), 21:13'. The only other attestation of the spelling *tam-di* (10:7) occurs later in the same line as a.ab.ba, so it might be elegant variation (see fn. 554), though admittedly the manuscripts are fragmentary, so that none is preserved with both spellings.

manuscripts, or bear compositions which resemble those attested in Assur, so the main centre for the production of royal inscriptions under TP I seems to have been Assur, the then capital. It is possible that the relative orthographic consistency of the small objects is due to their deriving from inscriptions devised by a circle of master scribes in Assur. By contrast, the exceptional orthography of no. 15, which was engraved on campaign, might be due to its originating in circumstances where sources from Assur could not be consulted.

The second explanation is that the inscription is pseudepigraphic, written for a later king. It is situated in proximity to inscriptions of Šalmaneser III (nos. 21-24), who is thus an obvious candidate for the role of forger.[738] The spellings which are unusual for TP I are not unusual for Šal III.

Against the hypothesis of pseudepigraphy one could argue that in the time of Šal III the main concern of kings was to push the boundaries of empire further than their predecessors, so that to fabricate evidence that TP I had reached the source of the Tigris before Šalmaneser would have undermined Šalmaneser's own propagandistic interests.[739] Nonetheless, we hold that the orthographic features (anomalous for TP I but not for Šal III) coupled with the proximity of the 'TP I' inscription to an inscription of Šal III amount to a strong case for pseudepigraphy. From the angle of self-presentation, we presume that Šal III aimed to foster a (spurious) association with an illustrious predecessor.

4.10 *Plene* spellings in feminine plurals

Some manuscripts follow a pattern in the spelling of forms which contain the morpheme *-āt-* or its variant *-ēt-* (i.e. feminine plural nouns and adjectives).

The pattern involves two variables: whether or not the vowel *ā* in the morpheme *-āt-* (= *ē* in *-ēt-*) is spelled *plene*, and whether the relevant word is in the 'free' form (*status rectus*) or a 'bound' form (*status constructus* or *status possessivus*). It can be summarised as follows:

738 The existence of similarities between the rock inscriptions of TP I and Šal III was hinted at by Borger, *Einleitung* (1961) 121: 'Die zwei Felsinschriften ... berichten ganz kurz über Feldzüge gegen Na'iri; sie sind mit den Felsinschriften Salmanassars III. zu vergleichen.'

739 I thank Karen Radner (pers. comm.) for this observation.

	'free' form	'bound' forms
plene spelling	often	rarely

For example, contrast *um-ma-na-a-te* 'troops' ('free') with *um-ma-na-at nak-ri* 'the troops of the enemy' and *um-ma-na-te-šu* 'his troops' ('bound').

In the following, all mention of *plene* spelling refers to the morpheme *-āt-* (*-ēt-*), so that a spelling such as *hi-ib-la-ti-i-ka* 'your losses' will count as non-*plene* for the purposes of our discussion, though it does contain a *plene* spelling.

4.10.1 Some evidence from Assyrian manuscripts

In order to establish whether a manuscript respects the pattern just described, it is necessary for it to contain a substantial number of feminine plural nouns and adjectives spelled syllabically. Many manuscripts, even long and well-preserved ones, are disappointingly poor in them. The richest group of sources are Assyrian royal inscriptions, and it is several of these that establish the pattern's existence beyond doubt: MSS 1-5 of TP I 1, Sargon's 8th campaign (TCL III+), Room II at Khorsabad and MS A1 of Asb's Prism A. Other manuscripts will be mentioned after them.

The numerical data is presented in tabular form below. In collecting this data, we ignored spellings in which the morpheme *-āt-* (*-ēt-*) was written as part of a cvc sign (e.g. *kib-rat*, *gi-sal-lat*), those where insertion of *plene -a-* would have given rise to *-a-a-* (e.g. *qa-bu-a-te*),[740] those where a seeming *plene* spelling could in fact be a way of representing a hiatus (e.g. *a-ri-a-at* for /ari'at/, see fn. 572), and any other spellings where it is uncertain whether *-a-* is phonologically motivated or not (see § 5.4.2).

4.10.1.1 TP I 1, MSS 1-5

We first give the attestations from individual manuscripts, then a summary table. In the first two tables, where the evidence of individual manuscripts is marshalled, '+' denotes the presence of *plene* spelling, '-' its absence, 'n/a' means that the manuscript omits the relevant word, and '[…]' that the relevant portion of the manuscript is lost in a lacuna.

740 The sign sequence *-a-a-* was used to represent /āya/ and the like.

Free forms:

	MS 1	MS 2	MS 3	MS 4	MS 5
i.80 *ba-ma-a-te*	+	+	+	[...]	+
ii.8 *pa-áš-qa-a-te*	+	+	+	+	[...]
ii.15 *ba-ma-a-te*	+	+	n/a	+	[...]
ii.21 *gu-ru-na-a-te*	+	n/a	+	n/a	[...]
ii.77 *pa-áš-qa-a-te*	+	+	+	+	+
iii.19 *pa-áš-qa-a-te*	+	+	+	+	+
iii.26 *ba-ma-a-te*	+	+	+	+	+
iii.35 *ṣi-ra-a-te*	-	-	+	+	+
iii.54 *gu-ru-na-a-te*	+	-	+	-*n*[*a-te*]	+
iii.55 *ba-ma-a-te*	+	+	+	+	[...]
iii.74 *ṣa-a-te*	+	+	+	+	+
iv.7 *ṣi-ra-a-te*	-	+	n/a	+	-
iv.19 *gu-ru-un-na-a-te*	+	-	+	+	+
iv.43 *ṣi-ra-a-te*	-	-	-	+	[...]
iv.53 *né-re-be-*(*e*)*-ti*	-	-	-	-	-
iv.54 *šup-šu-qa-a-te*	+	+	+	+	+
iv.69 *ti-tur-ra-a-te*	+	+	+	+	+
v.16 *ṣa-a-te*	+	+	+	+	+
v.95 *ba-ma-a-te*	+	+	+	+	[...]
vi.1 *gap-ša-a-te*	+	+	+	+	[...]
vi.7 *ba-ma-a-te*	+	+	+	+	[...]
vi.31 *qi-in-na-a-te*	+	+	+	+	[...]
vi.49 *ma-da-a-tu*	+	+	+	+	+
vi.98 *dan-na-a-te*	-	-	+	-	-
vii.87 *si-qur-ra-a-te*	+	+	+	-	+
viii.50 *ṣa-a-te*	+	+	+	+	+
viii.53 *si-qur-ra-a-tu*	+	+	+	+	+

Bound forms:

	MS 1	MS 2	MS 3	MS 4	MS 5
i.53 *mi-iṣ-re-te-šú-nu*	-	-	-	-	- [*-šu-nu*]
i.77 *šal-ma-at*	-	-	-	-	-
i.81 *i-da-at*	-	-	-	-	-
i.85 *si-te-et*	-	-	-	-	-
i.85 *um-ma-na-te-šu-nu*	-	-	-	-	-
ii.1 *si-te-et*	-	-	-	-	-
ii.7 *gir-re-te-šu-nu*	-	-	-	-	...*-r*]*e-*⌜*te*⌝*-šu-nu*
ii.10 *um-ma-na-te-ia*	-	-	-	-*n*[*a-t*]*e-*	-
ii.16 *um-ma-na-at*	-	-	-	-	-
ii.19 *um-ma-na-at*	-	[...]	-	-	[...]
ii.23 *šal-ma-at*	-	n/a	n/a	n/a	-

ii.40 *nap-ša-a-te-šu-nu*	-	-	+	-	+
ii.43 *um-ma-na-te-ia*	-	-	-<*na*>-*a-te-*	-	[...]
ii.55 *ṣa-at*	-	-	-	-	-
iii.12 *si-te-et*	-	-	-	-	*si-te-*[*et*]
iii.13 *um-ma-na-te-šu-nu*	-	-	-	-	-
iii.23 *šal-ma-at*	-	[...]	n/a	-	-
iii.36 *um-ma-na-at*	-	-	-	-	-
iii.40 *um-ma-na-te-ia*	-	-	-	-	-
iii.48 *um-ma-na-te-šu-nu*	-	-	-	-	-
iii.53 *šal-ma-at*	-	-	-	-	[...]
iii.53 *ba-ma-at*	-	n/a	n/a	-	n/a
iii.76 *um-ma-na-te-šu-nu*	-	-	-	-	-
iii.78 *šal-ma-at*	-	-	-	n/a	-
iii.93 *um-ma-na-te-ia*	-	-	-	-	-
iii.98 *um-ma-na-te-šu-nu*	-	-	-	-	[...]
iv.10 *um-ma-na-te-šu-nu*	-	-	-	n/a	(-<*na*>-⌜*te*⌝-)
iv.27 *si-te-et*	-	-	-	-	-
iv.27 *um-ma-na-te-šu-nu*	-	-	-	-	-

Summary table:

	MS 1		MS 2		MS 3		MS 4		MS 5	
	free	bound	free	bound	free	bound	free	bound	free	bound
plene	22	0	20	0	23	2	21	0	15	1
non-*plene*	5	29	6	25	2	24	3 +1?	25 +1?	3	21+1?

(the doubtful spellings on MS 4 are -*n*[*a-te*] and -*n*[*a-t*]*e*)
(the doubtful spelling on MS 5 is *si-te-*[*et*])

4.10.1.2 Sargon's 8th Campaign (TCL III+)

We first give the attestations, then a summary table:

Free forms:

plene (total 49): 6 *ad-na-a-ti*, 27 *gap-ša-a-ti*, 61 *dal-pa-a-te*, 63 *hi-da-a-ti*, 82 *ru-qe-e-te*, 95 *mah-ra-a-te*, 97 *ṣa-a-ti*, 100 *li-la-a-ti*, 114 *dam-qa-a-te*, 116 *ma-ta-a-te*, 116 *kib-ra-a-ti*, 117 *la-la-na-a-te*, 127 *dal-pa-a-ti*, 135 *ba-ma-a-te*, 143 *pa-aš-qa-a-ti*, 152 *ṣa-a-ti*, 155 *dal-pa-a-te*, 158 *nak-ra-a-ti*, 159 *re-ša-a-ti*, 166 *ma-'-da-a-ti*, 204 *qar-ba-a-te*, 223 *as-ma-a-ti*, 241 *pul-ha-a-ti*, 242 *di-ma-a-ti*, 245 *rab-ba-a-te*, 249 *di-ma-a-te*, 250 and 253 *li-lá-a-te*, 256 *rap-ša-a-te*, 261 *nak-la-a-te*, 262 *qi-ra-a-te*, 265 *la-la-na-a-ti*, 266 *rab-ba-a-ti*, 287 *dan-na-a-te*, 291 *bi-ra-a-ti*, 314 *ma-ta-a-ti*, 315 *ṣa-a-ti*, 327 *pul-ha-a-te*, 329 *paš-qa-a-te*, 331 *ti-ka-a-ti*, 359 *dan-na-*[*a-t*]*e*, 359 [*qa-ta*]*-na-a-te*, 360 *ṣip-ra-a-te*, 379 and 392 *dan-na-a-te*, 392 *qal-la-a-te*, 393 *dan-na-a-te*, 409 *rap-ša-a-te*, 415 *ṣi-ra-a-te*

non-*plene* (total 9): 93 *nu-ul-la-ti*, 130 *ia-la-te*, 182 *a-šam-ša-ti*, 186 *qi-ra-te*, 214 *pa-áš-qa-te*, 268 *a-šam-ša-ti*, 321 *mar-ṣa-ti*, 325 *pa-áš-qa-te*, 372 *še-l*[*a*]*-l*[*a*]*-te* (on 292 *ma-'-at-ta-tu* see § 4.7.3).

Bound forms:

suffixed, ***plene*** (total 8): 40 *ma-ta-a-ti-šu-nu*, 41 *ma-ta-a-ti-šú-nu*, 95 *hi-ṭa-a-te-šu*, 166 *qi-ra-a-te-šú-nu*, 216 *tar-ma-a-te-šu*, 219 *qi-ra-a-te-šu*, 274 *qi-ra-a-te-šú-nu*, 299 *bi-ra-a-te-šú*; **6 non-*plene***: 187 *tuk-la-ti-šu*, 221 *tuk-la-te-šú*, 287 *bi-ra-ti-šú*, 295 *qi-ra-te-šú-nu*, 298 *tuk-la-te-šú*, 409 *um-ma-na-te-ia*

construct,[741] ***plene*** (total 4): 362 *nàr-ma-ka-a-te*, 363 *hu-ru-pa-a-te*, 395 *nàr-ma-ka-a-ti*, 395 *a-sa-la-a-te*; **non-*plene*** (total 15): 10, 27 and 142 *um-ma-na-at*, 150 *ša-ha-at*, 245 *šin-na-at*, 256 *um-ma-na-at*, 267 *hi-im-ma-at*, 318 *i-da-at*, 361 *a-za-na-at*, 362 *a-sa-al-la-te*, 384 *qar-na-at*, 393 *še-la-at*, 394 *a-za-na-te*, 396 *mìn-da-at*, 407 *at-ma-na-at*

Summary table:

	free	bound
Plene	49	12 (8 suff, 4 const)
Non-*plene*	9	21 (6 suff, 15 const)

For 'free' forms the same tendency is apparent as on the other manuscripts, while the proportion of *plene* spellings in 'bound' forms is much higher (indeed in the majority). Possible reasons for this will be discussed below.

4.10.1.3 Asb Prism A, MS A1

We first give the attestations, then a summary table:

Free forms:

Plene (total 48): i.11 *te-né-še-e-ti*, i.22 *rik-sa-a-te*, i.23 *ri-šá-a-te*, i.34 *a-šá-a-te*, i.50 *ṣip-pa-a-ti*, i.63 *ep-še-e-ti*, i.63 *an-na-a-ti*, i.66 *ṣi-ra-a-te* , i.116 *rik-sa-a-te*, i.120 *sur-ra-a-te*, i.128 *a-ma-a-te*, i.128 *an-na-a-te*, ii.69 *da-ṣa-a-ti*, iii.73 *si-ma-a-te*, iii.80 *ṭu-ub-ba-a-ti*, iii.117 *si-ma-a-te*, iii.127 *an-na-a-te*, iv.21 *a-ma-a-ti*, iv.21 *an-na-a-te*, iv.38 *hi-ṭa-a-te*, iv.77 *ep-še-e-ti*, iv.77 *an-na-a-ti*, iv.82 *re-ba-a-te*, iv.85 *ka-ma-a-ti*, iv.88 *šab-sa-a-te*, iv.124 *tuk-la-a-te*, v.36 *a-ma-a-ti*, v.36 *an-*[*na*]*-a-ti*, vi.31 *pu-uz-ra-a-ti*, vi.65 *pa-az-ra-a-ti*, vi.84 *ha-za-na-a-ti*, vi.124 *da-ra-a-ti*, vii.1 *re-še-e-ti*, vii.26 *lib-ba-a-ti*, vii.91 *sur-ra-a-te*, vii.120 *ru-qé-e-ti*, vii.121 *kul-ta-ra-a-te*, viii.14 *ad-na-a-ti*, viii.68 *sur-ra-a-te*, ix.60 *ar-ra-a-ti*, ix.66

741 On f. pl. construct forms seemingly ending in *-āti* and *-āte* on this manuscript see § 4.4.6.

mu-še-ni-qa-a-te, ix.76 *i-la-a-ti*, ix.78 *gaš-ra-a-te*, ix.110 *ad-na-a-te*, ix.127 *ma-'-da-a-ti*, x.78 *eš-re-e-ti*, x.96 *re-šá-a-te*, x.107 *ri-šá-a-te*; **non-*plene***: none.

Bound forms:

suffixed, ***plene*** (total 8): i.37 *eš-re-e-ti-šú-un*, i.129 *šip-ra-a-te-šú-un*, i.130 *sur-ra-a-te-šú-un*, ii.53 *gir-re-e-ti-šú*, iii.40 *šal-ma-a-ti-šú-nu*, iii.116 *eš-re-e-ti-šú-nu*, iv.64 *sek-re-e-ti-šú*, x.106 *ep-še-e-te-šú*; **non-*plene*** (total 3):[742] vi.109 *si-ma-te-e-šá*, x.97 *ep-še-te-e-šú*, x.105 *i-ta-te-e-šú*.
construct, 0 ***plene***; 1 **non-*plene***: iv.81 *ri-he-et*

Summary table:

	free	bound
Plene	48	8 (8 suff, 0 const)
Non-*plene*	0	4 (3 suff, 1 const)

Special discussion is necessary for certain cases not listed above. At vi.114 (*aššur-bāni-apli ultu qereb māt elamti*(elam.ma^{ki}) *lem-né-ti ušeṣṣânni* 'Assurbanipal will rescue me from the middle of the evil land of Elam') we interpret *lem-né-ti* as a singular form with literary anaptyctic vowel (*lemnetu* : *lemuttu* = *damqatu* : *damiqtu*).[743]

Attestations of the words *birītu* 'fetter' and *izqātu* (or *iṣ qāti*) 'handcuffs' present problems:[744] are they plural? Are they in the *status constructus*? Re plurality, spellings of *birītu* (*bi-rɪ-ti*, *bi-rɪ-tú*) are ambiguous:[745] supposing cv-cv for /cvc/, they could represent *birīt* (sg.); supposing also Neo-Assyrian use of UD for TE (see fn. 282), they could represent

742 In the light of *-u-* rather than *-tu-*, and of the rarity of two *plene* spellings within one word in Neo-Assyrian, one could also make a case to the effect that máš.gi$_6$-*u-a* is equivalent to *šu-na-tu-u-a*. However, given the many uncertainties (e.g. *u* could also represent /w/) it seemed best to exclude it.

743 On these vowels see George, *Gilgamesh* (2003) 432, with refs, and, for a historical explanation, Hess, *Kaskal* 7 (2010) 109.

744 The attestations are as follows: i.131 *bi-re-ti ... iš-qa-ti*, ii.109 *iš-qa-ti ... bi-re-ti*, iii.59 *iš-qa-ti ... bi-re-ti*, v.4 *bi-re-tú*, ix.22 *bi-re-tú*.

745 If one followed AHw's supposition that the singular form is *birtu*, then spellings such as *bi-re-ti* would very likely be plural, but CAD's assignation of the relevant spellings to *birītu* on semantic grounds (link between places, link in chain) seems plausible. (Borger, *BIWA*, transliterates *-re-*, suggesting he regards the forms as plural). The alleged attestation at *Malku* I 94 is phantom (see Hrůša, *malku* = *šarru* (2010) 203).

birêt (pl.); the reading, derivation and number of *izqātu*? are uncertain.[746] As regards being in the *status constructus*, since all the attestations are (with one probably erroneous exception)[747] followed by an.bar (the sumerogram for *parzillu* 'iron'), it is possible that a nominal hendiadys is at work: literally 'fetters, iron' rather than 'fetters of iron'.[748] Owing to a dearth of evidence (material-words are usually written sumerographically, and the orthography/morphology of the relevant manuscripts is not 'good' enough to judge whether the object preceding the material is *status constructus* or *status rectus*) it is hard to confirm or refute this hypothesis. Since they are spelled non-*plene*, the attestations of *birītu* and *izqātu* would only gainsay the pattern if they turned out to be both plural and *status constructus*. We reserve judgment.

On spellings of the type '-*ca-te-e*-suffix' see the phonological discussion below.

4.10.1.4 *Gilgameš* VI MS **a**

This manuscript has sufficiently few relevant forms that a summary table is not necessary:

Free forms

i.4 (*Gilg*. VI 4) *a-ṣa-a-ti*, ii.17' (52) *šu-ut-ta-a-ti*, ii.25' (60) *ni-qé-e-ti* (for *unīqēti* ?), ii.40' (73) [*pi-š*]*á-a-ti u er-*[*re*]*-ti*, v.26' (158) *ke-ez-re-e-ti u ha-ri-me-ti*

Bound forms

iii.11' (*Gilg*. VI 86) *pi-šá-ti-ia u er-r*[*e-ti*]*-ia*, iii.16' (90) *p*[*i*]*-šá-ti-ki*, iii.17' (91) *pi-šá-ti-ki ù er-re-ti-ki*

---

746 CAD reads *iṣ qāti*, lit. 'wood of the hand', but von Soden, *AfO* 20 (1963) (ditto AHw 408b) sees problems with this interpretation, and suggests instead a loan from Aramaic *ḥizqā* / *'izqᵉṯā* 'ring', *plurale tantum* in Akkadian. Von Soden's objections to the CAD interpretation can be circumvented by supposing that the expression (genitival in origin) turned into a single word. This would explain spellings such as *iṣ-qa-tum* on manuscripts where the ending has to be taken seriously, and – the meanings of the constituent elements having become less important with their fusion into a single word – how one could have an *iṣqātu* of iron. We consider the matter unresolved.

747 Manuscript A1 is the only one to omit an.bar after *bi-ri-ti* at ii.109, and at iii.59 (another attestation of the same expression) it is present. At i.131, in a similar expression, *bi-ri-ti* and *iš-qa-ti* are both followed by an.bar. Most likely at ii.109 MS A1 omits an.bar in error (lipography).

748 See the Old Babylonian likely examples of 'hendiadys of material' in Wasserman, *Style and Form* (2003) 11.

The free forms are spelled *plene* five times out of seven. Interestingly, both cases where the *plene* spelling is missing are of the type Word_1-*plene* *u* Word_2-non-*plene.* Whether this is coincidence (and, if not, what the explanation is) cannot at present be established. The bound forms (which are all suffixed) are spelled non-*plene* five times out of five.

Though the evidence from this manuscript would not suffice alone to establish the existence of the pattern, since the pattern is known to exist from other sources it seems fair to suppose that the writer of this manuscript knew and implemented it.

For more on this manuscript see § 4.7.2.

4.10.2 Glimmers of the situation in Babylonian

The manuscripts cited above are all in Assyrian script, hence presumably written by Assyrians. The question thus arises: did Babylonians follow the convention? Problems of evidence make this question hard to answer: it is difficult to find manuscripts in Babylonian script which have enough syllabic spellings of feminine plurals to tell whether they conform to the pattern or not.

For Old Babylonian, we accordingly analysed a group of manuscripts, namely letters from the AbB corpus. Since royal and non-royal letters behave differently, we give counts for them separately. Our sources are all the letters in AbB II and IV, and also the additional Hammurapi letters in AbB I-XIII, as listed by Michael Streck.[749] Many spellings could be parsed as both singular and plural; where there was no reason to suppose plurality (e.g. *bīt* ^{munus}*sé-ek-re-tim*, AbB II 131:9), we assumed the form to be singular, and disregarded it.[750] Admittedly a minority of such spellings probably *are* plurals, but this should not seriously affect the tendencies which emerge from our counts. Cases where there were some grounds for parsing the form as plural, but this was not certain, we included

749 Streck, "Das "Perfekt" *iptaras* im Altbabylonischen der Hammurapi-Briefe", in Nebes (ed.), *Tempus und Aspekt* (1999) 103 n. 13 ('Stand 1995'). Streck lists additional Hammurapi letters outside the AbB series, and more have appeared in Veenhof's AbB XIV. It was not our purpose to sift all Hammurapi letters, simply to assemble a body of them large enough to yield patterns.

750 Note in particular the exclusion of *daqqatum*/*daqqātum* (*da-qa-at* II 87:14, 27, 28; *da-qa-t*[*um*] 143:29; *da-qa-ti* 144:12). AHw 163a apparently interprets these spellings as plurals, but this is uncertain (see esp. 143:29).

with a question mark. We excluded proper names, both of people and places. The following evidence was collected:

Royal

Free, ***plene*** (25 occurrences): *a-wa-a-tim* (II 11:11), *a-wa-a-*[*tim*] (II 11:27), *ri-ib-ba-a-tim* (II 21:5), *iš-ta-ra-a-tim* (II 34:6, 34:9), *ke-ez-re-e-tum* (II 34:12), *iš-ta-ra-a-tim* (II 34:15), *ke-ez-re-e-tim* (II 34:17), *iš-ta-ra-a-tim* (II 34:23), *pí-ha-a-tim* (II 54:6, 13), *te-re-e-tim* (II 54:25), *ša-al-ma-a-t*[*im*] (II 54:25), *pí-ha-a-tim* (II 70:12), *a-wa-a-t*[*im*] (IV 9:13), *aš-la-a-tim* (IV 21:13, 27), *tup-pa-a-tim* (IV 22:4, 26:9), *a-wa-a-tim* (IV 40:23, 34), *pí-il-ka-a-tim* (IV 99:8), *i-la-a-tim* (V 135:4, 135:11), *ap-pa-ra-a-tim* (XIII 5 r.5'); **non-*plene*** (4 occurrences): *ṣa-la-tim* (II 15:6, 23), *na-ak-ka-ma-tim* (XIII 8:9), *nam-ri-ia-tim* (XIII 48:5).

Suffixed, ***plene*** (6 occurrences): *a-wa-a-tu-šu-nu* (II 9:21), *a-wa-a-ti-šu-nu* (II 12:17), *a-wa-a-tu-šu-n*[*u*] (II 74:26), *a-wa-a-ti-šu-nu* (IX 190:25, XIII 10:8, 27:13); **non-*plene*** (8, maybe 9 occurrences): *a-wa-ti-šu* (II 1:17, 9:18, 19:10), *ne-ep-re-ti-šu-*[*n*]*u* (IV 83:10), *ma-ra-ti-ša* (XIII 18:8, 18:19), [*m*]*a-a-ra-ti-ša* (XIII 18:26), *ši-ma-ti-šu* (XIII 22:11); maybe also *ku-nu-uk-k*[*a-t*]*i-šu-nu* (XIII 48 r.6').

Construct, ***plene*** (3 occurrences): *tup-pa-a-at* (IV 32:6), *ri-ib-ba-a-*[*a*]*t* (XIII 9:4), *ri-ib-ba-a-at* (XIII 9:12); **non-*plene*** (7 occurrences): *e-mu-qá-at* (II 5:12), *ši-ta-at* (II 16:4), *i-ta-at* (II 36:5), *ka-ni-ka-at* (II 48:12, 52:11), *ši-ta-at* (IV 17:24, 28:12).

Non-royal

Free, ***plene*** (3 occurrences): *a-wa-a-tim* (II 112:20, 128:7), *a-wa-a-tum* (IV 111:30); **non-*plene*** (36, maybe 37 occurrences): *tup-pa-tim* (II 46:13), *ša-ap!-ra-ti* (II 82:22), *gu-ul-gu-ul-la-tim* (II 88:11), u_4*-ma-tim* (II 88:25), *ka-aq-qà-ra-tim* (II 90:22), *ši-pa-tim* (II 92:25), *tup-pa-ti* (II 104:10), *ṣú-ha-ra-t*[*i*]*m* (II 108:13), *ki-na-tim* (II 109:20), *en-ke-tim* (II 140:7, 9, 141:7), *ki-na-tim* (II 154:18), *um-ma-na-tim* (II 161:10), *tup-pa-tim* (II 161:24), [*tup*]*-pa-tim* (II 162:7), *la-bi-ra-tim* (II 162:7), [*eš-š*]*e-tim* (II 162:8), *tup-pa-tim* (II 162:15), *a-ma-tim* (II 162:17), *tup-pa-tim* (II 162:21), *e-le-tim* (II 177:16), *wa-ri-da-tim* (II 177:16), *ki-na-tim* (II 178:14), *pí-il-ka-tim* (IV 50:6, 11), *ši-ma-tum* (IV 56:11), *ši-ma-tum-ma* (IV 69:38), *a-wa-tim* (IV 75:8), *il-ka-tim* (IV 117:7), [*i*]*l-ka-tim* (IV 118:17), *ša-hi-la-tim* (IV 145:12), *ha-ar-ra-na-tim* (IV 150:27), *a-wa-tum* (IV 157:3', 10'), *pí-il-ka-tim* (IV 160:9') (uncertain: *eš-še-tim*, II 88 r.15').

Suffixed, ***plene*** (1 occurrence): *ú-né-e-ti-šu* (II 121:9); **non-*plene*** (16 occurrences): *ka-ni-ka-ti-šu-nu* (II 90:31), *né-mé-le-ti-šu* (II 107:28), *a-wa-ti-ša* (II 109:21), *ni-pa-ti-ka* (II 114:13, 15), *ma-ra-ti-šu* (II 126:5), *hi-ib-la-ti-šu-nu* (IV 60:16), *ma-na-ha-ti-šu* (IV 68:21, 25), *a-wa-ti-ia* (IV 69:17), *a-wa-ti-šu* (IV 69:32), *te-er-qé-ti-ši-na* (IV 111:26), [*hi*]*-ib-le-tu-ú-a* (IV 134:9), *hi-ib-le-ti-šu* (IV 134:17), *hi-ib-la-ti-i-ka* (IV 137:6), *a-wa-ti-ni* (IV 146:21).

Construct, ***plene***: (none); **non-*plene*** (4 occurrences): *ši-ta-at* (II 85:32), *qá-ta-at* (II 113:10), *pi-il-ka-at* (IV 57:9), *hi-ib-le-et* (IV 134:13).

This evidence can be summarised as follows:

	Royal			Non-royal		
	free	bound		Free	bound	
Plene	25	6 suff	3 const	3	1 suff	0 const
Non-*plene*	4	8(+1?)	7	36(+1?)	16	4

Within royal letters, *plene* spellings prevail in free forms, but are minoritarian in bound forms. In this tendency, the Old Babylonian royal letters agree with the Assyrian evidence. However, *plene* spellings of suffixed forms are much more common in Old Babylonian royal letters than on Assyrian manuscripts.

More particularly, as can be seen from the attestations above, Old Babylonian royal letters exhibit a contrast in suffixed forms which Assyrian manuscripts do not: in the sample studied, *plene* spelling is usually present with bisyllabic suffixes (*a-wa-a-tu-šu-nu* 'their words', etc.), but usually absent with monosyllabic suffixes (*ma-ra-ti-ša* 'her daughters', etc.).

As for Old Babylonian non-royal letters, *plene* spellings of feminine plurals are very rare in them *tout court.*

We have not performed a similar study for the first millennium, owing to the state of the evidence,[751] but it is worth noting that the Cyrus Cylinder follows neither the Neo-Assyrian nor the Old Babylonian royal pattern: it uses *plene* spellings in all forms of feminine plurals:

Free forms: 2 *[ki-i]b-ra-a-tim,*[752] 11 *kul-lat ma-ta-a-ta ka-li-ši-na*, 14 *dam-qa-a-ta*, 16 *rap-ša-a-tim*, 23 *ri-ša-a-tim*, 24 *rap-ša-tim*, 29 *kib-ra-a-ta*

Bound forms, **suffixed**: 6 *si-ma-a-ti-šu-nu*, 14 *ep-še-e-ti-ša*, 25 *si-ma-ti-šú-nu*, 26 *ep-še-e-ti-[ia]* (restored after line 14); **construct**: 5 *si-it-ta-a-tim ma-ha-za,*[753] 20 *kib-ra-a-ti er-bé-et-tim*, 35 *a-ma-a-ta du-un-qí-ia*

751 Neo-Babylonian letters from Assyrian royal archives are potentially treacherous sources, as they may be subject to Neo-Assyrian influence. Late Babylonian letters probably stem from a period when Akkadian was dead or dying, so it would be preferable to study them after the situation in earlier periods has been worked out.

752 Though the following word is lost in a lacuna, *[ki-i]b-ra-a-tim* stands at the end of its line, so it is unlikely to be a construct form.

753 The spelling with *-tim* could conceivably be an indication that this is a hendiadys rather than a genitive construction, in which case *si-it-ta-a-tim* would be a 'free' form.

What this can tell us about Babylonian phonology is uncertain. The problems will be discussed in the following.

4.10.3 Phonological interpretation

As noted in § 5.4.2.2, *plene* spellings were sometimes inserted as aids to reading rather than as flagposts of phonologically salient characteristics. One might, therefore, wonder in the Neo-Assyrian pattern documented above they were simply used to help readers distinguish feminine plurals from feminine singulars, e.g. sg. *šarrate* 'queen' vs pl. *šarrāte* 'queens'. This seems unlikely, however: feminine plurals are spelled *plene* where there can be no ambiguity in number, to wit the following four cases from TCL III+: *ad-na-a-ti* (line 6, this word has no singular), *ma-ta-a-te* (116, sg. *māte*), *ṣa-a-ti* (152, sg. *ṣīti*), *qi-ra-a-te* (166, sg. *qirīte*). We cannot disprove the idea that the pattern originated as a way of distinguishing singulars from plurals and subsequently spread to all *status rectus* feminine plurals through convention, but other interpretations seem preferable. For one thing, this would leave the curious behaviour of the Old Babylonian royal *status possessivus* unaccounted for.

We interpret *plene* spellings in the foregoing cases as representing a 'special' feature (e.g. stress, length, intonation) or combination of features which attached to the relevant vowels and which the writers of our manuscripts regarded as phonologically salient.

The simplest inference from our evidence is that, in Neo-Assyrian, the *a* of the feminine plural morpheme *-āt-* (ditto *e* for the by-form *-ēt-*) had a 'special' feature in 'free' forms which it lost in 'bound' forms, when a possessive suffix or dependent genitive was added.[754] This loosely recalls the behaviour of certain Neo-Assyrian nouns with monosyllabic stems, which lose the *plene* spelling when put into a form other than *status rectus* singular.[755]

The phonological transformations cannot just be thought of as the special feature moving to a different syllable, for the *plene* spelling does not usually move with it: not all manuscripts with spellings like *šar-ra-a-te* 'queens' also have spellings like *šar-ra-te-e-šu* 'his queen'

754 This is a reminder that the pronunciation of individual parts of Akkadian words was not necessarily stable. For additional evidence on this point see Worthington, *ZA* 100/1 (2010) 100–101.

755 Worthington, *JNES* 69/2 (2010).

(though some do). At least two possibilities arise: **a)** no move occurred, and the relevant feature was simply lost in 'bound' forms; **b)** a 'special' feature did move, but what had given rise to the *plene* spelling in free forms was a combination of features, not the 'special' feature by itself. For example, let us assume that the *a* in *šarrāte* was always long, and that in free forms it was also stressed. A vowel which was both long and stressed might acquire some additional characteristic (e.g. super-length) or simply greater phonological salience, resulting in *plene* spelling. If this were so, what would happen in forms like *šarrātešu*? *Ex hypothesi*, the *a* would remain long, but the stress would move to *e*. Neither vowel would be spelled *plene*, because neither would have the combination of length *and* stress. At present we cannot decide between these (and other) possibilities.[756]

On TCL III+ constructs are only spelled *plene* when preceding vocalic *Anlaut*, so that resyllabification takes place, e.g. *narmakāt erê* pronounced /nar–ma–kā–te–rê/. This may be evidence that the 'special' feature represented by *plene* spelling was lost in a closed syllable. But there is the complication that, in the long booty list, items of the same material might have been stressed to distinguish them: bówls of copper, láces of copper.

It is intriguing that on TCL III+ none of the suffixed forms spelled *plene* have three strong radicals, whereas *tuklātešu*, which has three strong radicals, is thrice spelled non-*plene*. Whether this is significant or coincidental cannot at present be established.

On Asb A MS A1 all suffixed forms have a *plene* spelling, though its position varies. Eight cases are of the type *-ca-a-ti*-suffix, while three are of the *-ca-te-e*-suffix type. We can see no reason for this difference, and cautiously suggest that the writer was confused about how to spell feminine plural words with suffixed pronouns (cf. § 4.5.2.5). In most cases he spelled them like the 'free' form, but when he did not, he suggestively moved the *plene* spelling forward, to the position where we would expect to find it if the addition of a suffix did indeed cause a shift of 'special' feature.

756 That genitive constructions caused the shift of a 'special feature' (stress) was already suspected by Gunkel *apud* Zimmern, *ZA* 8 (1893) 124 by analogy with Hebrew. However, Zimmern, *ZA* 10 (1895) 14 found that, on a tablet whose layout seems to follow metric schemes (for a recent discussion see West, *Iraq* 59 (1997) 176–178), a construct phrase usually counts for more than one metrical unit when the last word has a suffix pronoun.

It is difficult to draw hard and fast phonological conclusions, not least because the number of manuscripts considered is quite small. Nonetheless, it seems fair to conclude that, in the perception of some Neo-Assyrians, there was indeed some sort of movement, but this is not the whole story.

Old Babylonian exhibits a variant of the pattern, where the length of the suffix (measured in syllables) plays a part. The difference between royal and non-royal letters is unlikely to reflect phonological differences (unless perhaps the royal letters preserve archaisms), and is probably simply due to more economical orthography. This is turn may be connected with the (presumably) lower average educational level of private letter writers vs royal ones.

Whether the spellings on the Cyrus Cylinder attest to a vernacular phonological change from Old Babylonian or simply to different spelling traits (falsely archaising?) is uncertain. Similarly, whether the pattern (and its underlying phonology) featured in earlier stages of Assyrian cannot at present be established.

Spellings of feminine plurals in different varieties of Akkadian will be a useful source of information to future researchers of Akkadian phonology and linguistic diversification.[757] But recognition of the pattern is also useful in assessing the orthographic consistency of individual writers.

4.10.4 What about *-ūt-*?

On manuscripts in Neo-Assyrian script, *plene* spellings of the masculine plural morpheme *-ūt-* are rare for any forms (free or bound).[758] On some manuscripts, there are sufficient attestations to establish a clear contrast between *plene -āt-* and non-*plene -ūt-* in the *status rectus.*

The interest of this is that, *a priori*, one would assume masculine *-ūt-* to behave exactly like feminine *-āt-*. At least in writing, however, it does not. If our argument to the effect that the pattern in *plene* vs non-*plene* spellings of *-āt-* reflects a change in pronunciation, then the difference in spelling between *-ūt-* and *-āt-* may be inferred to reflect a phonological

757 It is worth noting in passing that the *ā* of the G infinitive is very rarely spelled *plene*, even in Old Babylonian royal letters. This too is matter requiring documentation and explanation.

758 An instance is *mar-ṣu-ú-te* (TCL III+ 413). Is the fact that the word appears at the end of the line relevant here? Or is this a Babylonianism? (Or both?).

difference. We would thus have a demonstration that morphemes which look as if they should behave identically do not always do so. Applied to other facets of the language, this principle could even undermine such basic assumptions as that *iprus* and *aprus* were stressed in the same way.

4.11 Spellings of verb-final contracted vowels before *-ma*

As is well known, verb-final contracted vowels in Akkadian at large are usually spelled *plene* (e.g. *il-qu-ú* for *ilqû* 'they took'). Less is known about how these vowels are spelled when a suffix is added, so that they are no longer in verb-final position (e.g. *ilqûšu* 'they took him'). Here we shall discuss the effects on spelling of the addition of *-ma.*[759] The results will prove to be of interest for the rationales of cuneiform orthography.

For convenience of reference we shall speak of '*ilqû-ma* forms', meaning 'verbal forms terminating in a contracted vowel followed by *-ma*', and '*ilqû* forms', meaning 'verbal forms terminating in a contracted vowel followed by zero'. All references to *plene* spelling in the following discussion should be understood to pertain to the contracted vowel.

A number of manuscripts consistently spell *ilqû-ma* forms non-*plene*, contrasting with *plene* spelling of *ilqû* forms. One example is the sole extant manuscript of Sargon's 8th Campaign (TCL III+). This manuscript includes 15 attestations of *ilqû-ma* forms, all spelled non-*plene*,[760] contrasting with 57 attestations of *ilqû* forms, all spelled *plene* except for a case of haplography (or sandhi spelling) in line 143.[761] Twice there is a contrast

759 For the effect of the addition of the ventive plural morpheme *-nim* see Worthington, *ZA* 100/1 (2010).

760 *iš-mu-ma* (39, 69), *iṣ-lu-ma* (80), *ú-taq-qu-ma* (113), *im-lu-ma* (143), *il-leq-qu-ma* (172), *ip-tu-ma* (173), *iš-mu-ma* (213), *la-mu-ma* (240), *ih-ṭu-ma* (310), *e-lu-ma* (344), *is-lu-ma* (346), *mul-lu-ma* (387), *ip-tu-ma* (416), *id-ku-ma* (325).

761 ***û***: *ip-tu-ú* (23), *la (ap)-pa-rak-ku-ú* (32), *ú-šar-bu-ú* (60), *i-du-ú* (66), *iš-mu-ú* (67), *il-qu-ú* (80), *i-du-ú* (81, 93), [*ú-ad-du*]*-ú* (100), *uq-ṭam-mu-ú* (102), *uṣ-ṣu-ú* (114), *ib-ba-nu-ú* (115), *aq-qu-ú* (123), *ip-pa-rak-ku-ú* (132), *ú-pat-tu-<ú> ú-ru-uh* (or sandhi? 143), *i-šu-ú* (164), *ba-šu-ú* (170), tuk-*ú* (170), *ú-rab-bu-ú* (171), *ú-še-mu-ú* (177), *ú-šam-ru-ú* (191), *ir-šu-ú* (192), *i-šat-tu-ú* (201), *i-šab-bu-ú* (201), *ip-pa-rak-ku-ú* (209), *iq-bu-ú* (213), *ih-bu-ú* (220), *i-šu-ú*[?] (225), *i-šu-ú* (228), *šu-ṣu-ú* (241), *i-šu-ú* (243), *ba-šu-ú* (244), *ú-ad-du-ú*[?] (250), *iš-šu-*[*ú*] (252), *la-mu-ú* (270), *na-du-ú* (272), *i-šu-ú* (322), *ma-lu-ú* (327), *i-du-ú*[?] (337), *in-na-áš-šu-ú* (338), *i-naq-qu-ú* (341), *i-n*[*am-bu*]*-ú*[?] (342), *du-uš-šu-ú* (351),

between the spelling of an *ilqû* form (*plene*) and that of the corresponding *ilqû-ma* form (non-*plene*): *iš-mu-ú* (line 67) vs *iš-mu-ma* (39, 69, 213), *ip-tu-ú* (23) vs *ip-tu-ma* (173, 416).

Interestingly, though contracted vowels are not spelled *plene* before *-ma* on this manuscript, non-contracted etymologically long ones are: *hu-du-du-ú-ma* (21), *šu-zu-zu-ú-ma* (191), *e-ta-at-ti-qa-a-ma* (128), *za-'-na-a-ma* (223), *šu-ut-tu-qa-a-ma* (326), *it-'u-la-a-ma* (370). It is thus clear that the writer of this tablet was not using or omitting *plene* spellings in III-weak verbs at whim. Rather, there was a system.

Still under Sargon, the same system appears at Khorsabad. **1)** The Khorsabad Cylinder has four attestations of *ilqû-ma* forms, each spelled non-*plene* on all manuscripts,[762] contrasting with fifteen attestations of *ilqû* forms, each spelled *plene* on all manuscripts;[763] by contrast, non-contracted vowels before *-ma* are twice spelled *plene.*[764] **2)** Room XIV at Khorsabad has two attestations of *ilqû-ma* forms, both spelled non-*plene*,[765] contrasting with four attestations of *ilqû* forms, all spelled *plene.*[766] **3)** The Annals (rooms II, V and XIII) have six attestations of *ilqû-ma* forms, each spelled non-*plene* on all manuscripts,[767] contrasting with thirty attestations of *ilqû* forms, each – with a single exception on only one manuscript (line 167, probably lipographic) – spelled *plene* on all manuscripts;[768] by contrast, non-contracted vowels before *-ma* are sometimes spelled *plene.*[769]

---

ba-šu-ú (368), [*b*]*u-un-nu-ú* (379), *šu-tam-lu-ú* (385), *ú-mal-lu-ú* (398), *i-šu-ú* (405), *ra-mu-ú* (420); ***â***: *il-qa-a* (108), *ú-mal-la-a* (144), *ú-šar-ba-a* (161), *ú-šal-sa-a* (207), *al-qa-a* (218), *ú-nam-ma-a* (266), *ih-tal-la-a* (370).

762 *ib-šu-ma* (8), *ip-tu-ma* (10), *im-šu-ma* (23), *ir-bu-ma* (38).

763 *ú-še-eṣ-ṣu-ú* (3), *šu-ut-bu-ú* (7), *id-du-ú* (9), *ur-ru-ú* (18), *ú-šar-mu-ú* (20), *ú-še-eṣ-ṣu-ú* (32), *i-du-ú* (36), *na-du-ú* (44), *ma-lu-ú* (47), *ṣe-bu-ú* (52), *na-bu-ú* (58), *ir-te-'u-ú* (72), *ú-sah-hu-ú* (76); *ú-qa-ta-a* (27), *ú-šar-ma-a* (73).

764 *pe-te-e-ma* (37), *ú-maš-ši-i-ma* (46).

765 *ú-šat-bu-ma* (21), *liš-tab-ru-ma* (74).

766 *ú-še-ṣu-ú* (2), *ba-šu-ú* (3), *ú-qat-tu-ú* (54), *ip-par-ku-ú* (74).

767 *i-du-ma* (121), *iš-šu-ma* (122), [... *iš-m*]*u-ma* (171), [*iṣ*]-*lu-ma* (189), *iš-mu-ma* (274, 282).

768 ***û***: *ih-ṭu-ú* (67), *id-du-ú* (81, 82), *am-nu-u* (109), *ú-rab-bu-ú* (167 II; V *ú-rab-bu*), *ib-šu-ú* (196), *ú-mal-lu-ú* (207), *i*[*p-t*]*u-ú* (211), *i-šu-ú* (239), *i-du-ú* (247), *ú-rab-bu-ú* (247), *ip-par-ku-ú* (249), [*ka-m*]*u-ú* (374), *na-šu-ú* (388), *ik-lu-ú* (395), *im-nu-ú* (406), *i-šu-ú* (443); ***â***: *it-ba-a* (54), *ir-šá-a* (68), *il-qa-a* (72a), *ú-ra-a* (75), *ú-še-ṣa-a* (155), *áš-ma-a* (182), *al-qa-a* (202), *ik-la-a* (257), *ul-la-a* (262), *ú-šar-ba-a* (263), *ú-šar-da-a* (336), *iš-šá-a* (384), *ir-ma-*⌜*a*⌝ (397), [*liš-ba*]-*a* (460, cf. *Prunk* 194).

A surprise appears in the Khorsabad *Prunk*-inscription. This has 34 attestations of *ilqû* forms, all spelled *plene* on all manuscripts,[770] and five attestations of *ilqû-ma* forms. Of these, four are spelled non-*plene* on all manuscripts,[771] but one is spelled *plene* on all four manuscripts (*iṣ-lu-ú-ma*, line 28). This is exceptional at Khorsabad, and it is likely that all four manuscripts go back to a single ancestor in which the *plene* spelling appeared through oversight. As elsewhere in Sargon's inscriptions, non-contracted vowels before *-ma* can be spelled *plene*: *e-ki-mu-ú-ma* (136, 163), *ip-pat-qu-ú-ma* (163).

Sargon's habit of spelling *ilqû-ma* forms non-*plene* is maintained by the Chicago Cylinder under his successor Sennacherib. This includes 29 *ilqû* forms, all spelled *plene*,[772] and four *ilqû-ma* forms, all spelled non-*plene.*[773]

The same pattern appears in the *Neo-Babylonian Laws.*[774] These include eleven attestations of *ilqû* forms, all spelled *plene*,[775] and four attestations of *ilqû-ma* forms, all spelled non-*plene.*[776] As under Sargon, non-contracted vowels before *-ma* can be spelled *plene*: *ta-leq-qé-e-ma* (r i.18'), *i-leq-qé-e-ma* (r i.34').

---

769 *id-bu-bu-ú-ma* (59, 133, 412), *in-na-bi-du-ú-ma* (133), *is-hu-pu-u-ma* (421); *ad-ke-e-ma* (62); *ik-la-a-ma* (401).

770 ***û***: *ú-še-ṣu-ú* (5), *ba-šu-ú* (7, 20, 21), *ik-lu-ú* (28), *id-du-ú* (38), *iṣ-lu-ú* (55), *il-qu-ú* (55), *ba-šu-ú* (56), *ik-lu-ú* (69), *ba-šu-ú* (75, 80), *ip-par-ku-ú* (85), *ba-šu-ú* (87), *i-šu-ú* (87), *i-du-ú* (96), *ú-rab-bu-ú* (96), *ip-par-ku-ú* (100, 114), *ba-šu-ú* (133), *ka-mu-ú* (135), *i-šu-ú* (142), *iš-mu-ú* (147), *ú-ša-an-nu-ú* (152), *ir-mu-ú* (157), *ma-lu-ú* (163), *i-šu-ú* (169), *ip-par-ku-ú* (190); ***â***: *ik-la-a* (79, 113, 122), *ú-šar-da-a* (128), *ú-rat-ta-a* (161), *liš-ba-a* (194).

771 *im-ma-šu-ma* (11), *ú-šat-bu-ma* (16), *iš-mu-ma* (148), *liš-*[*tab*]*-ru-ma* (190).

772 ***û***: *ba-šu-ú* (i.34), *i-šu-ú* (i.77, iii.21, vi.70, iv.77, v.21, v.33), *iš-mu-ú* (ii.34), *ú-šab-šu-ú* (iii.9), *ib-šu-ú* (iii.13), *ir-šu-ú* (iii.41), *id-du-ú* (iv.36), *ú-šab-šu-ú* (v.24), *iš-mu-ú* (v.66), *na-du-ú* (v.88), *i-šal-lu-ú* (vi.7), *id-ku-ú* (vi.18), *ú-ṣu-ú* (vi.34), *i-nam-bu-u* (vi.75), *i-šem-mu-u* (vi.80); ***â***: *i-šá-a* (iv.7), *e-te-el-la-a* (iv.22), *di-ka-a* (v.35), *al-sa-a* (v.75), *ú-šar-da-a* (vi.4), *ú-mal-la-a* (vi.10), *ir-ma-a* (vi.44), *ú-rat-ta-a* (vi.61), *ú-šar-ba-a* (i.12).

773 *id-du-ma* (ii.75), *id-ku-ma* (iv.34), *is-se-hu-ma* (v.17), *ip-tu-ma* (v.31).

774 Edited by Driver and Miles, *The Babylonian laws, vol. 2* (1955) 336–346. See also Roth, *Law Collections* (1995) 143–149 (normalisation based on collation) and 253 (bibliography).

775 *i?-na?-áš?-šu-ú* (i.29'), *il-qu-ú* (ii.10), *in-nu-ú* (iii.11), *i-leq-qu-ú* (iii.22), *im-ṭu-ú* (iii.27), *in-nu-ú* (iii.31), *ti-šu-ú* (iii.34), *il-qu-ú* (r.i.8'), *ti-šu-ú* (r.i.9'), *ta-leq-qu-ú* (r.ii.3'), *i-leq-qu-ú* (r.ii.39').

776 *ib-šu-ma* (ii.17), *ú-še-du-ma* (iii.5, iii.8), *iq-bu-ma* (iii.24).

There are doubtless other sources where the pattern applies, and it will be the task of future scholarship to identify them, and to establish whether all the sources which display it have anything else in common.

While it is clear that the pattern was important to certain writers, many others (probably: the great majority) seem to be completely oblivious to it. Thus for example MS A1 of Esarhaddon's Nineveh prism includes the following spellings of *ilqû-ma* forms: *ú-šab-šu-ma* (i.27), *im-ma-hu-ma* (i.41), *is-si-hu-ma* (i.43), *iš-mu-u-ma* (i.83), *id-du-u-ma* (iv.29), *ú-ṣal-lu-ma* (iv.41), *iš-mu-u-ma* (v.29). Four are non-*plene*, three are *plene*. Likewise, in the letters of the Babylonian scholar Bēl-ušēzib to the Neo-Assyrian king we meet *lu-ṣu-ú-ma* (SAA X 111 r.16), *ú-še-en-nu-ú-ma* (X 112 r.15), *id-ku-ú-⸢ma⸣* (X 112 r.24) alongside non-*plene i-ger-ru-ma* (XVIII 124:11).

Thus the abandonment of *plene* spelling before *-ma* can hardly be attributed to a pan-Akkadian (or even pan-Babylonian or pan-Neo-Babylonian) phonological rule, for the exceptions are too numerous,[777] and attested on tablets written by writers whom we may presume to have been highly competent (e.g. the letters of Bēl-ušēzib). It is, of course, conceivable that the sources which consistently spell *ilqû-ma* forms non-*plene* all reflect a dialectal peculiarity in which such a rule existed.

Whatever the phonological situation, it seems clear that some highly skilled writers consciously decided to standardise their spellings of *ilqû-ma* forms.[778] Whether this also means that they adhered to only one style of pronunciation where several were possible is uncertain; but either way, a decision of this sort, i.e. to spell a group of morphologically-phonologically equivalent forms in the same fashion even though different spellings were possible, betokens a high degree of linguistic self-awareness.

In this connection it is worth citing the remarks of Aage Westenholz apropos of a spelling pattern in Old Babylonian lexical lists from Nippur, which can be interpreted as distinguishing two different vowels (perhaps contracted *u* and contracted *o*):

> If *ô* was phonemically distinct from *û*, why didn't the scribes bother to distinguish them [except in some Nippur lexical lists, MW]? And if it be an-

777 Contrast *-nim*, before which *ilqû* forms are rarely spelled *plene*, in any variety of Babylonian (Worthington, *ZA* 100/1 (2010)).

778 Is it also possible that writers' perception of whether *-ma* counted as a word in its own right played a part?

> swered: because it wasn't necessary – if we can read the texts without error, so could they – we may ask again: why then did some of the Nippur scribes attempt the distinction? Part of the answer to that question surely lies in the character of the lexical texts themselves—they were the students' glossaries for their introductory Sumerian. They may have flaunted their knowledge of the fancy Sumerian syllabary by applying it to their native Akkadian. Or it may have been an abortive, unnecessary spelling reform by some *edubbâ* master, aiming at greater phonetic accuracy, like that of Emperor Claudius.[779]

The problem faced by Westenholz was analogous to that which we face in divining the rationales behind the spelling of the contracted vowel in *ilqû-ma* forms. A difference is, however, that in our case the 'school' context is no longer applicable. We dimly begin to see, therefore, the possibility of Akkadian spelling and its various innovations becoming a theme in modern reconstructions of Mesopotamian intellectual history.

4.12 Conclusions

In 1949, Classicist Alphonse Dain poured scorn on editions which devoted too much space to what he regarded as orthographic trivia:

> Je m'élève contre ceux qui, en vertu d'un religieux respect de la matière écrite, s'attachent à noter dans les apparats critiques, non pas tant la leçon que la manière dont la leçon est transcrite. Ce zèle remonte à plus d'un siècle. Déjà Merkel, en 1852, relevait dans l'apparat critique de son édition d'Apollonius de Rhodes tous les cas de non accentuation des prepositions dans le Laurentianus ; ce fait n'a de soi aucune importance. … Donc, sauf dans des cas exceptionnels, il est vain d'encombrer un apparat critique de notations de variantes qui ne sont pas vraiment des variantes.[780]

Whether or not Dain's recommendations to editors be thought wise in Classics, to follow them in Assyriology would be disastrous. For there is much that we still have to clarify in matters of Akkadian spelling, and it is only through the painstaking accumulation of data that hypotheses will turn into facts. As we observed in § 3.5.7, and indeed as previously recognised by Simo Parpola,[781] even the difference between *ina* and *i-na* can be important. Thankfully, there is plenty of data – orthography

779 Westenholz, *ZA* 81 (1991) 19.
780 Dain, *Les Manuscrits* (1949) 159.
781 Parpola, *LAS II* (1983) 444.

is one of the aspects of Mesopotamian civilisation which are most plentifully documented.

Sometimes, the study of orthography leads to the identification of general principles applicable to a wide array of writings, sometimes resulting in the elucidation of oddities and the vindication of the relevant writers. Such is the case with sandhi spellings (several types of which are not generally recognised) and 'soft' auto-correction. On other occasions, the study of orthography can help us to understand how writers chose between alternative spellings of the same word. Such is the case of man vs lugal as spellings or *šarru* 'king'.

There are also orthographic patterns internal to manuscripts which, however one interprets them phonologically, betoken a high degree of consistency in individual writers. Such is the case of *plene* spellings in feminine plurals and in verbal contracted vowels before *-ma*. By studying features of this kind we can form an opinion of a writer's spelling habits which can in turn inform our interpretation of difficult spellings (see e.g. § 5.4.5 on *ašratu*).

The likelihood that many more patterns of all these types remain to be found makes it inevitable that the study of orthography and textual criticism will, for Akkadian, be inextricable for the foreseeable future.

5 How easily were scholarship and literature sight-read in the first millennium?

> Dobbiamo attribuire agli scribi mesopotamici una grande capacità di lettura delle loro tavolette, certo ingigantita ... dalla memorizzazione di parte dei contenuti.
>
> Giorgio Cardona[782]

Discussions of ease of reading in Ancient Mesopotamia are usually oriented towards the identification of different bands of literacy, correlating with the uses which literacy served. Thus it has been persuasively argued that people solely concerned with utilitarian documents (letters, contracts, etc.) made do with a restricted repertoire of signs and sign values, while people who interacted with scholarly writings and literature would have had more extensive knowledge.[783]

Here we will tackle a different question about ancient reading, namely the degree of ease experienced in sight-reading[784] by the transmitters of literary and scholarly compositions. Give or take minor complications,[785] this is tantamount to enquiring into the ease of sight-reading experienced

782 Cardona, "Il sapere dello scriba", in Rossi (ed.), *La memoria del sapere* (1988) 16.

783 To the above two bands, Veldhuis, "Levels of Literacy", in Radner and Robson (eds), *Handbook of Cuneiform Culture* (2011) adds a third, for those who had a deep understanding of the historical development of cuneiform, and knew signs and sign values only attested in lexical lists.

784 I.e. reading something without having seen it before. On the reasons for this restriction and the complexity of defining the unfamiliar in relation to Akkadian see § 5.2.1.

785 As remarked in § 1.5, the writers of our extant manuscripts may often have been 'apprentices' rather than 'experts'. In principle, apprentices might have found reading harder than experts. That said, if, *ex hypothesi*, apprentices had advanced sufficiently far in the acquisition of literacy for them to be entrusted with the production of manuscripts which were supposed to be authoritative, it seems logical to infer that, in the textual typologies which they had specialised in (omens, medicine, incantations, narrative, prayers, etc.), they were at least very close to being fully literate by the standards of the day.

by people who, by the standards of the time, were fully literate in the relevant textual typology.

Did such individuals simply move their eyes across the line, as you are doing now, decoding the cuneiform signs so automatically that they were barely aware they were doing it? Or was it a slower, more arduous process, one which involved leaps and pauses, fit and starts, doubts and ponderings? In other words, was it more like a modern Assyriologist sight-reading his or her native language, or was it more like a modern Assyriologist sight-reading cuneiform?[786] We will refer to the latter scenario as a 'fits and starts' model of reading.

The reason for undertaking this enquiry is that its findings are of some importance for issues of textual change: the harder transmitters found it to read their sources, the more opportunities would arise for inadvertence or misunderstanding. Of course, these undesirables could set in even if the fact of reading *per se* was unproblematic – one need only think of Giorgio Manganelli's radio editors (§ 2.3.3). But it seems reasonable to suppose that, if the act of reading *was* challenging in itself, it would have increased the likelihood of corruption.[787]

We shall first summarise previous statements on the issue, then review a number of differences between ancient and modern reading, and finally proceed to the analysis of cuneiform spellings – from which, we shall argue, it can be deduced that reading cuneiform was not, even for fully literate people, as smooth a process as reading is for us today.[788]

Our analyses of spellings will concentrate on the first millennium, as the vast majority of scholarly and literary manuscripts are from this period. The extent to which our findings apply also to the second millennium is uncertain, since there are at least four reasons for envisaging differen-

786 References to Assyriologists reading cuneiform 'fluently' (e.g. Wilcke, *Wer las* (2000) 48 'Das kann jeder Assyriologe bestätigen, der Keilschrift fliessend lesen kann, …') should usually be understood as referring to re-reading manuscripts which one has already studied, rather than sight-reading unseen manuscripts.

787 With exceptionally conscientious and able transmitters, this need not have been the case: difficulties in reading might have kept them on the ball, and made them think hard about what they were transmitting. However, this does not seem to have been the general trend.

788 There can, obviously, be no universally applicable answer to the question of how easy cuneiform was to sight-read. Quite apart from issues of textual typology (see § 5.2.3), it may be supposed that – just as today – some people were more fluent readers than others. Nonetheless, it does not seem unreasonable to enquire into general trends.

ces in ease of reading between the two millennia.[789] First, the language of scholarship and literature in the first millennium was often archaic vis-à-vis contemporary vernacular Babylonian. Hence, even if they were native speakers of vernacular Babylonian, most first millennium transmitters would probably have encountered things which were unfamiliar and/or obscure to them (cf. fn. 539). Second, the vernacular died out in the first millennium.[790] While the details of this process are poorly understood, it seems fair to suppose that it would have exacerbated the problems of linguistic alienation. Third, for the first millennium we are often dependent on manuscripts written by Assyrians, which in many cases probably went back to Babylonian originals. Assyrian transmitters had to cope with a foreign idiom and sometimes a foreign script, both of which could have reduced their ease of reading (§ 3.7).[791] Fourth, first millennium scholarly and literary orthography required the reader to know more sign values (esp. cvc ones)[792] than in the second millennium[793] – an increase in complexity which is presumably linked to the fact that, the less they were written and spoken, the more Akkadian and cuneiform became the preserve of specialist professionals.[794]

Our discussion will centre on clay manuscripts (tablets, prisms, cylinders, etc.), clay being the support for writing which is most abundantly ex-

789 Thus also Wilcke, *Wer las* (2000) 33.

790 A letter from Sargon turning down a request from his correspondent that he be allowed to write in Aramaic (SAA XVII 2) suggests that Assyrian was minoritarian as a written language already in the late eighth century.

791 Assyrians would in principle have had the same problems in the second millennium, but owing to the distribution and likely textual history of our extant manuscripts this does not concern us.

792 With a small number of exceptions, cvc signs in Old Babylonian are usually used at the end of words to represent mimation. Woodington, *Grammar* (1982) 19 reports that, in the first 20 letters of AbB IX, 85.3 % of cvc signs are used for this purpose.

793 See however Labat, *Création* (1935) 22–23 on *Ee* manuscripts from Kiš preferring cv-vc to cvc, in contradistinction to Assur manuscripts (both groups are first millennium).

794 Cf. Cardona, "Il sapere dello scriba", in Rossi (ed.), *La memoria del sapere* (1988) 15: 'Si può mantenere in vita un universo di testi in una lingua morta, che nessuno più parla ... ma che continua ad essere intesa nella cerchia degli specialisti ... Il testo scritto può quindi crescere a un livello quanto si vuole alto di complessità e difficoltà, svincolato com'è dalla comprensione dell'ascoltatore e dal contesto di enunciazione. Al lettore incombe il peso della comprensione, ma è anche vero che non ci sono limiti per questa decifrazione; egli potrà tornare sul testo tutte le volte che vorrà'.

tant. There was, however, a long tradition of writing cuneiform on wooden tablets,[795] and in the first millennium wax tablets and papyrus were also used. Many of the things said here about cuneiform written on clay probably apply to them too.

Across many cultures and writing systems, people find the passive activity of reading easier than the active occupation of writing.[796] This was probably true of Mesopotamia.[797] Hence inferences about ability in reading cannot be made on the basis of proficiency in writing: someone who shows serious signs of inexperience in writing might yet have been much better as a reader. However, as we are interested in people who presumably wrote to a high standard, this concern is of secondary importance here.

5.1 Previous statements

Statements by Assyriologists on how easy sight-reading was for individuals who counted as fully literate in the domains of scholarship and literature by the standards of the day are surprisingly rare. Accordingly, as for certain other issues discussed in this book, it is not easy to gauge what the consensus across the field is, or indeed if one exists.

Occasionally, views about the ease of reading can be teased out by inference. For example, Edward Chiera wrote 'I should think that it took the Assyrian scribes as long to master their writing as it takes the pupils of today to acquire a good knowledge of reading and writing English'.[798] This would suggest that, for Chiera, once their scribal training was complete, Babylonians and Assyrians read as fluently and easily as modern English speakers. By contrast, Stefano Seminara and Bert Kouwenberg suggest that some *plene* spellings were used to help the reader recognise short words as words in their own right rather than mistake them for parts of adjacent words (§ 5.4.2.1). Implicit in this suggestion is the notion that, if these *plene* spellings had not been used, readers would have been con-

795 Clancier, *RA* 99/1 (2005) 98. See also refs in Rutz, *JCS* 58 (2006) 91a.

796 See e.g. Brayman Hackel, "Rhetorics and Practices of Illiteracy or The Marketing of Illiteracy", in Moulton (ed.), *Reading and Literacy* (2004) on people being able to read but not write in Early Modern England. Cf. Millard, *Reading and Writing* (2000) 154 on the Hellenistic and Roman worlds.

797 Thus also Wilcke, *Wer las* (2000) 48: 'Die Lesefähigkeit war … sicher immer wesentlich stärker entwickelt als die active Beherrschung der Schrift'.

798 Chiera, *They Wrote on Clay* (1939) 165.

fused by the absence of word spacing (an important issue, about which more will be said below). On this point, therefore, Seminara and Kouwenberg lean towards a 'fits and starts' model of reading.[799] Nicholas Postgate suggests that, when Assyrians needed a logogram for *pattu'u* 'open' (as a designation of a chariot), they chose DUH rather than BAD because the latter could have been misunderstood as sumun // *labīru* 'old'.[800] Here again we have the implication that readers could be mislead by the ambiguities of cuneiform, and that some writers went out of their way to help them.

Decades earlier, an unusually explicit statement about the ease of reading appeared from the pen of Godfrey Driver. Apparently with fully literate individuals in mind, Driver wrote of 'the difficulty of reading' and 'bewilderment of the reader'.[801] His contention was that reading Akkadian would have been rendered difficult by the fact that the same signs could be used syllabically or sumerographically.[802] This idea is worth dwelling on, for it is not as straightforward as it might seem.

There is admittedly one sense in which a passage written in both sumerograms and syllabograms is harder to read than one written in syllabograms alone: it requires more knowledge on the part of the reader (more signs, and more sign values). Beyond this, however, the case for the 'difficulty' of sumerograms ceases to be so clear-cut.

In principle, there is the complication of deciding whether a sign or signs should be read syllabically or sumerographically, but in many cases this ambiguity would not arise. For a start, there are signs which almost only function as determinatives or sumerograms, i.e. they are very rarely or never read syllabically. Examples include lú 'man', lugal 'king', uru 'town', dumu 'son', é 'house', anše 'donkey', $murub_4$ 'middle', edin 'steppe', gal 'great', gigir 'chariot', íd 'river', u_4 'day'. Secondly, the plural marker meš is a strong indicator that the preceding sign or signs

799 See also Seminara, *L'accadico di Emar* (1998) 112, observing that *plene* spellings of *u* at word ends in Emar lexical lists could have been a way of marking word ends. Presumably, Seminara has ease of reading in mind as the reason for this hypothetical procedure, though it should be noted that in lexical lists it is hardly necessary to mark word ends, so one would have to suppose that the procedure originated in other contexts, now lost.

800 Postgate, *SAAB* 4/1 (1990) 36.

801 Driver, *Writing* (1976) 67.

802 Variants of this idea surface sporadically in Assyriological writings, e.g. Talon, *Enūma eliš* (2005) x-xi 'Many Late Babylonian manuscripts [of *Ee*, MW] exhibit a tendency to use syllabic signs instead of logograms, even in the case of very usual ones, like ad for 'father' or $a^{meš}$ for 'water.' This … could be a sign of the need to give the reader a precise and unambiguous text'.

are sumerographic (see also § 5.4.7),[803] so on seeing e. g. AN MEŠ an experienced reader would know that they were very probably to be read dingir^{meš} 'gods'. Thirdly, in the first millennium the sign TIM likewise functions as marker of sumerography (see § 5.4.8). Fourth, some sumerograms consisting of more than one sign occurred frequently across cuneiform at large, and would have been easy to recognise as a group (a good example is kù.babbar 'silver').[804] If these interlocking principles are borne in mind, it transpires that, providing a reader had the necessary knowledge, it was possible for a manuscript to include a number of different sumerograms without becoming less simple or more ambiguous to read.

As for textual typologies which are written prevalently in sumerograms, such as omens or medical prescriptions,[805] here, of course, a great deal of knowledge is expected from the reader. But given this knowledge, decoding the signs is not as difficult as one might think: they mostly fall into easily recognisable groups, many of which recur frequently. The simple and formulaic structure of entries in these typologies is also helpful in keeping track of the meaning. To a modern reader, the method is very efficient,[806] and there is no reason to think that educated ancient readers would have found them less so. It is likely that we should think of sumerograms in such typologies as a 'shorthand'[807] of great practical convenience. See already Erle Leichty on the prevalently sumerographic orthography of *šumma izbu*:

803 In principle this applies also to the dual sign II, but being much narrower than meš, it can be harder to spot as a sign in its own right.

804 This example is a mixture of our first and third cases, since kù is overwhelmingly used sumerographically.

805 Cooper, "Mesopotamian Cuneiform, Sumerian and Akkadian", in Daniels and Bright (eds), *Writing Systems* (1996) 52 comments that sumerograms are also frequent in 'administrative texts, with their long lists and repetitive formulas'. Here a reader familiar with the context had a strong expectation of what would be recorded and how the record would be phrased, so reading was easier.

806 Modern readers of Akkadian typologies prevalently written in sumerograms often read the signs in Sumerian, without converting them into Akkadian. Finkel, "On Late Babylonian Medical Training", in George and Finkel (eds), *Studies Lambert* (2000) 139 n. 4 argues on the strength of syllabic spellings of Sumerian that this was true also for ancient readers.

807 Koch-Westenholz, *Babylonian Liver Omens* (2000) 10 comments that in some cases sumerograms in omens might 'not even represent coherently spoken Akkadian, they may have been read in a way resembling modern medical jargon which is filled with a hotch-potch of ungrammatical Latin and Greek'.

> At first glance, this makes the text look cryptic and ambiguous, but in actuality the writing system seems to be bound by rigid rules that eliminate almost all ambiguity and leave a concise, clear text. ... The writing system is little more than a scientific shorthand.[808]

One might compare the finding that Japanese college students read sentences more quickly when written in a combination of Kanji (ideographic) and Hiragana (syllabic) scripts than in Hiragana alone: though it presupposes greater knowledge, Kanji is more efficient.[809]

This is not to deny that, on occasion, the use of sumerograms could lead readers astray – with particularly ignorant or inattentive transmitters, this happened even in ways which to modern Assyriologists look surprisingly simple-minded (see § 3.4.6.1.1 on non-recognition of AD as a sumerogram for 'father'). But the notion that sumerograms made the reading of Akkadian 'difficult' requires nuance, and does not in itself compel the supposition of a 'fits and starts' model of reading.

In sum, then, the crop of previous statements about the ease of reading experienced by individuals who were fully literate in the relevant textual typology is meagre. Apart from the complicated issue of sumerograms, we have only a principle propounded by implication. Other discussions of Akkadian literacy seem not to treat the issue.[810]

---

808 Leichty, *šumma izbu* (1970) 27a and 29b. Leichty observes that, in *šumma izbu*, verbs which are usually written sumerographically almost always take the same phonetic complement (e.g. kur representing *ikaššad* 'he will conquer' takes *-ád* not *-ad*, cf. fn. 553). Cooper, "Mesopotamian Cuneiform, Sumerian and Akkadian", in Daniels and Bright (eds), *Writing Systems* (1996) 53 takes a similar view: the orthography 'resulted in easy-to-scan texts'. Frahm, *Einleitung* (1997) 247b speaks of a 'konventionalisierte "Kurzschrift" ... in verschiedenen Gattungen "wissenschaftlicher" Texte'. Cf. Driver, *Writing* (1976) 67 on sumerograms as 'a kind of abbreviated script or shorthand'.

809 Sakamoto and Maktia, "Japan", in Downing (ed.), *Comparative Reading* (1973) 443: 'All-Hiragana sentences required twice as much time'. Some allowance should presumably be made for the fact that mixed Kanji-Hiragana sentences were what the test subjects were used to seeing in the course of normal reading. But even so, the study's findings are striking.

810 Cooper, "Babbling on: Recovering Mesopotamian Orality", in Vogelzang and Vanstiphout (eds), *Oral or Aural?* (1992) 110 might appear to, but in fact he only comments explicitly on the proportion of people who might achieve full literacy by the standards of the time – not on what those standards were.

5.2 Differences between ancient and modern reading

The consensus across comparative studies of reading in modern times is that the degree of ease which fully literate readers enjoy does not change from one writing system to another.[811] *A priori*, this might seem to furnish an argument against the 'fits and starts' model of reading: if the Chinese and Japanese can read their newspapers as easily as users of the Roman alphabet read theirs, why should we suppose that Akkadian readers found it any more difficult? The reason is, that there are important differences (both material and cultural) between ancient and modern reading. We will set these out in the following.

5.2.1 Issues of exposure and familiarity

As common sense suggests, and experience in the modern classroom confirms, through practice one can become highly proficient at reading particular cuneiform passages or manuscripts, without yet becoming a confident or fluent reader of the script at large.

The reason why this simple point needs underscoring is that familiarity probably played a much bigger role in helping Babylonian and Assyrian readers than it does in our experiences of reading (see already Giorgio Cardona in the epigraph to this chapter). This is due to several circumstances.

For a start, there is a difference in the extent of exposure to written matter. From labels to instructions to adverts to insurance policies to websites to 'text messages', modern readers are bombarded with writing to be sight-read on a daily basis. In many pre-modern societies there was much less such exposure. Classicist Jocelyn Small remarks of the Graeco-Roman world that 'The … quantity of written matter in antiquity … is nothing compared to the amount with which we are bombarded today'.[812] Similarly, Henry Chaytor commented that 'The ordinary man

---

811 For example, see Gibson and Levin, *The Psychology of Reading* (1975) 165 (with reference to a UNESCO survey): 'The skilled readers of one system are able to read as efficiently as skilled readers of another'; Rayner and Pollatsek, *The Psychology of Reading* (1989) 59 know of 'no reliable evidence that there are any marked differences among writing systems either in how rapidly they can be read by skilled readers or in how easily they can be learned by beginning readers'.

812 Small, *Wax Tablets of the Mind* (1997) 22.

of our times probably sees more ... written matter in a week than the medieval scholar saw in a year'.[813] This is probably a fair summary also for the Akkadian-reading world.

Indeed, Ancient Mesopotamian scribal culture, and especially the earlier stages of scribal education, seem to have been primarily oriented towards the intensive study of a restricted number of literary and scholarly 'classics' (which had to be copied and re-copied, and perhaps also learned by heart).[814] It seems reasonable to surmise, therefore, that much engagement with written literature and scholarship would have involved re-reading manuscripts one had already read.[815]

There is a further difference in availability: discounting those who had recourse to a few exceptional assemblages of tablets, most Mesopotamian readers would probably have had access to a range of writings which by today's standards seems vanishingly small.[816] Availability goes hand in hand with motivation in learners. A study of Japanese literacy deems the availability of 'many good reading materials at low prices' to be one of five key factors in enabling a literacy level of 99 % among

---

813 Chaytor, *From Script to Print* (1945) 10. The 34 doctors of 16th Century Amiens, a town of c. 20.000 inhabitants, owned on average 33 books each (Chartier, *Lectures et lecteurs* (1987) 88–89).

814 On learning by heart see § 1.2.3. It is of course possible that there were vigorous and complex oral traditions which did not find their way into writing (see Clancier, *Bibliothèques* (2009) 292, with refs), but they do not impinge on the issues here discussed.

815 We are not claiming that Akkadian scribal culture was oriented towards the familiar *because of* the difficulties of the script. This was the contention of Havelock, *Literate Revolution* (1982), who maintained that 'syllabaries' placed a 'restriction ... upon the range and scope of oral statement' (p. 96). Havelock compared the descriptions of the flood in *Gilg.* XI and *Iliad* XII, concluding that 'the deficiencies of cuneiform as an instrument of acoustic-visual recognition have discouraged the composer from packing into his verse the full variety of expression which such a description calls for' (p. 172). As regards this, one can only concur with Halverson, *Journal of the History of Ideas* 53/1 (1992) 161: 'That the difficulties of the Semitic scripts tended to confine them to recording the familiar and typical and to center on religion and myth seems a particularly unwarranted generalization'. We are simply claiming that much of what Babylonians and Assyrians read would have been familiar to them – either in the sense that they had seen the passage itself before (perhaps even on the self-same manuscript), or in the sense that they had previously seen something very similar.

816 Royal libraries (esp. those of Assurbanipal) were, unsurprisingly, very rich. In other centres of learning, not only was the number of compositions held much smaller, but they were not always held in their entirety (cf. § 3.3.4, esp. fn. 437).

the Japanese population.[817] In the same vein, John Ingulsrud and Kate Allen hold that an ample supply of congenial reading matter is a significant motivating factor for Chinese learners.[818] Another scholar comments that, though ‘many children do learn to read with a very limited book environment’, there is nonetheless ‘international agreement on the importance of a rich supply of books in the literacy learner’s environment at school, and home, and elsewhere’.[819] It is doubtful whether Mesopotamian readers would have had the benefit of these facilities. Related to this is the matter of personal inclination: Mesopotamians did not, as far as we know, read for pleasure.[820] This too would have limited the amount read.

Finally, we need to spend a word on the complexity of the notion of ‘familiarity’ in connection with Akkadian reading. Many textual typologies in Akkadian scholarship are highly repetitive. This is true both in the sense that different entries on the same manuscript are often similar to each other (in orthography, vocabulary and structure), and also in the sense that there is much similarity running through all relevant entries on all relevant manuscripts. Thus it is holds true for many typologies that an experienced reader faced with a completely new manuscript would be assisted in decoding the signs by having already read a good deal of very similar matter.[821] The notion of ‘unseen’ is not, then, as simple to apply as it looks. The familiar and unfamiliar could mingle inextricably within the same manuscript, and even the same sentence: well known passages could be encountered in unfamiliar orthography, hand-writing or layout; passages containing (mostly) familiar wording and orthography might turn up with variants of either type; simple (i. e. familiar) signs could be used to write difficult words, and (though more rarely) easy words could

817 Sakamoto and Maktia, “Japan”, in Downing (ed.), *Comparative Reading* (1973) 444.

818 Ingulsrud and Allen, *Learning to read in China* (1999) 130: ‘Part of the success of literacy in Japan is due to the amount of material available for beginning readers’.

819 Downing, “Other Extraneous Factors”, in Downing (ed.), *Other Extraneous Factors* (1973) 177 and 178.

820 Charpin, *Reading and Writing* (2010) 67. Cf. Foster, *Before the Muses* (2005) 47: the Akkadian-speaking world had ‘no broad reading public in the modern sense’.

821 To take the example of medical prescriptions, though it is too much to claim that ‘Once you have read one medical prescription, you have read them all’, it seems fair to say that ‘Once you have read two hundred medical prescriptions, you will find it much easier to read any others’.

be written with difficult signs. In view of these complexities, attempting a closer definition of 'familiar' in connection with Babylonian and Assyrian reading is difficult, and the concept is most useful at its most vague.

Taking all this into account, it seems fair to conclude that most Akkadian readers, even those who counted as fully literate by the standards of the relevant textual typology, had less experience of exposure to unfamiliar written matter than modern readers. Though an assessment in quantitative terms cannot be attempted, it therefore is likely that ancient readers who counted as fully literate by the standards of the times would have been less skilled than modern readers in dealing with the unfamiliar in its many forms.

5.2.2 The relevance of unfamiliar manuscripts

We argued in the previous section that, owing to the difficulty of getting hold of them, ancient readers would have had considerably less exposure and access than we do to completely unfamiliar writings in the spheres of literature and scholarship. On the strength of this, it might be thought that the question of how transmitters dealt with unfamiliar manuscripts has little bearing on the issue of textual transmission, because it happened so rarely. This would, however, be too dismissive.

For a start, we should envisage movements of manuscripts and people. For much of Mesopotamian history, the evidence for movement of individual people has not yet been assembled, so that it is difficult to draw a general picture. However, a ground-breaking study by Michael Jursa surveys the situation in first-millennium Babylonia (with particular reference to the fifth and sixth centuries).[822] He finds that the main axis of travel was along the Euphrates (Uruk, Marad, Borsippa, Babylon, Sippar), with Babylon being the most important node in the network. Not all cities were equally well linked to each other, and Nippur in particular seems to have been relatively isolated. That said, people movements were frequent, both in the service of institutions and for private purposes, for reasons of many kinds, from business ventures to lawsuits. The situation painstakingly reconstructed by Jursa cannot, of course, be assumed to have obtained in all periods of Mesopotamian history – an important difference being that in his period the whole of Babylonia was under a single government, while this was not always true in the second millennium.

822 Jursa in Jursa, Hackl, Janković, Kleber, Payne, Waerzeggers and Weszeli, *Economic History of Babylonia* (2010) 62–140.

That said, Assyrian merchants made it to central Anatolia in the early second millennium, and the frequent movement of people between cities seems likely for much of Mesopotamian history. It seems a fair assumption that some of them would have carried tablets. A tablet of solar omens from Middle Babylonian Nippur states in its colophon that it was copied from a writing board from Susa![823]

Additional evidence comes from references to allochthonous exemplars in the colophons included in Hunger's volume *Babylonisch-assyrische Kolophone* (we consider first-millennium ones only).[824] We tabulate them below. The numbers in the table cells refer to the colophon numbers in Hunger. When a locality which has its own column lacks its own row or vice versa, this is because it is not attested in the relevant function.[825]

		exemplar supplied to							
		Babylonia			Assyria				
		Bab.	Nipp.	Uruk	Assur	Kalhu	Khors.	Sult.	Nin.
exemplar supplied by	'Akkad'				222, 229(?), 271, 274, 275, 276				318, 328, 336
	Assur				n/a			380(?)	350
	Babylon	n/a	119	84, 86, 90 var., 106	203 (var.), 225, 227, 232, 252, 273, 277, 278, 292	293, 302, 307, 312		379, 381, 406	
	Borsippa	[152], 156		75, 89					
	Eridu	153			292				
	Kutha								349
	Larsa				292				
	Nippur		n/a	110	292				
	Sippar				292				
	Ur				292				
	Uruk			n/a	292, 211, 212				
	Assur				n/a		350		
	'Land of Assur'				272	307			318, 328, 336
	Nineveh				203				n/a

823 See Rutz, *JCS* 58 (2006) 64.

824 For allochthonous exemplars in Uruk see Clancier, *Bibliothèques* (2009) 258–259, drawing on more ample sources than the above table, but confirming that for allochtonous exemplars Uruk relied chiefly on Nippur, Babylon, and Borsippa.

825 None of Hunger's 17 colophons from Borsippa mention an allochthonous tablet as exemplar, though no. 140 declares itself to be a copy of an inscription of Hammurabi's in the É.nam.ti.la temple at Babylon.

Since some of Hunger's numbers identify a colophon attested on multiple manuscripts, precise quantifications on the strength of the above table are hazardous. Nonetheless, while colophons referring to an allochthonous exemplar are in a minority, there is a substantial number of them, testifying to interaction between many different scribal centres.[826] If one bears in mind the countless tablets which are surely lost, and scales up, it will become apparent to anyone who doubted it that there were, in absolute terms, significant numbers of allochthonous exemplars round and about Mesopotamia – certainly in the first millennium, and probably already in the second (and earlier?).[827]

It further seems likely that, in at least some of the movements of tablets, the person who carried the tablet from place to place simply acted as go-between.[828] When this happened, recipients would find themselves confronting unfamiliar manuscripts, and opportunities for misunderstanding would arise.

The same would happen when manuscripts turned up out of the ground. While this is best documented for royal inscriptions, which indeed anticipated their being found and instructed future rulers in how to treat them, other typologies could be involved from time to time.[829]

Instances of the written tradition gaining the upper hand over the oral tradition can indeed be inferred from errors which transmitters would not have made, had they known the composition. Unsurprisingly, there are

---

826 Can we distil profiles for individual cities? The fact that exemplars from many centres were current in Neo-Assyrian Assur probably reflects the intellectual ferment of Assyria in this period (cf. fn. 317). The fact that Babylon supplied exemplars to many cities probably reflects its traditional status as a centre of learning. (Thus also Clancier, *Bibliothèques* (2009) 259–260, commenting that Babylon probably had especially comprehensive holdings of tablets). Beyond these fairly obvious points, matters become highly speculative, not least owing to the scantiness of the evidence.

827 Clancier, *Bibliothèques* (2009) 95 suggests that allochthonous exemplars were procured in the first place so as to 'suivre l'enseignement d'un maître en la matière … ou …se procurer un manuscrit rare'.

828 Another possible scenario, supposed by Clancier, *Bibliothèques* (2009) 258 (and implicit in Pearce, "Statements of Purpose: Why the Scribes Wrote", in Cohen, Snell and Weisberg (eds), *Studies Hallo* (1993) 187b), is that the owners of the extant tablet travelled to the exemplar's town to copy it *in situ*, taking their copy home with them. This must indeed have happened from time to time, but presumably not to the exclusion of the scenario discussed above.

829 See Rutz, *ZA* 101/2 (2011) 296 n. 12 (*utukkū lemnūtu*), complementing CAD N/ 1 310b-311a.

several instances in the West,[830] but they are also found in Mesopotamia proper. Some examples were collected in § 3.3.4.

In sum, even if completely unfamiliar manuscripts were a relative rarity, throughout the millennium and more over which textual transmission occurred, a large number of instances would have amassed. Within each line of transmission, their impact in terms of textual change would have been cumulative. Hence the cumulative influence on transmission of how transmitters dealt with completely unfamiliar manuscripts could have been very significant.

5.2.2.1 Allochthonous exemplars at Nineveh

It is generally thought that the best sources for first millennium literature and scholarship are the Ninevite libraries. It is a noteworthy feature of these collections that they absorbed an enormous influx of tablets from all over the empire.[831] Copyists at Nineveh were therefore faced with numerous exemplars they had never previously seen, and whose writers or owners were not available for oral clarification. Probably through a combination of somnolence and ignorance (see §§ 2.3.3 and 5.2.3), Ninevite copyists could slip up in spectacular fashion (several examples in §§ 3.3.1 and 3.3.2) – so much so as to foster the suspicion that the generally higher standard of Ninevite manuscripts is due not to editorial excellence at Nineveh, but simply to the fact that Ninevite copyists had access to first-class exemplars.

Irving Finkel comments as follows on Ninevite medical manuscripts:

> Tout ce qu'on peut arriver à trouver en eux ne sont que les efforts de présentation des scribes du collège de Ninive lesquels écrivaient pour le roi ce qu'ils avaient colligé des textes anciens, et ce comme des bibliothécaires en chef et non pas comme des médecins.[832]

---

830 Cf. George, *Gilgamesh* (2003) 85 on aberrant spellings of the name 'Gilgameš' in Syria: 'Clearly, somewhere in the long history of transmission the original logographic function of GIŠ had been forgotten and scribes had made the assumption that this sign, like those that followed it, was syllabic' (note also the spelling *-bar-ra*, showing that *maš* was misunderstood as *bar*). Similarly, Valério, *Journal of Language Relationship* 6 (2011) argues that the toponym *ha-ni-rab-bat* (or *ha-ni*-gal-*bat*) was misunderstood as *ha-ni-gal-bat* by peripheral transmitters (*rab* and *gal* being two readings of the same sign). (I owe this reference to Ilya Yakubovich). On transmitters' unfamiliarity with names which appeared in the texts they transmitted see also § 2.4.3.

831 See Frame and George, *Iraq* 67/1 part two (2005) esp. 277–279.

832 Finkel, *JMC* 4 (2004) 26.

It seems likely that this observation can be extended to Nineveh scribes' efforts in other domains of Mesopotamian intellectual culture.

5.2.3 Issues of textual typology

The range of writings in Babylonian and Assyrian is immense, and, however one gauges it (e.g. orthography, vocabulary, morphology, syntax), their level of difficulty is variable.

Some textual typologies were probably not too difficult to sight-read. As was first pointed out by Johannes Renger,[833] and has since been reiterated by other scholars (also for Old Babylonian letters),[834] Old Assyrian letters use a small repertoire of cuneiform signs, each with a small number of readings. Simo Parpola observes that simplifications of this kind were also current in the first millennium: a letter written by a minor Assyrian official in the Zagros states he has no scribe, and it is therefore likely that he wrote the letter himself. This tallies with unusual spellings in the letter, in particular the avoidance of cvc signs (replaced with cv-vc).[835] In general, utilitarian letters probably required less knowledge and effort to decode than other typologies. Readers would have been further helped by the letters' down-to-earth vocabulary and, often, by their knowledge of the contexts referred to.

Many signs and sign-values were specific to particular textual typologies. This is especially true of scholarship (e.g. medical prescriptions, omens, astronomy). A modern scholar who is expert in one of these do-

833 Renger, *ZA* 71 (1971) 33: 'Das altassyrische Syllabar zeichnet sich durch eine außerordentliche Beschränkung in der Zeichenwahl aus. ... Wesentlichen Einfluß auf die Ausgestaltung des Syllabars mag ... die Tatsache gehabt haben, daß die Texte in der Regel nicht von professionellen Schreibern, sondern von den Kaufleuten selbst geschrieben wurden (auch ein Grund für viele der Schreibfehler)'.

834 E.g. Wilcke, *Wer las* (2000) 33. See further refs in Charpin, *Comptes Rendus de l'Académie des Inscriptions et Belles-Lettres* (2004) 489 n. 30. Koch-Westenholz, *Babylonian Liver Omens* (2000) 15 speaks of the 'simple syllabic cuneiform' of the Old Babylonian period.

835 Parpola, "The Man Without a Scribe and the Question of Literacy in the Assyrian Empire", in Pongratz-Leisten, Kühne and Xella (eds), *Fs. Röllig* (1997). Parpola (p. 321 n. 17) comments that 'To put the matter in perspective, it may be noted that even the syllabary of such an expert scribe as Mar-Issar, attested in an extensive correspondence (SAA X 347-370), does not include more than 225 graphemes (170 syllabograms + 55 ideograms)'.

mains would be completely baffled on attempting to read in another without due preparation, and there is no reason to think that the situation would have been different in antiquity.

The degree and type of training which individual readers and writers received presumably depended on the professional trajectory which training was to prepare them for. For example, it is likely that people who were to have careers in administrative contexts, preparing and processing utilitarian documents, received different training from people who were to be involved in things such as literature and scholarship.[836] Irving Finkel's reasoning on this point seems compelling:

> Very little is known about the training [healers, MW] had to undergo, but obviously the first step for candidates would have been the painful acquisition of literacy. No doubt a given proportion of trainee scribes who were led to undertake the great work would emerge as possessing mixed ability, and it seems a reasonable assumption that mediocre students would be discouraged from pursuing a career of esoteric scribal learning. Such scribes would thus be prone to find their professional niveau in the world of commerce in small-time contract or letter-writing, and it would only be a minority of literate graduates who went on into the complex world of the priesthood, divination guilds, or magic and medicine.[837]

Even if the differences arose principally in the final stages of training, they could still be very significant. For example, ignorance of certain sumerograms would have rendered some scholarly corpora (e. g. omens) all but impenetrable to the uninitiated.

If the transmitters who contributed to the complex textual history which underlies our extant manuscripts only ever dealt with the typologies they were expert in, this issue might not be important for the purposes of understanding the mechanisms of textual change. But this was prob-

---

836 This distinction would be less rigid today: a civil servant who spends the working day on administrative papers might well go home and read a novel with the same ease and smoothness as a novelist. But our putative civil servant lives in a culture which offers him or her much more practice in reading at large (§ 5.2.1). Also, as far as we can tell, modern administrative papers are more fulsome and complex than ancient notes.

837 Finkel, "On Late Babylonian Medical Training", in George and Finkel (eds), *Studies Lambert* (2000) 141. The model outlined by Finkel resembles that proposed in Plato's *Laws*, vii.809e-810b: 'The children must work hard at their letters until they can read and write, but as far as reaching a high level of speed or calligraphy is concerned, those whom nature has not helped along in the prescribed number of years should be released' (after Harris, *Ancient Literacy* (1989) 100).

ably not the case, cf. Wilfred Lambert's comment on a Middle Assyrian manuscript of *Tamarisk and Date Palm*: 'The suspicion is aroused that it comes from a scribe more accustomed to writing letters and contracts than literature'.[838] Classicists will not be surprised to hear this – Eric Turner remarked that 'Some of the most precious texts of Greek literature survive only in copies made by scribes whose normal employment was copying documents'.[839] Kuyunjik copyists in particular seem to have been confronted with a diversity of textual materials which they were not equal to understanding in full (refs in § 5.2.2.1).

For these reasons, it is almost meaningless to ask in abstract terms how easy cuneiform was to read, or how literate a person was: typology plays a large role. This is why we specified that we are interested in the sight-reading skills of people who were fully literate by the standards of the relevant textual typology.

5.3 Potential obstacles to smooth sight-reading

Students of pre-modern cultures know that sight-reading was not always easy, even for those who were trained in it.[840] William Harris comments that reading in antiquity could be 'physically harder than it is for us'.[841] Medievalist Paul Zumthor paints a similar picture: '[La lecture] ... demeure difficile. [Elle] exige initiative, action physique en même temps que hardiesse intellectuelle'.[842] A more fulsome statement appears from Alphonse Dain:

> Les œuvres de l'antiquité étaient peu adaptées à la lecture ... Si les chœurs de Sophocle, sortis de la main de l'auteur, se présentaient sans colométrie, sans séparation de mots, sans signes de lecture ou d'exécution, ... le lecture devait en être difficile. Dépourvue de signes de lecture, une page d'un dialogue de Platon ou d'une pièce de théâtre devait être très malaisée à dechiffrer.[843]

838 Lambert, *BWL* (1960) 152 (but why Lambert considers it to be 'neither a library copy nor a school exercise' is not explained).

839 Turner, *Greek Papyri* (1980) vii.

840 From what I can see, though, discussion of how smooth and easy reading of the unfamiliar was for people who should be considered to be fully literate by the standards of the age is rare in many fields.

841 Harris, *Ancient Literacy* (1989) 5 n. 6.

842 Zumthor, *La lettre et la voix* (1987) 115–116.

843 Dain, *Les Manuscrits* (1949) 94.

Here we shall review factors which might have caused difficulties for Babylonian and Assyrian sight-readers.

First, there is the complexity inherent in the cuneiform script: individual signs were polyvalent;[844] occasionally, rare (cryptographic or super-learned) sign values were used;[845] words were written without spaces between them, making it hard to tell where they started and stopped;[846] there was no punctuation, making it harder to identify clause or sentence boundaries;[847] and most words could be spelled in several different ways, making them harder to recognise. (Spacing and punctuation are discussed further in § 5.3.1). Unsurprisingly, all these features cause problems for modern learners of cuneiform. Akkadian orthography's penchant for prioritising etymology over vernacular pronunciation might have added to its readers' vexations.

To the purely 'cognitive' complications it is useful to add some practical ones. For our concern with textual change leads us not only to wonder what proficiency ancient sight-readers might theoretically demonstrate under ideal laboratory conditions, but what they could do in the conditions they actually faced on a daily basis. These were considerably more adverse than those familiar to readers in industrialised countries.

First, there is the problem of deciphering the manuscript's ductus and the writer's individual handwriting. Just as some scrawls are hard to decipher today, so it may be presumed *a priori* that this was sometimes the case in antiquity. Indeed, comments by modern editors support this suspicion.[848] Philippe Clancier comments for Late Babylonian that 'Les tab-

---

844 As noted in § 5.2.3, with refs, letters of various periods used restricted repertoires of signs and readings. The majority of compositions which were transmitted, however, presuppose a much wider range.

845 An extreme example are the omens remarked on by Gadd, *JCS* 21 (1967), where the protases are written in numbers. We still do not know how to read them.

846 Cardona, "Il sapere dello scriba", in Rossi (ed.), *La memoria del sapere* (1988) 16 holds that, partly owing to layout, 'Anche l'occhio dello scriba più esperto non avrebbe potuto cogliere *d'emblée* le articolazioni o meglio le parole chiave di un testo, ma avrebbe dovuto percorrere tutto lo spazio scritto'.

847 Admittedly, the layout of some typologies assisted in working out syntax. In literary manuscripts, line ends often coincided with syntactic boundaries. Many entries on *šumma*-typologies (laws, omens, medical recipes, etc.) consisted in a single sentence (though one still had to identify the clause boundaries). But no such help was forthcoming e. g. with letters.

848 For example Veldhuis, *JCS* 52 (2000) 80: 'Very cursive and difficult to read'. Of course there is always the possibility that a tablet which looks badly written today in fact subscribed to calligraphic conventions widespread on many other

lettes littéraires et savantes ... sont généralement bien plus soignées et normalisées que les textes de la pratique',[849] and similar observations have been made by others.[850] But even if transmitters of literature and scholarship did not often have to contend with poor handwriting as such, ductus might have been a more serious obstacle.[851]

Second, there could be the problem of format (especially sign size and line spacing): some tablets were written with very small signs and/or lines very close together, and one can only suppose that reading them strained the eye.[852] It is noteworthy that one of the greatest Cuneiformists of modern times remarks that the dearth of space between lines of cuneiform on certain manuscripts renders them 'almost illegible'.[853]

---

tablets generated in the same scribal setting, now lost, and that within that setting they were read with great ease. This is very unlikely to apply to all such cases, however.

849 Clancier, *Bibliothèques* (2009) 70.

850 Millard, *Reading and Writing* (2000) 167 reports that, in the Graeco-Roman-Jewish world, 'effort' was needed to read documents which had been written only for the moment, in cursive handwriting. Sommerfeld, *Tutub* (1999) 12 notes that at Old Akkadian Tutub tablets intended only for the moment were inscribed less deeply and with fewer wedges in each sign, to save effort.

851 In the first place one thinks of archaic sign forms, and Babylonians reading Assyrian script and vice versa (see fn. 320), but research into cuneiform palaeography is likely to reveal further complexities.

852 A modern scholar – Hilprecht, *Transactions of the American Philosophical Society, New Series* 18/3 (1896) 225 – speaks openly of his 'overtaxed eyesight' incurred through studying small fragments. The ancient scholar Nabû-zuqup-kēna wrote in a colophon that *ana tāmarti ištar-šuma-ēreš māriya ultu* $1\frac{1}{2}$ *šanāte* [...] *digla ukabbir-ma zamar ubahhiš-ma ab-r*[*i*?...]. Beyond the fact that he did something for one and a half years for the benefit of his son's education, the translation is very uncertain. The phrase *digla ukabbir* is sometimes understood to mean something like 'I overtaxed my eyesight' (CAD B 186a) or 'I ruined my eyesight' (CAD D 136b), but – as recognised by CAD K 5b and Hunger, *Kolophone* (1968) 93 – this is uncertain. It might also mean something like 'I made great use of my eyesight'. Von Soden, AHw 169a is non-committal: he translates literally 'machte er "dick"'. Otherwise, for the idea of diminishing eyesight, the dictionaries cite five attestations of *diglu* + *maṭû* (G, D and Š). There might of course have been several ways of saying the same thing, but from the range of the five attestations – medical symptoms, a curse, a complaint and a letter (SAA X 294) – one wonders whether *diglu* + *kabāru* would be unidiomatic as a way of saying that one became shortsighted.

853 Lambert, *BWL* (1960) v: '[My] copies of tablets are an attempt at compromise between the 'freehand' and 'accurate' schools. I do not believe that the scientific

Third, there is the state of preservation of the manuscript to be read. Tablets whose surface is even slightly damaged can become very hard to read,[854] so transmitters would have been at a disadvantage when tackling worn manuscripts.

Fourth, there are the physical circumstances in which reading was done. In the case of cuneiform inscribed three-dimensionally (i.e. on clay or stone), lighting conditions – not only ambient luminous intensity, but also the position of the light source – would have been very important, more so than with two-dimensional scripts.[855]

Of course, all of these difficulties could be compounded by poor eyesight (see fn. 852). Most ancient readers probably did not have recourse to lenses.[856]

So much for factors which *might* have made cuneiform difficult to sight-read. In the following we will attempt, on the evidence of cuneiform

---

value of a copy is enhanced by its being almost illegible. I have therefore normally put space between the lines of script'.

854 Cf. e.g. Jacobsen, *King List* (1939) 19: 'Any copyist knows how difficult it can be to read a figure like this if the surface of the text is in the least bit scratched or damaged'; Jursa, *Bēl-rēmanni* (1999) 19: 'Bei einer leicht beschädigten Tafeloberfläche sind [Verlesungen, MW] leicht möglich, wenn nicht auf den Kontext geachtet wird'.

855 Wilcke, "Inschriften 1983–1984 (7.–8. Kampagne)", in Hrouda (ed.), *Isin* (1987) 83 'Das Lesen von Keilschrifttexten setzt besondere Lichtverhältnisse voraus, die in einem "Klassenzimmer" nur schwer zu gewinnen wären, müsste jedoch jeder Schüler an einem Fenster mit von links einfallendem Licht plaziert sein'.

856 Layard, *Discoveries* (1853) 197–198 reported the discovery in Nimrud of 'a rock-crystal lens, with opposite convex and plane surfaces' (now BM 90959), whose properties 'could scarcely have been unknown to the Assyrians'. *Per se*, the find of a lens at Nimrud would not be implausible: likely lenses are known from the much earlier palace in Knossos (see Sines and Sakellarakis, *American Journal of Archaeology* 91/2 (1987)). The principal difficulty is rather that there is no mention or depiction of lenses in Mesopotamian writings or iconography. Gasson, *The Ophthalmic Optician* 9 December (1972) 1270 notes as a 'possibility … of conjectural interest' that the object, whose size and shape match 'the facial orbital aperture', was used as a lens by someone 'having a marked presbyopic error'; but also remarks that it could have been used solely as a means of decoration'. Indeed, an alternative interpretation is that Layard's find was not a lens at all, but a piece of inlay – thus the British Museum webpage (accessed 28.ix.2011), noting that this view is corroborated by the findspot 'beneath a heap of fragments of beautiful blue opaque glass, apparently the enamel of some object in ivory or wood, which had perished' (Layard p. 198). Whether this intriguing artefact truly served as a lens is doubtful. (I thank Yoram Cohen for alerting me to the 'Nimrud lens').

spellings, to produce some sort of picture of what actually happened. First, however, a short digression is necessary on how much importance – in terms of ease of sight-reading – should be attributed to the absence of word spacing and punctuation in Akkadian cuneiform.

5.3.1 Excursus on spacing and punctuation

In 1927 Joseph Balogh held it as self-evident that 'Das Lesen des antiken Buchs haben die ungegliederten Zeilen, die sog. "scriptio continua" ungemein erschwert',[857] connecting this to the now discredited view that reading was normally done aloud (see fn. 945). This model of reading long proved influential, to wit the following from Klaus Junack (who goes on to refer to Balogh):

> Eine Handschrift, selbst kalligraphisch exakt und ohne individuelle Eigenwilligkeit in der Buchstabengestaltung (von daher fast den modernen Drucktypen vergleichbar), aber in der *scriptio continua* geschrieben, kann nicht gelesen werden, wie wir es tun, d. h. kann nicht durch ausschließlich optisches Erfassen der deutlich gegliederten Worteinheiten aufgenommen und verstanden werden.[858]

A similar view was more recently taken by Paul Saenger, in the course of assembling an argument that silent reading began to be widespread in consequence of spaces being introduced between words.[859] Saenger cites modern studies of reading, and his contentions were built on by Jocelyn Small.[860]

Unfortunately, studies of reading on modern test subjects are not so clear in their findings as Saenger suggests. When test subjects were required to read both spaced and unspaced Thai (which is normally unspaced), it was found that they read spaced script very slightly faster than unspaced, but not so much faster for the difference to be impres-

857 Balogh, *Philologus* 82 (1926–1927) 227. Delz, "Textkritik und Editionstechnik", in Graf (ed.), *Einleitung in die lateinische Philologie* (1993) 63 notes that the division of words often caused problems for copyists of Latin (an example is cited in § 3.2.19).

858 Junack, „Abschreibpraktiken und Schreibergewohnheiten", in Epp and Fee (eds), *New Testament Textual Criticism* (1981) 283.

859 Saenger, *Spaces* (1997).

860 Small, *Wax Tablets of the Mind* (1997) 19 with note on Small's p. 253.

sive.[861] The authors of another, similar, study on Thai concluded somewhat lamely that their results gave 'qualified support' to the idea that inter-word spaces facilitate reading.[862] Other researchers have studied the eye movements of readers reading both spaced and unspaced English, and, finding that spaced reading was not appreciably faster, concluded that it was word recognition rather than the spaces *per se* which determines the ease of reading, though they conceded that spacing could facilitate this.[863] Our impression of studies such as these is that they are still at a pioneering stage: many are based on small samples, and interpretive consensus still has to form. Without disputing the great intellectual value of explorations such as they undertake, it seems unwise for the time being to take their conclusions as scientific fact.

There are also two difficulties of principle with exporting results generated for modern languages to the world of cuneiform. The first is that, as noted in § 5.2.1, most ancient readers of cuneiform were probably less practised in sight-reading than the modern readers used as test subjects (the eight subjects in the experiment by Kohsom and Gobet all had at least a first-level degree). Therefore ancient sight-readers might well have been more disadvantaged by the absence of spaces than modern subjects. Secondly, the ambiguities of the cuneiform script probably often made the recognition of word boundaries harder than in most modern scripts, so that results generated on the basis of less ambiguous modern scripts are of doubtful applicability to cuneiform. All in all, the results of modern tests cannot, even if one were persuaded of their reliability, be assumed to hold true for cuneiform.

A modern scenario which may offer a closer parallel to reading cuneiform than those in the above-cited experiments is provided by the Vai people of Liberia, studied in the 1970s by Sylvia Scribner, Michael Cole and their team. The literacy rate was around 20 %.[864] Several features

---

861 Kohsom and Gobet, "Adding spaces to Thai and English: Effects on reading", in (Anonymous) (ed.), *Proceedings* (1997). The *p* value for their finding that spaces help to read faster is 0.08. The reaction to this paper by Saenger, *Spaces* (1997) 13–14 seems overly enthusiastic.

862 Winskel, Radach and Luksaneeyanwin, *Journal of Memory and Language* 61/3 (2009).

863 Epelboim, Booth and Steinman, *Vision Research* 34 (1994). See the critique by Rayner and Pollatsek, *Vision Research* 36 (1996), and the reply by Epelboim, Booth and Steinman in the same volume.

864 Over 20 % of adult males were literate in the Vai script, while 28 % had 'some knowledge of some script' (including the Roman and Arabic scripts) (Scribner

of the Vai script are noteworthy from the perspective of ease of sight-reading:

> There are many ambiguities in the way the Vai script represents spoken Vai. Some of these ambiguities arise because the script does not incorporate standard symbols or conventional marks for displaying phonological features that are crucial in comprehending spoken Vai, such as vowel tone. In addition, as we have pointed out …, the higher-order units that carry meaning are not set off in the script. A string of syllabic characters runs across the page without division into words or phrases. A single character on a page, depending on its semantic function, may represent a one-syllable word (many Vai words consist of a single syllable), or it may be the initial, middle or final syllable of a polysyllabic word. Just as there are no divisions into words, there are often no divisions into utterances or sentence units.[865]

Though the parallels are not exact, the Vai script nonetheless loosely matches cuneiform in that its signs are polysemous, and need to be decoded; also in the fact that the orthography is defective. For our purposes it is, then, interesting that Scribner and Cole found that the Vai script was not always sight-read with ease:[866] 'Our observations of Vai script literates deciphering letters from friends [...] had so impressed us with the complexity of the skills involved in reproducing spoken Vai from the written page that we considered it a complex search for meaning and likened it to a problem-solving process'.[867] (For the strategies adopted by Vai readers in this 'problem-solving process' see § 5.6).

The Vai evidence provides corroboration to the intuitively plausible idea that, with a script so full of ambiguities as cuneiform, and in a setting where there was much less exposure to writing than we are used to, the absence of word and sentence spacing would have caused sight-readers

---

and Cole, *The Psychology of Literacy* (1981) 63). The figure for adult males is given because 'In Vai society literacy functions are predominantly carried out by men' (ibid.).

865 Scribner and Cole, *The Psychology of Literacy* (1981) 165.

866 As for learning the script, Scribner and Cole, *The Psychology of Literacy* (1981) 66 record the following: 'On the average, it was reported that two to three months of lessons were required to achieve some functional literacy, although some people admitted to needing more time, even a year, to complete the process. Of course, it is not entirely clear what "completing the process" meant to our informants, who were virtually unanimous in telling us that if they found a particular letter or document difficult to understand they routinely consulted with an acquaintance reputed to be especially knowledgeable. Some students do not complete the process. Various reasons were cited for this failure, including the verdict that learning the script was too hard'.

867 Scribner and Cole, *The Psychology of Literacy* (1981) 164.

problems. We also take encouragement from the judgment of first-rate modern scholars with great experience of handling ancient manuscripts in other fields – Eric Turner commented on 'the strain of breaking up letters into words' on Greek papyri.[868] In view of all this, we deem it reasonable to suppose that the lack of spacing and punctuation was a hindrance to the sight-reading of Akkadian cuneiform.

5.4 Spellings calculated to assist readers in decipherment

It is now time to discuss instances in which ease (or otherwise) of sight-reading Akkadian can be inferred from spellings.

It is our contention that certain spellings (and spelling habits) were intended to assist the ancient reader.[869] Strategies such as those to be discussed here are by no means used consistently, and it was surely possible (though probably more difficult) to read without them. Nonetheless, they are interesting as indications of the sort of 'traps' which writers thought sight-readers might fall into, and also of the fact that writers expected readers to fall into traps at all.

One strategy for helping readers was already met with above: the use of 'enriched' sandhi spellings to help in the recognition of word beginnings (see § 4.4.2). Here we shall discuss more cases. Our survey is by no means exhaustive (see e.g. Leichty in fn. 553).

---

868 Turner, *Greek Papyri* (1980) 99. (Contrast Johnson, *Readers and Reading Culture* (2010) 20, who implies that with 'thorough training' it was possible to read unspaced Latin 'readily and comfortably', but it is not clear whether this comment applies to sight-reading).

869 Compare the 'lectional aids' occasionally used in Greek bookrolls to help the reader identify word boundaries in *scriptio continua*: non-elisions of vowels, apostrophes to mark elision, diaeresis over iota and upsilon *Anlaut*, diastole (to indicate that a letter group should be separated into two words), sub-placed sling (to indicate that a group of letters form a single word), breathings or accents (to disambiguate a letter group). On these see Johnson, "The Ancient Book", in Bagnall (ed.), *Oxford Handbook of Papyrology* (2009) 262 (whose wording we have followed for several items). Johnson notes that the rarity of reading aids can be explained by bookrolls' not being 'designed for … ease of use, much less mass readership' (p. 262): 'The bookroll seems … an egregiously elite product intended in its stark beauty and difficulty of access to instantiate what it is to be educated' (p. 263). On reading aids in Greek see also Junack, "Abschreibpraktiken und Schreibergewohnheiten", in Epp and Fee (eds), *New Testament Textual Criticism* (1981) 283–284. Reading aids were arguably more necessary in Akkadian literature, owing to the polyvalency of cuneiform signs.

5.4.1 Double consonants as aids to parsing

A Neo-Assyrian letter includes the following spellings of verbs in the perfect tense: *it-tu-ar* (i.e. *ittuar* 'he returned'), *as-sap-par* (i.e. *assapar* 'I sent'), *a-sap-rak-ka* (i.e. *assaprakka* 'I sent you'). In all three cases, spelling the first radical double requires more strokes of the stylus than spelling it single (i.e. there are more wedges in IT and AS than I and A).[870] Why, then, does the writer twice write the first radical double (the more demanding option) and once single (the easier option)?

On some manuscripts, variation of this kind may simply be whimsical, but for this letter Nicholas Postgate offers an ingenious explanation: the writer went to the trouble of writing the first radical in the perfect double when to write it single would have created ambiguity with the present tense,[871] but wrote it single when this did not create ambiguity.[872] Thus the reader's ease of parsing took precedence over the writer's convenience of writing, but convenience was sought when ambiguity did not arise.

There are probably many more manuscripts where this rationale can be discerned.

5.4.2 *Plene* spellings as aids to reading

Plene spellings are generally, and with good reason, interpreted by Akkadianists as indications that the relevant vowel possessed a 'special' feature (such as length or stress) which Akkadian speakers' notions of phonological salience led them to mark in writing. They are, therefore, a useful (if vastly under-exploited) source of evidence for the reconstruction of Akkadian phonology.

It is, then, all the more important to recognise that *plene* spellings do not always have the function of marking a 'special feature' possessed by a vowel. Sometimes, they are instead inserted to help the reader interpret the signs correctly. We shall term two such uses 'augmentative' and 'disambiguatory'.

---

870 This is not always the case in cuneiform. For example, *i-si* requires more strokes than *is-si-*.

871 The spellings *i-tu-ar* and *a-sap-par* (which in cuneiform is the same as *a-šap-par*) could be interpreted as presents, and indeed elsewhere in the letter these very spellings are used to represent presents.

872 Postgate, *Iraq* 35/1 (1973) 24 n. 10.

It follows from the existence of 'augmentative' and 'disambiguatory' *plene* spellings that, even when a *plene* spelling occurs in a context where it is phonologically explicable (e.g. a long vowel), it might actually be the case that phonological considerations alone would not have sufficed to include it, and that it was rather inserted as an aid to reading. We are unable to cite a manuscript where this is demonstrably the case, but it is a complication which should be borne in mind by future researchers.

5.4.2.1 Augmentative *plene* spellings

Stefano Seminara and Bert Kouwenberg (see § 5.1) have suggested that *plene* spellings were added to words which would otherwise have been written with a single cuneiform sign,[873] to lend them more orthographic bulk and forestall the likelihood that they be misinterpreted as part of adjacent words. For such cases we propose the label 'augmentative *plene* spellings'.

The possibility of augmentative *plene* spellings can affect our normalisations of Akkadian, e.g. in respect of the length of the vowel in the negative particle which AHw normalises as *lā* and CAD as *la.* Similarly, if it were certain that the *plene* spelling of *pû* 'mouth' in the *status constructus* (e.g. *ina pi-i* X 'in the mouth of X') were phonologically motivated, this would have knock-on consequences for the reconstruction of Akkadian morphology: it would be evidence for the presence of the genitive case marker in the *status constructus.* If on the other hand the *plene i* is just augmentative (*ina pī* X), nothing morphological can be deduced from it.

5.4.2.2 Disambiguatory *plene* spellings

Sometimes *plene* spellings were inserted to help the reader select the correct reading for a particular cuneiform sign.[874] We propose to call such cases 'disambiguatory *plene* spellings'.

873 Seminara, *L'accadico di Emar* (1998) 109: '[La *scriptio plena*, MW] serve a dare maggiore consistenza grafica a quelle parole che, per essere monosillabiche, rischierebbero di confondersi con le sequenze grafemiche contigue (*ki-i*, *la-a*, *lu-ú*, *pí-i*, "bocca" …, etc.)'. For a similar view applied to Akkadian at large see Kouwenberg, *The Akkadian Verb* (2011) 492. The notion was perhaps implicit in *GAG* § 7e: 'Im Inlaut unterbleibt die Schreibung der Länge allerdings sehr oft, besonders bei mehrsilbigen Wörtern'.

874 See already Westenholz, *ZA* 81 (1991) 13 and Kouwenberg, *The Akkadian Verb* (2011) 206 n. 32. It would be logical for this use to be more wide-ranging in lexical lists than in connected text (e.g. a-a A = *ša-a*; A I/1 111, Civil, Green and

In Old Babylonian, disambiguatory *plene* spellings were frequent with the polyvalent sign AH (which can also represent *uh*, *ih* and *eh*). This is seen most clearly in spellings of the word *ahum* 'arm': *a-ah-ka* 'your arm' (AbB IV 137:7), *a-[a]h-šu-nu* 'their arm' (140:18), *a-ah* 'arm of …' (18:14), etc. Here the A sign is probably not telling us there is anything special about the relevant vowel: it is simply telling us to read AH as *ah* (not *uh* etc.).

Later, disambiguatory *plene* spellings were frequent with the aleph sign (which could represent aleph plus any vowel, preceding or following).[875] For example, in *ú-ma-'i-i-ra-an-ni* (*Ee* III 13 MS a), the *plene* spelling is probably not telling us that there is anything special about the vowel *i*: it is simply telling us to read *uma''iranni* (preterite) as opposed to *uma''aranni* (present).

Whereas the *plene* spelling in *uma''iranni* may well be eliminating a genuine ambiguity (in the sense that without it an ancient reader might not have known whether the form was present or preterite),[876] with cases such as *a-ah-šu* there is no ambiguity: given a few extra seconds, and perhaps a bit of looking backwards and forwards, the reader could work out what AH-*šu* represented. The function of the *plene* spelling must simply be to speed things up. For our purposes, then, it is all the more interesting: its presence confirms the suspicion that the polyvalence of the AH sign was expected to slow readers down to a significant extent.

Disambiguatory *plene* spellings also occur when normal orthographic conventions would give rise to a two-sign sequence consisting in consonant+*u* followed by *šam*. For the sign which represents *šam* can be read *ú*, so the foregoing CU sign might trick readers into reading CU-*ú*- rather than CU-*šam*-. To prevent this, an extra *šam* sign could be inserted: the first, to be read *ú*, served no function except to show the reader that the second one must be read *šam* (not *ú*): CU-*ú-šam*-…

Lambert, *MSL XIV* (1979) 205), since the interpretation of lexical entries was complicated by the absence of context (Westenholz ibid.). However, we have not examined the lexical lists systematically. Our discussion above cites examples only from connected passages.

875 An aleph sign not yet having emerged in Old Babylonian, other means were used to represent glottal stops in writing.

876 One could of course object to this that *Sprachgefühl* would have resolved the issue. But in the case of literature in the first millennium, when the Akkadian of the works themselves was archaising (not least in matters of verbal tense) and spoken Akkadian was dying out, some readers might well have been unsure.

This strategy is sometimes adopted in spellings of *mušamqit* 'who causes … to fall': *mu-ú-šam-qit* (Asn II 1 i.7, iii.130, 3:13, 26:41).[877] The fact that the attestations cluster in the reign of Assurnaṣirpal II creates the impression that the spelling was championed by an individual royal scribe, and lost currency at the end of that scribe's career.

Another likely example is *lu-ú-šam-ṣa-a* (*Ee* II 140 MS C, Neo-Assyrian script). On a Neo-Assyrian manuscript, this could be understood as an Assyrianism,[878] but since other manuscripts of this line go out of their way to write *ša-am* rather than *šam*, almost certainly for purposes of disambiguation, it seems likely that this was also the intention on MS C.

A likely disambiguatory *plene* spelling not involving *šam* occurs in *lu-ú-ba-ra* (*Adapa* Frag. B (Amarna) line 31').[879] Here, ensuing BA might have led the reader to read LU as *dib*.[880] When the same word occurs later on the MS (line 63', *lu-ba-ra*) the *plene* spelling is omitted – this is consistent with the possibility that the reader was now expected to recognise the word, having met it above.

If the stative element *dà-a-ri* in the name *šarru-lū-dà-a-ri* 'may the king be everlasting' (e.g. RINAP 3/1 no. 17 ii.92) is unlikely to be the participle *dāri* (see Kouwenberg, *The Akkadian Verb* (2011) 206), it should simply be taken from the adjective *darû* 'everlasting'. Hence the *plene* spelling *-a-* is not phonologically motivated, but serves as a hint to the reader that the sign GAG is to be read *dà*.

The writers who decided on the above spellings were offering help to their readers. What sort of reader were they expecting? The Amarna manuscript of Adapa may have been produced with the needs of Egyptian learners of Akkadian in mind, and Assurnaṣirpal's inscriptions could be argued (though we doubt this) to have been designed for legibil-

877 Izre'el, *JANES* 20 (1991) 51–52 notes that here the *plene* spelling 'cannot be explained as reflecting a historically long vowel', and proposes to compare spellings such as *lu-u-nak-kil* (*Ee* VI 9). We hold *mu-ú-šam-qit* to be a special case, because *plene* spellings of initial *mu* in *mu*-participles are rare, while *plene* spellings of initial *lu* in precatives are quite common in Neo-Assyrian.

878 As just stated, Neo-Assyrian often has a *plene* spelling at the start of Š precatives, even when it apparently serves no purpose of disambiguation.

879 See Izre'el, *Adapa* (2001).

880 I do not know whether *dib* as a reading of LU is attested at Amarna (it is not listed by Cochavi-Rainey, *The Akkadian dialect of Egyptian Scribes* (2011) 24), but even if not, I do not find this too troubling. The corpus of Mesopotamian letters at Amarna is extremely small, so we have a very limited impression of the sign values which Mesopotamians expected Egyptians to know.

ity by as wide an audience as possible. The *Ee* manuscripts, however, were presumably aimed at typical users of literary manuscripts, i. e. individuals who were fully (or almost fully) literate in the relevant textual typology.

5.4.3 Splitting the syllable *šam* as an aid to reading

Another strategy to prevent readers from misreading CV-*šam* as CV-*ú* was to split the syllable /šam/ into two signs: *ša-am* or *šá-am.*[881] Though writers were of course free to write *ša-am* or *šá-am* rather than *šam* if they wanted to, in the first millennium they tended to use *šam.* If they chose not to use it after CV, there is a strong likelihood that disambiguation was the reason for this.[882]

Examples: at *Ee* I 35, MS M has *i-pu-ša-am-*[*ma*] (MS 'a' has ambiguous *i-pu-šam-ma*). At II 140, MS a has *lu-šá-am-ṣa-a*, while MSS e and f have *lu-ša-am-ṣa-a.* As seen above, MS C has *lu-ú-šam-ṣa-a.* Only MS J has the ambiguous spelling *lu-šam-ṣa-a.* When the same verbal form recurs two lines later, MSS a, e, f and J repeat themselves. (MS C omits II 142).

5.4.4 *ša*$_1$ vs *šá*

From the late second millennium onwards, writers had the choice between the signs ŠA and ŠÁ to write the syllable /ša/.[883] Many manuscripts, in many different textual typologies, oscillate between ŠA and ŠÁ, apparently at whim.[884] It is, then, all the more interesting that some do not de-

---

881 The reason for concentrating on the splitting of *šam* is that the sign representing it is the only one to be used commonly with both CVC and V values. If other signs had this ambivalence, eqivalent considerations would presumably apply to them.

882 It is even possible that some writers made a general habit of splitting the syllables /sam/ and /šam/ (same sign), to prevent confusion. E.g. at *Gilg.* VI 13 all three manuscripts split /sam/ in the word *sammat*, *sa-am-ma-ti* (MS A_1), *sa-am-mat* (MSS Q_1 and $\mathbf{a}_1$). At *Gilg.* XI 134 the two manuscripts with *appalsamma* 'I looked' (C and T_1) spell it as *ap-pal-sa-am-ma.* This issue could usefully be investigated statistically, though a huge corpus would be necessary.

883 In theory other signs were also available (e. g. ŠÀ), but by convention these were almost never used for the syllable /ša/. (For exceptions at Susa see fn. 239).

884 Innumerable examples could be given. Here are some sundry ones: the Cyrus Cylinder; the Nimrud Monolith of Asn II (no. 17); the Al-Rimah stele of AN III (no. 7); the Nimrud stele of ŠA V (no. 1); the Sippar manuscript of *Ee* II

ploy these two signs at random, but use them in ways which help the reader. There are three main ways in which this was done, plus another which is a variant of the second.

5.4.4.1 always *šá*, except *ša*$_1$ for disambiguation

Alongside manuscripts which (at least in their preserved portions) always use ŠÁ (see § 4.8.2), there are some which almost always use it, but for various reasons switch to ŠA in a minority of cases. One of the reasons for this switch is to help the reader, by forestalling ambiguities of reading arising from the polyvalency of ŠÁ. Here are some examples:

Manuscript A of *Gilg.* VI uses ŠÁ 32 times,[885] while ŠA appears only once, at ii.21 (= *Gilg.* VI 65): *ša ka-a-a-nam-ma šu-gu-ra-a na-šak-ki.* Since the syllable /ša/ is followed by *k*, if ŠÁ had been used readers might have read it as *nik*, whereas ŠA forestalled the ambiguity. There is one other place on the (extant portions of the) manuscript where ŠÁ is followed by a velar and so ambiguity might have arisen, but here the preceding sign ends in *š*, so disambiguation was not necessary: *ú-na-áš-šá-ku* (ii.19 = *Gilg.* VI 63).

Manuscript B of *Gilg.* I uses ŠÁ 36 times,[886] and ŠA only four. The latter can all be interpreted as avoiding ambiguity: *ša ka-la-a-mi* (B_3 i.4'= *Gilg.* I 6) – as above, ŠA has the advantage over ŠÁ that it cannot be read *ník*; [*lu-bu-š*]*i-ša-ma* (B_2 iii.42 = *Gilg.* I 143) – the ensuing MA could have led the reader to suppose that the sign ŠÁ (= GAR) stood sumerographically for a form of the verb *šakānu*; *a-na mil-ki ša a-bi-šú* (B_2 iii.45 = *Gilg.* I 146) – the use of ŠA saves the reader from erroneously interpreting *a* as a *plene* spelling: *šá-a-*; *ki-iṣ-ru ša* ^{d}*a-nim* (B_1 v.47 = *Gilg.* I 248) – the sign sequence ŠÁ AN (AN = ^{d}) could have been read as a form of the verb *šakānu* (gar-*an*).

(George and Al-Rawi, *Iraq* 52 (1990)); MS C of *Gilg.* XI; MS **a** of the *Dialogue of Pessimism* (*BWL* plate 37), MS G of *Gilg.* XII.

885 10 occurrences as word: i.6, i.11, ii.1, ii.18, ii.29, ii.30, v.8, v.10, v.29, v.30; 22 occurrences within words: i.3, i.9, i.10, i.11 (*2), i.20, i.21, i.36, i.37, i.38, i.41, ii.6, ii.12, ii.19, ii.29, ii.35, ii.37, ii.39, [iii.8'], [iii.14'], v.12, v.13.

886 Line numbers after *Gilg.* I rather than the MS itself – ŠÁ as word: 8, 11, 13, 14, 15, [18], 150, 152, 157, 186, 200, 239, 288; ŠÁ as syllable: [100], 101, 159, 161, 188, 189 (*2), 191 (*2), 193, 195, 203, [212], 215, 219, 231, 235, 243, 272, 276, 284, 289, catchline.

The 'banquet stele' of Asn II (no. 30) uses ŠÁ 73 times,[887] and ŠA only three: *tu-ug-da-ša-ra* (line 49), ^{d}*ša-la* 'Šala' (line 56) and mu *i-si-ni-šú ša* iti.ziz *taš-ri-ih-tu* / mu-*ša ab-bi-ma* 'I named the name of his festival in the month Shebat "Splendour"' (lines 74-75). In line 49, ŠA is probably used because the following *r* might have caused readers to interpret ŠÁ as *gar*; similarly, in line 74, with a month in the offing, ŠÁ might have been mistaken for the number 'four'. The god's name in line 56 is always spelled with ŠA, never ŠÁ.[888]

5.4.4.2 *ša*$_1$ for the word, *šá* for the syllable

We proceed now to the second way in which some writers used the distribution of ŠA and ŠÁ to forestall ambiguities. This was to use ŠA for the independent word *ša* (as both preposition and pronoun) but ŠÁ for the syllable *ša* within a larger word.[889] When it is clear that a manuscript conforms to this pattern, exceptions can be studied with profit, sometimes yielding unexpected insights into textual history and ancient *Sprachgefühl.* We will duly present some manuscripts which conform to the pattern, attempting along the way to account for any exceptions they display.

The letters of the Neo-Assyrian scholar Akkullānu (SAA X 84-108) conform to the pattern without exception. Though most letters do not offer enough evidence to prove their conformity to the pattern if considered in isolation (though 100 does, and arguably 96 and 104 too), the

887 As word (50 occurrences): 4 (*2), 6, 7 (*2), 10, 14, 16, 18, 19, 22, 23, [30], 31, 33 (*3), 34 (*2), 35 (*2), 38, 40, 41 (*2), 50, 54, 79, 81, [95], 98, 103, 105 (*2), 116, 117 (*2), 118, 126, 131, 132, 133, 134, 142 (*2), 143, 148 (*2), 150, 151; within word (23 occurrences): 4, 8, 10, 12, 13, 16, 17, 24, 27, 30, 34, 36, 37, 38, 41, 52, 75, 82, 84, 100, 101, 137, 141.

888 See Schwemer, "Šāla. A. Philologisch", in Streck et al. (eds), *RlA XI* (2008) 565: '*^{d}*Šá-la* auch im 1. Jt. Bisher nicht belegt'. The consistency is all the more striking as *plene* versions of the name (*ša-a-la*) are found, showing that the spelling was not absolutely fixed.

889 To my knowledge this pattern was first observed by Heidel, *Sumer* 9 (1953) 186: 'With the exception of VII:43, the sign *šá* is used nowhere else [on this manuscript, MW], nor in the duplicate (CT XXVI, Pls. 1-37), as a relative particle'. Heidel's observation was applied more widely by Tadmor, Landsberger and Parpola, *SAAB* 3/1 (1989) 51 n. 32, stating that Neo-Assyrians normally wrote the word *ša* with the sign *ša*$_1$ (citing some exceptions; for more see § 4.8.2), and indeed that most Neo-Assyrians 'never used <šá> for writing the pronoun [i.e the word *ša*, MW], reserving it exclusively for the spelling of longer words'.

numbers across the letters as a whole are impressive: 83 occurrences of *ša*$_1$ as a word, and 24 occurrences of *šá* as a syllable.[890]

Tiglath-pileser III's 'summary inscription 7', a large tablet fragment found at the South-West Palace in Nimrud, contains 41 occurrences of *ša*$_1$ as a word, and 26 occurrences of *šá* as a syllable.[891] There is only one clear exception to this pattern: at obv. 3 ŠÁ is used for the word *ša*; for this, no cogent explanation can be offered (inadvertence?).

The extant manuscripts of Sennacherib's Rassam cylinder, presented by Eckart Frahm in a *variorum* edition, generally conform to the pattern. The cases where all the manuscripts agree are all in conformance with the pattern.[892] The exceptions,[893] where the manuscripts disagree, are as follows:

890 ***ša*$_1$ as word** (83 occurrences): 84:6, [84:17], 84 r.8, 87 r.7', [89:4'], 89 r.9, 90:5, 90:7 (*2), 90:13, 90:17, 90:19, 90:20, 90:21, 90 r.9', 90 r.19', 19:25e, 90 s.1, 90 s.2, 90 s.3, 91 :7, 91:11, 92:8, 93:7, 94:6, 94 r.6', 94 r.7', 94 r.10', 95:11, 95:12, 95:17, 95 r.9', 95 r.14', 95 r.18', 95 r.19' (*2), 95 r.25e (*2), 96:5, 96:6, 96:7, 96:11, 96:16, 96:24, 96 r.3, 96 r.6, 96 r.8, 96 r.11, 96 r.12, 96 r.13, 96 s.3, 97:5', 97 r.2, 97 r.5, 97 r.6, 98 r.4, 98 r.7, 99:5, 99:6, 100:13, 100:17, 100:28, 100:29, 100:33, 100 r.1, 100 r.3 (*2), 100 r.6, 100 r.7, 100 r.14, 101 r.7, 102:6', 103 r.2', 103 r.3', 104:5', 104:8', 104 s.2, 105:4', 105:22', 107:6, 107:7, 107 s.1, [108 r.8']; ***šá* as syllable** (24 occurrences): 89:6', 89 r.8, 90 r.15', 93:10, 96:8, 96 e.22, 96 r.9, 98:8, 98 r.14, 100:6, 100:11, 100:15, 100:20, 100 r.7, 100 r.8, 101 r.5, 103 r.2', 104:7', 104:12', 104:16', 104 r.4, 104 r.9, 105:10', 107:14.

891 ***ša*$_1$ as word**: 2, [3], 3, 4, 8 (*3), 9 (*2), 10, 13, 14, 15, 17, 18, 24 (*2), 26 (*2), 27, 29, 32 (*3), 35, 36 (*2), 38 (*3), 39 (*2), 40, 42, 47, r.4', r.7', r.16', r.17', r.24', r.26', r.27' (probably belongs here, but following signs are fragmentary), r.29', r.35'; ***šá* as syllable**: 3, 11, 12, 13, 15, 16, 19 (*2), 20, 22, 25, 30, 46 (*2), [r.2'], r.19', r.27', r.28', r.30' (*2), r.31', r.32', r.33' (*2), r.34' (*sic*!), r.35. At r.16', where Tadmor transliterates *ša-rēši*, *ša* is not visible in the copy. At rev. 19' it is not clear whether to read *mišihti qaqqariša* (Tadmor) or *mišihti qaqqari ša* (CAD M/1 122b).

892 We give the attestations by the prism's line number. We cannot verify how many (nor which) manuscripts are extant in each of the following cases, though according to Frahm's *apparatus criticus* the extant manuscripts are unanimous, and the overall pattern is clear: ***ša*$_1$ as word** (46 occurrences): 5, 6, 7, 9 (*2), 10, 15, 18, 21, 22, 23, 24, 26, 28, 31 (*2), 36, 39, 41 (*2), 42, 43, 45, 46, 47, 49 (*2), 53, 55, 59, 61, 62, 63, 64, 66, 69, 70, 71, 72, 73, 75, 83, 85, 89, 91, 93; ***šá* as syllable** (44 occurrences): 1 (*2), 2, 3, 4, 19 (*2), 21, 24, 27, 39, 40 (*2), 42, 44, 52, 59, 69, 70, 72, 73, 74 (*3), 74 (*3), 75 (*4), 76, 78 (*2), 80 (*2), 83, 84, 85, 88 (*2), 89, 92, 93.

893 The occurrence of MA for *ša*$_1$ at the start of line 49 on MS BB is not a real exception to the pattern, as it does not involve the substitution of *ša*$_1$ and *šá* or vice versa. It is an error of sign similarity.

Line 49: *ša nība lā īšû* 'which have no number': MSS Z, AA, and e have *ša*$_1$; MSS A, FF, LL have *šá*.

Line 51: *ša lā nībi* 'without number': MSS A, F, AA, FF, MM, DDD have *šá*; MS Z has *ša*$_1$.

Line 57: *ša nība lā īšû* 'which have no number': MSS Z, AA, LL have *ša*$_1$; MSS A and FF have *šá*.

It is striking, and can hardly be coincidental, that these cases all cluster around variations of the same phrase. Why is this? We think it likely that *ša lā* 'without', originally two separate words, had come to be thought of as a single word.[894] The development would be analogous to others discussed below. In line 51 MS Z opts for an 'etymological' spelling, with *ša* as a word in its own right. We suggest that in lines 49 and 57 the spelling of *ša lā nībi* (where *šá* is easily explicable through the supposition of a single word *šalā*) somehow, perhaps through misunderstanding, influenced the spelling of the synonymous phrase *ša nība lā īšû.*[895]

The manuscripts of Sargon's Khorsabad cylinder all basically conform to the pattern.[896] Seeming exceptions can be explained:[897]

a) In line 16, MS C2 has *ki-i šá~áš-šu-ri* 'like that of Assur'. As it is the only exception on the manuscript, this is very probably a sandhi spelling, reflecting crasis of *ša* and *aššuri.* Hence one can deduce from the spelling with *šá* that the person with whom it originated pronounced *ša aššuri* as /šaššuri/.

b) In line 51, MSS P2 and C1 have *ṭup-pa-a-te ša-a-a-ma-nu-te,* while MSS L1 and L2 have *ṭup-pa-a-te šá-a-a-ma-nu-ti/te.* The phrase clearly means something like 'the tablets about the purchases', but it is unlikely that it was originally a genitive construction: one would expect

894 In line 57 one could think of another explanation: *dictée intérieure* might have converted *ša* 'which' into a possessive suffix of the foregoing noun *tāhāzi* 'battle' (*tāhaziša* 'her battle' instead of *tāhāzi ša* 'battle which'). This would however leave *šá* in line 49 (*limētišunu ša*) unaccounted for, and given the similarity of the phrases it is likely that a single solution applies to them.

895 Another possibility is that *ša nība lā īšû* was considered a single 'word', but we think this less likely.

896 *ša* as a word (48 occurrences): 3, 6, 7, 8, 9, 10, 11, 14, 16, 17, 18, 19, 20, 21, 22, 23, 25, 26, 27, 28, 29, 31, 32, 32, 33, 35, 36, 38, 40, 44, 45, 45, 47, 48, 50, <51> (see discussion above), 52, 54, 58, 59, 60, 67, 68, 69, 70, 73, 76; *šá* within a word (24 occurrences): 1, 3, 4, 5, 10, 13, 18, 22, 27, 30, 41, 43, 48, 49, 49, 51, 56, 56, 62, 68, 73, 74, 75, 76. For exceptions see discussion above.

897 For the identification of exceptions we are dependent on Fuchs's *apparatus criticus.*

ṭuppāt rather than *ṭuppāte*,[898] and the *plene* spelling would be unexpected (§ 4.10). Both these considerations suggest that the original wording was *ṭuppāte ša šāyimānūte*, and that the initial *šá* of *šāyimānūte* was omitted by haplography on an ancestor manuscript. In this analysis, the transmitters of the tradition(s) represented by MSS P2 and C1 faithfully reproduced what they found on their exemplar (even though it was wrong), whereas the transmitters of the tradition(s) represented by MSS L1 and L2 interpreted the phrase as a genitive construction, and hypercorrected ŠA to ŠÁ.

c) In line 54, all manuscripts spell the foreign name 'Šauška' with ŠA. This is a special case: the reader might not know the name (see § 2.4.3 and fn. 830), so ŠA could have been used in preference to ŠÁ as an aid to reading, to prevent ambiguity (ŠÁ has several syllabic readings, whereas ŠA does not).

d) Lines 67-70 are about the building of city gates. For each gate, all manuscripts except MS C1 describe its orientation with the phrase *ša mehret*(igi-*et*) 'facing (a cardinal point)'. MS C1, by contrast, consistently uses *šá*. Since, discounting *ṭup-pa-a-te ša-a-a-ma-nu-te* in line 51 (see above), these are the only exceptions on MS C1, the suspicion arises that the writer of MS C1 did not intend to spell *ša mehret*, but a word beginning with /ša/. It is possible that the writer interpreted the signs ŠA ŠI IT on the exemplar as representing *šāsīt* 'which calls out to (a cardinal point)' (f. participle of *šasû*, in apposition to *abullu* 'gate').[899] Thus e.g. line 68:
enlil–mukīn–išdī–āliya mullissu–muddeššat–hiṣbi zikrī abul enlil u mullissu šá-ši-it iltani ambi '"Enlil–is–the–maker-firm–of–the–foundations–of–my–city" (and) "Mullissu–is–the–renewer–of–plentifulness" I named as the names of the gate(s) of Enlil and Mullissu which call(s) out to the North'.

---

898 It is true that sometimes feminine plurals are spelled with the ending *-āte* even in the construct state, but this does not seem to apply to the manuscripts of the Cylinder, whose morphology is generally 'good'. One cannot argue by analogy with seeming masculine plural construct states in *-ūte* (for expected *-ūt*), which are attested on manuscripts of the Cylinder, because the interchangeability between TE and UD in Neo-Assyrian script (see refs in fn. 282) means that a spelling such as *a-ši-bu-te* could stand for *a-ši-bu-ut.*

899 In this analysis, the writer of MS C1 interpreted ŠI as an Assyrian spelling of /si/. Compare MS C1's *iq-bu-u-ni* in line 55, where the presence of *plene* spelling is, as argued in Worthington, *ZA* 100/1 (2010), phonologically Assyrian and the use of U (rather than Ú, as on MSS P2, L1 and L2) is orthographically Assyrian.

It should be stressed that we are suggesting that a transmitter *thought* this to be the intended wording.[900]

Another manuscript which uses ša for the word *ša* and šá for the syllable /ša/ within larger words is Sennacherib's Chicago prism.[901] There are three exceptions, and given how solidly the pattern is attested on this manuscript, they require close scrutiny.

a) The first two cases occur nearby in identical constructions, and shall be treated together:

> *šemerī aṣ-pi hurāṣi* ki.sag *ebbi* ***šá*** *rittīšunu / amhur* (vi.13-14)
> *patrāt šibbī hurāṣi kaspi* ***šá*** *qablīšunu ēkim* (vi.15)[902]

In both sentences, the phrases *ša rittīšunu* (lit. 'of their hands') and *ša qablīšunu* (lit. 'of their hips') are sandwiched between a direct object and the verb which governs it. The most obvious way to take these phrases is as qualifiers of the direct objects, in a construction like English 'the-book-on-the-shelf'. In this interpretation, Sennacherib would tell us that he took the-ornaments-on-their-hands and the-swords-at-their-hips.[903] However, in this construction we would expect ša rather than šá.

Accordingly, we suppose that the person responsible for the sequence of signs extant on the Chicago prism understood *ša rittīšunu* and *ša qablīšunu* as noun-like expressions, analogous to e.g. *ša zumbē* 'that of flies', i.e. 'fly whisk' (attested in two inscriptions of Sargon).[904] The phrase *ša*

---

900 Another possibility is that the transmitter correctly understood *ša mehret*, but regarded it as one word.

901 *šá* within words (51 occurrences): i.5, i.8, i.10, i.13, i.68, i.70, i.79, ii.9, ii.22, ii.62, ii.68 (*2), iii.1, iii.51, iii.76, iii.77, iii.80, iv.6, iv.7, iv.10, iv.19, iv.45, v.8 (*3), v.62, v.65, v.67, v.73, v.81 (*2), v.82, v.83, vi.2, vi.3, vi.4, vi.5, vi.34, vi.42, vi.43, vi.44 (*2), vi.45 (*2), vi.52, vi.65, vi.71 (*2), vi.72, vi.73, vi.76; *ša* as word (89 occurrences): i.13, i.14, i.20, i.26, i.27, i.37, i.38, i.40, i.52, i.54, i.67, i.77, i.82, ii.3, ii.8, ii.18, ii.24, ii.33, ii.34, ii.50, ii.61, ii.71 (*2), ii.74, ii.75, ii.80, iii. 4, iii.8, iii.13, iii.19, iii.20, iii.21, iii.26, iii.27, iii.31, iii.39, iii.53, iii.59, iii.65, iii.66, iii.77, iv.15, iv.29, iv.33, iv.35, iv.36, iv.39, iv.41, iv.44, iv.47, iv.51, iv.56, iv.57, iv.66 (*2), iv.70 (*2), iv.71, iv.73, iv.74, iv.77 (*2), v.5, v.21, v.31, v.32, v.33, v.38 (*2), v.56, v.59, v.60, v.63, v.64, v.72, v.85, v.88, vi.4, vi.7, vi.17, vi.20, vi.25, vi.34, vi.36, vi.39, vi.49, vi.55, vi.63, vi.70, vi.74. For the three exceptions see above.

902 The sentence with *ša qablīšunu* occurs almost verbatim also on the Jerusalem prism, where it is the only exception to the pattern (see fn. 907).

903 It is normal for *ša* to be used instead of other prepositions in constructions of this type.

904 Of course any speaker of Babylonian or Assyrian would have recognised the independent origin of *ša* in such expressions, but it seems plausible that they could nonetheless have been thought of as a single word, and spelled accordingly. Note

qabli 'that of the hips' is known from other sources to have been so used with the meaning 'sash' (here it would be 'waist-trappings'),[905] whereas this would be the first attestation for *ša ritti* (which would mean 'wrist-trappings'). In this interpretation, *ša rittīšunu* and *ša qablīšunu* were understood as resumptions, analogous to *maddattu* in certain passages of Assurnaṣirpal II's inscriptions which likewise refer to the receipt of tribute.[906] The sense would, then, be:

> 'As their wrist-trappings I received bracelets of pure … gold; … as their waist-trappings I received swords of silver and gold'.

Quite possibly, this understanding was faulty, and the 'book-on-the-shelf' construction was the intended meaning.

b) The third case of ŠÁ for expected ŠA on the Chicago prism occurs at vi.69, in the building narrative: *naṣmadī sīsî parî* ***šá*** *emūqī rabâti īšû* 'teams of horses and mules which possess great strength'. Here we have no explanation for the use of ŠÁ other than to suppose a lapse on the part of the writer. This lapse could be of two kinds: correctly understanding *ša* as 'which' but forgetting to spell it as the pattern would require; or misunderstanding *ša*, i. e. taking it as a possessive suffix attached to *parî* (*parîša* 'its mules', with 'it' referring to the temple). Of these two possibilities, we find the latter more persuasive, because the same sentence contains another syntactically peculiar case of possessive -*ša* referring to the temple (vi.70, *ki-sal-la-šá*).

---

the possibility of an extreme case on two Late Babylonian medical tablets where the entire complex *ša libbiša* 'that of her womb', i. e. 'foetus' may be treated as a noun, being given a further possessive suffix (Finkel, "On Late Babylonian Medical Training", in George and Finkel (eds), *Studies Lambert* (2000) 174). The doubt arises because one attestation is restored, and the other (BM 42313+ r.11') has vanished along with the article's footnote 32.

905 In addition to the dictionaries, see George, "Babylonian Texts from the Folios of Sidney Smith, Part Three", in Guinan, de Jong Ellis, Ferrara, Freedman, Rutz, Sassmannshausen, Tinney and Waters (eds), *Studies Leichty* (2006) 180:6 for a Late Babylonian attestation.

906 E.g. RIMA 2, p. 197, lines 54-56: *madattu ša māt kirruri simesi simera ulmania adauš hargāya harmasāya sīsê kūdanī alpī immerī karānu*(? geštin^{meš}) *diqārī siparri madattašunu amhur* 'I received the tribute of the lands of …, horses, mules, oxen, wine, bronze casseroles, as their tribute' (the construction translates awkwardly into English!). (Owing to the fact that *maddattu* 'tribute' is frequently spelled with a single *d* – even when it has double *t* – in royal inscriptions whose language is Assyrianised, I normalise it on the assumption that in Neo-Assyrian the *dd* had simplified to *d*; cf. fn. 536).

Sennacherib's Jerusalem prism respects the pattern,[907] with a single exception (*šá* [muru]$b_4^{meš}$-*šú-nu*, i.e. *ša qablīšunu*, vi.12). We explain this in the same way as the same phrase on the Chicago prism.

Another manuscript which seems to conform to the pattern is a cylinder of Esarhaddon (RIMB 17), though ideally one would like more attestations.[908]

5.4.4.3 *šá* for the word, *ša*$_1$ for the syllable

Above we saw that some Neo-Assyrian manuscripts use *ša* for the independent word and *šá* for the syllable. Other manuscripts (we only know of Neo-Babylonian ones), do the opposite: they use *šá* for the independent word, and *ša* for the syllable within a word.

One manuscript which (in its preserved portions) does this consistently is *Ee* IV MS a.[909] The only exception to the pattern occurs in the second line of the colophon (*šá-ṭa-ri* '(piece of) writing'), colophons being a *locus classicus* for unusual orthography (see also *u-kin* instead of *ú-kin* in the fourth line).[910] Overall, this manuscript exhibits a high level of orthographic consistency, and we have more to say about it elsewhere (see § 4.8.3 on consistent use of *šu*$_1$; § 5.4.5 on *-tum*).

Another manuscript which exhibits this pattern is *Ee* I MS a.[911] There are however two[912] apparent exceptions.[913] The first occurs in line 110 (see fn. 386):

---

907 *ša* as a word (79 occurrences): i.12, i.13, i.18, i.23, i.25, i.32, i.33, i.35, i.47, i.48, i.61, i.70, ii.7, ii.16, [ii.22], ii.32, ii.47, ii.58, ii.67 (*2), ii.70 (*2), ii.75, [iii.4], iii.8, iii.11, iii.16, iii.18 (*2), iii.23, iii.27, iii.35, iii.45, iii.52, iii.68, iv.11, iv.27, iv.30, iv.33, iv.35, iv.38, iv.41, iv.45, iv.49, iv.58, iv.59, iv.62 (*2), iv.63, iv.65, iv.66, iv.68, iv.69, iv.76, v.13, v.23, v.24, v.25, v.29, v.30, v.47, v.49, v.54 (*2), v.61, v.73, v.76, vi.5, vi.13, vi.16, vi.25, vi.29, vi.31, vi.32, vi.33, vi.41, vi.44, vi.48, vi.54; *šá* within a word (50 occurrences): i.2, i.4, i.7, i.10, i.12, i.64, ii.8, ii.59, ii.64 (*2), ii.78, iii.24 (*sic*!), iii.44, iii.67 (*sic*!), iii.68, iii.71 (*sic*!), iv.5, iv.14, iv.38, v.1 (*3), v.17, v.52, v.55, v.57, v.62, v.69, v.70, v.71, v.77, v.78, vi.1, vi.2, vi.34, vi.35, vi.36 (*3), vi.37 (*2), vi.46, vi.47, vi.50 (*2), vi.51 (*3), vi.53, vi.55.

908 *ša* as a word (4 occurrences): 6, 8, 12, 21; *šá* within a word (4 occurrences): 18 (*2), 20 (*2).

909 *ša* as syllable (19 occurrences): lines 4, 6, 15, 23, 31, 32 (*2), 37, 42, 124, 132, 134 (*2), 135, 138 (*2), 139, 140, 145; *šá* as independent word (9 occurrences): 17, 18, 31, 33, 119, 128, 129, 143, 145.

910 On unusual orthography in colophons see Hunger, *Kolophone* (1968) 4–6.

911 The manuscript is written in Babylonian script, and therefore we give it a lowercase siglum. According to Langdon, *Penitential Psalms* (1927) xvi, it was 'found with tablets of the age of Sargon of Assyria', which establishes the end of the

⌜dingir[meš]⌝ *la šup-šu-⌜hu⌝ i-za-ab-bi-lu šá a-ri*[…]

If at the end of the line we had the word *šārī* 'the winds', we would expect this to be spelled with *ša*$_1$. Perhaps a transmitter understood it as *ša âri*[*ša*] 'that of her opposing', i. e. 'what was needed to oppose her' (cf. the use of *âru* at II 88 etc.).[914]

The second exception occurs in line 138:

⌜*me*⌝*-lám-me ma uš taš šá a i-liš um-*[…]

On the evidence of parallel manuscripts, the signs *uš taš šá a* should make up the verbal form *uštaššâ* 'she made carry' (*-ma* goes with *melammē*). If the signs are so read, the pattern is ruptured. While this might happen through inadvertence, we should again consider the possibility of misun-

eighth century BC as a *terminus ante quem.* On p. xvi and plates xxxi-xxxv, Langdon wrongly gives the tablet's siglum as Kish 1927-71. Paul Collins, to whom I am very grateful for looking into the matter, reports that the siglum is in fact Kish 1924.790+1813+2081 (Kish 1924-790 being correctly given by Langdon in his transliteration). Thanks to the good offices and flexibility of Paul Collins, several signs on the tablet were very kindly collated by Aage Westenholz and Inger Jentoft, who also supplied me with photographs. I express my heartfelt gratitude to them. Inger Jentoft noticed that the tablet has some signs which do not appear in Langdon's copy (perhaps because it was joined afterwards).

912 In line 17, MSS a and b read *ša abbîšu a-lid-su-nu* 'his forefathers' begetter', while MSS F and H (KAR 118 and KAR 163, both from Assur) have *ša abbîšu šá-liṭ-su-nu* 'his forefathers' *šāliṭu*'. If one were to regard *a-lid-su-nu* as a corruption of *šá-liṭ-su-nu*, then we would have to suppose that an ancestor manuscript had *šá* for the syllable within a word, which would contravene the pattern. However, it seems at least as likely that *šá-liṭ-su-nu* is a corruption of *a-lid-su-nu* (cf. line 19, *ana ālid abīšu* 'to his father's begetter').

913 At *Ee* I 147 and 151, other manuscripts have *šu-ut.* It is unclear (coll. Aage Westenholz) whether MS 'a' has *šu-ut* or *ša*$_1$ (lines 146 and 150 in Langdon's copy). Borger, *MesZL* (2004) 665 *sub* 566 remarks on this ambiguity in Neo-Babylonian script: 'šu-ut und ša schwer zu unterscheiden'. If the writer did intend *ša*, this could have arisen as a misreading of *šu-ut* (for such a case see Heeßel, *Divinatorische Texte I* (2007) 111, note to line 9), and/or in the belief that ŠA represented a sumerogram for the word *ša* in its masculine plural form *šūt* (see Landsberger and Hallock, "Neo-Babylonian Grammatical Texts", in Landsberger, Hallock, Jacobsen and Falkenstein (eds), *MSL IV* (1956) 137 (NBGT I 213), where Sum. ša$_1$ is equated with Akk. *ša*$_1$).

914 There are several problems with this line, including the variants at its end and the ending *-a* on other manuscripts' *šup-šu-ha* (if stative, who is the subject? If infinitive or verbal adjective, what does it agree with or depend on?). Is it possible that in some traditions *šupšuha* was accusative?

derstanding – e.g. *me-lám-me ma-nit-tiš* 4-*a i-liš.* This would not give much sense, but transmitters did not always understand what they wrote.

5.4.4.4 *šá* for the syllable, the word written with both signs

The fourth distribution of ŠA and ŠÁ is a variant of the second (§ 5.4.4.2): whereas in the second pattern ŠA and ŠÁ were respectively used for *ša* the word and *ša* the syllable, in the fourth pattern *ša* the syllable is always spelled ŠÁ, while *ša* the word is spelled either ŠA or ŠÁ, apparently at whim.

Manuscripts which exhibit this distribution include the following:

A Nineveh prism of Esarhaddon[915] spells the word *ša* 57 times with ŠÁ and 62 times with ŠA.[916] By contrast, the syllable /ša/ is always written with ŠÁ (56 attestations).[917]

Asb F1 spells the word *ša* 54 times with ŠÁ and 34 times with ŠA.[918] By contrast, the syllable /ša/ is written with ŠÁ almost every time (33 attesta-

915 Published by Thompson, *Prisms* (1931), who reports that its state of preservation is 'perfect except for a light stroke of the pick' (p. 7).

916 ŠÁ as word: i.6, i.10 (*2), i.29, i.34, i.35, i.45 (*2), i.46, i.50, i.59 (*2), i.80, ii.23, ii.45, ii.46, ii.52, ii.58, iii.15, iii.39, iii.41, iii.44, iii.49, iii.52, iii.54, iii.62, iii.64, iv.26, iv.29, iv.32, iv.33, iv.34, iv.35, iv.42, iv.47 (*2), iv.50, iv.53, iv.73, iv.78, iv.79, v.15, v.20, v.21, v.28, v.31, v.34 (*2), v.63, vi.13, vi.30, vi.32, vi.44 (*2), vi.45, vi.69, vi.75; ŠA as word: i.5, i.6, i.8, i.21, i.24, i.41, i.53, i.83, ii.4, ii.8, ii.19, ii.20, ii.23, ii.28, ii.41, ii.56, ii.67, ii.68, ii.78, iii.1, iii.9, iii.10, iii.22, iii.50, iii.57, iii.72, iv.2, iv.12, iv.35, iv.37, iv.40, iv.46, iv.48, iv.59, iv.69, iv.82, iv.83, v.3, v.10, v.12, v.17, v.20, v.23, v.27, v.37, v.38, v.40, v.41, v.45, v.71, v.75, v.76, v.77, v.79, vi.5, vi.6, vi.15, vi.16, vi.19, vi.20, vi.24, vi.66.

917 ŠÁ as syllable: i.2, i.19, i.57, i.71, i.78, i.86, ii.4, ii.5, ii.13, ii.35, ii.37, ii.40, ii.44, ii.64, ii.78, ii.81, iii.16, iii.37, iii.67, iii.70, iii.82, iv.16 (*2), iv.36, iv.50, iv.85, v.1, v.6, v.35, v.48, v.59, v.63, v.81, vi.7, vi.21, vi.26, vi.29, vi.31, vi.32, vi.33, vi.35 (*2), vi.37 (*2), vi.41 (*2), vi.47, vi.51 (*2), vi.53, vi.56, vi.57, vi.61, vi.62, vi.64, vi.67.

918 ŠÁ as word: i.27, i.49 (*2), ii.11, ii.24 (*2), ii.43 (*2), ii.56 (*2), ii.61, ii.70, iii.17, iii.34, iii.40, iii.47, iii.48, iii.49, iii.53, iii.58, iii.63, iii.66, iii.70, iii.72, iii.74, iii.80, iii.82, iv.49, iv.59, iv.67, iv.72, v.4, v.13, v.15 (or syllable? ^{giš}*šá šadādi*, could be a single word), v.16, v.18, v.22, v.39, v.45, v.58, v.61 (or syllable? ^{lú}*šá* [*pēthalli*], could be a single word), v.65, vi.6, vi.8, vi.13, vi.14, [vi.17], vi.22, v.24, vi.31, vi.37, vi.53, vi.58, vi.62; ŠA as word: [i.19], i.38, i.41, i.54, i.57, i.65, i.72, ii.12, ii.16, ii.26, ii.48, ii.51, ii.68, ii.75, iii.32, iii.38, iii.54, iii.58, iv.20, iv.43, iv.48, iv.55, iv.57, iv.58, iv.60, iv.65, v.19, v.21, v.22, v.60, v.72, vi.12, vi.35, vi.50.

tions).[919] The only exceptions occur at vi.31: an.dùl-*ša šá ša-la-me*. Here it seems to be the sequence of so many ŠAs which has somehow 'thrown' the writer (though why an.dùl-*ša šá ša-la-me* was written rather than an.dùl-*šá ša šá-la-me* is unclear).

A Nimrud cylinder of Esarhaddon (ND 1126),[920] virtually perfectly preserved, consistently spells the syllable *ša* with ŠÁ (6 times),[921] while for the word *ša* it alternates between ŠÁ (3 times) and ŠA (17 times).[922]

This distribution could be *bona fide* in its own right, but it can also be interpreted as a corruption of the second pattern: writers with a preference for the quicker-to-write ŠÁ who were copying manuscripts which conformed to the second pattern might well sporadically convert the exemplar's ŠA to ŠÁ, while leaving ŠÁ unchanged. Indeed, since it is difficult to see any useful function the distribution here discussed could serve in its own right, the supposition that it is a distortion of the second pattern is perhaps to be preferred.

5.4.5 *-tum* as a marker of singular word ends

MS a of *Ee* IV has the peculiarity that singular nouns and adjectives with stem-final *t* usually end in *-tum* in the *status rectus* singular, regardless of their function in the sentence (i. e. in terms of second millennium grammar, regardless of their grammatical case):[923]

2 *ma-li-ku-tum* 'rulership' (gen.)
11 *za-na-nu-tum* 'sustenance' (acc.)
14 *šar-ru-tum* 'kingship' (acc.)
22 *a-ba-tum* 'destruction' (acc.)
32 *pu-uz-ra-tum* (gen.)

---

919 ŠÁ as syllable: i.16, i.17, i.28, i.29, ii.15, ii.30, ii.37, ii.44, ii.60, ii.64, ii.66, ii.70, iii.34, iii.67, iii.71, iii.75, iii.79, iv.5, iv.36, iv.68, iv.69, v.15, v.19, v.31, v.33, v.35, v.60, v.66, vi.3, vi.6, vi.26, vi.31, vi.49. For line vi.31 see discussion above.

920 See Wiseman, *Iraq* 14/1 (1952).

921 ŠÁ as word: 7, 42, 46; ŠA as word: 3, 4, 11, 15 (*2), 22, 26 (*2), 29, 31, 32 (*2), 33, 35, 41, 42, 54.

922 ŠÁ as syllable: 16, 23, 35, 44, 67, 53.

923 This is also true of masculine plurals in *-ūtu*: 1 *ru-bu-tum*, 3 and 5 *ra-bu-tum*, 127 *ka-mu-tum*, catchline *ra-bi-ú-tum*. This might be thought to signify a connection in the writer's mind between the m. pl. morpheme *-ūtu* and the abstract f. sg. ending *-ūtu*, which has sometimes been envisaged by modern scholars. But since apart from *rubûtum* 'nobles' they are all attributes of the gods, they could be honorific nominatives.

38 ^{kuš}*iš-pa-tum* 'quiver' (acc.)
129 *ti-a-ma-tum* 'Tiamtu' (gen., perhaps honorific nom., § 4.5)
141 *aš-ra-tum* 'place' (acc.)

The exceptions are TAM-TIM 'sea' (line 41, gen.) and límmu-TIM 'four' (line 42, *erbetti šārī* 'four winds'), but these are special cases: TAM-TIM is a fossilized spelling used for any singular form of *tâmdu* 'sea';[924] in límmu-TIM, -TIM is a phonetic complement which attaches to sumerographic spellings regardless of the relevant word's grammatical case, probably as an aid to reading (see § 5.4.8).

By contrast, *status rectus* feminine plurals on this manuscript end not in *-tum*, but in *-āti*/*-ēti*:

14 *gim-re-e-ti*
18 *lem-né-e-ti*
136 *nik-la-a-ti*

Now, it could be argued that *aš-ra-tum* (line 141) and *pu-uz-ra-tum* (line 32), listed as singulars above, are actually plurals. This is indeed the view adopted by AHw, which interprets *aš-ra-tum* as a plural of *ašru* in the meaning 'Stätte' (83a *sub* 4a) and (885b *sub* B7) *pu-uz-ra-tum* as a plural of *puzurtum.* Similarly, CAD H 160a has *ašrātum* 'the localities', and many translators have plurals.[925]

However, without prejudice to how the line 'should' run, or ran originally, it seems safe to infer that, in the mind of the person who generated the sequence of signs extant on MS a, *aš-ra-tum* and *pu-uz-ra-tum* were singulars. For there is not only the ending *-tum* (which in itself would not be probative), but also the absence of *plene* spelling: the three unequivocal feminine plurals in the *status rectus* (listed above) are spelled *plene.* On a manuscript as carefully spelled as this one (see the introduction to § 5.4.4.3), this coupling of features (no *plene*, *-tum* rather than *-ti*) is highly suggestive. At least for the writer of this manuscript, then, we should follow CAD A/ii 454b in positing a lexeme *ašratu* (attested only once elsewhere), which CAD suggests is 'a poetic word for heaven'.

924 It is possible that the spelling TAM-TIM was indeed chosen in line 41 because the word stood in the genitive, but most likely the writer was adopting a ready-made spelling of the word rather than deciding *sponte sua* to spell it with *-tim.*

925 Foster p. 462 reads *ašrātu* and translates 'firmament'. CAD P 558b bottom (and B 347a) interprets the spelling *pu-uz-ra-tum* as a form of *bussurtu* 'tidings' (not clear whether singular or plural). AHw's skepticism of this was presumably induced by the elision of *u*, which is unexpected after an etymologically double consonant.

For *pu-uz-ra-tum* some may see the fact that the writer understood it as singular as evidence that it is in fact a form of *bussurtu*, but it is also possible that a word *puzratum* 'hiddenness' should be posited.

Be that as it may, it seems safe to re-state that the writer of this tablet consistently spelled words with stem-final *t* in the *status rectus* singular using the sign *-tum*. This contrasts with the spellings of other words in the *status rectus* singular, which on at least three occasions have 'correct' *status rectus* singular genitive endings: *i-na ki-šib-bi* (122), *pa-di-i* (130), *a-na pi-i šá-ṭa-ri* (second line of colophon). There are three exceptions, two of which can be explained quite easily: *šu-ul-mu~u* (34) as an enriched sandhi spelling (§ 4.4.2), and *i-na* PU-HUR (15) as a fossilised spelling.[926] The ending on the third case, *na-ki-ru* (215), is harder to explain away, but here the layout of the tablet is relevant: it looks from Leonard King's copy as if the writer thought that RU was (or was part of) a different word from *na-ki*, in which case *na-ki* would have the expected genitive ending.

We suggest that the writer's use of *-tum* at the end of nouns and adjectives whose stem ends in *t* was an aid to reading (and parsing).[927] If this is so, it worked: it contributed to the recognition of *ašratu* vs *ašrātu*.

5.4.6 *-tu* as a marker of nom./acc. singular

The sole extant manuscript of Sargon's 8th campaign, TCL III+, displays great consistency in its spelling of case endings in the *status rectus* singular. The genitive always ends in *i* or *e* and the nominative in *u*, as expected in 'good' grammar.

Spellings of the accusative therefore become all the more curious: here there is a cleavage between nouns and adjectives with stem-final *t* (which are nearly all feminine), and all other nouns and adjectives. The first group always has nominative and accusative case marker *-u* (almost always spelled *-tu*₁), whereas the second group exhibits both *a* and *u* as accusative endings. We list the instances:[928]

---

926 Cf. *Ee* V 126, *ana ma-har* PU-HUR-*ku-un* 'before your assembly' very probably represents /puhrikunu/. Another possible case is YOS III 200:17 (*ina* PU-HUR-*šú-nu* 'in their assembly').

927 For a possible parallel (but with much more slender evidence) see the discussion of LUM on *Gilg.* VI MS **a** in § 4.7.2.

928 We exclude place names, adverbial accusatives (e.g. *qaq-qa-ru* at 75, 145, 254; *gi-mir-tu* at 89, 164, 247 and 422), and accusatives in long lists of booty where

Stem ending in *-t*

41 cases of *-tu*$_1$: gal-*tu* (18), *pu-luh-tu* (21), *ka-bit-tu* (41), *be-lu-tu* (66), *ta-šim-tu* (81 and 93), *kab-tu* (94), *gul-lul-tu* gal-*tu* (95), *si-dir-tu* (111), *taš-ri-ih-tu* (119), *ka-ṣir-tu* (120), *ma-'-at-tu* (134), *ir-tu* (142), gal-*tu* (147), *šu-tur-tu* (153), *šah-ra-ar-tu* (158), *di-im-ma-tu* (158), *a-nu-un-tu* (194), *te-li-tu* (208), *er-re-tu* (210), *pu-ú-tu* (215), *ma-at-tu* (219), *mi-ni-tu* (225), gal-*tu* (231), *ba-ṭil-tu* (243), *si-kil-tu* (244), *šá-[ha]-tu* (252), *kit-mur-tu* (257), *ma-'-at-tu* (274), *ma-ṣar-tu* (278), *bíl-tu ma-da-at-tu* (312), *ur-tu* (333), *ta-[k]ul-tu* (341), gal-*tu* (343), *i-šit-tu kit-mur-tu* (351), *šu-qul-tu* (376), *pu-luh-tu* (420), *ma-at-tu* (421)
2 cases of *-tú*: *gi-lit-tú* (192), *šu-bul-tú* (228)
2 cases of *-tum*: íd-*tum* (17), í[d-*tu*]*m* (79)
1 (apparent) case of *-ta*: *nap-ša-ta* (193)

Stem not ending in *-t*

54 attestations of *-u*: an.ta-*ú* (8), ki.ta-*ú* (10), *ta-lu-ku* (13), *ṣil-lu* (16), *gir-ru* (24), *pet-hal-lum* (25), *kal-la-bu* (26), gal-*ú* (54), *ap-pu* (55), *sap-hu* (57), *lib-bu* (61), *qe-e-pu* (73), *qaq-qa-ru* (75), *ki-it-ru* (85), *šu-ri-pu* (101), *ma-'-du* (103), *mu-lu-ú mu-rad-du* (128), *ta-ha-zu* (138), *mu-lu-ú ù mu-rad-du* (144), *ak-lu* (151), *nu-u-ru* (155), *qu-ú-lu* (158), *a-ṣu-ú si-ih-ru ù ta-a-ru* (173), *na-gu-ú* (194), *pal-gu* (203), *ta-ra-nu* (206), *šid-du* (215), *dan-nu* (217), *ma-'-du* (225, 228), *as-mu* (229), *sah-hu* (230), *šam-ru* (251), *na-gu-ú* (253), *ma-la-ku* (254), *ha-a-a-ṭu* (255), *bu-šu-ú ma-ak-ku-r[u]* (257), *kal-la-bu* (258), *ta-lu-ku* (317), kur-*ú dan-nu* (322), an.ta-*ú* (323), *da-rag-gu* (325), *aq-ru* (340), *il-ku tup-šik-ku* (410), *gir-<ra>?-nu* (414), *ṣu-lu-lu* (416), *mu-ni-ih-hu* (420)
19 attestations of *-a*: *me-te-qa* (20), *re-e-ma* (59, sandhi poss.), *qi-nam* (98), *né-ra-ra* (107), *re-e-ha* (147), *lem-na* (155), *mi-i-na* (164), *hal-la* (173), *iṣ-ṣa* (227), *ni-i-ba* (228), *ṣir-pa* (229), *pa-na* (252), *mu-la-a* (322), *ni-ba* (325), *gir-ra qa-at-na me-te-qa su-ú-qa* (330), *ni-i-ba* (405)

The two instances of *-tú* could be read *-ta*$_5$, but they both occur at the end of their line, and it looks from Thureau-Dangin's copy as if the writer simply switched from *tu*$_1$ to *tu*$_2$ in order to avoid overrunning the margin (*tú* being a much narrower sign than *tu*$_1$).

The big surprise occurs in line 193: *nap-ša-ta i-še-'u-ú* 'they sought life', which appears to involve an accusative ending in *-ta*. While this is not impossible, we think it more likely that *nap-ša-ta* represents /napšat/, i.e. it is a truncated spelling resulting from crasis of *napšatu iše''û* into /napšatiše''û/ (see § 4.4.7). There are comparable instances of redundant word-final vowels on this manuscript: *a-ka-ma ger-ri-ia* 'the

case might have been forgotten (*ta-kil-tu* at 366; *ši-bir-tu* at 369). None of these (nor instances of *casus pendens*, e.g. *dan-nu* at 179) would contradict the pattern if included, however.

dust-cloud from my campaign' for /akāmgerriya/, *li-i-ti* ^d^*a-šur* 'the victory of Aššur' (lines 146 and 152) for /lītaššur/, and probably *a-ši-bu-tu nagî* 'who inhabit the district' (line 192) for /āšibūtnagî/. Therefore, despite appearances to the contrary, *nap-ša-ta* does not properly contravene the pattern to this manuscript's use of accusative endings.

Quite how firmly the writer was wedded to the pattern becomes further apparent in the phrase *um-ma-ni ma-'a-at-ta-tu* 'my vast army' (line 292). Here he first wrote a singular accusative in *-ta*, then corrected himself to *-tu* (without erasing the unwanted *-ta*; 'soft auto-correction', see § 4.3).[929]

The distribution of accusative singular endings cannot possibly be due to coincidence. What, then, is the explanation? As there seems to be no plausible phonological or morphological reason why the cleavage might exist, so it is likely that the reason should be sought in the realm of orthography. Our view is that the writer standardized the spelling of noun ends to make them easier to recognize. This was easily done for nouns with stem-final *t*, but not done for other nouns because too many different cuneiform signs would have been involved (almost one per stem-final consonant), so the gain in ease of word recognition would have been too small.

5.4.7 The use of MEŠ to mark sumerograms

Traditionally, the sign MEŠ functions as a marker of plurality. However, as several scholars have observed,[930] it sometimes appears in cases where grammar or idiom suggests that a sumerogram conceals a singular word. Here are some examples:

---

929 Compare *ummānšunu ma'attu ušamqit* 'I felled their vast army' (line 421) and *ummānšu ma'du … idkâm-ma* 'he roused his vast army …' (line 103). An alternative interpretation is *ummānī ma'attātu* 'the numerous troops', but the secondary plural formation *ma'attātu* would, though linguistically conceivable in Neo-Assyrian (see Hämeen-Anttila, *Sketch* (2000) 43 on *piqittāte* rather than *piqdāte* as a secondary plural of *piqittu*), be odd on this manuscript. The expected form *ma'dāti* appears in line 166. Also, it would be odd on this manuscript for a feminine plural form to end in *-tu*. (A further problem with *ummānī ma'attātu* is that one would arguably expect a possessive suffix after *ummānu*, but its absence could be explained away as lipography).

930 E.g. Cole in fn. 932; cf. Weeden, *WdO* 39/1 (2009) 84.

ka-la-a-at ^{giš}gigir^{meš}-[*šu*] '[his] chariot(ry) was held back' (Middle Assyrian)[931]
^{giš}gigir^{meš} / *ha-lup*(MS:*lap*)*-ta* 'armoured chariot' (TP I 1 iv.94-95)
gu$_4$^{meš} *šanûm-ma* 'another ox'[932] and ki-*TIM*^{meš} (both early Neo-Babylonian)[933]
gaz^{meš}*-šu-nu ma-'a-tu* 'a mighty defeat of them' (AN II 1:14)
bīt ŠE.PAD^{meš}*-šu ma-at-ti* 'his abundant *grain* store' (TCL III+ 189)
ŠE.PAD^{meš}*-su ma-at-tu* 'his abundant *grain*' (TCL III+ 219)
ŠE.PAD^{meš}*-su-nu ma-'-at-tu* 'their abundant *grain*' (TCL III+ 274)
na$_4$^{meš} *a-qar-tu*$_{(2)}$ 'precious stone' (Sar XIV 63, Esar NinA-F ep.5 A ii.75)[934]
ud^{meš} *an-né-e* 'this day' (Asb F iv.75 // A vi.2, MS F49)
erim^{meš} mè^{meš}*-ia* 'my combat troops' (Asb B v.80 MS B9)
arad^{meš}*-ti-ia* 'thralldom to me' (Asb B vii.71 MS D36)
^{giš}gišimmar^{meš}$_{(2)}$ 'date palm' (*Tamarisk and Date Palm* 12 and 19 MS **c**)[935]

Three cases occur on Assurbanipal's MS F2: mè^{meš}*-ia* (F v.47 // A vi.68), geštin^{meš} (F vi.46 // A x.83) and the attestations of gìr$^{\text{ii.meš}}$-(*ia*) below. In all three instances MS F2 is the only manuscript to display the unexpected MEŠ. At Asb F v.36, MS F6 has alam^{meš} where all other manuscripts have alam.

In the above (and similar) cases, the unexpected MEŠ should probably be understood as an aid to reading: it indicates to the reader that the preceding sign or group of signs is to be read sumerographically. A particularly interesting case is *a-sa*-gi^{meš} // *a-sa-kan* 'I placed' (Asn II 1 iii.2 var.): here MEŠ indicates that the sign GI (sumerogram of Akkadian *qanû* 'reed') should be read aloud as /kan/.

There is a possible case already in Old Babylonian: di.ku$_5$^{meš} as subject of *ṣubāssu elišunu iddi-ma* 'He threw his garment over them' (CT 48, no. 3:22). However, in the absence of further examples from this period, Claus Wilcke's explanation that the writer wrote MEŠ out of habit,

931 TN epic 'iii'.35.

932 With Cole, *Archive* (1996) 133 n. to line 9.

933 Cole, *Archive* (1996) 270 line 31, reading ki-*tim* "MEŠ". The sign group ki-*TIM* should be understood as an orthographic fossil (§ 5.4.8), and the MEŠ sign probably indicates this.

934 As noted by Fuchs *ad loc.*, the parallel passage *Prunk* 180 has na$_4$ (no MEŠ!) *a-qar-tum*.

935 Lambert, *BWL* (1960) 152 found the alternation of spellings with and without MEŠ 'most peculiar', but if MEŠ does not mark plurality the inconsistency is less troubling.

di.ku$_5^{\text{meš}}$ 'judges' being a commonly occurring sequence of signs, may be preferable.[936]

Since one plural marker renders the other redundant, in principle MEŠ and HI.A (traditionally also a plural marker) should not co-occur. Again in principle, MEŠ and the dual marker should not co-occur because they contradict each other. Nonetheless, there are cases in which MEŠ follows HI.A or the dual marker:

hi.a.meš:

> *si-ta-at* érin$^{\text{hi.a.meš}}$-*šu-nu* … *i-tu-r*[*u-n*]*i* (AN II 1:17-19)
> u$_8$.udu$^{\text{hi.a.meš}}$ (Asb A vi.93 varr.)
> érin$^{\text{hi.a.meš}}$-*ia* (F iv.17 var., A v.98 MS A3, A ix.127 MS A2)

ii.meš:

> gìr$^{\text{ii.meš}}$-*ia* (AD II 1:70)
> igi$^{\text{ii.meš}}$-*šu* (AD II 1:85)
> gìr$^{\text{ii.meš}}$-*ia* (TN II 5:38)
> igi$^{\text{ii.meš}}$-*šú-nu* (Asn II 1 i.117 var.)
> gìr$^{\text{ii.meš}}$-*ia* (Asb A iii.19 var.)
> á$^{\text{ii.meš}}$-*ia* (Asb F iv.24 var.)
> gìr$^{\text{ii.meš}}$-(*ia*) (Asb MS F2: F iii.26, F iii.38 (//A iv.115); A iv.123)

The function of MEŠ in such cases is uncertain. It may, as in the foregoing examples, serve as an aid to reading. Another possibility is that HI.A and the dual marker have simply come to be regarded as part of the relevant sumerogram, so that MEŠ marks the forms as non-singular.

This would be most likely to happen with sign groups that occurred frequently. Good candidates would include sumerographic spellings of double body parts (hands, eyes, etc.). It is rare for one only to be referred to, so the dual sign is almost always present. This is probably why occasionally it is present even though the word is grammatically singular, e.g. [ig]i^{ii}-*šú ina* ugu-*hi* / [*t*]*a-tu-qut* 'his eye fell on it' (SAA X 50 r.5-6) and gìr^{ii} lú.kúr *lem-na* (TCL III+ 155): *lem-na* is difficult as f. pl. stative, so probably gìr^{ii} lú.kúr represents *šēp nakri* (accusative singular).[937] Perhaps érin$^{\text{hi.a}}$-*šu-nu ma-at-tu* (TCL III+ 421) also belongs here.

---

936 Wilcke, "A Riding Tooth. Metaphor, Metonymy and Synecdoche, quick and frozen in Everyday Language", in Mindlin, Geller and Wansbrough (eds), *Figurative Language* (1987) 102 n. 104.

937 The attractiveness of an emendation to *lem-na-*<*te*> is lessened by the fact that on this manuscript *lem-na-a-te* would be more likely (see § 4.10.1).

Where MEŠ following a sumerogram is difficult to interpret as a plural marker,[938] Akkadianists may have recourse to the supposition that it was an aid to reading.

5.4.8 The use of -*TIM* to mark sumerograms

There is a peculiarity to the use of the sign TIM when it is ostensibly used as a phonetic complement to sumerograms: on manuscripts which otherwise give genitives the ending *-i/e*, TIM is used as a complement even for words which stand in the nominative and accusative. The use of TIM does not, then, indicate pronunciation /ti(m)/. Rather, it has simply become a standard spelling accompanying the sumerogram: a fossilised spelling. Rykle Borger called sign groups such as zi-*tim* and ki-*tim* 'logographische Einheiten'.[939]

Why did such cases come into being? In our view, they are aids to reading. In the first millennium, the sign TIM is very rarely required to represent the spoken sounds /tim/ or /dim/. Therefore, readers knew as a rule of thumb that, whenever they saw it, there was a good chance it was being used as phonetic complement to a sumerogram. From here it is only a short step to using it as a marker of sumerography.[940]

5.5 Recapitulation on ancient misreadings in § 3.3

As we saw in § 3.2.1, Hugo Radau wrote already in 1908 that 'even Babylonians could and actually did misread [i.e. misidentify, MW] their own signs'. This statement was borne out by the evidence assembled in § 3.3 above. Though we saw that matters are more complex than Radau imagined, and that in many cases it is impossible to distinguish errors of sign identification on the part of a reader from *lapsus styli* on the part of a writer, there are nonetheless numerous cases where transmitters can be shown to have failed in identifying the signs on their exemplar. We also

938 For an example of such a case see the comment by Rochberg, *JAOS* 116/3 (1996) 476 n. 4.

939 Borger, *MesZL* (2004) 411 (KI) and 279 (ZI).

940 A special case is ki-*TIM*, which Deller, "Die Briefe des Adad-Šumu-Uṣur", in Röllig and Dietrich (eds), *1st Fs von Soden* (1969) 48 and Parpola, *LAS II* (1983) 117 have argued to represent the word *qaqqar*- 'earth, soil' (not *erṣetu* 'earth') in Neo-Assyrian.

encountered cases where, though the signs were correctly identified, they were incorrectly read (i.e. assigned the wrong value).

These errors are valuable sources of information about how easy or otherwise ancient readers found it to read cuneiform. The more such errors we find, the stronger the evidence for difficulties in reading becomes.

Their errors need not imply that readers were aware of having difficulties. Indeed, it is likely that some of the readers we encountered in § 3.3 bulldozed their way through a passage with a touching faith they were getting it all right, when they were actually getting it badly wrong. For our purposes, however, the very fact that readers who appear to have been advanced in their study of cuneiform could be under this misapprehension would be significant in itself: it would show just how treacherous cuneiform was.

Not all errors by readers are evidence of straight-forward failure to decode the script. For 'external' complications which might have beset reading (unfamiliar ductus, poor handwriting, poor lighting, damage to the surface of the manuscript) are obscured from us. Hence errors by readers do not necessarily tell us about difficulties in reading at the cognitive level. Nonetheless, they tell us about the difficulties in reading as it was done in practice. This is in itself a great boon in understanding the mechanisms of transmission and textual change.

We will not here review the many errors by readers discussed in § 3.3. Suffice it to say that it is clear that readers could and did make all sorts of mistakes, sometimes in the most surprising ways. It would, therefore, have been perfectly natural for meticulous writers to have chosen spellings with a view to helping readers. This adds plausibility to the interpretations proposed in § 5.4.

5.6 Towards a model of ancient sight-reading

The evidence we have assembled for the ease (or otherwise) with which cuneiform was sight-read in antiquity is of two kinds: writers offering help to their readers, and – in previous chapters – transmitters misunderstanding their exemplars.

Quite apart from practical difficulties posed by lighting, damage to tablet surface etc., the conclusion seems inescapable that the ambiguities of the script itself could mislead even readers who were fully literate in the relevant textual typology, resulting in erroneous textual changes. Unseen cuneiform was apparently not as straightforward for the ancients as reading a newspaper is for us: for a significant proportion of transmitters, reading the unfamiliar (in whichever of its many forms) was not always a smooth process, but one which unfolded in fits and starts. This does not just apply to unpractised individuals writing utilitarian documents, but to writers of manuscripts of high intellectual merit, who were in the final stages in their training, if not beyond. How far purely cognitive difficulties (inherent in the ambiguities of the script) were exacerbated by practical ones (lighting, eyesight, script size etc.) is difficult to determine.

Since we know that signs were misidentified and misinterpreted, and also that cuneiform was not always easy to sight-read, it seems logical to suppose that all these facts belong together. Coupled with somnolence or other types of distraction, we begin to see how hair-raising corruptions such as hypercorrection of *ušardâ* to *ušaršida* (§ 3.4.6.1) could arise.

It is, however, worth repeating what we said in § 2.3.3: the difficulties of cuneiform would simply have exacerbated textual distortions which, as many cultures show, happen universally. The arguments advanced in other chapters about the desirability of more conjectures in Assyriology stand independently of the present chapter.

So, if sight-reading cuneiform was not simply a matter of looking at the signs and decoding them with zero effort, as we do with a newspaper, how did decoding work? What strategies were used?

The many 'helpful' spellings cited in § 5.4 suggest that ancient sight-readers of cuneiform were expected to decipher a line a bit at a time – not to sweep their eyes across it as we do with our script, reading it as a matter of course. For consideration of six or seven signs together would have made the 'helpful' spellings redundant, so the fact that they appear suggest that fewer signs were considered. A good example is the sequence *ša ka-a-a-nam-ma šu-gu-ra-a na-šak-ki*, where at the start of the line *ša* was used instead of *šá* to prevent the reading *nik-ka-* (*Gilg.* VI 65 MS A, § 5.4.4.1). Here one has the impression that the reader was expected to move through the line reading maybe three or four signs at a time, and go back to try again if the result did not make sense.

In this connection it is worth citing Henry Chaytor's characterisation of the 'mental attitude' of medieval readers, who were 'confronted not by the beautiful productions of a university press, but by a manuscript often crabbed in script and full of contractions': their 'instinctive question, when deciphering a text, was not whether [they] had seen, but whether [they] had heard this or that word before; [they] brought not a visual but an auditory memory to the task'.[941] In the same vein, Paul Zumthor comments that 'Le mode d'encodage des graphies mediévales faisait de celles-ci une base d'oralisation'.[942] It seems likely that we should envisage similar processes in readers of cuneiform.

An interesting ethnographic parallel is provided by readers of the Vai script, whose ambiguities (no word division etc.) loosely recall those of cuneiform (§ 5.3.1):

> Vai readers have had to elaborate special techniques for discovering higher-order semantic units. One common technique, which we heard over and over again, consists of "recycling"—saying strings of syllables aloud repeatedly, varying vowel tones and lengths until they "click" into meaningful units.[943]

Indeed,

> The overwhelming majority of script literates we met read aloud or subvocally; even when reading silently, their lip movements suggested that the articulatory-sound system of language was actively engaged.[944]

This habit of 'clicking' offers a suggestive model for how ancient readers of cuneiform dealt with the unfamiliar, whether in the shape of completely unseen passages or just new variants to a familiar passage. (It should be stressed that from this we do not conclude cuneiform to have always, or even usually, been read aloud. For a long time this was thought to be the norm in antiquity, but this is no longer so).[945]

It is finally worth remarking that many details of how cuneiform was sight-read may eventually be gleaned from large statistical analyses of the

941 Chaytor, *Bulletin of the John Rylands Library* 26 (1941–1942) 51.

942 Zumthor, *La lettre et la voix* (1987) 108.

943 Scribner and Cole, *The Psychology of Literacy* (1981) 165.

944 Scribner and Cole, *The Psychology of Literacy* (1981) 179.

945 That reading in antiquity was done aloud was mentioned as self-evident by Nietzsche, *Jenseits von Gut und Böse* (1886) section 247: 'Der antike Mensch las, wenn er las – es geschah selten genug – sich selbst etwas vor, und zwar mit lauter Stimme; man wunderte sich, wenn jemand leise las, und fragte sich insgeheim nach Gründen'. The first large-scale argument to this effect was assembled by Balogh, *Philologus* 82 (1926–1927) (see § 5.3.1). This view has met with growing scepticism in recent years (e.g. Valette-Cagnac, *La lecture à Rome* (1997) 69–70, esp. n. 128), culminating in the cogent rebuttal by Gavrilov, *The Classical Quarterly* 47/1 (1997), who has argued that the *locus classicus* (i.e. Ambrose in Augustine's *Confessions*), which is probably what Nietzsche had in mind, is not evidence of attitudes to reading in general, but only of attitudes to reading by a master in the presence of his disciples. On the possibility of silent reading of Akkadian see Charpin, *Reading and Writing* (2010) 41–42.

incidence of different error types. For example, it has been observed that in Modern English readers make a disproportionate number of errors on the words 'the' and 'and', and it has been inferred from this that they tend to be read not as self-standing words, but as units with surrounding words.[946] If such findings could ever be made for cuneiform, they would have a sizeable contribution to make to the understanding of how the script was read, and such awareness would in turn very likely enhance the understanding of mechanisms of textual change.

946 Drewnowski and Healy, *Memory and Cognition* 5/6 (1977).

6 Some issues of edition and interpretation

> There is no reason to suppose that the tradition of a Middle Babylonian poem was exempt from those accidents that are an inherent feature of this sublunary world.
>
> Martin West[947]

The matters discussed in this book are not without import for the edition and interpretation of Akkadian writings. For example, we have seen that it is profitable to study manuscripts individually, with particular attention to their orthography (and morphology and phonology, these sometimes being hard to disentangle from it). It follows that, as already remarked by Rykle Borger (*JCS* 18/2 (1964) 50) almost 40 years ago, it is an invaluable service to other researchers for editors to present transliterations in *Partitur* format.

Here we shall discuss two more points: how is one to choose between variants? And to what extent is one justified in formulating conjectures when the manuscripts are not senselessly garbled?

6.1 Choosing between variants

How to choose between variant readings on different manuscripts of the same passage?[948] Alas, we have no easy answers: the decision needs to be taken on a case-by-case basis, following one manuscript for one word, and maybe another for the next ('eclectic' procedure), all the while recognising that often our knowledge of Akkadian is not refined enough to tell us which variant is better.[949]

---

947 West, *Iraq* 59 (1997) 187, proposing to emend the line sequence in the first two stanzas of *Ee* to 1-2-7-8, 3-4-5-6 (see § 2.1).

948 At present, owing to the small number of manuscripts on which any given word or line is attested, this difficulty is rarely felt for Akkadian. It will become more acute, however, as more manuscripts are published.

949 Compare West, *Iran* 46 (2008) 123a: an editor 'is putting before the (generally less expert) reader the text as it should read in his considered opinion, while providing … the materials for the reader to assess his jugdments and, if he sees fit, to come to different ones'.

What we can do, is to point out the inadequacy of certain short-cuts. For a start, it is well known among textual critics that older manuscripts do not necessarily offer better readings than later ones.[950] Similarly, it is hazardous to invoke the principle that 'Variant A could have been corrupted into variant B, but not vice versa; therefore variant A is older'.[951] The principle is logically rigorous, but difficult to implement for Akkadian: many variants are susceptible to multiple explanations of how they came into being, so it is usually very difficult to exclude the 'vice versa'. This difficulty is exacerbated by our ignorance of transmission history. The following sections discuss three more short-cuts. We then comment on dangers which beset the comparison of duplicates.

6.1.1 *Codex optimus*

The so-called '*codex optimus*' procedure involves adopting all the readings of the manuscript which (for whatever reason or reasons) the editor regards as 'best' overall, relegating other manuscripts' variants to the *apparatus criticus*.[952]

One could say in this procedure's favour that it documents *a* version of a composition as it was known to an individual person,[953] but if one allows for the possibility of somnolence in transmitters (§ 2.3.3), the version thus reconstructed does not necessarily correspond to the conscious in-

950 See fn. 138 and cf. Rubio, "Sumerian Literature", in Ehrlich (ed.), *From an Antique Land* (2009) 39: 'Although it may seem counterintuitive, Ur III versions of compositions attested later on in Old Babylonian do not necessarily offer a more reliable text'.

951 This principle was used repeatedly by Jacobsen, *King List* (1939) e. g. p. 17 on the numbers 840 and 720: 'While it is easy to see how … (840) passing through a damaged form … can become … (720) in a later copy, the opposite development is improbable'. (Where we have '…', Jacobsen reproduces cuneiform signs).

952 The first influential advocacy of this procedure seems to be that of Bédier, *Romania* 54 (1928). Following up a devastating critique of 'Lachmann's method' (see fn. 268) of choosing between variants on the basis of stemmatic considerations (see fn. 269), and an exposure of the weaknesses of an alternative method proposed by dom Quentin, Bédier argued – 'au seul domaine que j'ai fréquenté, celui des lettres françaises' (p. 335) – that in the last resort editors could only really rely on their personal taste, and so they would do well to tamper with extant manuscripts as little as possible.

953 Bein, *Textkritik* (2008) calls this procedure the *Leithandschriften-Prinzip* and comments that Medievalists use it for the reason mentioned above.

tentions of any single person. Further, in Assyriology, where so many manuscripts are broken, reconstructing a version of a composition as it was known to a single individual is usually an unrealistic ambition.

In other disciplines, some scholars object that the eclectic procedure results in a text which is extant on no single manuscript:

> Modern eclectic methods ... [result, MW] in a running text that has absolutely no support from any known manuscript, version, or patristic writer ... The original text of modern eclecticism thus becomes a phantom mirage with no real existence as soon as its readings are taken in sequence.[954]

Maurice Robinson wrote this apropos of the New Testament, for which thousands of manuscripts are extant. Though one can see the attraction of his position, one should ask oneself: given the length and complexity of transmission involved, would one expect to find the exact sequence of original words preserved on any one manuscript? The odds are surely against this.[955] This is all the more true of Akkadian compositions, where the number of extant manuscripts per line is very often one or two.

More generally, there is simply no reason to think that any one manuscript will always offer the best readings.

6.1.2 *Eliminatio codicum descriptorum*

In other disciplines, stemmata are sometimes used to choose between variants. The principle is that, given a manuscript which is wholly derivative from other extant manuscripts ('*codex descriptus*'), it (and any unique variants it possesses) can be disregarded in the reconstruction of the original wording (so-called *eliminatio codicum descriptorum*), as it has nothing of its own to contribute.[956] Mechanical rules for the identification of

---

954 Robinson, "The Case for Byzantine Priority", in Black (ed.), *New Testament Textual Criticism* (2002) 125–126.

955 See also the reply to Robinson by Silva, "Responses", in Black (ed.), *Responses* (2002) 146–148, with an entertaining thought experiment. Borger, *Theologische Rundschau* 52/1 (1987) 9 maintains for the New Testament that the evaluation of variants on a case-by-case basis ('innere Kritik', 'Eklektizismus') is 'wohl der bessere Weg' vis-à-vis the *codex optimus* procedure (which Borger calls 'Bevorzugung gewisser Handschriften').

956 See e.g. Borger, *Theologische Rundschau* 52/1 (1987) 39 'Hoskier ... hat erkannt, daß seine Nr. 57 ... eine Abschrift nach dem Druck von Colinaeus (1534) ist und daher völlig wertlos'. Note also Spalinger, *JAOS* 94 (1974) 317a: 'The next two editions of Assurbanipal's prisms are D and K. At most they can be dated to

codices descripti have sometimes been proposed, in attempts to reduce the element of subjectivity.

Attractive though this method sounds, it is not always easy or useful to implement. For a start, even when a stemma can be constructed, there is an intrinsic complication to the *eliminatio codicum descriptorum*: it is very difficult to show that a manuscript is *solely* derived from particular sources.[957] One would usually have to reckon with the possibility that its writer imported variants from other sources – oral or written, remembered or consulted (see §§ 1.2.3 and 1.4.4).

For Akkadian, the *eliminatio* can rarely be practised, owing to the difficulty of establishing stemmata for Akkadian compositions. In the rare cases where a distinctive genealogical link can be established between two recensions, it is usually hard to say which is ancestor and which is descendant.

6.1.3 The 'majority text'

It is a basic tenet of textual criticism that counting the manuscripts which witness to different variants is not a reliable way of determining which variant is original.[958] For secondary formulations could gain ascendancy over the original wording during the process of transmission, and end up being attested more widely. Accordingly, a 'majority text', produced by following the majority of manuscripts wherever a choice arises, has no guarantee of being the most authentic text.

However, whether one regards 'original' as synonymous with 'superior' is bound up with the issue of authorial *Urtext* discussed in § 2.1. With well-known authors such as Plato or Dante, the aim of reconstituting the

---

a few years after B and differ little from that inscription. For that reason they will be disregarded here.'

957 Cf. Reeve, "*Eliminatio codicum descriptorum*: a methodological problem", in Grant (ed.), *Editing Greek and Latin Texts* (1989) esp. 25: contamination always being possible, 'No manuscript ... can be proved to derive its inherited readings entirely from another'.

958 West, *Textual Criticism and Editorial Technique* (1973) 49. This was recognised by Borger, *Theologische Rundschau* 52/1 (1987) 58, noting that 'die absolute Mehrzahl aller Handschriften den Urtext natürlich nicht hervorzaubern kann'; perhaps also by Lambert, *BSOAS* 52/3 (1989) 544. For a rebuttal of the 'majority text' principle in New Testament studies see Fee, "The Majority Text and the Original Text of the New Testament", in Epp and Fee (eds), *Studies in New Testament Textual Criticism* (1993).

wording willed by the author is clearly a worthwhile one, however difficult it may be in practice. In the largely authorless world of Akkadian cuneiform, the endeavour is arguably not only hopeless but also less meaningful.

In the few cases where we have enough manuscripts of a passage to make for a (hopefully) representative sample of how it was transmitted in different times and places, what counting manuscripts can achieve is to give us a sense of variants' diffusion in antiquity. For the purposes of cultural and literary history, this is information worth having (cf. § 2.1).

But what about grammar and orthography – can counting manuscripts help us assess an odd form or spelling, and help us decide if it is erroneous? This is the contention of Rykle Borger apropos of the verbal form *ib-ši-mu* in an inscription of Assurbanipal (B vii.68): Borger rejects a reading *ib-lim-mu* in favour of *ib-ši-mu*, one of his reasons being that it would be implausible for all six extant manuscripts to have the unusual spelling with double *m*.[959]

Caution is required here: it is true that, if they chose their spellings independently of each other, six different writers would have been unlikely to spell *iblimū* as *ib-lim-mu*. The question is, were the spellings chosen independently? So long as the possibility exists that the six manuscripts derive from a common source through copying,[960] transmission of an unusual spelling such as *ib-lim-mu* for *iblimū* cannot be ruled out.[961] In § 2.4.3 we saw two instances where four manuscripts have a corruption (*šallassunu*, *tûša-milkī*) and only one has the correct wording (*šallūssunu*, *pīša-milkī*), so six is not a very impressive number. Borger's line of argument would be strengthened if it were shown that there were substantial orthographic disagreements among the manuscripts for other words, but this would require detailed examination which has not yet been undertaken.

Let us consider another case. Manuscripts of *Ee* offer multiple attestations of the verbal form *ay innenâ* 'may it not be changed'. Since *ay* is normally followed by the preterite, one expects the second *n* of *innenâ* to

959 Borger, *BIWA* (1996) 111.

960 Borger maintains that Assurbanipal's inscriptions were written at dictation (see fn. 29). If this were shown to be true, his argument would be stronger, but at present no such demonstration exists.

961 This is not to reject Borger's conclusion that the reading *ib-ši-mu* is preferable to *ib-lim-mu* (indeed, his adduction of parallels with *ib-ši*[*m-mu*] is very compelling). We are only pointing out that the orthographic part of the argument is not probative.

be single not double. Strikingly, however, of the eight spellings which are sufficiently well preserved to show whether the second *n* is single or double, one is single (II 162 MS a) and seven are double (II 162 MSS C, k and M; III 64 MSS c, h and i; III 122 MS a). Why this strong preference for double spellings? It is well known that consonants sometimes geminate (probably for purely orthographic reasons) at morpheme boundaries, but this explanation is unlikely to apply to the problematic *innennâ*, for the morpheme boundary falls not after *n* but in the middle of the contracted *â*. We suspect instead that the writers confused the recherché construction *ay innenâ* with the very similar but much more vernacular construction *lā innennâ* 'it must not be changed', attested several times in *Ee* (I 158, II 44, III 48, III 106, IV 7), where the second *n* is legitimately double (*lā* + present). If this interpretation is correct, the spellings of *innenâ* show that counting manuscripts is not always the best guide to linguistic 'correctness'.

Another illustration of this principle was offered in § 3.3.3, where we saw that all manuscripts but one corrupted *ištu* 'from' into *išdu* 'base'.

6.1.4 Treacherous duplicates

For the reasons given in § 2.3.2, we should be wary of allowing one manuscript to condition our understanding of another, even if they are nearly identical. We shall cite two examples from René Labat's 1939 edition of the Hemerologies.

Labat wrote that the variant u_4-*mu* (singular) in place of $u_4^{meš}$ (plural) 'exclut pour *ūmē*(meš) une traduction "pour ses jours"'. In our view, this attributes too much authority to the variant. The writer of the variant u_4-*mu* might well have objected to the translation 'pour ses jours', but that does not mean this was the only understanding current in antiquity, or that it was the best.[962]

On a different passage, Labat remarked that 'Le texte porte sag giš.ku. On pourrait supposer une erreur du scribe pour sag.pa.kil (= *nissatu*) ; mais la comparaison avec V R 49, col. X, 20 : giš.ku.in.mà.mà montre que la copie d'Assur est correcte: sag = *elû* (II 1 = élever, brandir)'.[963] We believe that Labat's conjecture has value, and that the duplicate does

962 Labat, *Hémérologies* (1939) 59 n. 33.
963 Labat, *Hémérologies* (1939) 136 *ad* 63.

not suffice to discount his suggested emendation. Again, we think it useful to envisage some fluidity of understanding in antiquity.

We cite these two instances not as evidence of wrong-headed thinking, far from it; rather as illustrations of an attitude of editorial tentativeness which, though understandable and arguably necessary in 1939, now seems excessive.

As remarked in § 1.6, the discovery of a new manuscript cannot disprove a conjecture. It can show that an extant version circulated more widely than we previously knew, or that variants to it existed, but this was already the case *ex hypothesi.* The new manuscript's variant could itself be the result of a conjecture or corruption by an ancient transmitter, and we have seen that ancient conjectures were not always good. Modern conjectures are thus in a different situation from, say, restorations, where the find of a new fragment can show a suggested restoration to be wrong *for a particular manuscript*,[964] though even here one cannot exclude that other, broken or lost, manuscripts ran as the suggestion did.

Nonetheless, the study of variants across duplicate manuscripts has a central place in Akkadian textual criticism. For by studying cases where it is clear that transmitters misunderstood something, and determining how the misunderstanding arose, we can generate parameters within which to formulate conjectures of our own.

6.2 Formulating conjectures

We noted in § 1.6 that, by and large, Akkadianists are reluctant to formulate conjectural emendations ('conjectures' for short) except when the extant text is senselessly garbled.[965] It is our expectation that increased

964 'Die Erfahrung lehrt leider, daß nach Zusammenschlüssen von erwogenen schönen Ergänzungen oft betrüblich wenig übrigbleibt' (Borger, *Nachrichten der Akademie der Wissenschaften in Göttingen. 1. Philologisch-historische Klasse* Jahrgang 1991/2 42). By contrast, if a restoration of one manuscript is contradicted by the find of a different manuscript, this need not prove the restoration wrong, as the two manuscripts could have witnessed to different versions or recensions.

965 Borger, *Theologische Rundschau* 52/1 (1987) 22 approves a conjecture in the New Testament (*pollōj*, dative of measure, at Matthew 10:31 and Luke 12:7), but this is on the strength of Syriac translations which appear to rely on the conjectured reading. On p. 37 he finds the conjectured reading *prōtēs* at Acts 16:12 to possess a 'hohen Wahrscheinlichkeitsgrad'. (In several places Borger's essay

text-critical vigilance will lead to the recognition that many extant formulations are problematic (and corrupt) without being senseless, and to conjectures about how said formulations might have run before corruption.

6.2.1 The fallibility of manuscripts

Obviously, correcting ancient manuscripts is a delicate matter, not least because it runs the danger of circularity noted by Alfred Housman in the epigraph to this volume's Introduction. Yet, as is standard in fields of research dealing with written sources, we should not let manuscripts bully us into accepting their readings when we have good reason to believe that ours are better.

We have seen that, alongside instances of great faithfulness and skill, there were cases in which ancient transmitters display almost unbelievable misunderstanding. The hopelessly unidiomatic corruption of *ištu* 'since' into *išdu* 'base' (§ 3.3.3) is perhaps the most striking example we encountered, but it does not stand alone even in this book, and doubtless many additional instances will be found by future researchers.

As more evidence accumulates of how corruptions arose, and our understanding of the mechanisms of textual change refines, editors may propose conjectures with increasing confidence. Naturally, it will always be essential to know what signs are actually on the manuscripts. But, in textual typologies where compositions were transmitted many times over, with plenty of scope for the intrusion of corruptions, extant manuscripts are not necessarily good authorities. If a conjecture both gives better sense than what we find on extant manuscripts by the standards of the Akkadian-speaking world, and is consistent with what we know of the mechanisms of textual change in the relevant typology, then it is at the very least worth making.

6.2.2 The conjectural aspect

The proposal that more conjectures should be attempted in Assyriology may well prove controversial: who are we, it might be asked, to set about 'correcting' ancient manuscripts when they are not drastically

expresses the view that conjectures should never be displayed in the main text, only in the *apparatus criticus*).

wrong? We would, the argument might continue, be throwing ourselves onto mere surmise, irresponsibly squandering the solid textual source base which we are so lucky to have.

To objections such as these, one must reply in two steps. First, it is true that introducing conjectures to the study of ancient manuscripts places interpretation where previously there seemed to be solid fact,[966] and one can sympathise with the view that solid facts were preferable. Second, however, as noted at many junctures in this book, the 'solid facts' were not actually as solid as they seemed: transmitters could alter, misunderstand, and alter because of misunderstanding.

It should also be borne in mind that much Akkadian literature and scholarship is known to us from a number of manuscripts per line which, by the standards of many other disciplines, is extremely small. Often, a particular word, line, sentence or entry is only extant on one manuscript. In such cases we have no way of telling how wide a reception the extant text enjoyed, and what variants it might have been in competition with. If the extant text arose through inadvertence (e. g. *dictée intérieure*), it does not even reflect the intention of the person who introduced it. Under these circumstances, if a conjecture solves a problem, it seems painless to adopt it.[967]

In formulating conjectures on the basis of perceived grammatical oddity, of course we run the risk of introducing regularity where it did not exist. For example, a medical symptom is thus described: *šumma*

966 Textual critics in other fields are well aware of this, e. g. Dain, *Les Manuscrits* (1949) 171: 'Le seul fait de choisir une leçon, d'en faire la critique, c'est déjà prononcer un jugement dans l'ordre de l'histoire du texte'; Hanna, *Middle English Manuscripts* (1996) 181: 'the interpretive gesture inherent in textual criticism'. See also Hanna's p. 64: 'Those who have edited' – textual criticism being a routine element of editing in Middle English studies – 'know only too well that the task they perform is an interpretive act, not especially different from the critical [i.e. literary-critical, MW] act'. For Cerquiglini, *Éloge de la variante* (1989) 73 'La critique textuelle, discipline rigoureuse et austère, est la praxis non dite de la théorie littéraire'.

967 When a corrupt or suspectedly corrupt passage is attested on many manuscripts, one must – unless it were supposed that transmitters reproduced faults despite recognising them as such (see the introductory comments to § 3.4.6) – take note that this is how the composition was known to many readers in antiquity, so the corrupted version has its place in Akkadian literary history. But even so, conjecturing how the passage might originally have run is a valuable exercise, for it can bring into focus questions about issues such as changing literary sensibilities and the ways in which literature was received.

amīlu sa úr-*šú ka-la-šu-ma tab-ku* (BAM 130:19). Plural *tabkū* is at odds with singular *kalāšu-ma*; and why unidiomatic *-ma*? Hence elsewhere we have suggested emending *ka-la-šu-ma tab-ku* to *ka-la-šu* gu_7-*šu* '... all hurts him', which has a loose parallel (CT 23, 1:1).[968] To us this emendation seems judicious, as we think these oddities would be most likely to arise through an error of sign identification, and very unlikely to have been introduced deliberately, but this is admittedly impressionistic, and the contention cannot be proven.

In formulating conjectures, sense is the most important guide of all.[969] Here there arise problems created by cultural distance (§ 2.2.1.3). We are used to seeing Akkadian speakers doing and saying what, by our standards, are the strangest things. Therefore, we must be ready to bend our notions of what is semantically odd.[970] If however a conjecture can turn a passage into something which (as far as we can tell) gives better sense *by the standards of the Akkadian-speaking world*, then it becomes attractive. Below, we shall give what we believe to be two such examples from *Gilgameš*.[971] First, however, some remarks are in order on a further point of method.

6.2.3 *Lectio difficilior potior*?

An old maxim of textual criticism has it that *lectio difficilio potior*, i. e. the reading (or variant) which is most likely to be original is that which is most 'difficult'. The idea is that transmitters would usually effect transformations from things they did not understand into things they did understand (or from things they found more strange to things they found less strange) rather than *vice versa*. The principle is sometimes invoked by Akkadianists,[972] sometimes used tacitly (e. g. fn. 130).

968 Worthington, *BSOAS* 72/1 (2009) 154.

969 According to Reiner, *JCS* 25/1 (1973) 17 n. 17, 'Failure to notice that the item [i.e. reading, MW] selected makes little sense is the cause for most erroneous interpretations in Assyriology'.

970 Cf. West, *Iran* 46 (2008) 125 on the Iranian *Gāthās*: 'Of course the poems are often difficult to interpret, and we cannot assume that whatever we do not understand must be corrupt'. (He argues, however, that 'The difficulties of interpretation should not paralyse textual criticism but stimulate and guide it').

971 For a simpler example of a conjecture, see § 2.4.4 on KA ṢAB.

972 E.g. Lambert, *JNES* 33/3 (1974) 294 *ad* 29: of the variants *ēma* and *ša*, '*ema* [which is a much rarer word than *ša*, MW] has preference as the *lectio difficilior*'. (Cf. Lambert, *BSOAS* 52/3 (1989) 544–545, apparently criticising acceptance of

However, the idea that Akkadian transmitters only made things clearer is not tenable. Many instances are cited in this book where, for whatever reason, they garbled things in the most diverse and surprising ways.

More generally, the notion of 'difficult' requires closer definition:

> When we choose the "more difficult" reading, ... we must be sure that it is in itself a plausible reading. The principle should not be used in support of dubious syntax, or phrasing that it would not have been natural for the author to use.[973]

Latin textual critic Josef Delz comments further that the principle of *lectio difficilio potior* can be of limited use ('wenig hilfreich'): the border between 'difficult' and 'impossible' readings is not always easily drawn.[974] Sometimes, the very facts which make the 'easier' reading such may add up to a strong case for its being preferred to the 'more difficult' one.[975]

Laurie Pearce comments with good sense that when a 'difficult' variant or reading which hovers on the brink of implausibility can easily be understood as a corruption of an 'easy' variant or reading – e.g. *maharša* 'her equal' ('difficult') vs *māhirša* 'her rival' ('easy') at *Ee* II 56 – then preference should in the first instance be accorded to the 'easy' variant or reading.[976]

'*Lectio difficilior*' is not, then, a concept to be invoked as if its validity and usefulness were self-evident. Perhaps it would contribute to clarity if the relevant arguments were made without using the phrase '*lectio difficilior*' at all.

---

the *lectio difficilior* 'when it makes sense only by ad hoc assumptions'); Moran, *JAOS* 103/1 (1983) 257 on *muppašir* and *mupaššir* in *Ludlul* I 9 (see § 3.3.2): *muppašir* 'seems to me the more difficult and therefore probably the original reading'. See also Landsberger, *JCS* 8/3 (1954) 130 n. 336: '*Puršu-rutta*, verglichen mit Variante *Purpu-ruta* ist lectio difficilior'.

973 West, *Textual Criticism and Editorial Technique* (1973) 51.

974 Delz, "Textkritik und Editionstechnik", in Graf (ed.), *Einleitung in die lateinische Philologie* (1993) 59: 'Der Unterschied zwischen 'schwierig' und 'unmöglich' ist im Einzelfall fließend'. This is illustrated by the variants *mupaššir* and *muppašir* at *Ludlul* I 9 (see § 3.3.2): while *muppašir* is clearly preferable, it is not clear that, as Moran would have it, it is also the *lectio difficilior.* In a sense, by defying the standard parallelism *ezēzu* G vs *pašāru* N, it is *mupaššir* which is *difficilior.* Obviously, it depends on exactly what one means by *difficilior.*

975 See e.g. Priestley, *Mnemosyne* 60 (2007) for a compelling case in favour of the reading 'robe' over the *lectio difficilior* 'plough' in an early Greek poem.

976 Pearce, *JAOS* 127/3 (2007) 372.

6.2.4 Enkidu as a powerful king

In § 2.2.1.3.1 we met the two dreams experienced by Gilgameš in the first Tablet of his Epic (Standard version). Here we shall conjecture an emendation to a line in the first dream, which uses a simile in connection with the kissing of feet.[977]

The line in question (I 255) is fragmentary, but it can be restored from II 107:[978]

I 255	F_1 v.29	[				]^{meš}-*šu*
	P v.35	[*ki-i*	*šèr-ri la*]-⌜'⌝-*i*		*ú-na-šá-qu*	gìr[^{meš}-*šú*]
II 107	X_2 ii.9'	*ki-i*	*šèr-ri la-'-i*		*ú-n*[*a-áš-šá-qu* gìr^{ii}-*šu*]	
	k ii.6'	*ki-ma*	*šèr-ri la-'-*⌜*i*⌝		[	]

The two identical lines can, then, be reconstructed as follows:

kī(ma) šerri la'î unaššaqū šēpīšu 'They kissed his feet like ...'.

In Tablet I, the foot kissing happens to a meteor in Gilgameš's dream. In Tablet II it happens to Enkidu. Since the meteor symbolises Enkidu (see § 4.7.1.1), these two episodes of foot-kissing are really only one, which is first foretold in the dream, and then duly takes place. Hence we need not be troubled by the image of a meteor having feet (see fn. 676).

Current interpretations understand the simile to involve a *šerru la'û* 'small child', though there are divergences of interpretation as regards the import. For CAD L 114a, the simile refers to the people doing the kissing, 'as if they were small children'. For Andrew George, it refers to the feet being kissed, 'like a little baby's'.

A 'small child' / 'a little baby' is clearly what we have on both manuscripts.[979] The phrase surfaces elsewhere in *Gilgameš* (III 210)[980] and indeed Akkadian literature, including *Erra* I 48 and *Ištar's Descent*

977 Streck, *Bildersprache* (1999) 214 observes that Enkidu attracts the largest number of images in Akkadian 'epic' (thirty).

978 After George, http://www.soas.ac.uk/nme/research/gilgamesh/standard/, accessed 31.v.2011.

979 It is absent from the Old Babylonian version, see OB II 11 and 21.

980 *adi kī šerri la'î nikaššadu niz*[*mat*]*ni* 'until, like little babies, we attain our desire' (said to Gilgameš by the high officials of Uruk on the occasion of his departure for the Cedar Mountain). Interference from this line might have affected the transmission of I 255 // II 107 (see § 1.2.3).

Ass. 38.[981] Nonetheless, it seems an odd image here. George observes that 'Adults commonly find babies' feet irresistible',[982] so in principle the idea of kissing feet 'as to a little baby' makes sense. The problems, as we see them, are twofold: **a)** in Mesopotamia the kissing of feet was standard as a gesture of submission to gods and kings, so to couple foot kissing with babies is incongruous in an Akkadian context; more specifically, **b)** one has the impression that Enkidu excited awe rather than tenderness in those who first saw him.[983] One could of course argue that the beauty of the imagery lies precisely in its incongruity, but in our view a different explanation commends itself.

We conjecture that *šerru la'û* 'small child' / 'little children' is a corruption of (phonetically similar) *šarru le'û* 'powerful king'. The image of kissing feet 'as to a powerful king' seems fitting for the excited crowd doing obeisance to the newly arrived Enkidu, who proposes to challenge their overbearing ruler.

Whether the switch between the phrases should be thought of in terms as a metathesis of vowels (*e…a* becoming *a…e*) or whether the fact of having identical radicals was responsible, or indeed whether both these factors played a part, is uncertain. The same applies to whether the similarity of the signs ŠÈR and ŠAR in Neo-Assyrian script is relevant.[984] Be that as it may, the substitution was probably facilitated by the resulting phrase's being well known.

At the moment, the simile is found on only two manuscripts, one from Babylon and one from Nineveh, both with *šerru la'û.* With so little evidence, it is premature to speculate on how widely *šerru la'û* circulated. If new manuscripts show it to have been widespread, we must accept that this is how the Epic was widely understood, just as future generations of scholars will have to accept that we sing of 'five gold rings' and not 'five gold wrens' (§ 2.1).

---

981 Cf. attestations in CAD L 114a and Š/ii 319a; note also virtually synonymous *ṣehru la'û* (Wilcke, *ZA* 75 (1985) 200 line 54). *Erra* I 48 uses *šerru la'û* as a source of imagery (*kī šerri la'î*) – is it quoting *Gilgameš*?

982 George, *Gilgamesh* (2003) 802.

983 Cf. the shepherds' reaction to first seeing Enkidu at II 40-42.

984 On this similarity see George, *Gilgamesh* (2003) 889 *ad* 148 // 151 // 154: 'Confusion between the signs ŠAR and HIR [=ŠÈR, MW] was rife at Nineveh'.

6.2.5 Ea, the wall and Ūta-napišti: who talks to who?

In *Gilgameš* Tablet XI, Ūta-napišti explains to Gilgameš that he survived the Flood thanks to a message from the god of wisdom, Ea. Since Ea was not supposed to inform mankind of the disaster which loomed over them, let alone save them, he had recourse to a stratagem: rather than tell Ūta-napišti directly, he did so by an interposed medium, so that strictly speaking he was not telling Ūta-napišti at all.

This outline seems uncontroversial enough, but when one reads the relevant portion of the Epic, the details turn out to be very confusing. We give George's composite text and his translation, which is representative of how the passage is understood by modern scholars:[985]

ninšiku ea ittišunu tame-ma
amāssunu ušannâ ana kikkišu
ki-ik-kiš ki-ik-kiš i-gar i-gar
ki-ik-ki-šu ši-me-ma i-ga-ru hi-is-sa-as
šuruppakû mār ubara-tutu
uqur bīta bini eleppa

With them the Prince Ea was under oath likewise,
(but) repeated their words to a reed fence:
'Reed fence, reed fence! Brick wall, brick wall!
Listen O reed fence! Pay heed, O brick wall!
O man of Šuruppak, son of Ubār-Tutu,
demolish the house, build a boat!'
(*Gilg.* XI 19-24)

We see two difficulties here, one of sense and one of morphology. In terms of sense, Ea's speech begins addressed to the fence and wall, but then switches in mid flow, turning into an address to Ūta-napišti. If the audience was supposed to infer that there are in fact two speeches, one from Ea to the fence and wall, and one from them to Ūta-napišti, then the occurrences are presented in a *very* condensed and rather confusing manner. Though in theory a case might be made that this is some form of literary sophistication, this does not convince.[986] In terms of morphol-

985 See e.g. Schott and von Soden, *Das Gilgamesh-Epos* (1988) 93–94, Röllig, *Das Gilgamesch-Epos* (2009) 116–117, Maul, *Das Gilgamesch-Epos* (2008) 140–141.

986 A further, if slight, oddity in sense is that, though we are told that Ea repeated the god's *amātu* to the fence and wall, in the speech we hear this is not quite what happens: he does not repeat their plan as such. This observation is slight enough that I would not consider proposing an emendation on the strength of

ogy, if the wall and fence are vocatives in both line 21 and 22, why do we find 'correct' vocatives with zero ending (*ki-ik-kiš*, *i-gar*) in line 21, but nominative-looking forms (*ki-ik-ki-šu*, *i-ga-ru*) in line 22? This discrepancy does not arise from the composite text's conflation of two traditions – MS j makes the distinction.[987] The co-occurrence of difficulties in sense and grammar is suggestive: we infer that the passage is corrupt. This inference is reinforced by the fact that a simple change dissolves the difficulties.

We conjecture that, in line 22, the recension extant on MS j originally ran something like *kikkišu šemi igāru hissus* 'The fence listened, the wall *remembered*' (on *hissus* and its meaning see fn. 989). The translation would run thus:

> With them the Prince Ea was under oath likewise,
> (but) he repeated their *amātu*[988] to a reed fence:
> 'Reed fence, reed fence! Brick wall, brick wall!'
> The reed fence listened, the wall *remembered*:
> 'O man of Šuruppak, son of Ubār-Tutu,
> Demolish the house, build a boat!'

There would still be elements of condensation: **a)** Ea's words to the fence and wall would not be reported in full – but then again they do not need to be, as we are given the gist of what he said (i. e. we are told that he repeated the *amātu* of the other gods). **b)** The fence and wall would not get their own *verbum dicendi*, but this seems condensation at an acceptable level in *Gilgameš*. In fact, if the original form of *hasāsu* did mean to 'remember',[989] then this would be an ingenious substitute for a *verbum dicendi*: the notion of remembering, which by definition connects two episodes removed in time, would serve as link between hearing the message from Ea and delivering it to Ūta-napišti. So much for the difficulties in sense. As regards morphology, in the passage as we reconstructed it there would be no inconsistency.

---

it alone. However, since it is something which will get tidied up through the emendation proposed on other grounds, it seems worth mentioning.

987 No other manuscript is complete for both lines. MS J_2 has [*k*]*i-ik-ki-š*[*u*] in line 21 (unlike MS j), and MS W_1 has [*k*]*i-i*[*k-k*]*i-šu* in line 22.

988 The sense of *amātu* here appears to be something like 'resolution'.

989 We suggest Gt stative *hissus* as this differs from extant *hissas* in only one vowel, but bigger distortions are not out of the question. For AHw, *hasāsu* in the Gt stem does not mean 'remember', but there are so few attestations that this is very uncertain. CAD H 124a does translate a Gt form of *hasāsu* as 'remember': *erēša hissas* 'Remember (their importance for) the ploughing!'.

How did the putative corruption originate? At least two possibilities can be envisaged, and choosing between them does not seem important. What matters is that the conjectured textual change is plausible. **a)** Different versions of *Atra-hasīs*, where the episode originated, offer different accounts of it: some appear to dispense with the fence and wall altogether, others explicitly involve a dream.[990] There seems to have been some fluidity about the details in this episode.[991] One possibility, then, is that a transmitter of *Gilgameš* contaminated the version of line 22 conjectured by us with another version (perhaps from *Atra-hasīs* rather than a *Gilgameš* narrative), in which Ea made a long speech to the fence and wall. This hypothetical transmitter would have failed to notice (or correctly to interpret) the discrepancy between zero-ending in line 21 and *u*-ending in line 22, but this would be no bigger a sin than many others chronicled in this book. For someone who was not attentive to matters of orthography (or who was used to dealing with carelessly written manuscripts, on which paying attention to spellings was not worthwhile), stative *še-mi* could have looked like a spelling of the imperative, particularly if that was what he (or she?) expected to find. The only conscious change, then, would have been *hissus* to *hissas*, which a transmitter of the sort envisaged would have effected painlessly, presuming the exemplar to contain an error. **b)** Another possibility is that *hissus* changed to *hissas* through an error of phonetic similarity. A subsequent transmitter could then have changed *še-mi* to *ši-me* on the strength of *hissas.*

One could of course conjecture even further, e. g. that a line with *verbum dicendi* for the fence and wall was omitted. *Per se*, this is entirely plausible, but conjecturing lines out of thin air is a risky business. On present knowledge, then, we content ourselves with the above suggestions, which seems to us to solve the difficulties in a plausible manner.[992]

990 Indeed, Ea claims to have sent Ūta-napišti a dream at XI 197, though this is by no means evident when the subterfuge is first recounted. Unwitting authorial inconsistency? Or a further sign of Ea's duplicity?

991 That the version of the episode in *Gilgameš* differs from other accounts of it is noted by George, *Gilgamesh* (2003) 510 n. 226.

992 Additional remarks on the passage, with reference to lines 32-34 (*anāku īde-ma azakkara ana ea bēliya* / [*am-g*]*ur bēlī ša taqbâ atta kīam* / [*at*]*ta'id anāku eppuš* 'I understood and spoke to Ea, my master: "I hereby concur, my master, with what you told me thus. I have paid attention; I shall do it"'): *anāku īde* is generally translated as 'I understood', but *edû* never otherwise seems to mean 'to understand'. The sense is probably 'I knew (who the message really came from)'. The word *kīam* 'thus' is common in Old Babylonian letters, where it refers to the content of a message, but rare in literature. In our *Gilgameš* passage it presumably

refers to the very unusual way in which Ea delivered his message rather than to the message's content (though cf. XI 38 *u atta kīam taqabbâššunūti* 'Well, you shall address them as follows …'). Some translations allow for both senses, but we suspect that Röllig's 'was du da sagst' requires modification; ditto Schott/von Soden, who omit it altogether. To avoid ambiguity, it might best be translated as 'in this way'.

7 Summary

> Peinliche Genauigkeit und erneute Prüfung ist bei diesen schwierigen Fragen unbedingt nothwendig; sonst werden wir hier schwerlich vorwärts kommen.
>
> Paul Haupt[993]

It is a commonplace in other fields of research that manuscripts cannot be trusted. The possibility that extant text is in some way wrong has far-reaching repercussions on the study of the ancient world, and it is necessary to bolster our defences.

To this end, three activities need to be conducted in parallel: we need to understand the orthographic conventions which ancient writers employed; we need to develop an awareness of the sorts of corruptions which arose, and how; we need to scrutinise extant text in the light of what we know about orthography and the mechanisms of textual change, and ask ourselves if it might in some way be wrong. When we suspect that it is wrong, we might propose a conjecture about how it originally ran, or how it was intended to run.

All of this has at one time or another been acknowledged and applied by Akkadianists, but owing probably to the lack of formal discussion of such matters, implementation is neither coherent nor systematic.

This book has attempted a systematisation of the problems and analytical methods, offering a framework within which errors may be identified and accounted for, and conjectures proposed. The likelihood of errors by transmitters is all the greater if one accepts the 'fits and starts' model of ancient sight-reading argued for in chapter 5.

At several junctures we dwelled on the importance of studying manuscripts individually. We saw that close analysis of their orthography and morphology can have surprisingly wide-ranging implications.

There is much more to do, and hopefully this book will entice others into doing it.

---

993 Haupt, *Zeitschrift für Keilschriftforschung* 2 (1885) 269.

8 References

Abusch, T. 1983. "The Form and Meaning of a Babylonian Prayer to Marduk", *JAOS* 103, 3–15

Abusch, T. 1986. "Ishtar's Proposal and Gilgamesh's Refusal: An Interpretation of "The Gilgamesh Epic", Tablet 6, Lines 1–79", *History of Religions* 26, 143–187

Abusch, T. 2002. *Mesopotamian Witchcraft: toward a history and understanding of Babylonian witchcraft beliefs and literature* (AMD 5). Leiden: Brill

Abusch, T. 2011. "The Revision of Babylonian Anti-Witchcraft Incantations: The Critical Analysis of Incantations in the Ceremonial Series Maqlû", in G. Bohak, Y. Harari, S. Shaked (eds), *Continuity and Change in the Magical Tradition.* Leiden: Brill, 11–41

Adams, J. N. 2007. *The Regional Diversification of Latin 200 BC–AD 600.* Cambridge: Cambridge University Press

Adams, J. N. Forthcoming. *Social Variation and the Latin Language.* Cambridge: Cambridge University Press

Al-Rawi, F. N. H., George, A. R. 1995. "Tablets from the Sippar Library V. An Incantation from *Mīs pî*", *Iraq* 57, 225–228

Albright, W. F. 1918. "The Babylonian Sage Ut-Napištim Rûqu", *JAOS* 38, 60–65

Albright, W. F. 1957. *From the Stone Age to Christianity: monotheism and the historical process.* Garden City, NY: Doubleday

Annus, A., Lenzi, A. 2010. *Ludlul bēl nēmeqi: The Standard Babylonian Poem of the Righteous Sufferer* (SAACT 7). Helsinki: The Neo-Assyrian Text Corpus Project / The Foundation for Finnish Assyriological Research

Aro, J. 1955. "Studien zur mittelbabylonischen Grammatik", *StOr* 20, 1–175

Bagnall, R. S. 2011. *Everyday Writing in the Graeco-Roman East* (Sather Classical Lectures 69). Berkeley: University of California Press

Balogh, J. 1926–1927. ""Voces Paginarum". Beiträge zur Geschichte des lauten Lesens und Schreibens", *Philologus* 82, 84–109, 202–240

Beaulieu, P.-A. 1997. "The Cult of AN.ŠÁR/Aššur in Babylonia after the Fall of the Assyrian Empire", *SAAB* 11, 55–73

Bédier, J. 1928. "La tradition manuscrite du *Lai de l'ombre.* Réflexions sur l'art d'éditer les textes anciens. Premier article", *Romania* 54, 161–196

Bédier, J. 1928. "La tradition manuscrite du *Lai de l'ombre.* Réflexions sur l'art d'éditer les anciens textes. Deuxième article", *Romania* 54, 321–356

Bein, T. 2008. *Textkritik – eine Einführung in Grundlagen germanistisch-mediävistischer Editionswissenschaft: Lehrbuch mit Übungsteil.* Frankfurt am Main: Peter Lang

Berger, P.-R. 1973. *Die neubabylonischen Königsinschriften: Königsinschriften des ausgehenden babylonischen Reiches* (AOAT 4/1). Kevelaer: Butzon & Bercker; Neukirchen-Vluyn: Neukirchener Verlag

Biggs, R. D. 1993. "Descent of Ištar, line 104", *NABU*, no. 74, pp. 58–59

Bird, G. D. 2010. *Multitextuality in the Homeric Iliad: the witness of the Ptolemaic papyri* (Hellenic Studies 43). Washington, DC: Center for Hellenic Studies

Black, J. A. 1998. *Reading Sumerian Poetry.* London: Athlone Press

Bloch, S. J. 1940. "Beiträge zur Grammatik des Mittelbabylonischen", *Orientalia* 9, 305–347

Böck, B. 2007. *Das Handbuch Muššu'u "Einreinbung": Eine Serie sumerischer und akkadischer Beschwörungen aus dem 1. Jt. vor Chr.* (Biblioteca del próximo oriente antiguo 3). Madrid: Consejo Superior de Investigaciones Científicas

Borger, R. 1956. *Die Inschriften Asarhaddons Königs von Assyrien* (AfO Bh. 9). Osnabrück: Biblio-Verlag

Borger, R. 1957. "Assyriologische und altarabistische Miszellen", *Orientalia* 26, 1–11

Borger, R. 1961. *Einleitung in die assyrischen Königsinschriften. Erster Teil* (HdO Ergänzungsband 5). Leiden: Brill

Borger, R. 1962. "Kleinigkeiten zur Textkritik des Kodex Hammurapi", *Orientalia* 31, 364–366

Borger, R. 1964. "Review of Lambert, *Babylonian Wisdom Literature*", *JCS* 18/2, 59–56

Borger, R. 1967. "Das dritte "Haus" der Serie bīt rimki (VR 50–51, Schollmeyer HGŠ Nr. 1)", *JCS* 21, 1–17

Borger, R. 1974–1977 [1978]. "Textkritisches zur Prisma-Inschrift Tiglatpileser's I.", *AfO* 25, 161–165

Borger, R. 1987. "NA^{26} und die neutestamentliche Textkritik", *Theologische Rundschau* 52, 1–58

Borger, R. 1991. "Ein Brief Sîn-idinnams von Larsa an den Sonnengott sowie Bemerkungen über "Joins" und das "Joinen"", *Nachrichten der Akademie der Wissenschaften in Göttingen. 1. Philologisch-historische Klasse* Jahrgang 1991, 39–81

Borger, R. 1996. *Beiträge zum Inschriftenwerk Assurbanipals – Die Prismenklassen A, B, C = K, D, E, F, G, H, J und T sowie andere Inschriften – Mit einem Beitrag von Andreas Fuchs.* Wiesbaden: Harrassowitz

Borger, R. 2004. *Mesopotamisches Zeichenlexikon* (AOAT 305). Münster: Ugarit-Verlag

Borger, R. 2006. *Babylonisch-assyrische Lesestücke (3., revidierte Auflage)* (AnOr 54). Rome: Pontificio Istituto Biblico

Brayman Hackel, H. 2004. "Rhetorics and Practices of Illiteracy or The Marketing of Illiteracy", in I. F. Moulton (ed.), *Reading and Literacy in the Middle Ages and Renaissance* (Arizona Studies in the Middle Ages and Renaissance 8). Turnhout: Brepols, 169–183

Brown, D. 2000. *Mesopotamian Planetary Astronomy-Astrology* (CM 18). Leiden: Brill

Brown, D. 2008. "Increasingly Redundant: The Growing Obsolescence of the Cuneiform Script in Babylonia from 539 BC", in J. Baines, J. Bennet, S. Houston (eds), *The Disappearance of Writing Systems: Perspectives on Literacy and Communication.* London: Equinox, 73–101

Brown, D., Linssen, M. 1997. "BM 134701 = 1965-10-14,1 and the Hellenistic period eclipse ritual from Uruk", *RA* 91, 147–166

Bryan, E. J. 1999. *Collaborative meaning in Medieval Scribal culture: The Otho Lazamon* (Editorial Theory and Literary Criticism). Ann Arbor: The University of Michigan Press

Cardona, G. R. 1988. "Il sapere dello scriba", in P. Rossi (ed.), *La memoria del sapere: forme di conservazione e strutture organizzative dall'antichità a oggi.* Rome: Laterza, 3–28

Cavigneaux, A. 1981. *Textes scolaires du temple de Nabû ša harê* (Texts from Babylon 1). Baghdad: State Organisation of Antiquities & Heritage, Republic of Iraq

Cavigneaux, A. 1993. "Review of Cohen, *Lamentations*", *JAOS* 113, 251–257

Cerquiglini, B. 1989. *Éloge de la variante: Histoire critique de la philologie.* Paris: Éditions du Seuil

Champan Bates, R. 1937. *L'Hystore Job: adaptation en vers français du Compendum in Job de Pierre de Blois* (Yale Romanic Studies 14). New Haven: Yale University Press

Charpin, D. 1989. "Corrections, ratures et annulation: la pratique des scribes mésopotamiens", in R. Laufer (ed.), *Le texte et son inscription.* Paris: CNRS, 57–62

Charpin, D. 1995. ""Lies natürlich ..." À propos des erreurs de scribes dans les lettres de Mari", in M. Dietrich, O. Loretz (eds), *Vom Alten Orient zum Alten Testament: Festschrift für Wolfram Freiherrn von Soden zum 85. Geburtstag am 19. Juni 1993* (AOAT 240). Kevelaer: Butzon & Bercker; Neukirchen-Vluyn: Neukirchener Verlag, 43–55

Charpin, D. 2004. "Lire et écrire en Mésopotamie: une affaire des spécialistes?", *Comptes Rendus de l'Académie des Inscriptions et Belles-Lettres* 148/1, 481–508

Charpin, D. 2008. *Lire et écrire à Babylone.* Paris: Presses Universitaires de France

Charpin, D. 2010. *Reading and Writing in Babylon.* Cambridge, MA: Harvard University Press

Chartier, R. 1987. *Lectures et lecteurs dans la France d'Ancien Régime.* Paris: Éditions du Seuil

Chaytor, H. J. 1941–1942. "The Medieval Reader and Textual Criticism", *Bulletin of the John Rylands Library* 26, 49–56

Chaytor, H. J. 1945. *From Script to Print.* Cambridge: Cambridge University Press

Chiera, E. 1939. *They Wrote on Clay: The Babylonian Tablets Speak To-day.* Cambridge: Cambridge University Press

Civil, M. 2004. *The Series DIRI = (w)atru* (MSL 15). Rome: Pontificio Istituto Biblico

Civil, M., Green, M. W., Lambert, W. G. 1979. *Ea A = nâqu, Aa A = nâqu, with their Forerunners and Related Texts* (MSL 14). Rome: Istituto Pontificio Biblico

Clanchy, M. 1993. *From Memory to Written Record: England, 1066–1307.* Oxford: Blackwell

Clancier, P. 2005. "Les scribes sur parchemin du temple d'Anu", *RA* 99, 83–104

Clancier, P. 2009. *Les bibliothèques en Babylonie dans la deuxième moitié du Ier millénaire av. J.-C.* (AOAT 363). Münster: Ugarit-Verlag

Cochavi-Rainey, Z. 2011. *The Akkadian dialect of Egyptian Scribes in the 14th and 13th centuries BCE* (AOAT 374). Münster: Ugarit-Verlag

Cogan, M. 1977. "Ashurbanipal Prism F: Notes on Scribal Techniques and Editorial Procedures", *JCS* 29, 97–107

Cole, S. W. 1996. *The Early Neo-Babylonian Governor's Archive from Nippur* (OIP 114). Chicago: Oriental Institute

Conner, R. P., Sparks, D. H., Sparks, M., Anzaldúa, G. 1997. *Cassell's encyclopedia of queer myth, symbol, and spirit: gay, lesbian, bisexual, and transgender lore.* London: Cassell

Cooper, J. S. 1975. "The Conclusion of Ludlul II", *JCS* 27, 248–249

Cooper, J. S. 1977. "Gilgamesh Dreams of Enkidu: The Evolution and Dilution of Narrative", in M. de Jong Ellis (ed.), *Essays on the Ancient Near East in Memory of Jacob Joel Finkelstein* (Memoirs of the Connecticut Academy of Arts & Sciences 19). Hamden, Conn.: Archon Books for the Academy, 39–44

Cooper, J. S. 1978. *The Return of Ninurta to Nippur* (AnOr 52). Rome: Pontificium Institutum Biblicum

Cooper, J. S. 1992. "Babbling on: Recovering Mesopotamian Orality", in M. E. Vogelzang, H. L. J. Vanstiphout (eds), *Mesopotamian Epic Literature: Oral or Aural?* Lewiston, NY: The Edwin Mellen Press, 103–122

Cooper, J. S. 1996. "Mesopotamian Cuneiform, Sumerian and Akkadian", in P. Daniels, J. Bright (eds), *The World's Writing Systems.* Oxford: Oxford University Press, 37–57

Cooper, J. S. 2005. "Right writing: Talking about Sumerian orthography and texts", *ASJ* 22, 43–52

Cribiore, R. 2009. "Education in the Papyri", in R. S. Bagnall (ed.), *The Oxford Handbook of Papyrology.* Oxford: Oxford University Press, 320–337

Crowder, R. G., Wagner, R. K. 1992. *The psychology of reading: an introduction.* New York: Oxford University Press

Dahood, M., Deller, K., Köbert, R. 1965. "Comparative Semitics: Some Remarks on a Recent Publication", *Orientalia* 34, 35–44

Dain, A. 1949. *Les Manuscrits.* Paris: Société d'édition « Les belles lettres »

Dalley, S., Walker, C. B. F., Hawkins, J. D. 1976. *The Old Babylonian Tablets from Tell Al Rimah.* London: British School of Archaeology of Iraq

De Odorico, M. 1994. "Compositional and Editorial Processes of Annalistic and Summary Texts of Tiglath-Pileser I", *SAAB* 8, 67–112

de Vaan, J. M. C. T. 1995. *"Ich bin eine Schwertklinge des Königs": die Sprache des Bel-ibni* (AOAT 242). Münster: Ugarit-Verlag

Delitzsch, F. 1906. "Zu W. Andrae's Bericht vom 8. Mai 1906", *MDOG* 32, no. 4, pp. 25–27
Deller, K. 1957. "Zur sprachlichen Einordnung der Inschriften Aššurnaṣirpals II. (883–859)", *Orientalia* 26, 14–56
Deller, K. 1962. "Studien zur neuassyrischen Orthographie", *Orientalia* 31, 186–196
Deller, K. 1969. "Die Briefe des Adad-Šumu-Uṣur", in W. Röllig, M. Dietrich (eds), *lišān mithurti – Festschrift Wolfram von Soden zum 19.vi.1968 gewidmet von Schülern und Mitarbeitern* (AOAT 1). Kevelaer: Butzon & Bercker; Neukirchen-Vluyn: Neukirchener Verlag des Erziehungsvereins, 45–64
Delnero, P. 2007. "Pre-verbal /n/: function, distribution, and stability", in J. Ebeling and G. Cunningham (eds), *Analysing Literary Sumerian: corpus-based approaches.* London: Equinox, 105–143
Delnero, P. 2010. "Sumerian extract tablets and scribal education", *JCS* 62, 53–69
Delnero, P. Forthcoming. "Memorization and the Transmission of Sumerian Literary Compositions", *JNES*
Delz, J. 1993. "Textkritik und Editionstechnik", in F. Graf (ed.), *Einleitung in die lateinische Philologie.* Stuttgart: Teubner, 51–73
Donbaz, V. 1990. "Two Neo-Assyrian Stelae in the Antakya and Kahramanmaraş Museums", *ARRIM* 8, 5–24
Downing, J. 1973. "Other Extraneous Factors", in J. Downing (ed.), *Comparative Reading.* New York: Macmillan, 169–180
Drewnowski, A., Healy, A. F. 1977. "Detection Errors on *the* and *and:* evidence for reading units larger than the word", *Memory and Cognition* 5, 636–647
Driver, G. R. 1976. *Semitic Writing from Pictograph to Alphabet.* London: Oxford University Press for the British Academy
Driver, G. R., Miles, J. C. 1955. *The Babylonian laws, vol. 2* (Ancient codes and laws of the Near East 1/ii). Oxford: Clarendon Press
Durand, J.-M. 1979. "Un commentaire à *TDP* I, AO 17661", *RA* 73, 153–170
Durand, J.-M. 1988. "*Yasûm « Médecin »", *NABU,* no. 66, p. 46
Ebeling, E. 1931. *Tod und Leben nach den Vorstellungen der Babylonier.* Berlin: Walter de Gruyter
Ebeling, E. 1949. "Beschwörungen gegen den Feind und den bösen Blick aus dem Zweistromlande", *ArOr* 17, 172–211
Edzard, D. O. 1959. "Review of A. Finet, *L'accadien des lettres de Mari*", *ZA* 53, 304–308
Edzard, D. O. 1976–1980. "Keilschrift", in D. O. Edzard, P. Calmeyer, A. Moortgat, H. Otten, W. Röllig, W. Von Soden, D. J. Wiseman (eds), *Reallexikon der Assyriologie, vol. V.* Berlin: De Gruyter, 544–568
Elat, M. 1982. "Mesopotamische Kriegsrituale", *BiOr* 39, cols. 5–25
Elman, Y. 1975. "Authoritative Oral Tradition in Neo-Assyrian Scribal Circles", *JANES* 7, 19–32
Epelboim, J., Booth, J. R., Steinman, R. M. 1994. "Reading unspaced text: Implications for theories of eye movements", *Vision Research* 34, 1735–1766
Epelboim, J., Booth, J. R., Steinman, R. M. 1996. "Much Ado About Nothing: the Place of Space in Text", *Vision Research* 465–470

Fales, F. M., Postgate, J. N. 1995. *Imperial administrative records. Part 2, Provincial and military administration* (SAA 11). Helsinki: Helsinki University Press

Falkenstein, A. 1941. *Literarische Keilschrifttexte aus Uruk.* Hildesheim: G. Olms

Farber, W. 1982. "Altbabylonische Adverbialendungen auf *-āni*", in G. van Driel, T. J. H. Krispijn, M. Stol, K. R. Veenhof (eds), *Zikir šumim: Assyriological Studies Presented to F. R. Kraus on the Occasion of his Seventieth Birthday.* Leiden: Brill, 37–47

Farber, W. 1987. "Neues aus Uruk: Zur "Bibliothek des Iqīša"", *WdO* 18, 26–42

Farber, W. 1989. *Schlaf, Kindchen, Schlaf! Mesopotamische Baby-Beschwörungen und -Rituale.* Winona Lake: Eisenbrauns

Fee, G. D. 1993. "The Majority Text and the Original Text of the New Testament", in E. J. Epp, G. D. Fee (eds), *Studies in the Theory and Method of New Testament Textual Criticism.* Grand Rapids, MI: W.B. Eerdmans, 183–210

Ferrara, A. J. 1976. "Texts and Fragments 91–96", *JCS* 28, 93–97

Feyerabend, P. 1975. *Against Method: outline of an anarchistic theory of knowledge.* London: NLB

Finet, A. 1954. "Liste des erreurs de scribes", in J. Bottéro, A. Finet (eds), *Répertoire analytique des tomes I à V.* Paris: Imprimerie Nationale, 93–113

Finet, A. 1956. *L'accadien des lettres de Mari* (Académie royale de Belgique. Classe des lettres et des sciences morales et politiques. Mémoires. Collection in 8o. 2. sér., t. 51, fasc. 1). Bruxelles: Palais des académies

Finet, A. 1986. "Allusions et réminiscences comme source d'information sur la diffusion de la littérature", in K. Hecker, W. Sommerfeld (eds), *Keilschriftliche Literaturen, Ausgewählte Vorträge der XXXII. Rencontre Assyriologique Internationale.* Berlin: Dietrich Reimer, 13–17

Finkel, I. L. 1988. "Adad-apla-iddina, Esagil-kin-apli, and the series SA.GIG", in E. Leichty, M. de Jong Ellis, P. Gerardi (eds), *A scientific humanist: studies in memory of Abraham Sachs.* Philadelphia: University of Pennsylvania Museum of Archaeology and Anthropology, 143–159

Finkel, I. L. 2000. "On Late Babylonian Medical Training", in A. R. George, I. L. Finkel (eds), *Wisdom, Gods and Literature: Studies in Assyriology in Honour of W. G. Lambert.* Winona Lake: Eisenbrauns, 137–223

Finkel, I. L. 2004. "Old Babylonian Medicine at Ur: lettre aux éditeurs", *JMC* 4, 26

Finkel, I. L. 2006. "On an Izbu VII Commentary", in A. K. Guinan, M. deJ. Ellis, A. J. Ferrara, S. M. Freedman, M. T. Rutz, L. Sassmannshausen, S. Tinney, M. W. Waters (eds), *If a Man Builds a Joyful House: Assyriological Studies in Honor of Erle Verdun Leichty* (CM 31). Leiden: Brill, 139–148

Finkelstein, J. J. 1963. "The Antediluvian Kings: A University of California Tablet", *JCS* 17, 39–51

Foster, B. R. 2003. "Late Babylonian Schooldays: An Archaising Cylinder", in G. J. Selz (ed.), *Festschrift für Burkhart Kienast zu seinem 70. Geburtstage dargebracht von Freunden, Schülern und Kollegen* (AOAT 274). Münster: Ugarit-Verlag, 79–87

Foster, B. R. 2005. *Before the Muses: An Anthology of Akkadian Literature.* Bethesda, MD: CDL Press
Foster, B. R. 2007. "Review of Radner, *Die Macht des Namens*", *JAOS* 127, 369–371
Foster, B. R. 2009. "Akkadian Literature", in C. S. Ehrlich (ed.), *From an Antique Land: An Introduction to Ancient Near Eastern Literature.* Lanham: Rowman & Littlefield, 137–214
Foxvog, D. 1978. "Royal Inscriptions at Berkeley", *RA* 72, 41–46
Frahm, E. 1997. *Einleitung in die Sanherib-Inschriften* (AfO Bh. 26). Wien: Selbstverlag des Instituts für Orientalistik der Universität Wien
Frahm, E. 2011. *Babylonian and Assyrian Text Commentaries. Origins of Interpretation* (Guides to the Mesopotamian Textual Record 5). Münster: Ugarit-Verlag
Frame, G. 2004. "The Order of the Wall Slabs with the Annals of Sargon II in Room V of the Palace at Khorsabad", in G. Frame (ed.), *From the Upper Sea to the Lower Sea. Studies on the History of Assyria and Babylonia in Honour of A. K. Grayson.* Leiden: Nederlands Instituut voor het Nabije Oosten, 89–102
Frame, G., George, A. R. 2005. "The Royal Libraries of Nineveh: New Evidence for King Ashurbanipal's Tablet Collecting", *Iraq* 67, 265–284
Frankena, R. 1960. "Nouveaux fragments de la sixième tablette de l'Épopée de Gilgameš", in P. Garelli (ed.), *Gilgameš et sa légende* (CRRA 7). Paris: Klincksiek, 113–122
Frayne, D. 1990. *The Old Babylonian Period* (RIME 4). Toronto: University of Toronto Press
Friedrich, J., Kammenhuber, A. 1998. *Hethitisches Wörterbuch, Band III. Lieferung 13.* Heidelberg: Universitätsverlag C. Winter
Fuchs, A. 1993. *Die Inschriften Sargons II. aus Khorsabad.* Göttingen: Cuvillier Verlag
Gadd, C. J. 1925. "On Two Babylonian Kings", *StOr* 1, 25–33
Gadd, C. J. 1967. "Omens Expressed in Numbers", *JCS* 21, 52–63
Gasson, W. 1972. "The oldest lens in the world: A critical study of the Layard lens", *The Ophthalmic Optician* 9 December, 1267–1272
Gavrilov, A. K. 1997. "Techniques of Reading in Classical Antiquity", *The Classical Quarterly* 47, 56–73
Gelb, I. J. 1949. "The Date of the Cruciform Monument of Maništušu", *JNES* 8, 346–348
Gelb, I. J. 1961. *Old Akkadian Writing and Grammar* (Materials for the Assyrian Dictionary 2). Chicago: Chicago University Press
Gelb, I. J. 1963. *A Study of Writing.* Chicago: The University of Chicago Press
Geller, M. J. 2003. "Review of Hämeen-Anttila, *A Sketch of Neo-Assyrian Grammar*", *BSOAS* 65, 562–564
Geller, M. J. 2010. *Ancient Babylonian Medicine: Theory and Practice.* Chichester: Wiley-Blackwell
George, A. R. 1986. "Sennacherib and the Tablet of Destinies", *Iraq* 48, 133–146

George, A. R. 1992. *Babylonian Topographical Texts* (OLA 40). Leuven: Peeters

George, A. R. 1993. "Ninurta-pāqidāt's Dog-Bite and Notes on Other Comic Tales", *Iraq* 55, 63–75

George, A. R. 2003. *The Babylonian Gilgamesh Epic: Introduction, Critical Edition and Cuneiform Texts.* Oxford: Oxford University Press

George, A. R. 2005. "In search of the é.dub.ba.a: the ancient Mesopotamian school in literature and reality", in Y. Sefati (ed.), *"An Experienced Scribe who Neglects Nothing". Ancient Near Eastern Studies in Honor of Jacob Klein.* Bethesda, MD: CDL Press, 127–137

George, A. R. 2006. "Babylonian Texts from the Folios of Sidney Smith, Part Three", in A. K. Guinan, M. de Jong Ellis, A. J. Ferrara, S. M. Freedman, M. T. Rutz, L. Sassmannshausen, S. Tinney, M. W. Waters (eds), *If a Man Builds a Joyful House: Assyriological Studies in Honor of Erle Verdun Leichty* (CM 31). Leiden: Brill, 173–185

George, A. R. 2007. "The Civilizing of Ea-Enkidu : An Unusual Tablet of the Babylonian Gilgameš Epic", *RA* 101, 59–80

George, A. R. 2009. *Babylonian Literary Texts in the Schøyen Collection* (Cornell Studies in Assyriology and Sumerology 10). Bethesda, MA: CDL Press

George, A. R. 2010. "Babylonian Literary Texts in the Schøyen Collection, Nos. 18 and 19", *NABU*, no. 5, pp. 5–6

George, A. R. Forthcoming. *Babylonian Divinatory Texts Chiefly in the Schøyen Collection* (Cornell Studies in Assyriology and Sumerology). Bethesda, MA: CDL Press

George, A. R., Al-Rawi, F. N. H. 1990. "Tablets from the Sippar Library II. Tablet II of the Babylonian Creation Epic", *Iraq* 52, 149–157

George, A. R., Al-Rawi, F. N. H. 1996. "Tablets from the Sippar Library VI. Atra-hasīs", *Iraq* 58, 147–190

George, A. R., Al-Rawi, F. N. H. 1998. "Tablets from the Sippar Library VII. Three Wisdom Texts", *Iraq* 60, 187–206

Gesche, P. 2001. *Schulunterricht in Babylonien im ersten Jahrtausend v. Chr.* (AOAT 275). Münster: Ugarit-Verlag

Gibson, E. J., Levin, H. 1975. *The Psychology of Reading.* Cambridge, MA: MIT Press

Glassner, J.-J. 2005. *Mesopotamian Chronicles* (Writings from the Ancient World 19). Brill: Leiden

Goetze, A. 1945. "The Akkadian dialects of the Old Babylonian mathematical texts", in O. Neugebauer, A. Sachs (eds), *Mathematical Cuneiform Texts.* New Haven: The American Oriental Society and the American Schools of Oriental Research, 146–151

Goetze, A. 1965. "An Inscription of Simbar-Šīhu", *JCS* 19, 121–135

Gonda, J. 1975. *Vedic Literature* (A History of Indian Literature). Wiesbaden: Harrassowitz

Goodnick Westenholz, J. 1997. *Legends of the Kings of Akkade* (Mesopotamian Civilizations 7). Winona Lake: Eisenbrauns

Goodnick Westenholz, J. 2011. "Who was Aman-Aštar?", in G. Barjamovic, J. L. Dahl, U. S. Koch, W. Sommerfeld, J. Goodnick Westenholz (eds), *Akkade is King: A Collection of Papers by Friends and Colleagues Presented to Aage Westenholz on the Occasion of his 70th Birthday, 15th May 2009* (PIHANS 118). Leiden: Nederlands Instituut voor het Nabije Oosten, 315–332

Gooseens, G. 1942. "L'Accadien des clercs d'Uruk", *Le Muséon* 55, 61–86

Gordon Carter, I. 1933. "Some Songs and Ballads from Tennessee and North Carolina", *Journal of American Folklore* 46, 22–50

Gragg, G. B. 1972. "Observations on Grammatical Variation in Sumerian Literary Texts", *JAOS* 92, 204–213

Grayson, A. K. 1963. "The Walters Art Gallery Sennacherib Inscription", *AfO* 20, 83–96

Grayson, A. K. 1975. *Assyrian and Babylonian Chronicles* (TCS 5). Locust Valley, NY: J. J. Augustin

Grayson, A. K. 1991. *Assyrian Rulers of the Early First Millennium BC I (1114–859)* (RIMA 2). Toronto: University of Toronto Press

Grayson, A. K. 1991. "Old and Middle Assyrian Royal Inscriptions—Marginalia", in M. Cogan, I. Eph'al (eds), *Ah, Assyria: studies in Assyrian history and ancient Near Eastern historiography presented to Hayim Tadmor.* Jerusalem: The Hebrew University of Jerusalem, 264–266

Grayson, A. K. 1996. *Assyrian Rulers of the Early First Millennium BC II (858–745)* (RIMA 3). Toronto: Toronto University Press

Grayson, A. K. 2000. "Murmuring in Mesopotamia", in A. R. George, I. L. Finkel (eds), *Wisdom, Gods and Literature. Studies in Assyriology in Honour of W. G. Lambert.* Winona Lake: Eisenbrauns, 301–308

Grayson, A. K. and Novotny, J. Forthcoming. *The Royal Inscriptions of Sennacherib, King of Assyria (704–681 BC), Part 1* (RINAP 3/1). Winona Lake: Eisenbrauns

Gurney, O. R. 1954. "Two Fragments of the Epic of Gilgamesh from Sultantepe", *JCS* 8, 87–95

Gurney, O. R. 1956. "The Sultantepe Tablets (Continued). V. The Tale of the Poor Man of Nippur", *AnSt* 6, 145–164

Gurney, O. R. 1957. "The Sultantepe Tablets (Continued). VI. A Letter of Gilgamesh", *AnSt* 7, 127–136

Gurney, O. R. 1960. "A Tablet of Incantations against Slander", *Iraq* 22, 221–227

Gurney, O. R. 1983. *Middle Babylonian Legal and Economic Texts from Ur.* London: British School of Archaeology in Iraq

Gutas, D. 2010. *Theophrastus On First Principles (known as his Metaphysics)* (Philosophia Antiqua 119). Leiden: Brill

Haas, V. 2006. *Die hethitische Literatur.* Berlin: De Gruyter

Hackl, J. 2010. "Uruk, syllabic, and other peculiarities in LB orthography", *NABU*, no. 16, pp. 16–19

Hagen, F. Forthcoming. *An Ancient Egyptian Literary Text in Context: The Instruction of Ptahhotep* (OLA 218). Leuven: Peeters

Hallo, W. W. 1977. "Haplographic Marginalia", in M. de Jong Ellis (ed.), *Essays on the Ancient Near East in Memory of Jacob Joel Finkelstein* (Memoirs of the Connecticut Academy of Arts & Sciences 19). Hamden, Conn.: Archon Books for the Academy, 101–103

Halverson, J. 1992. "Havelock on Greek Orality and Literacy", *Journal of the History of Ideas* 53, 148–163
Hämeen-Anttila, J. 2000. *Sketch of Neo-Assyrian Grammar* (SAAS 13). Helsinki: The Neo-Assyrian Text Corpus Project
Hanna III, R. 1996. *Pursuing History: Middle English Manuscripts and their Texts.* Stanford: Stanford University Press
Hanna III, R. 2000. "The Application of Thought to Textual Criticism in All Modes—with Apologies to A. E. Housman", *Studies in Bibliography* 53, 163–172
Harris, W. V. 1989. *Ancient Literacy.* Cambridge, MA: Harvard University Press
Haupt, P. 1885. "Einige Verbesserungen und Nachträge zu meinen Akkadischen und Sumerischen Keilschrifttexten", *Zeitschrift für Keilschriftforschung* 2, 267–284
Havelock, E. A. 1982. *The Literate Revolution in Greece and its Cultural Consequences.* New Haven: Yale University Press
Hecker, K. 1974. *Untersuchungen zur akkadischen Epik* (AOAT 8). Kevelaer: Butzon und Bercker; Neukirchen-Vluyn: Neukirchener Verlag
Heeßel, N. P. 2000. *Babylonisch-assyrische Diagnostik* (AOAT 43). Münster: Ugarit-Verlag
Heeßel, N. P. 2001/2002. ""Wenn ein Mann zum Haus des Kranken geht ..."", *AfO* 48/49, 24–49
Heeßel, N. P. 2007. *Divinatorische Texte I: Terrestrische, teratologische, physiognomische und oneiromantische Texte* (KAL 1). Wiesbaden: Harrassowitz
Heeßel, N. P., Al-Rawi, F. N. H. 2003. "Tablets from the Sippar Library XII. A Medical Therapeutic Text", *Iraq* 65, 221–239
Heidel, A. 1953. "The Octagonal Sennacherib Prism in the Iraq Museum", *Sumer* 9, 117–187
Herrero, P. 1975. "Une tablette médicale assyrienne inédite", *RA* 69, 41–53
Hess, C. W. 2010. "Towards the Origins of the Hymnic Epic Dialect", *Kaskal* 7, 101–122
Hilgert, M. 2002. *Akkadisch in der Ur III-Zeit* (IMGULA 5). Münster: Rhema
Hilprecht, H. V. 1896. "Old Babylonian Inscriptions Chiefly from Nippur. Part II", *Transactions of the American Philosophical Society, New Series* 18, 221–282
Horowitz, W., Lambert, W. G. 2002. "A New Exemplar of Ludlul bēl nēmeqi Tablet I fom Birmingham", *Iraq* 64, 237–245
Horowitz, W., Wasserman, N. 2004. "From Hazor to Mari and Ekallatum: A Recently Discovered Old-Babylonian Letter from Hazor", in C. Nicolle (ed.), *Nomades et sédentaires dans le Proche-Orient ancien* (CRRAI 46). Paris: Éditions Recherche sur les Civilisations, 335–344
Housman, A. E. 1921. "The Application of Thought to Textual Criticism", *Proceedings of the Classical Association* 18, 67–84
Housman, A. E. 1926. *M. Annaei Lucani Belli Civilis libri decem.* Oxford: Blackwell
Houwink Ten Cate, P. H. J. 1968. "Muwatallis' "Prayer to Be Spoken in an Emergency," An Essay in Textual Criticism", *JNES* 27, 204–208

Hrůša, I. 2010. *Die akkadische Synonymenliste malku = šarru: Eine Textedition mit Übersetzung und Kommentar* (AOAT 50). Münster: Ugarit-Verlag

Huehnergard, J. 1989. *The Akkadian of Ugarit* (HSS 34). Atlanta, GA: Scholars Press

Hunger, H. 1968. *Babylonisch-assyrische Kolophone* (AOAT 2). Kevelaer: Butzon & Bercker; Neukirchen-Vluyn: Neukirchener Verlag

Hunger, H. 1989. *Schreiben und Lesen in Byzanz: die byzantinische Buchkultur* München: Beck

Ingulsrud, J. E., Allen, K. 1999. *Learning to read in China: sociolinguistic perspectives on the acquisition of literacy.* Lewiston, NY: Mellen

Izre'el, S. 1991. "On the Person-Prefixes of the Akkadian Verb", *JANES* 20, 35–56

Jacobsen, T. 1939. *The Sumerian King List* (AS 11). Chicago: University of Chicago Press

Izre'el, S. 2001. *Adapa and the South Wind: language has the power of life and death* (Mesopotamian Civilizations 10). Winona Lake: Eisenbrauns

Jeyes, U. 1989. *Old Babylonian Extispicy: Omen Texts in the British Museum* (Uitgaven van het Nederlands Historisch-Archaeologisch Instituut te İstanbul 64). Istanbul: Nederlands Historisch-Archaeologisch Instituut te İstanbul

Johnson, W. A. 2009. "The Ancient Book", in R. S. Bagnall (ed.), *The Oxford Handbook of Papyrology.* Oxford: Oxford University Press, 256–281

Johnson, W. A. 2010. *Readers and Reading Culture in the High Roman Empire: a study of elite communities.* Oxford: Oxford University Press

Junack, C. 1981. "Abschreibpraktiken und Schreibergewohnheiten", in E. J. Epp, G. D. Fee (eds), *New Testament Textual Criticism: Its significance for Exegesis.* Oxford: Clarendon Press, 277–293

Jursa, M. 1999. *Das Archiv des Bēl-rēmanni* (PIHANS 86). Leiden/Istanbul: Nederlands Historisch-Archaeologisch Instituut te İstanbul

Jursa, M., Hackl, J., Janković, B., Kleber, K., Payne, E. E., Waerzeggers, C., Weszeli, M. 2010. *Aspects of the Economic History of Babylonia in the First Millennium BC* (AOAT 377). Münster: Ugarit-Verlag

Jursa, M., Weszeli, M. 2004. "Neunzehn, syllabisch", *NABU,* no. 56, pp. 56–57

Kienast, B. 1977. "*qabal lā mahār*", *JCS* 29, 73–77

Kilmer, A. D. 1982. "A Note on an Overlooked Word-Play in the Akkadian Gilgamesh", in G. van Driel, T. J. H. Krispijn, M. Stol, K. R. Veenhof (eds), *Zikir šumim: Assyriological Studies Presented to F. R. Kraus on the Occasion of his Seventieth Birthday.* Leiden: Brill, 128–132

King, L. W. 1912. *Babylonian Boundary-Stones and Memorial-Tablets in the British Museum.* London: Printed by Order of the Trustees

Kinnier Wilson, J. V. 1956. "Two Medical Texts from Nimrud", *Iraq* 18, 130–146

Kinnier Wilson, J. V. 1961. "Lugal ud melambi nirgal: New Texts and Fragments", *ZA* 54, 71–89

Kinnier Wilson, J. V. 1962. "The Kurba'il Statue of Shalmaneser III", *Iraq* 24, 90–115 and plates xxx, xxxiii-xxxv

Kinnier Wilson, J. V. 1968. ""Desonance" in Akkadian", *Journal of Semitic Studies* 13, 93–103

Knudsen, E. E. 1986. "Review of Greenstein, *The Phonology of Akkadian Syllable Structure*", *BiOr* 43, 723–730

Koch-Westenholz, U. 2000. *Babylonian Liver Omens: The chapters Manzāzu, Padānu and Pān tākalti of the Babylonian Extispicy Series mainly from Aššurbanipal's Library* (CNI Publications 25). Copenhagen: The Carsten Niebuhr Institute of Near Eastern Studies / Museum Tusculanum Press

Kohsom, C., Gobet, F. 1997. "Adding spaces to Thai and English: Effects on reading", in (Anonymous) (ed.), *Proceedings of the 19th Annual Meeting of the Cognitive Science Society*. Hillsdale: Erlbaum, 388–393

Kouwenberg, N. J. C. 2003. "Evidence for Post-Glottalised Consonants in Akkadian", *JCS* 55, 75–86

Kouwenberg, N. J. C. 2005/2006. "Review of Luukko, *Grammatical Variation in Neo-Assyrian*", *AfO* 51, 331–334

Kouwenberg, N. J. C. 2011. *The Akkadian Verb and its Semitic Background* (Languages of the Ancient Near East 2). Winona Lake: Eisenbrauns

Kraus, F. R. 1968. *Briefe aus dem Archive des Šamaš-hāzir in Paris und Oxford (TCL 7 und OECT 3)* (AbB 4). Leiden: Brill

Krecher, J. 1957–1971. "Glossen. A. In sumerischen und akkadischen Texten", in E. F. Weidner, W. von Soden, P. Calmeyer, D. O. Edzard, A. Falkenstein, A. Moortgat, H. Otten, W. Röllig, D. Wiseman (eds), *Reallexikon der Assyriologie, vol. III*. Berlin: De Gruyter, 431–440

Kruschwitz, P. 2010. "Romanes eunt domus!", in T. V. Evans, D. O. Obbink (eds), *The Language of the Papyri*. Oxford: Oxford University Press, 156–170

Labat, R. 1935. *Le poème babylonien de la création*. Paris: Libraire d'Amerique et d'Orient

Labat, R. 1939. *Hémérologies et ménologies d'Assur*. Paris: Librairie d'Amerique et d'Orient

Labat, R. 1951. *Traité akkadien de diagnostics et pronostics médicaux* (Collection de travaux de l'académie internationale d'histoire des sciences 7). Paris: Académie Internationale d'Histoire des Sciences

Læssøe, J. 1956. "A Prayer to Ea, Shamash and Marduk, from Hana", *Iraq* 18, 60–67

Lambert, W. G. 1954–1956. "An Address of Marduk to the Demons", *AfO* 17, 310–321

Lambert, W. G. 1960. *Babylonian Wisdom Literature*. Oxford: Oxford University Press

Lambert, W. G. 1962. "A Catalogue of Texts and Authors", *JCS* 16, 59–77

Lambert, W. G. 1967. "The Gula Hymn of Bullutsa-rabi", *Orientalia* 36, 105–132

Lambert, W. G. 1969. "A Middle Assyrian Medical Text", *Iraq* 31, 28–39

Lambert, W. G. 1974. "Dingir.šà.dib.ba Incantations", *JNES* 33, 267–270 and 272–322

Lambert, W. G. 1989. "Review of *JEOL* vol. 29, 1985–1986", *BSOAS* 52, 544–546

Lambert, W. G. 1997. "The Assyrian Recension of Enūma eliš", in H. Waetzold, H. Hauptmann (eds), *Assyrien im Wandel der Zeiten (CRRAI 39)* (Heidelbeger Studien zum Alten Orient 6). Heidelberg: Heidelberger Orient-Verlag, 77–79

Lambert, W. G. 2007. *Babylonian Oracle Questions.* Winona Lake: Eisenbrauns

Lambert, W. G. 2011. "Notes on *Malku = šarru*", *NABU*, no. 28, pp. 36–37

Landsberger, B. 1934. *Die Fauna des alten Mesopotamien nach der 14. Tafel der Serie HAR-ra* (Abhandlungen der Philologisch-historischen Klasse der Sächsischen Akademie der Wissenschaften). Leipzig: S. Hirzel

Landsberger, B. 1954. "Assyrische Königsliste und "Dunkles Zeitalter" (Continued)", *JCS* 8, 106–133

Landsberger, B. 1958. "Corrections to the Article, "An Old Babylonian Charm against Merḫu"", *JNES* 17, 56–58

Landsberger, B. 1965. *Brief des Bischofs von Esagila an König Asarhaddon* (Mededelingen der Koninklijke Nederlandse Akademie van Wetenschappen, afd. Letterkunde. Nieuwe Reeks deel 28, no. 6). Amsterdam: Noord-Hollandsche Uitg. Mij

Landsberger, B., Hallock, R. 1956. "Neo-Babylonian Grammatical Texts", in B. Landsberger, R. Hallock, T. Jacobsen, A. Falkenstein (eds), *Materialien zum Sumerischen Lexikon IV.* Rome: Pontificium Institutum Biblicum, 129–207

Langdon, S. 1927. *Babylonian penitential psalms to which are added fragments of the epic of creation from Kish in the Weld Collection of the Ashmolean Museum, excavated by the Oxford-Field Museum Expedition* (OECT 6). Paris: Geuthner

Layard, A. H. 1853. *Discoveries in the ruins of Nineveh and Babylon: with travels in Armenia, Kurdistan and the desert: being the result of a second expedition undertaken for the Trustees of the British Museum.* London: John Murray

Leichty, E. 1970. *The Omen Series šumma izbu* (TCS 4). Locust Valley, NY: J. J. Augustin

Leichty, E. 2011. *The Royal Inscriptions of Esarhaddon, King of Assyria (680–669 BC)* (The Royal Inscriptions of the Neo-Assyrian Period 4). Winona Lake: Eisenbrauns

Levine, L. D. 1973. "The Second Campaign of Sennacherib", *JNES* 32, 312–317

Livingstone, A. 1988. "A note on an epithet of Ea in a recently published creation myth", *NABU*, no. 65, pp. 45–46

Livingstone, A. 1989. *Court Poetry and Literary Miscellanea* (SAA 3). Helsinki

Livingstone, A. 2007. "Ashurbanipal: Literate or Not?", *ZA* 97, 98–118

Llop, J., George, A. R. 2001/2002. "Die babylonisch-assyrischen Beziehungen und die innere Lage Assyriens in der Zeit der Auseinandersetzung zwischen Ninurta-tukulti-Aššur und Mutakkil-Nusku nach neuen keilschriftlichen Quellen", *AfO* 48/49, 1–23

Lord, A. B. 1960. *The Singer of Tales.* Cambridge, MA: Harvard University Press

Luiselli, R. 2010. "Authorial Revision of Linguistic Style in Greek Papyrus Letters and Petitions (AD i-iv)", in T. V. Evans, D. O. Obbink (eds), *The Language of the Papyri.* Oxford: Oxford University Press, 71–96

Luukko, M. 2004. *Grammatical Variation in Neo-Assyrian* (SAAS 16). Helsinki: The Neo-Assyrian Text Corpus Project

Maas, P. 1927. "Textkritik", in A. Gercke, E. Norden (eds), *Einleitung in die Altertumswissenschaften.* Leipzig: B. G. Teubner, 1–18. (The pages in this book are not numbered consecutively; Maas's is the second chapter)

Maas, P. 1966. *Greek Metre (translated by Hugh Lloyd-Jones).* Oxford: Clarendon Press

Manganelli, G. 2008. *Vita di Samuel Johnson* (Piccola Biblioteca 577). Milan: Adelphi

Maul, S. M. 1992. "*kurgarrû* und *assinnu* und ihr Stand in der babylonischen Gesellschaft", in V. Haas (ed.), *Außenseiter und Randgruppen: Beiträge zu einer Sozialgeschichte des Alten Orients* (Xenia 32). Konstanz: Universitätsverlag Konstanz, 159–171

Maul, S. M. 2005. *Die Inschriften von Tall Ṭābān (Grabungskampagnen 1997–1999): die Könige von Ṭābētu und das Land Māri in mittelassyrischer Zeit* (Acta Sumerologica Supplementary Series 2). Tokyo: Institute for Cultural Studies of Ancient Iraq, Kokushikan University

Maul, S. M. 2008. *Das Gilgamesch-Epos.* München: C. H. Beck

Maul, S. M., Strauß, R. 2011. *Ritualbeschreibungen und Gebete I* (Keilschrifttexte aus Assur literarischen Inhalts). Wiesbaden: Harrassowitz

Mayer, W. 1971. *Untersuchungen zur Grammatik des Mittelassyrischen* (AOAT, Sonderreihe 2). Kevelaer: Butzon & Bercker; Neukirchen-Vluyn: Neukirchener Verlag

Mayer, W. 1983. "Sargons Feldzug gegen Urartu – 714 v. Chr. Text und Übersetzung", *MDOG* 115, 65–132

Mayer, W. R. 1987. "Ein Mythos von der Erschaffung des Menschen und des Königs", *Orientalia* 56, 55–68

Mayer, W. R. 1990. "Sechs Šu-ila-Gebete", *Orientalia* 59, 449–490

Meissner, B. 1922. "Die Eroberung der Stadt Ulhu auf Sargons 8. Feldzug", *ZA* 34, 113–122

Michalowski, P. 1989. *The Lamentation over the Destruction of Sumer and Ur.* Winona Lake: Eisenbrauns

Militarev, A., Kogan, L. 2000. *Semitic Etymological Dictionary, vol. 1 Anatomy of man and animals* (AOAT 278/1). Münster: Ugarit-Verlag

Millard, A. R. 1994. *The Eponyms of the Assyrian Empire* (SAAS 2). Helsinki: The Neo-Assyrian Text Corpus Project

Millard, A. R. 2000. *Reading and Writing in the Time of Jesus* (The Biblical Seminar 69). Sheffield: Sheffield Academic Press

Miller, J. L. 2004. *Studies in the origins, development and interpretation of the Kizzuwatna rituals* (Studien zu den Boghazköy-Texten 46). Wiesbaden: Harrassowitz

Montanari, E. 2003. *La critica del testo secondo Paul Maas* (Millennio medievale 41). Firenze: SISMEL edizioni del Galluzzo

Moorey, P. R. S. 1994. *Ancient Mesopotamian Materials and Industries: The Archaeological Evidence.* Oxford: Clarendon Press

Moran, W. L. 1983. "Notes on the Hymn to Marduk in *Ludlul Bēl Nēmeqi*", *JAOS* 103, 255–260

Nemirovskaya, A. V. 2008. "lú as a logogram for *mamma* in the standard babylonian epic of Gilgamesh", *NABU*, no. 78, pp. 110–112

Nietzsche, F. 1886. *Jenseits von Gut und Böse: Vorspiel einer Philosophie der Zukunft.* Leipzig: C. G. Naumann

Nougayrol, J. 1968. "Review of von Soden, Röllig, *Das akkadische Syllabar (2. Aufl.)*", *RA* 62, 161–163

Nougayrol, J. 1968. "Textes suméro-accadiens des archives et bibliothèques privées d'Ugarit", in J. Nougayrol, E. Laroche, C. Virolleaud, C. F. A. Schaeffer (eds), *Ugaritica V: Nouveaux textes accadiens, hourrites et ugaritiques des archives et bibliothèques privées d'Ugarit: commentaires des textes historiques (première partie).* Paris: Imprimerie Nationale / Librairie Orientaliste Paul Geuthner, 1–446

Nurullin, R. 2012. "Philological Notes on the First Tablet of the Standard Babylonian Gilgameš Epic", *Babel und Bibel* 6, 189–208

Nurullin, R. 2012. "The Name of Gilgameš in the Light of Line 47 of the First Tablet of the Standard Babylonian Gilgameš Epic", *Babel und Bibel* 6, 209–224

O'Hara, J. J. 2007. *Inconsistencies in Roman Epic.* Cambridge: Cambridge University Press

Oakley, S. P. 1998. *A Commentary on Livy Books VI-X. Volume II, Books VII-VIII.* Oxford: Oxford University Press

Oelsner, J. 1976. "Review of Gurney, UET VII", *ZA* 65, 285–293

Olmstead, A. T. E. 1916. *Assyrian Historiography: A Source Study* (University of Missouri studies. Social science series 3/1). Columbia, MO: University of Missouri

Oppenheim, A. L. 1977. *Ancient Mesopotamia: Portrait of a Dead Civilization.* Chicago: Chicago University Press

Otten, H. 1980–1983. "Kopien von Keilschrifttexten (bei den Hethitern)", in D. O. Edzard, P. Calmeyer, H. Otten, W. Röllig, E. von Schuler, W. von Soden, D. J. Wiseman (eds), *Reallexikon der Assyriologie, vol. VI.* Berlin: De Gruyter, 211

Parker, B. 1954. "The Nimrud Tablets, 1952: Business Documents", *Iraq* 16, 29–58

Parkinson, R. 2004. "The History of a Poem: Middle Kingdom Literary Manuscripts and their Reception", in G. Burkard (ed.), *Kon-Texte: Akten des Symposions "Spurensuche—Altägypten im Spiegel seiner Texte", München, 2. bis 4. Mai 2003.* Wiesbaden: Harrassowitz, 51–63

Parpola, S. 1983. *Letters from Assyrian Scholars to the Kings Esarhaddon and Assurbanipal. Part II: Commentary and Appendices* (AOAT 5/2). Kevelaer: Butzon & Bercker; Neukirchen-Vluyn: Neukirchener Verlag

Parpola, S. 1988. "Proto-Assyrian", in H. Waetzoldt, H. Hauptmann (eds), *Wirtschaft und Gesellschaft von Ebla: Akten der internationalen Tagung, Heidelberg, 4.–7. November 1986* (HSAO 2). Heidelberg: Heidelberger Orientverlag, 293–298

Parpola, S. 1993. *Letters from Assyrian and Babylonian Scholars* (SAA X). Helsinki: Helsinki University Press

Parpola, S. 1997. "The Man Without a Scribe and the Question of Literacy in the Assyrian Empire", in B. Pongratz-Leisten, H. Kühne, P. Xella (eds), *ana šadî labnāni lū allik. Beiträge zu altorientalischen und mittelmeerischen Kul-*

turen. Festschrift für Wolfgang Röllig (AOAT 247). Kevelaer: Butzon & Bercker; Neukirchen-Vluyn: Neukirchener Verlag, 315–324

Parsons, P. 2007. "Copyists of Oxyrhynchus", in A. K. Bowman, R. A. Coles, N. Gonis, D. Obbink, P. J. Parsons (eds), *Oxyrhynchus: A city and its texts* (Graeco-Roman Memoirs 93). London: The Egypt Exploration Society, 262–270

Pearce, L. 1993. "Statements of Purpose: Why the Scribes Wrote", in M. E. Cohen, D. C. Snell, D. B. Weisberg (eds), *The Tablet and the Scroll: Near Eastern Studies in Honor of William W. Hallo.* Bethesda, MD: CDL Press, 185–193

Pearce, L. 2007. "Review of Talon, *Enūma eliš (SAACT)*", *JAOS* 127, 371–373

Pearce, L. E., Doty, T. 2000. "The Activities of Anu-belšunu, Seleucid Scribe", in J. Marzahn, H. Neumann (eds), *Assyriologica et Semitica: Festschrift für Joachim Oelsner anlässlich seines 65. Geburtstages am 18. Februar 1997* (AOAT 252). Münster: Ugarit-Verlag, 331–341

Pedersén, O. 1986. *Archives and libraries in the city of Assur: a survey of the material from the German excavations. Part 2* (Studia Semitica Upsaliensia 8). Uppsala: Almqvist & Wiksell

Pinches, T. G. 1924. "Hymns to Pap-due-garra", in Anonymous (ed.), *Centenary Supplement of the Journal of the Royal Asiatic Society, being a selection of papers read to the Society during the celebrations of July, 1923.* London: The Royal Asiatic Society, 63–86

Poebel, A. 1939. *Studies in Akkadian Grammar* (AS 9). Chicago: Chicago University Press

Poebel, A. 1943. "The Assyrian King List from Khorsabad (continued)", *JNES* 2, 56–90

Postgate, J. N. 1973. "Assyrian Texts and Fragments", *Iraq* 35, 13–36

Postgate, J. N. 1990. "The Assyrian Porsche?", *SAAB* 4, 35–38

Postgate, J. N. 1992. *Early Mesopotamia. Society and Economy at the Dawn of History.* London: Routledge

Priestley, J. 2007. "The φαρος of Alcman's Partheneion 1", *Mnemosyne* 60, 175–195

Radau, H. 1908. *Letters to Cassite Kings from the Temple Archives of Nippur* (The Babylonian Expedition of the University of Pennsylvania Series A, Cuneiform Texts 17/i). Philadelphia: University of Pennsylvania

Radner, K. 2005. *Die Macht des Namens – Altorientalische Strategien zur Selbsterhaltung* (SANTAG 8). Wiesbaden: Harrassowitz

Rassam, H. 1892. *Asshur and the Land of Nimrod.* Cincinnati: Curts & Jennings

Rayner, K., Pollatsek, A. 1989. *The Psychology of Reading.* Englewood Cliffs, NJ: Prentice-Hall

Rayner, K., Pollatsek, A. 1996. "Reading unspaced text is not easy: Comments on the implications of Epelboim et al.'s study (1994) for models of eye movement control in reading", *Vision Research* 36, 461–465

Reade, J. E. 1998–2001. "Ninive (Nineveh)", in D. O. Edzard, M. Krebernik, J. N. Postgate, W. Röllig, U. Seidl, M. Stol, G. Wilhelm (eds), *Reallexikon der Assyriologie, vol. IX.* Berlin: De Gruyter, 338–433

Reeve, M. D. 1989. "*Eliminatio codicum descriptorum*: a methodological problem", in J. N. Grant (ed.), *Editing Greek and Latin Texts: papers given at the Twenty-Third Annual Conference on Editorial Problems, University of Toronto, 6–7 November 1987*. New York: AMS Press, 1–35

Reiner, E. 1960. "Plague Amulets and House Blessings", *JNES* 19, 148–155

Reiner, E. 1973. "How We Read Cuneiform Texts", *JCS* 25, 3–58

Reiner, E. 1982. "The Reading of the Sign LIŠ", *RA* 76, 93

Reiner, E. 1984. "*Damqam īnim* revisited", *StOr* 55, 177–182

Reiner, E., Civil, M. 1967. "Another Volume of Sultantepe Tablets", *JNES* 26, 177–211

Renger, J. 1971. "Überlegungen zum akkadischen Syllabar", *ZA* 71, 23–43

Reynolds, L. D., Wilson, N. G. 1991. *Scribes and Scholars: A Guide to the Transmission of Greek and Latin Literature*. Oxford: Clarendon Press

Robert, J., Robert, L. 1964. "Bulletin épigraphique", *Revue des études grecques* 77, 127–259

Robert, J., Robert, L. 1976. "Bulletin épigraphique", *Revue des études grecques* 89, 415–595

Robinson, M. A. 2002. "The Case for Byzantine Priority", in D. A. Black (ed.), *Rethinking New Testament Textual Criticism*. Grand Rapids, MI: Baker Academic, 125–139

Robson, E. 2008. *Mathematics in Ancient Iraq: A Social History*. Princeton: Princeton University Press

Rochberg, F. 1996. "Personifications and Metaphors in Babylonian Celestial Omina", *JAOS* 116, 475–485

Röllig, W. 2009. *Das Gilgamesch-Epos* (Reclam Bibliothek). Stuttgart: Philipp Reclam jun.

Rollston, C. A. 2010. *Writing and Epigraphy in the World of Ancient Israel: Epigraphic Evidence from the Iron Age* (Archaeology and Biblical Studies 11). Atlanta: Society of Biblical Literature

Römer, W. H. P. 1990. ""Weisheitstexte" und Texte mit Bezug auf den Schulbetrieb in sumerischer Sprache", in O. Kaiser (ed.), *Texte aus der Umwelt des Alten Testaments 3: Weisheitstexte, Mythen und Epen*. Gütersloh: G. Mohn, 17–109

Roth, M. T. 1995. *Law Collections from Mesopotamia and Asia Minor* (Writings from the Ancient World 6). Atlanta, GA: Scholars Press

Rubio, G. 2000 [2005]. "On the Orthography of the Sumerian Literary Texts from the Ur III Period", *ASJ* 22, 203–225.

Rubio, G. 2009. "Sumerian Literature", in C. S. Ehrlich (ed.), *From an Antique Land: An Introduction to Ancient Near Eastern Literature*. Lanham: Rowman & Littlefield, 10–75

Russell, J. M. 1999. *The Writing on the Wall: studies in the architectural context of late Assyrian palace inscriptions*. Winona Lake: Eisenbrauns

Rüster, C. 1988. "Materialien zu einer Fehlertypologie der hethitischen Texte", in E. Neu, C. Rüster (eds), *Documentum Asiae Minoris antiquae: Festschrift für Heinrich Otten zum 75. Geburtstag*. Wiesbaden: Harrassowitz, 295–306

Rutz, M. T. 2006. "Textual Transmission between Babylonia and Susa: A New Solar Omen Compendium", *JCS* 58, 63–96

Rutz, M. T. 2011. "Threads for Esagil-kīn-apli: The Medical Diagnostic-Prognostic Series in Middle Babylonian Nippur", *ZA* 101, 294–308
Sachs, A. 1952. "Babylonian Horoscopes", *JCS* 6, 49–75
Saenger, P. 1975. "Colard Mansion and the Evolution of the Printed Book", *The Library Quarterly* 45, 405–418
Saenger, P. H. 1997. *Space Between Words: The Origin of Silent Reading.* Stanford: Stanford University Press
Saggs, H. W. F. 1981. "Review of von Voigtlander, *Bisitun*", *JRAS* 113, 71–72
Sakamoto, T., Maktia, K. 1973. "Japan", in J. Downing (ed.), *Comparative Reading: cross-national studies of behavior and processes in reading and writing.* New York: Macmillan, 440–465
Sallaberger, W. 1999. *"Wenn Du mein Bruder bist, …": Interaktion und Textgestaltung in altbabylonischen Alltagsbriefen* (CM 16). Leiden: Brill
Sallaberger, W. 2008. *Das Gilgamesch-Epos – Mythos, Werk und Tradition.* München: C. H. Beck
Sassmannshausen, L. 2002. "Zur babylonischen Schreiberausbildung", *BaM* 33, 211–228
Schaudig, H. 2001. *Die Inschriften Nabonids von Babylon und Kyros' des Grossen samt den in ihrem Umfeld entstandenen Tendenzschriften: Textausgabe und Grammatik* (AOAT 256). Münster: Ugarit-Verlag
Schott, A. 1934. "Zu meiner Übersetzung des Gilgameš-Epos. (Reclams Universalbibliothek Nr. 7235.)", *ZA* 42 (NF 8), 92–143
Schott, A., von Soden, W. 1988. *Das Gilgamesh-Epos* (Universal-Bibliothek). Stuttgart: Philipp Reclam jun.
Schwemer, D. 2001. Die Wettergottgestalten Mesopotamiens und Nordsyriens im Zeitalter der Keilschriftkulturen. Wiesbaden: Harrassowitz
Schwemer, D. 2006–2008. "Šāla. A. Philologisch", in M. P. Streck, G. Frantz-Szabó, M. Krebernik, J. N. Postgate, U. Seidl, M. Stol, G. Wilhelm (eds), *Reallexikon der Assyriologie, vol. XI.* Berlin: De Gruyter, 565–567
Schwemer, D. 2007. *Abwehrzauber und Behexung: Studien zum Schadenzauberglauben im alten Orient.* Wiesbaden: Harrassowitz
Schwemer, D. 2007. *Rituale und Beschwörungen gegen Schadenzauber* (KAL 2). Wiesbaden: Harrassowitz
Schwemer, D. 2010. "Fighting Witchcraft before the Moon and Sun: a Therapeutic Ritual from Neo-Babylonian Sippar", *Orientalia* 79, 480–504
Scribner, S., Cole, M. 1981. *The Psychology of Literacy.* Cambridge, MA: Harvard University Press
Scurlock, J. 2006. *Magico-Medical Means of Treating Ghost-Induced Illnesses in Ancient Mesopotamia* (AMD 3). Leiden: Brill
Scurlock, J., Andersen, B. R. 2005. *Diagnoses in Assyrian and Babylonian Medicine.* Champaign: University of Illinois Press
Seminara, S. 1998. *L'accadico di Emar* (Materiali per il vocabolario sumerico 6). Rome: Università degli studi di Roma La Sapienza, Dipartimento di studi orientali
Silva, M. 2002. "Responses", in D. A. Black (ed.), *Rethinking New Testament Textual Criticism.* Grand Rapids, MI: Baker Academic, 141–150

Sines, G., Sakellarakis, Y. A. 1987. "Lenses in Antiquity", *American Journal of Archaeology* 91, 191–196
Singer, I. 1996. *Muwatalli's Prayer to the Assembly of Gods Through the Storm-God of Lightning (CTH 381).* Atlanta, GA: Scholars Press
Sjöberg, A. W. 2006. "Some Emar Lexical Entries", in A. K. Guinan, M. deJ. Ellis, A. J. Ferrara, S. M. Freedman, M. T. Rutz, L. Sassmannshausen, S. Tinney, M. W. Waters (eds), *If a Man Builds a Joyful House: Assyriological Studies in Honor of Erle Verdun Leichty* (CM 31). Leiden: Brill, 401–429
Sjöberg, Å. W., Bergmann, E., Gragg, G. B. 1969. *The Collection of the Sumerian Temple Hymns and the Keš Temple Hymn* (TCS 3). Locust Valley, NY: J. J. Augustin
Skeat, T. C. 1956. "The Use of Dictation in Ancient Book-Production", *Proceedings of the British Academy* 42, 179–208
Small, J. P. 1997. *Wax Tablets of the Mind: cognitive studies of memory and literacy in classical antiquity.* London: Routledge
Smick, E. B. 1967. "A lesson in textual criticism as learned from a comparison of Akkadian and Hebrew textual variants", *Bulletin of the Evangelical Theological Society* 10/2, 127–133
Smith, J. D. 2009. "Consistency and character in the *Mahābhārata*", *BSOAS* 72, 101–112
Sollberger, E. 1962. "Graeco-Babyloniaca", *Iraq* 24, 63–72
Sollberger, E. 1968. "The Cruciform Monument", *JEOL* 20, 50–70
Sommerfeld, W. 1999. *Die Texte der Akkade-Zeit. 1. Das Dijala-Gebiet: Tutub* (IMGULA 3). Münster: Rhema
Spalinger, A. 1974. "Assurbanipal and Egypt. A Source Study", *JAOS* 94, 316–328
Steinkeller, P. 1993. "Comments on the Seal of Aman-Eshtar", *NABU*, no. 9, pp. 7–8
Stol, M. 1981. *Letters from Yale* (AbB 9). Leiden: Brill
Streck, M. 1916. *Assurbanipal und die letzten assyrischen Könige bis zum Untergange Niniveh's. II. Teil: Texte. Die Inschriften Assurbanipals und der letzten assyrischen Könige* (VAB 7/2). Leipzig: J. C. Hinrichs
Streck, M. P. 1999. "Das "Perfekt" *iptaras* im Altbabylonischen der Hammurapi-Briefe", in N. Nebes (ed.), *Tempus und Aspekt in den semitischen Sprachen. Jenaer Kolloquium zur Semitischen Sprachwissenschaft* (Jenaer Beiträge zum Vorderen Orient 1). Wiesbaden: Harrassowitz, 101–126
Streck, M. P. 1999. *Die Bildersprache der akkadischen Epik* (AOAT 264). Münster: Ugarit-Verlag
Streck, M. P. 2000. *Das amurritische Onomastikon der altbabylonischen Zeit: Die Amurriter, die onomastische Forschung, Orthographie und Phonologie, Nominalmorphologie* (AOAT 271/1). Münster: Ugarit-Verlag
Streck, M. P. 2001. "Keilschrift und Alphabet", in D. Borchers, F. Kammerzell, S. Weninger (eds), *Hieroglyphen, Alphabete, Schriftreformen: Studien zu Multiliteralismus, Schriftwechsel und Orthographieneuregelung* (Lingua Aegyptia Studia Monographica 3). Göttingen: Seminar für Ägyptologie und Koptologie, 77–97

Streck, M. P. 2003. "Orthographie. B", in D. O. Edzard, M. P. Streck, M. Krebernik, J. N. Postgate, U. Seidl, M. Stol, G. Wilhelm (eds), *RlA 10/1–2*. Berlin: De Gruyter, 137–140

Streck, M. P. 2010. "Notes on the Old Babylonian Hymns of Agušaya", *JAOS* 130, 561–571

Streck, M. P., Wasserman, N. 2008. "The Old Babylonian Hymns to Papulegara", *Orientalia* 77, 335–358 and Tab. xxxvi-xxxvii

Streck, M. P., Wasserman, N. 2011. "Dialogues and Riddles: Three Old Babylonian Wisdom Texts", *Iraq* 73, 117–125

Strugnell, J. 1974. "A Plea for Conjectural Emendation in the New Testament, with a Coda on 1 Cor 4:6", *Catholic Biblical Quarterly* 36, 543–558

Suter, C. E. 2007. "Between Human and Divine: High Priestesses in Images from the Akkad to the Isin-Larsa Period", in J. Cheng, M. H. Feldman (eds), *Ancient Near Eastern Art in Context: Studies in Honor of Irene J. Winter by Her Students*. Leiden: Brill, 317–361

Tadmor, H. 1994. *The Inscriptions of Tiglath-Pileser III, King of Assyria. Critical Edition, with Introduction, Translations and Commentary*. Jerusalem: Israel Academy of Sciences and Humanities

Tadmor, H., Landsberger, B., Parpola, S. 1989. "The Sin of Sargon and Sennacherib's Last Will", *SAAB* 3, 3–51

Talon, P. 2005. *The Standard Babylonian Creation Myth Enūma eliš* (SAACT 4). Helsinki: The Neo-Assyrian Text Corpus Project

Tarrant, R. J. 1989. "The Reader as Author: Collaborative Interpolation in Latin Poetry", in J. N. Grant (ed.), *Editing Greek and Latin Texts: papers given at the Twenty-Third Annual Conference on Editorial Problems, University of Toronto, 6–7 November 1987*. New York: AMS Press, 121–162

Tertel, H. J. 1994. *Text and Transmission: An Empirical Model for the Literary Development of Old Testament Narratives* (Beihefte zur Zeitschrift für die alttestamentliche Wissenschaft 221). Berlin: De Gruyter

Thompson, H. 2011. *Tintin: Hergé and his Creation*. London: John Murray

Thompson, R. C. 1930. *The Epic of Gilgamish*. Oxford: Clarendon Press

Thompson, R. C. 1931. *The Prisms of Esarhaddon and Assurbanipal Found at Nineveh, 1927–8*. London: Printed by Order of the Trustees of the British Museum

Thompson, R. C. 1940. "A Selection from the Cuneiform Historical Texts from Nineveh (1927–32)", *Iraq* 7, 85–131

Thureau-Dangin, F. 1912. *Une relation de la huitième campagne de Sargon (714 av. J.-C.)* (TCL 3). Paris: Librairie Paul Geuthner

Tigay, J. H. 1982. *The Evolution of the Gilgamesh Epic*. Philadelphia: University of Pennsylvania Press

Timpanaro, S. 2010. *La genesi del metodo del Lachmann*. Novara: De Agostini

Tsumura, D. T. 1999. "Scribal Errors or Phonetic Spellings? Samuel as an Aural Text", *Vetus Testamentum* 49, 390–411

Turner, E. G. 1980. *Greek Papyri: An Introduction*. Oxford: Clarendon Press

Ungnad, A. 1915. *Babylonian Letters of the Hammurapi Period* (PBS 7). Philadelphia: University Museum

Ungnad, A. 1922. "Zwei neue Veröffentlichungen der Yale-Universität", *ZA* 34, 15–23

Ungnad, A. 1928–29. "Zum Sanherib-Prisma I R 37–42", *ZA* 38, 191–200

Valério, M. 2011. "Hani-Rabbat as the Semitic Name of Mitanni", *Journal of Language Relationship* 6, 173–183

Valério, M., Yakubovich, I. 2010. "Semitic word for "Iron" as Anatolian Loanword", in T. M. Nikolaev (ed.), *Исследования по Лингвистике и Семиотике: Сборник статей к юбилею Вяч. Вс. Иванова (Studies in Linguistics and Semiotics: A Collection of Articles for the Anniversary for Vyacheslav V. Ivanov)*. Moscow: Languages of Slavonic Culture, 108–116

Valette-Cagnac, E. 1997. *La lecture à Rome: rites et pratiques.* Paris: Belin

van Beethoven, L. 1988. *32 sonate per pianoforte, edizione tecnico-interpretativa di Artur Schnabel.* Milan: Edizioni Curci

van Orden, G. C. 1987. "A ROWS is a ROSE: Spelling, sound, and reading", *Memory and Cognition* 15, 181–198

Veenhof, K. R. 1972. *Aspects of Old Assyrian Trade and its Terminology* (Studia et Documenta ad Iura Orientis Antiqui Pertinenda 10). Leiden: Brill

Veldhuis, N. 1998. "TIN.TIR = Babylon, the Question of Canonization and the Production of Meaning", *JCS* 50, 77–85

Veldhuis, N. 2000. "Kassite Exercises: Literary and Lexical Extracts", *JCS* 52, 67–94

Veldhuis, N. 2003. "On the Curriculum of the Neo-Babylonian School", *JAOS* 123, 627–633

Veldhuis, N. 2006. "How Did They Learn Cuneiform? Tribute/Word List C as an Elementary Exercise", in P. Michalowski, N. Veldhuis (eds), *Approaches to Sumerian Literature: Studies in Honour of Stip (H. L. J. Vanstiphout)* (CM 35). Leiden: Brill, 181–200

Veldhuis, N. 2011. "Levels of Literacy", in K. Radner, E. Robson (eds), *The Oxford Handbook of Cuneiform Culture.* Oxford: Oxford University Press, 68–89

Vinaver, E. 1939. "Principles of Textual Emendation", in (Anonymous) (ed.), *Studies in French Language and Medieval Literature Presented to Prof. Mildred K. Pope.* Manchester: Manchester University Press, 351–370

Visicato, G. 2000. *The Power and the Writing: The Early Scribes of Mesopotamia.* Bethesda, MD: CDL Press

von Soden, W. 1944. "Aufsätze aus nichtorientalischen Zeitschriften", *ZA* NF 14, 238–239

von Soden, W. 1957–1958. "Zur Laut- und Formenlehre des Neuassyrischen", *AfO* 18, 121–122

von Soden, W. 1963. "*izqātu, išqātu*, "Kettenringe", ein aramäisches Lehnwort", *AfO* 20, 155

von Soden, W. 1969. "Bemerkungen zu einigen literarischen Texten in akkadischer Sprache aus Ugarit", *UF* 1, 189–195

von Soden, W. 1981. "Untersuchungen zur babylonischen Metrik, Teil I", *ZA* 71, 161–204 von Soden, W. 1990. ""Weisheitstexte" in akkadischer Sprache", in O. Kaiser (ed.), *Texte aus der Umwelt des Alten Testaments 3: Weisheitstexte, Mythen und Epen.* Gütersloh: G. Mohn, 110–188

von Voigtlander, E. N. 1978. *The Bisitun inscription of Darius the Great: Babylonian version* (Corpus Inscriptionum Iranicarum. l. Inscriptions of Ancient Iran, v. 2, pt. l). London: Lund Humphries

von Weiher, E. 1993. *Uruk. Spätbabylonische Texte aus dem Planquadrat U 18. Teil 4* (Ausgrabungen in Uruk-Warka. Endberichte 12). Mainz: Philipp von Zabern

Wagensonner, K. 2011. "A Scribal Family and its Orthographic Peculiarities. On the Scientific Work of a Royal Scribe and his Sons," in G. J. Selz, K. Wagensonner (eds), *The Empirical Dimension of Ancient Near Eastern Studies. Die empirische Dimension altorientalischer Forschungen* (Wiener Offene Orientalistik 6). Vienna: Lit, 645–701.

Walls, N. 2001. *Desire, Discord and Death: Approaches to Ancient Near Eastern Myth* (ASOR Books 8). Boston, MA: American Schools of Oriental Research

Warner, N., Weber, A. 2002. "Perception of epenthetic stops", *Journal of Phonetics* 29, 53–87

Wasserman, N. 2003. *Style and Form in Old Babylonian Literary Texts* (CM 27). Leiden: Brill

Wasserman, N. 2011. "Adzes, not Skirts in CUSAS 10. No. 7", *NABU*, no. 53, pp. 56–57

Weeden, M. 2009. "The Akkadian Words for "Grain" and the God Haya", *WdO* 39, 77–107

Weeden, M. 2010. *Hittite Logograms and Hittite Scholarship* (StBoT 54). Wiesbaden: Harrassowitz

Weeden, M. 2011. "Spelling, phonology and etymology in Hittite historical linguistics", *BSOAS* 74, 59–76

Weidner, E. F. 1931–1932. "Das Vokabular Martin A.", *AfO* 7, 271–275

Weidner, E. F. 1932–1933. "Assyrische Beschreibungen der Kriegs-Reliefs Aššurbânaplis", *AfO* 8, 175–203

Weidner, E. F. 1936–1937. "Das Vokabular Martin A. (Schluss)", *AfO* 11, 357 and Taf. VII-VIII

Weidner, E. F. 1937–1939. "Neue Bruchstücke über Sargons achten Feldzug", *AfO* 12, 144–148

Weißbach, F. H. 1918. "Zu den Inschriften der Säle im Palaste Sargon's II. von Assyrien", *ZDMG* 72, 161–185

Wenzel, S. 1990. "Reflections on (New) Philology", *Speculum* 65, 11–18

West, M. L. 1973. *Textual Criticism and Editorial Technique Applicable to Greek and Latin Texts.* Stuttgart: B. G. Teubner

West, M. L. 1997. "Akkadian Poetry: Metre and Performance", *Iraq* 59, 175–187

West, M. L. 1997. *The East Face of Helicon: West Asiatic Elements in Greek Poetry and Myth.* Oxford: Oxford University Press

West, M. L. 2008. "On Editing the Gāthās", *Iran* 46, 121–134

West, M. L. 2011. *Hellenica: Selected papers on Greek Literature and Thought. Volume I: Epic.* Oxford: Oxford University Press

West, M. L. 2011. *The Making of the Iliad: Disquisition and Analytical Commentary.* Oxford: Oxford University Press

West, M. L. Forthcoming. "Critical Editing", *Abhandlungen der Akademie der Wissenschaften in Göttingen*

Westenholz, A. 1974–1977. "Old Akkadian School Texts. Some Goals of Sargonic Scribal Education", *AfO* 25, 95–110

Westenholz, A. 1991. "The Phoneme /o/ in Akkadian", *ZA* 81, 10–19

Westenholz, A. 1996. "Review of Frayne, RIME 2", *BiOr* 53, cols 116–123

Westenholz, A. 2007. "The Graeco-Babyloniaca Once Again", *ZA* 97, 262–313

Westenholz, U., Westenholz, A. 1997. *Gilgamesh – Enuma Elish. Guder og mennesker i oldtidens Babylon.* Copenhagen: Spektrum

Wilcke, C. 1969. *Das Lugalbandaepos.* Wiesbaden: Harrassowitz

Wilcke, C. 1976. "Formale Gesichtspunkte in der sumerischen Literatur", *ASJ* 20, 205–316

Wilcke, C. 1977. "Die Anfänge der akkadischen Epen", *ZA* 67, 153–216

Wilcke, C. 1981. "*šumṣulu*, "den Tag verbringen"", *ZA* 70, 138–140

Wilcke, C. 1985. "Liebesbeschwörungen aus Isin", *ZA* 75, 188–209

Wilcke, C. 1987. "Inschriften 1983–1984 (7.–8. Kampagne)", in B. Hrouda (ed.), *Isin – Išān Bahrīyāt III: Die Ergebnisse der Ausgrabungen 1983–1984.* München: Verlag der bayerischen Akademie der Wissenschaften, 83–120

Wilcke, C. 1987. "A Riding Tooth. Metaphor, Metonymy and Synecdoche, quick and frozen in Everyday Language", in M. Mindlin, M. J. Geller, J. E. Wansbrough (eds), *Figurative Language in the Ancient Near East.* London: School of Oriental and African Studies, 77–102

Wilcke, C. 2000. *Wer las und schrieb in Babylonien und Assyrien: Überlegungen zur Literalität im Alten Zweistromland* (Sitzungsberichte der bayerischen Akademie der Wissenschaften, philosophisch-historische Klasse. Jahrgang 2000, Heft 6). München: Verlag der bayerischen Akademie der Wissenschaften

Wilcke, C. 2010. "Die Inschrift "Tukultī-Ninurtas I 1" – Tukultī-Ninurtas I. von Assyrien Feldzug gegen Gutäer und andere, nordöstliche und nordwestliche Feinde und der erste Bericht über den Bau seines neuen Palastes", in J. C. Fincke (ed.), *Festschrift für Gernot Wilhelm anläßlich seines 65. Geburtstages am 28. Januar 2010.* Dresden: Islet Verlag, 411–446

Wilhelm, G. 1971. "Eine altbabylonische Graphik im Hurro-Akkadischen", *UF* 3, 285–289

Winckler, H. 1897. *Altorientalische Forschungen.* Leipzig

Winskel, H., Radach, R., Luksaneeyanwin, S. 2009. "Eye movements when reading spaced and unspaced Thai and English: A comparison of Thai–English bilinguals and English monolinguals", *Journal of Memory and Language* 61, 339–351

Wiseman, D. J. 1952. "An Esarhaddon Cylinder from Nimrud", *Iraq* 14, 54–60

Woodington, N. R. 1982. *A Grammar of the Neo-Babylonian Letters of the Kuyunjik Collection.* (Unpublished PhD Thesis: Yale University)

Woods, C. E. 2004. "The Sun-God Tablet of Nabû-apla-iddina Revisited", *JCS* 56, 23–103
Worthington, M. 2005. "Edition of UGU 1 (=*BAM* 480 etc.)", *JMC* 5, 6–43
Worthington, M. 2006. "Dialect admixture of Babylonian and Assyrian in SAA VIII, X, XII[I], XVII and XVIII", *Iraq* 78, 59–84
Worthington, M. 2006. "Edition of BAM 3", *JMC* 7, 18–48
Worthington, M. 2009. "An Instructive Mistake on a Cuneiform Medical Tablet", *Chatreššar* 97–99
Worthington, M. 2009. "Review of Böck, *Muššu'u*", *BSOAS* 72, 153–155
Worthington, M. 2010. "*i-ba-aš-šu-ú* vs. *i-ba-aš-šu* from Old to Neo-Babylonian", in L. Kogan (ed.), *Language in the Ancient Near East.* Winona Lake: Eisenbrauns, 661–706
Worthington, M. 2010. "The lamp and the mirror, or: Some comments on the ancient understanding of Mesopotamian medical manuscripts", in A. Imhausen, T. Pommerening (eds), *Writings of Early Scholars in the Ancient Near East, Egypt, Rome, and Greece.* Berlin: De Gruyter, 189–199
Worthington, M. 2010. "A new phonological difference between Babylonian and (Neo)-Assyrian", *ZA* 100, 86–108
Worthington, M. 2010. "Some new patterns in Neo-Assyrian orthography and phonology discernible in nouns with monosyllabic stems", *JNES* 69, 179–194
Worthington, M. 2011. "On Names and Artistic Unity in the Standard Version of the Babylonian Gilgamesh Epic", *JRAS* 21, 402–421
Worthington, M. Forthcoming. "Literatures in Dialogue: A Comparison of Attitudes to Speech in Babylonian and Middle Egyptian Literature", in R. Enmarch, V. Lepper (eds), *Ancient Egyptian Literature: Theory and Practice.* London: The British Academy
Wyatt, N. 2007. "Making Sense of the Senseless: Correcting Scribal Errors in Ugaritic", *UF* 39, 757–772
Yamada, S. 2000. *The Construction of the Assyrian Empire: a historical study of the inscriptions of Shalmaneser III (859–824 B.C.) relating to his campaigns to the West* (Culture and History of the Ancient Near East 3). Leiden: Brill
Zaccagnini, C. 1993. "Notes on the Pazarcik stela", *SAAB* 7, 53–72
Zgoll, A. 2004. *Die Kunst des Betens. Form und Funktion, Theologie und Psychagogik in babylonisch-assyrischen Handerhebungsgebeten an Ischtar* (AOAT 308). Münster: Ugarit-Verlag
Zgoll, A. 2006. *Traum und Welterleben im antiken Mesopotamien: Traumtheorie und Traumpraxis im 3.–1. Jahrtausend v. Chr. als Horizont einer Kulturgeschichte des Träumens* (AOAT 333). Münster: Ugarit-Verlag
Ziegler, N. 2005. "Les vaisseux sanguins et *Enûma eliš*", *JMC* 5, 4–5
Ziegler, N. 2011. "Gilgameš : le roi héroïque et son ami", in J.-M. Durand, T. Römer, M. Langlois (eds), *Le jeune héros: Recherches sur la formation et la diffusion d'un thème littéraire au Proche-Orient ancien* (OBO 250). Fribourg: Academic Press, 289–306
Zimmern, H. 1893. "Ein vorläufiges Wort über babylonische Metrik", *ZA* 8, 121–124
Zimmern, H. 1895. "Weiteres zur babylonischen Metrik", *ZA* 10, 1–24

Zolyómi, G. 2007. "Variation in the multiword expression *igi bar* in the Old Babylonian period", in J. Ebeling and G. Cunningham (eds), *Analysing Literary Sumerian: corpus-based approaches.* London: Equinox, 316–350
Zumthor, P. 1987. *La lettre et la voix: De la littérature médiévale.* Paris: Seuil

Alphabetical index (selective)

Index locorum

Note – AbB, RIMA, RINAP and SAA and are cited by inscription or letter number (not by page number); references to RIMA and RIMB should be sought under the king's name, abbreviated as per p. xx.

AbB I **34**:9, 111; **27**:33, 170 *sub* 4); **31**:11, 170 *sub* 5)

AbB II **1**:17, 230; **5**:12, 230; **9**:18, 230; **9**:21, 230; **11**:11, 230; **11**:27, 230; **12**:17, 230; **15**:6, 230; **15**:23, 230; **16**:4, 230; **19**:10, 230; **21**:5, 230; **36**:5, 230; **34**:6, 230; **34**:9, 230; **34**:12, 230; **34**:15, 230; **34**:17, 230; **34**:23, 230; **46**:13, 230; **48**:12, 230; **52**:11, 230; **54**:6, 230; **54**:13, 230; **54**:25, 230; **70**:12, 230; **74**:26, 230; **82**:21, 190 fn. 638; **82**:22, 230; **82**:26, 103; **89**:22, 105; **83**:7, 105; **85**:32, 230; **88**:11, 230; **88**:25, 230; **88** r.15', 230; **89**:22, 105; **90**:22, 230; **90**:31, 230; **92**:25, 230; **96**:7, 13, 105; **98**:2, 190 fn. 638; **98**:14-15, 191 fn. 638; **100**:22, 191 fn. 638; **104**:10, 230; **106**:21, 103; **106**:29, 103; **107**:28, 230; **108**:13, 230; **109**:3, 169 *sub* 2); **109**:20, 230; **109**:21, 230; **112**:20, 230; **113**:10, 230; **114**:13, 230; **114**:15, 230; **114**:23, 191 fn. 638; **120**:8, 173; **121**:9, 230; **126**:5, 230; **128**:7, 230; **140**:7, 230; **140**:9, 230; **141**:7, 230; **146**:5, 191 fn. 638; **149**:8, 191 fn. 638; **154**:18, 230; **157**:1, 191 fn. 638; **158**:6-7, 182; **159**:r.10', 173; **161**:10, 230; **161**:24, 230; **162**:7, 230; **162**:8, 230; **162**:15, 230; **162**:17, 230; **162**:21, 230; **170**:15, 107; **172**:18, 191 fn. 638; **177**:16, 230; **178**:14, 230

AbB IV **9**:13, 230; **17**:24, 230; **18**:14, 267; **21**:13, 230; **21**:27, 230; **22**:4, 230; **26**:9, 230; **28**:12, 230; **32**:6, 230; **40**:23, 230; **40**:34, 230; **49**:9, 169 fn. 557; **50**:6, 230; **50**:11, 230; **53**:16 and 19, 173 fn. 572; **55**:6, 173; **56**:11, 230; **57**:9, 230; **60**:16, 230; **68**:21, 230; **68**:25, 230; **69**:17, 230; **69**:32, 230; **69**:38, 230; **72**:12, 182 fn. 603; **75**:8, 230; **83**:10, 230; **99**:8, 230; **111**:26, 230; **111**:30, 230; **113**:10-11, **182** fn. 603; **117**:7, 230; **118**:17, 230; **134**:9, 230; **134**:13, 230; **134**:17, 230; **137**:6, 230; **137**:7, 267; **138**:9, 170 *sub* 8); **140**:18, 267; **142**:5, 110; **145**:4, 182 fn. 603; **145**:12, 230; **146**:21, 230; **150**:27, 230; **157**:3', 230; **157**:12', 110; **160**:9', 230

AbB V **40**:5-6, 109; **135**:4, 230; **135**:11, 230; **161**:23, 169 fn. 559; **273** :6', 106

AbB VI **70** :16, 105; **168**:9, 191 fn. 638

AbB VII **91** line 6, 8, and 27, 193

AbB VIII **15**:38-39, 110; **53**:23, 193; **54**:24-25, 193

AbB IX **22**:4, 189; **107**:1, 181; **190**:25, 230; **250**:10-13, 192

AbB X **73**:12, 181; **170**:10, 177

AbB XI **11**:11, 109; **16** :9, 106; **27**:13 and 28, 176 fn. 580; **33**:13, 173; **35**:16, 111; **44**:3-4, 110; **85**:7, 173; **91**:r.5', 170 *sub* 9); **95**:6, 111; **178**:31, 177

AbB XII **163**:8, 170 *sub* 7); **172**:12'-14', 193

AbB XIII **5** r.5', 230; **8**:9, 230; **9**:4, 230; **9**:12, 230; **10**:8, 230; **18**:8,

www.ingramcontent.com/pod-product-compliance
Lightning Source LLC
Chambersburg PA
CBHW060038100426
42742CB00014B/2631
* 9 7 8 1 5 0 1 5 1 3 2 5 1 *